CW00553160

Welcome aboard: the "boat without oars..."
Prepare yourself for what might be the most
important journey of your entire life~
Sail the winds of the sun, stars and moon with a Family whose
history precedes the dawn of earthly time; become reunited with
your ancestral Family who, have sailed beyond the seven seas
and subsequently returned from the Realm of the Blessed...

"It is also in the interests of a tyrant to keep his people poor, so that they may not be able to afford the cost of protecting themselves by arms and be so occupied with their daily tasks that they have no time for rebellion."

~ Aristotle

heretic- *n*

1. a person who adheres to or believes in an ideology or belief system that is contradictory to established religious dogma, especially those concepts that are officially condemned by a religious or governmental institution and its pompous authorities

2. a person, whose teachings, opinions, beliefs, or theories on any given subject, are considered by those who claim authority in that field, to be extremely unconventional or unorthodox

3. a person who dares to openly challenge the ideas, cultural mores, taboo systems and mythologies of contemporaneous organized society and its popular authoritarian rule in an overtly public manner;

4. a person who openly opposes intellectual or theosophical chauvinism

A Lesson from the Tao~

Be one with the Tao
and allow it to nurture your essence;
Be one with Virtue
and allow your essence to become a reflection of the Tao;
Being one with Loss
Loss can bring you good fortune;
How can you fathom the subtle Mystery of Being one with Loss?
By understanding fully what is within you.

If we identify rituals or practices, which are outdated, immoral and corrupt, and in turn determine that it is in our best interest to rebel against such practices, it isn't enough to become armchair heretics and rail against it vociferously; we must take action. However, if we too become monsters while fighting monsters, all is lost, for it is certainly true that "Two wrongs don't make a right."

Civilization isn't won through intimidation and coercion, neither by chaotic anarchy. To be a heretic is not sufficient unto itself; heresy must be complimented by appropriately sustained sophisticated behavior.

~William Hearth

Ormus ‡
The Secret Alchemy of Mary Magdalene ~Revealed~
[Part A]

ORMUS‡ The Secret Alchemy of Mary Magdalene
is a five part volume which includes an
Introduction subtitled "~Revealed~ [part A]" (this very book)
and "~Revealed~ [part B]" sold separately.
Parts I , II and III are also sold separately.

This book ...
ORMUS‡ The Secret Alchemy of Mary Magdalene ~Revealed [Part "A"]~
... is the first of two {A & B} introductions to commonly accepted "facts" that concern the following works of fiction, which are sold as a series of novels in three parts:

ORMUS ‡ The Secret Alchemy of Mary Magdalene ~ Part I (a novel)
ORMUS ‡ The Secret Alchemy of Mary Magdalene ~ Part II (a novel)
ORMUS ‡ The Secret Alchemy of Mary Magdalene ~ Part III (a novel)
(Parts "B" is sold separately & Parts "I, II, and III" are sold separately as a three part set)

These and other books by William Hearth, are published by
ORMUS™ Publications & Booksellers LLC (USA)
In cooperation with;
ORMUS® Natural Science Laboratories Int'l (JAPAN)
ORMUS® Institute of Natural Science & Metaphysics LLC (USA)
ORMUS® Global Holdings LLC (USA)
ORMUS® Marine Mineral Japan Co, Ltd. (Japan)
ORMUS University Press™
Academie Des ORMEs™

ORMUS ǂ
The Secret Alchemy of Mary Magdalene
~ Revealed ~

[Part A]

William Hearth

"As above, So below."

Ormus® Publications and Booksellers LLC

In cooperation with:

Ormus University Press™

Ormus Global Holdings LLC

Ormus® Natural Science Laboratories Int'l

Ormus® Institute of Natural Science & Metaphysics LLC

Academie des Ormes™ (USA)

Ormus® Marine Mineral JAPAN Inc.

ORMUS® Institute of Natural Science & Metaphysics LLC
ORMUS® Natural Science Laboratories Int'
ORMUS™ Publications & Booksellers LLC
ORMUS® Marine Mineral Japan K.K.
ORMUS® Global Holdings LLC
ORMUS University Press™
Academie des Ormes™

International Head Office: (ALL inquiries)
For the Attention of:
ORMUS® Institute of Natural Science & Metaphysics LLC
1-50-105 Shuri Oonaka-cho
Naha, Okinawa
JAPAN 903-0823

www.ormus.net
www.ormus.org
www.williamhearth.com

International Telephone Inquiries:
Delaware, USA (302) 397-2462
Internet Inquiries:
http://www.WilliamHearth.com

This book: Printed USA
May 2008, Limited 2nd Edition *BookExpo America 2008 Proof 100 copies only.*
6x9 SOFTBOUND ISBN [10]: 0-9793737-3-5 [13]: 978-0-9793737-3-2

Previous editions:
6x9 SOFTBOUND ISBN [10]: 0-9793737-2-7 [13]: 978-0-9793737-2-5
6x9 SOFTBOUND ISBN [10]: 0-9793737-0-0 [13]: 978-0-9793737-0-1

ORMUS Publications & Booksellers LLC
SAN: 853-2966
(*for inquiries see NOTE below)
16192 Coastal Highway, Lewes, DE 19958 USA

*NOTE Kindly address *ALL* inquiries to the International Head Office (Japan) location (above-left), by Air-Mail only (or by eMail contacts located at http://www.WilliamHearth.com)

Limited Second Edition (BookExpo America 2008 Proof Limited to 100 copies)
Printed in USA, May of 2008

This is number ______ of ______ signed copies.

ORMUS‡ The Secret Alchemy of Mary Magdalene ~ Revealed [Part "A"]

____

~signed by William Hearth

♨

Mar *Master, Teacher, Wisdom, wizened*
As in master~craftsman *(especially metallurgy)*, *master~alchemist,* master~builder, master~mason, master~architect.

Yam *Ocean, Sea*
Example: Yam HaMelah (the Dead Sea)

MarYam *An Ocean of Wisdom*

Magdal /*Migdal*
Tower, Lighthouse
Beacon in the Night

Migdal-Eder *Tower of the flock*

MarYam *the* **Migdal-Eder**
A watchtower or lighthouse amidst an Ocean of Wisdom
(**The Lady of the Lake** *[great salt lake ~ Dead Sea]*)

"When you put your faith in television,
What you get is what you've got~
Cause when they own the information
They can bend it all they want."

~John Mayer

This book...

" ☉RMUS‡ The Secret Alchemy of Mary Magdalene ~***Revealed***~ [Part "A"]"

...is an introduction to a particular set of commonly accepted "facts" that are discussed and or disputed in William Hearth's much anticipated work of fiction:

" ☉RMUS‡ The Secret Alchemy of Mary Magdalene."

These so-called historical and theosophical "facts" are rapidly becoming the source of serious and widespread controversy, disagreement and in many instances, heated debate.

Dissent[1] and the attendant right to question authority in a gentle and sophisticated manner, is a good thing. It is the sociological treasure of a sophisticated and civilized society~ But this healthy attitude, being born of a heretical mind-set, is behavior that is all too often misunderstood and hence, degraded; however, so long as it remains nothing less than the distilled result of deductive reasoning, this open-minded approach to life should be both revered and protected by a civilized society.

We should accord all due respect to such considerate reasoning, regarding it as the very root of sanity. Sanity is sacred and as such, an enlightened heresy should be the commonly accepted root of a healthy lifestyle.

Take no man's word for it!

1 ***Dissent*** ~ to refuse to conform to the rules and beliefs of an established church, sociological or governmental authority's dogma. (The courage and wisdom to think differently at the appropriate moment.).

HOW TO USE THIS BOOK

Mirror, mirror, on the wall, who's the fairest of them all?

When we, as open-minded, independent thinkers, finally muster the courage to question authority, and act upon that decision, the need to perform alternative research will indubitably arise and that's when we will discover the sad truth of just how biased, bigoted and truly narrow-minded our centers of "higher education" and governmental institutions really are.

We will find ourselves amazed at how certain aspects of history are simply ignored by all mainstream encyclopedias, dictionaries and textbooks; each country, nation-state and its corporatist regime, force-feeding the global population various versions of history as they see fit~ i.e.: the version that supports that ruling party's current private agenda; whereas all the names, places, *words* and *ideas* of major significance are being literally *written in & out* of history on a daily basis.

We will discover that all ideologies and thought processes other than the homogenized package of "pasteurized" thought, touted by mainstream religion and orthodox academia, has been carefully disposed of. Consequently the only records we have left to us are the "sanitized" versions that were approved by either the "powers that be" or "the powers that have been," or "a power imminent and as yet concealed."

When we consider the fact that the original endowments of almost all greater seats of learning and their associated colleges of medicine were setup by one institutionalized religion or another, then it shouldn't surprise us to learn that these carefully edited mind-sets still prevail to date; each in their own way, deliberately choosing on our behalf, to ignore the single most important common denominator: *A common denominator that would harmonize all valid equations.*

In essence, what we have are the competing factions of a global technocracy, owned in the majority by oil companies, pharmaceutical giants, tobacco concerns, drug cartels and arms manufacturers *{the military industrial complex}* that vie for supremacy over several organized religious states.

National borders fade into obscurity, as these corporate-states impose their will on the worldwide stage; thus we are all becoming members and even "citizen~slaves" of various "states-of-mind." Like it or not, we are all forced to choose sides and align ourselves with one faction or another so that we can offer the basic necessities of water, food, clothing and shelter to our children and loved ones.

The Global Village in turn has become a killing-field, as opposed to a playing-field, where various media groups have positioned themselves to become the, extremely biased, self-serving, mealy-mouthed, *"league of umpires"* that we see and hear daily on most of our radio and television programs, each contending for prime-time brainwashing opportunities and a greater market-share of the blood-money. *Trade wars prevail at 50 cents per bullet. Mothers and children pay the price: in blood, sweat, tears and untold suffering. A disgusting state-of-affairs?* The understatement of all time*!*

Media conglomerates *profit from war! Media conglomerates are "in bed-dead" with the war machine, like yesterdays' worn-out gigolos, as it roles on into each new territory and sells us their images of blood, guts, gore and* ***fear.*** Meanwhile the sympathy pitch to donate your hard won money to repair all the damage they have done drones on. *They get you coming and going, and if you're not pretty damn careful they'll rape your wives, daughters* ***and sons*** *on the way in and on the way out.* They wreak havoc and destruction everywhere they go, and then have the audacity to ask you to pay for it again though donations to charities that they intentionally mismanage.

This is not to say that all Media magnets, reporters and journalists are immoral, but it is becoming rather difficult to differentiate between an investigative reporter and an Intelligence Operative who is dressed-up as a well-intended cameraman and his mouthpiece. Especially since so many of our favorite newscasters completely disappeared from the scene within months after the 9-11 series of events. *Anyone who spoke out against the militarists were quickly defrocked, discredited and excommunicated from the Church of Media: therefore~*

We have our task set-out before us, and it is a task of Herculean proportions to be sure. We have an obligation to set the record straight; an obligation to expose the lies and a duty to repair the damage caused by 2,000 years of intentional deceit and betrayal (or is it 6,000 years, or maybe more?)

But the Catholic Church is only 1600 years old you contend? Well, think again dear friends. The seeds of the Catholic Church were sown centuries *if not eons* before Mary Magdalene and her Beloved Family of Friends were even born.

What do you think? Can we fit six million years of *planetary* history into 800 pages? How about cramming six thousand years of *human* history into 200 pages? It might be compared to Hercules trying to clean the Augean stables, yes?

Remember, (the mythical?) King Augeas of Elis who kept a team of three thousand oxen? The barn-carpet had not been sent to the cleaners for over thirty years? Pheew! Well, how about all those papal bulls, whose mess hasn't been cleaned up in almost 1,666 years? Quite a stinky mess wouldn't you agree?

You know it's true, and you'll have to *think outside the box* if you expect to be l*iberated from that confessional,* particularly where religion and state-sponsored dogma and brainwashing are concerned. You will also want to question authority and our contrived ***his***torical (hysterical?) records in every instance. ...and don't be fooled by the so-called protestant, gnostic, atheist, pagan or heathen religions either! They're all built around the same blind superstitious ignorance.

This book doesn't endorse any particular organized religion; nor does it endorse any particular nation-state; we are not atheists, neither do we accept blindly the generally accepted ***his***tories that were written and rewritten by those individuals who, through bloody conflict, have wrested power from one another, generation after generation, during the past few thousand years.

To the contrary, this book constitutes a heresy of the greatest magnitude! Indeed, this is a heretic's book of heresies. It will no doubt offend many a pompous ass and anger various others, such as those individuals who wield a PhD in a manner that is utterly incompatible with the true spirit and nature of Genuine Chivalry; and who thereby are, in truth, unworthy to hold sway over the minds of the unsuspecting masses such as they do. This book, to put it mildly, is intended to be controversial in the extreme and in many instances down right scandalous. But scandal for scandal's sake alone is nothing but a cheap trick. So make no mistake, this book is not to be compared with the daily news, small-minded tabloids or a gossip column.

We dare to ask, "What is Truth?" and we have a follow-up question, "Who guards the guardians?"

We need to know, "Who gave them the right to demand that we accept their point of view at the point of a gun or a sword?"

Although many have asked these questions, few dare to answer publicly, bluntly and truthfully for fear of reprisals; as such behavior would spell the sure and certain excommunication from the Banking Cartels' elite circle and its Worldwide System of Financial Slavery.

We no longer live under the illusion that the sun shines out the arse of every person who has acquired a PhD nor of those who have attained to public office through democratic process.

*D*o you remember the very first Friday the 13th (not the movie) and its original significance; the day that *Jacques Bourguignon Molay* and his immediate associates were all summarily arrested?[2] Those great men and women

---

2 ***Templar Knights ~*** *All* Templars in France were to be arrested by the king's men on Friday, October 13th, 1307, their lands sequestered, along with all goods and possessions (especially their books and manuscripts).

However, the Templars had apparently received advance warning because, just before the arrests, the Grand Master himself, Jacques de Molay, had many a book and manuscript burned, knowing that copies of the most important documents were secure in other parts of the world.

Approximately seven years thereafter, in the month of March 1314, the Grand Master, Jacques de Molay, and the Preceptor of Normandy, Geoffroi de Charnay, were slowly roasted to death, in a final and unsuccessful attempt to force others to come forward with the information that the King so ardently desired.

The Templars however do not vanish from the stage of world power, history and politics. To the contrary, this is where their legacy begins...

Four years after Philippe IV suppressed the Order, Pope Harminius excommunicated the Scottish Templars and The Compagnonnage thereafter claimed to be the continuing Order:

"Our founder, Jacques Bourguignon Molay, (was) born in Sossay in 1243. (He was) Grandmaster of the Commandery in Jerusalem in 1285. He returned to France in 1301, bringing with him the secrets of the Orient. The king and the pope were jealous of his science, of his knowledge and his authority... He was executed on the outskirts of the city, but before his death, he gave his Master's Charter to Jean de Larmenie, who re-instituted our order. Our ancestors managed to ***purchase the head of our founder from the henchman, who had removed it from the body before it burned****. The* ***skull was kept at Evreux for two-hundred years*** *until Isaac Long – Knight - took it to Charleston, where it remained until 1781, when Franklin returned it to Mans, where it lay until this day in the Temple de la Fraternite.'* ~Leadership of the Knights Templar passed to John Larmenius in France. In reading his Charter of Transmission **one can't help but be aware of the degree of contempt that the French survivors held towards their *brothers* in Scotland:**

who championed Truth? Why do we never hear of them in our elementary schools' history lessons? Where then, does the authentic truth begin and end; dare we speak openly and candidly of the Ancient Truth? Is it safe for women to walk *that* street alone at night?

Suffice it to say that there is a grain of truth to be found in all religions, but with all due respect, none of them represent a perfect reflection of the Great Truth. In fact, few even come close any more. The world wallows in the excrement of all these outdated and immoral religious institutions (Agean Stables), that haven't had a good house cleaning for the past few thousand years. It would be ridiculous of course to imagine that we can suddenly clean up that mess and repair all the damage, in a few days, or even years (decades?), but these issues must be addressed and corrected; the sooner the better! The State of Denial must be addressed, dismissed and gently dismantled, in as painless a manner as possible. Of course the use of methods, which employ chaos and anarchy to this end, should ***NOT*** be considered as viable options, as these only lead to war as well.

So how then do we eat a twelve-ton watermelon? One bite at a time and the more who join in, the merrier!

Together we can do it. It's time for a quantum leap in consciousness on a planetary scale. So, let's get started...

In order to understand the Great Truth, one must first relinquish all the preconceived notions, corporatist programming and religious-jingoist dogma that has been foisted upon us, since we were children.

One must liberate oneself from all the false religious precepts and jingoist ideologies that form the psychological foundation (and subsequent security matrix) upon which all modern day societies hinge. For example: One might begin by erasing all the prime-time television jingles from ones subconscious (but that's easier said than done isn't it?).

Our code of behavior must be totally readjusted.

We have to push the RESET button, but only after careful preparation. It won't do us any good to jump from the pot into the frying pan. What we want, in fact, is to land in a cool, slow-moving mountain stream surrounded by wildflowers and warm sunlight, with picnic baskets waiting in the shade of the Ancient Elm and Oak Tree Groves.

In no uncertain terms, it should be stated that this book is intended as a travel-guide and general reference for the modern heretic; and for those, who have decided that, indeed, the time has arrived for us to think outside the box. This book includes a symbolic map. It is a map that leads us to consider

---

"I, lastly, by the decree of the Supreme Assembly, by Supreme authority committed to me, will, say and order that the Scot- Templars deserters of the Order be blasted by anathema, and that they and the brethren of St John of Jerusalem, spoilers of the demesnes of the Knighthood (on whom God have mercy), be outside the circle of the Temple, now and for the future."

So how much of this is true? Did Molay actually pass leadership to Larmenie? Or did some form of ***skullduggery*** occur? ***(and where's the skull of John the Baptist to be found these days? Whose skull is it that Mary Magdalene is often pictured with?)*** Did Molay pass leadership to a "pretender to throne" in order to preserve the *anonymity* of those who held the Sacred Knowledge in trust? Pretense to leadership is an egotistical affair, whereas the preservation of Sacred Knowledge is, perforce, an esoteric affair. One wonders!

points of interest that are well concealed in the woods of olde; points of interest which might otherwise be overlooked and left unnoticed.

It includes a treasure map as well, where ⊙ and ‡ mark the spot. It also includes a small collection of keywords and historical signposts designed to assist the frustrated masses in their effort to "think different" and in turn, to *act* differently; thereby leading them to a clear and concise understanding of what the ⊙ and ‡ symbols truly represent...

But will our modern-day, *convenience-store audience*, fall asleep, with popcorn in hand, long before the action begins? (Especially, when we consider the fact that the average young adult these days, has the attention span of a thirty-second *Barn-Carpet-Cola™* advertisement or a fifteen-second *iSnod™ smear-your-ear* commercial?)

Perhaps we should come out shooting, with guns blazing, in a hotel room, where our action hero is having sex with his two mistresses, while chatting to his wife on a mobile phone about tomorrow's dinner reservations at the White House?

Then !!!Whamm!!!

A nasty question rears its monstrously ugly head: *"Are we, as a society, really interested in the Truth; or do we pray mostly for mere distraction, dumb-down-monotony, and to simply be entertained for another two hours; thereby being spared the pain and frustration of our self-inflicted ignorance?"*

And Bammm!!!

Our Superstar just cut ***that*** *question's head off!*

Yeahh!!! Blood spurts out, spraying the bed and three naked bodies... eeeuuuww!!! ***coitus interuptus*** ~ But, two more nasty questions grow in its place. (and cut to commercial).

We will return after a word from our sponsors... What will our Superstar do next?

He puts his wife on hold, smiles reassuringly at the two sex kittens as he wrestles with the two new questions snapping furiously at his virgin ears (balls?)...

"Is our planetary and human history really so important after all? Is it even remotely relevant to us today, being caught up as we are, in our petty soap-opera micro-worlds with their sorted extramarital S&M affairs?"

Without even pausing for thought he answers confidently in his best Viennese accent, *"Let's just stick with "Sex in the Shitty," "Prostate Nation" and the "C-M&M News Channel." After all, the paparazzi and arms dealers can only exist so long as there are customers, right?"*

Ever notice how you *never* see a single gun advertisement on your Television screens? Hey! Who needs 'em, when we have so many sociopaths currently seated in government office; and Rambo has just been elected for a fifth term in the White House! But wait!!! Isn't that illegal, five terms in office? Nope: not since the 9-11 attacks; anything goes these days! Haven't you heard? We're under martial law ***baaybee***! The American population may be a danger to themselves and others! (Ain't that the truth!!!)

Will knowing the Truth affect the outcome of one's college examinations or job interview this week?

Will it improve our children's SAT scores? Probably not, ***since Truth has so little to do with what we are taught in school these days.*** It has even less to do with surviving the trials of today's modern corporate work environments.

When after all, the fine art of bending and stretching the truth is much more applicable to getting a job these days, as opposed to knowing the Truth and reporting it accurately.

The ability to fabricate perceived realities is the order-of-the-day, not to mention the concealment and outright distortion of Truth. Now that's a useful tool for tomorrow's best-girl, her wily wolf-man and their assorted coyote pups!

So, which of the two evils will you vote for in the coming elections; The Democrats or The Republicans? Which do you prefer, the left or right hand of the two-headed monster?

And which view of history will you adopt? The Gnostic? The Pistic? Which version of Islam do you prefer? Which sect of Buddhism? The Seventh Day Adventist's perhaps? Jehovah's Biznezz? Are the Hindu any better that the Shinto or Taoists? How about Quan-Yin's version? Zeus'? Thor's? Odin's? Sol Invictus? Which form of Judaism suits you? Or would the atheist states of China or Russia suit you better~ or take the middle road and live in France where the unions can fix anything by going on strike for several weeks at a time [cynical retoric]?

Do you think we've kept the facts straight, after six thousand years of blood-curdling strife has passed between the multifarious warring factions? It is a story that has been written and rewritten, time and time again, by those war mongers, who, each vying for control of the world and all its resources are prepared to commit any atrocity in the name of their greed, their god and their national pride and prejudice: In the name of their Lord.

It is our legacy that has been abused; passed around between several opposing parties like a gang rape, each having left the stain of their own private agenda upon it, each having imposed their own particular spin and slant to it, eventually reducing it to nothing more than yesterday's dirty-laundry, political-turmoil, the *daily news* of princes and pedophiles; all the while masquerading, sadly, as a children's lullaby~ a legacy now suspect of being little more than ancient myth and metaphor. But nothing could be further from the truth!

Once upon a time it was a chivalrous love story and it had a happy ending. It taught our children some very important lessons about compassion and right livelihood.

Once upon a time it denounced theft of resources. But all that is lost now to the annals (anus?) of history and various corrupt corporate shenanigans. We hardly have even a vestige of truth left to us. *History has been most unkind to us, the legacy having been perverted beyond all recognition.*

If there is anything we can say for sure about human beings, it is that, *"People see and hear what they want to see and hear," and "they rarely, if ever, report the details of any given event with reasonable accuracy."* Never mind the fact that devious minds have added insult to injury by intentionally altering the historical records to support their own self-serving activities.

Can we trust any historical record? We rarely get the facts straight concerning events and stories that transpired even a few weeks ago; even stories born only yesterday have been known to mysteriously morph, after the telling and retelling of the story: When only minutes after the fact, *witnesses disagree vehemently, especially on what they saw only seconds earlier.*

In the first instance, so much depends on the observers' point of view; our personal prejudices, emotions and mind-set, we all, being such fickle creatures at any given moment.

Three different eyewitnesses will give three separate accounts of any incident. We all know that this much is true and few will disagree with this, each of us having been the victims, at one time or another, of vicious gossip or rumors, (which of course was nothing but pure tripe even before its inception. Yes?).

In this discourse, "ORMUS‡ The Secret Alchemy of Mary Magdalene - *Revealed"* we are constantly challenged by this dilemma, as we investigate the time-honored question, "What is Truth?"

We are thwarted by the stumbling blocks of human frailty and fallibility, issues that in turn become mingled with our own pride, prejudice and general unwillingness to openly admit to ourselves and others, our inadequacies and failures.

A collage of personal issues inevitably compromise our sense of justice and damage any initial efforts aimed at achieving an understanding of ourselves and our neighbors, however sincere; ultimately our personal ego thwarts our attempts at achieving emotional and mental clarity. Meanwhile we search in vain for meaning in our lives and the reasons for our existence- *as the light slowly fades.*

Who and what are we, where did we come from and where are we going? How did we get here and why should we go wherever it is that we're going?

If we can't be honest with the person in the mirror today, dare we hope to find any measure of honesty among the writings of our predecessors? As we pursue this research into our past *and future*, is it reasonable for us to expect that they were any better-off than we are today? Why would the people of yesteryear have been any different from us?

We will never become the Master of the Moment so long as we continue to bear false witness against ourselves, and if there is a morsel of truth to be found in the ancient teachings, we will never be able to perceive it, much less accept it, unless we first, make certain, that fundamental changes occur in the way we live in the present tense. We must be prepared to change the way we feel, think and act *at this very moment*, today, and quite possibly in surprisingly drastic proportions.

Then again, do we need to know anything of the past, after all? Will a well-endowed investigation of the present suffice? Should we forget the concept of time entirely and look within for the answers? Where is within? Where does *"I"* begin and end? Who and what am *I?* What is this thing that *"I"* daily take for granted and call *my body?*

In this quest for Truth, if we rely solely upon the infinitely varied interpretations of widely contradictory reports, both ancient and modern, and events that supposedly occurred thousands of years ago, the uncompromising reality is this, that *Truth* and her old friend *Justice* will likely remain concealed by the mists time; and we shall be further frustrated by the fact that *Truth* and *Justice* will indubitably remain obscured, so long as they are cloaked in the veils of a mystery that is born of our own shortsightedness, denial and self-deceit.

Remember this: It was a group of people *just like our present day governors and professors,* who wrote history. Their feet stank just as much as ours do today. If that doesn't scare the bejeezus out of you, we don't know what will.

If there is however, any *Hope,* at all, of discovering the *genuine nature* of Truth and Justice, then that very Hope, *along with our salvation,* depends entirely upon our ability to see clearly and ACCEPT *that* Truth, *which stands before us today, in the here and now,* in all its glory. Again, the past, and all its ancient history, and all its winding roads, will only lead us down increasingly twisted trails that lead to little more than our continued bewilderment, whereas today's timeless Truth will set us free.

Friends;

This is a book filled with signposts...

Signposts that point to the here and now and to a Truth that is both, eternal and infinite.

It is a book filled with clues...

Clues, which are presented, for your pleasure, in no particular order.

It is a treasure-hunt... a quest that fulfills the promise, when finally, discovery is made.

It is a Grail-Quest if you will; that is presented in the chivalrous spirit of an age not long past. We pray that these clues will lead you to fountains of crystal clear waters.

Those among you who are destined to drink from the Grail, should persevere and in so doing you will surely rediscover these ancient wellsprings, which were set in place since the times-before-time. Here's your first clue: "Annat" of the Scared Union. Make a note of this word: Annat

Connect the dots as you find them. A pleasant picture will emerge for those who seek diligently.

And now as promised, some advice on:
How to Use This Book ~

Ok~ Be honest with yourself. Are the thoughts that you are thinking your own, or were they purloined from a set of dogmatic beliefs that you switched-over-to after abandoning the nonsense you were programmed to believe-in since birth?

How to make best use of this (or any) book?

Be honest with yourself!
Then respect yourself for having the
courage and compassion to do so!
Thereafter, perform your own independent investigations!
Take no man's or woman's word for it!
Don't be afraid to think, be and "act differently from your piers"!
But just because it's different or politically fashionable
doesn't make it right, so keep an open mind no matter what.

Still confused as to how to make best use of this book?

1. Next time you're in India and you've lost your wallet: Use the mysterious eyes on the back cover of this book to *mesmerize, confound and confuse* a cobra poised to strike at you, while you, *clever devil that you are*, reach round with your other hand, grab his tail, and toss him back into his basket!

2. Use this book to threaten the angry Indian fakir, who is trying to kick you, by waving it aggressively in the air like a Bible (when his audience throws money at ***you*** instead of *him*).

3. The next time you get lost in the Himalayas without a backpack or tent, use a few pages of this book to light your campfire.

4. Use the first or last blank page to write yourself a memo to remember to bring a butane lighter along next time you go camping in the Himalayas (to set the pages on fire in number 3, silly!)

5. Recycle this book (No, not for toilet paper, goofball!) Give it to an unsuspecting fool who thinks themselves already enlightened (*after you have read and digested the words of wisdom yourself of course!)*

6. Swat flies, scorpions, spiders and gnats (but only in self defense, ok?). PS this works not only in India, but in other countries as well! (*You know*, the fly swatting thing... but you'll get the most use out of it in tropical locations or on banana boats and slave-labor coffee farms, poppy farms and cocaine factories.)

7. If you have a lousy sense of humor, then just read the book with tears and a sad frown on your face... someone might come to your rescue.

8. Give this book to the poor cobra (to read while he's stuck in that basket) and tickle his belly as you give it to him.

Read this book from the beginning and resist the urge to skip around; you may skip an important point (clue) or two; or worse still, you may miss the Key Element that unlocks the alchemical codices, a Key that is hidden amongst the words and chapters of this very book.

DISCLAIMER

We remind you that this is a book of irreverent heresies.

There is no substitute for a good editor. But after all, editors are only human (or so they would have us believe) and good editors are hard to find: *Rare as hen's teeth!* Like any of us, they have their likes and dislikes, their prejudices and pet raves, they have their good days and their bad days. Then there are those few editors (the majority?) who, put job protection well ahead of *actually doing their job~* much less would they allow themselves to become involved in the process of actually expounding the Truth (heaven forbid). This certainly has an effect on serious authors with an agenda who, are politically inclined! Most will argue that Truth is relative, but in actual fact it isn't, because "Truth is that which never changes." It's *your point of view that's relative,* not the Truth.

So, if you're determined to defame all convention (as we are) and if you've set your heart upon the lofty goal of releasing yourself from the mental and emotional prisons that were built to restrain your free spirited attempts at enlightenment (as we are), one *must* be prepared to *go it alone!*

Thus, if all of the political and religious dogma seems to fall short of the goal~state, and you have determined that you want more out of life than the latest adds, fads and commercials on the TV can offer: then just relax (as we do), and rest assured that you are *not* alone: We're just far and few between. *There are many Others who do agree with You,* except that They are not so outspoken, as We tend to be. They're lying low, keeping their heads down, most of time (protecting their jobs and children), trying to keep a *very* low profile~ hence you will have to think for yourself at first, though you may feel quite isolated in pursuing your new-found definitions; and you will need to do some things on your own, if you want to break through the barriers that have been setup to keep you docile and subservient.

You may suddenly "see through" a few of your "hard-won" friends and discover more superficiality than you had previously imagined possible. You may even lose the respect of a few family members; but as you progress, your self-esteem will soar, and you will find new friends to share your urge to discover ever brighter and clearer, open spaces. So don't be afraid to explore and enjoy the more joyful aspects of this amazing universe in which we live.

Just beware, along the Way, of those people who claim that they want to "help" you and be cautious with people who want you to "help them."

As we remind you repeatedly that this is a book of irreverent heresies, we must also point out that, in this instance, finding a good editor who could perform in an unbiased, professional manner was more than a challenge; it was about as close as one can come to achieving the impossible! So we invoked the magic of the Little Red Hen Herself, and we went DIY all the way... (Do It Yourself). We did it the old fashioned way, that is to say, we did it all by our witty~bitty selves...

[smiley face with wizard's hat & beard goes here~ **<};o)>** "have a nice day"].

Because we have contravened so many politically correct attitudes, no doubt we will soon find ourselves in a position to "butt heads," on one point or another, with the vast majority of our readership; but*t* that's just part of the price we pay for the "freedom-of-thought," the "freedom-of-speech" and our "right-to-dissent;" particularly in those instances where, pressing the envelope of human bigotry is concerned. You see, the only problem with democracy is that, the majority are usually wrong; and that majority usually forget that the prime directive of any good democracy, is that it should *protect the rights of the* ***minority***. A fact that the majority tend to consciously ignore. The sad truth is that the vast majority of the people of the world are uneducated, and the few that are educated are biased in the extreme, over specialized and generally prone to intellectual chauvinism.

Here you have it, in all of its unmitigated, unadulterated importunity, *written as it were* ***for the minority!*** No doubt the second and third editions, etc. etc., will be more grammatically correct and no doubt, more than a few spelling errors will have been corrected. And oh! not to mention the fact that, a few dates or factoids may not have been set down perfectly (we need to leave a few crumbs for the academics and critics to moan and groan over! Otherwise they won't be able to justify their salaries and next year's ever-expanding budgets, bombastic entrance fees and those absurd tuition rates...) But, as for now, we hope that you will ex***or***cise[3] common sense and aspire to new heights of pristine cognition. In so doing, forgive us our humanity, while you dear reader, attempt to behave in a more sophisticated manner, however much it pains you to ***laugh*** alongside us, at our mistakes and folly! Have we cast our pearls before swine? We will leave the task of answering *that* question to (you) the reader's *own* discretion.

We have also taken a few liberties with the commonly accepted rules in formatting the "section breaks" and "page numbering" of this book. We know the rules, yet consciously choose to ignore them.

That having been said, we hereby acknowledge the fact that *we do err*; and there's no doubt about that. In turn, we offer our heartfelt apologies as such; but we just couldn't spend anymore time or money on protocol. We felt an urgent need to get this message out ASAP and hopefully, begin the process of reversing global warming and to bring an end to the senseless killing of our friends and neighbors 'round the world; *and that includes putting an end to any and all wanton and pointless slaughter of plants and animals (fauna and flora).*

Be kind to animals: Love them, don't eat them!

Respect the Seed Cycles! and help to insure that our future generations enjoy the right to the pursuit of happiness as we have. Be reverent of all plant-life and do not discount their contributions to our evolutionary process.

Homage to the Emerald Tablets of Thoth~ The Mighty Chlorophyll; wherein all the Secrets of Life are Written.

In closing this Disclaimer~ AGAIN We implore you, read this book from the beginning and resist the urge to skip around; you may overlook an important point (clue) or two; or worse still, you may miss the Key Element that unlocks the Alchemical Codices, a Key that is hidden amongst the words and chapters of this very book.

3 **exorcise~** conjure out or attempt to conjure out (an evil spirit) from a person or place : an attempt to exorcise an evil spirit to rid an individual of an evil spirit

We neither agree or disagree with the concepts and contents of this book.

It is provided for evaluation purposes only and to stimulate original thought.

The Publishers

A quotation from the "*Hope Fiend" himself*~
"Feel good and do no harm!"
Timothy Leary PhD.

AN ANCIENT ODE TO ORMUS
& A LOVE SUPREME

"I have a word of secret to tell thee,
a message to whisper unto thee:
It is a contraption that launches words,
a Stone that whispers.
Men its messages will not know;
Earth's multitudes will not comprehend."

"Heaven with Earth, it makes converse,
and the seas with the planets.
It is a Stone of Splendor;
To heaven it is yet unknown.
Let's you and I raise it
within my cavern, on lofty Zaphon."

- Ugarit tablet

See: "The Stairway to Heaven"
by Zecharia Sitchin

TABLE OF CONTENTS

ACKNOWLEDGEMENTS

I salute the Deva within you...

First of all I wish to acknowledge You the Reader and your genuine interest in all things sacred and truthful.

Secondly I would like to recommend "The Alchemy Key" by Stuart Nettleton. It is a book that will prove an invaluable resource to the sincere and diligent aspirant. See <http://www.ormus.net> for the latest information on how to access this most excellent and voluminous work. (Or just search the internet for it.)

Third: I salute the Deva, which resides within you! The Divine Light of Reason[4] which shines forth throughout the Universe, rooted in Divine Darkness (perfect peace, tranquility and stillness). The Blessed Darkness graciously harbors that Light and receives the Light wherever It may wander and fulfills all those who, wonder at the miracle of the simultaneous union and individuality of the Her Light and His Darkness. They belong to each other. The Light and Darkness (Yin Yang) are NOT opposites that attract~ They are complimentary components of a unified field. They BELONG to each other.

We acknowledge the Light and the Darkness as an inseparable pair and offer homage to the Holy Union of the Black Madonna and her Father-Son-Consort, the Christ.[5]

As the Universal Host of All Things She is nameless, She is a Perfect Void; She is the Ultimate Mystery and as such, remains indescribable.

She is Nothing and nothing doesn't exist... She is Paradox.

As the Mother of all things- They are namable, when the Holy Light refracts into myriad forms and states of matter, both imperfect and perfected, and as the ineffable Word of Godde; She/He is namable, as the Divine Intonation and Perfect Harmonic, the Common Denominator, Master Architect and Sacred PHI of Life with Its perfectly balanced manifestations: The Divine Paradigm.

"In Motion they separate, In stillness they fuse."
"Attempt the difficult, Approach the Impossible."

~from the T'ai Chi Ch'uan Classics

Peace Be With You

William Hearth

4 **Light of Reason** ~The Universal CHRIST (not necessarily the "Jesus" of Orthodox and Catholic Christianity, ***nor*** the Gnostic; ***more at~ the teachings of the Essene Jesus (Mar Yeshua the vegan)***

5 ***CHRIST~*** Anointed One: literally ***one whose DNA and light-body has been perfected:*** One who has emerged from the primordial chaos and having shared the Breath of Godde [as in, One who enjoys the benefits of the Manna of Heaven] is an accurate reflection of the Divine Paradigm; a Master Architect who knows how to access, transmit and construct the Sacred Blueprint of Life, the clear and present Voice of the Living Word ...anointed with ORMUS: having completed the fasting.

More at: The Living Word of the Living Godde given to Living Prophets for Living Men and Women; ***Kabalistic version ~*** "That which is spoken from mouth to ear~ the sharing of The Breath of Godde and Water of Life." ~ The Living Word. ~ A Living Fountain of Knowledge

"By human hands & feet, the New World shall be built." ~ Nicholas Roerich

~A SAPPHIC HYMN~[6]

Happy Bridegroom! Now has dawned
That day of days supreme,
When in thine arms, ' wilt hold at last
The Maiden of thy dreams.

6 **Sappho circa 610 B.C to 570 B.C** "...Sappho lived in the sixth century B.C. on the island of Lesbos, which is situated in the Northeastern Aegean. We do not know the exact date of her birth or death, but it has been suggested that she was alive from about 610 B.C to 570 B.C. Her family is known to have been wealthy merchants; Lesbos in the sixth century B.C. was very prosperous. That she lived a life of luxury, and loved beautiful clothes and ornaments is clear from several allusions in the fragments. In addition, it is known that women of Lesbos at this time were exceptionally liberated and moved freely in social and religious circles. Some of the other Lesbian poets of this period were Terpander and Alcaeus, and there were several other women poets."

~~> [continued on page 237]

DEDICATION ~ HOMAGE TO THE LADY OF THE LAKE

To All Courageous Troubadours
&
The Fyne Ladies Whom They Serve

For all those Women and Great Grand Mothers
whose names have been lost to antiquity.

It is, after all, due to your perseverance, loving~kindness
and upon occasion, your ruthless dedication to the
survival of your children, that we are all here today!

Thank you one and all for being so very patient with
your domineering Fathers and their haughty Sons.

Perhaps they'll all awaken now from their illusions of grandeur
and join the gentlemen in kissing your daughters' pretty feet!

LANGUE D'OC ~ LANDFALL "IN A BOAT WITH NO OARS"

A Romance language called *provencal*, or *langue d'oc.*

Troubadours composed poetry in a Romance language called *provencal*, or *langue d'oc.* The canso d'amor (love song) was one of the rich and varied poetic forms used by troubadours. In the canso, the poet imagines the lady of his desires as the model of virtue, and dedicates his talents to singing her praises. The troubadours' praise of physical love stood in direct contrast to traditional Christian morality. Their ideal of love and their praise of women influenced many writers, poets and song-writers; and even the clergy were often moved to entertaining an original thought on occasion!

Where is Languedoc?
What is the connection between Languedoc
and Mary Magdalene?
Who is the Migdal-Eder?

FOREWORD ~ QUESTIONS THAT MERIT ANSWERS

Mary Magdalene, a Master Alchemist?

Did Mary Magdalene act as mentor to the man whom we today incorrectly refer to as Jesus the Christ? If there was no Catholic Church during her lifetime, then why would Mary Magdalene have been considered a heretic and by whom?

Did Saul of Tarsus (and later, his following) wage a campaign of terror and character assassination against Mary Magdalene (and her descendents), even after his deceitful conversion, throughout the days of the early Ebionite Church (and later during the Templar executions and other Inquisitions directed by the Catholic Church)? Did Judas really betray Jesus and Mary, or did Saul of Tarsus and other detractors of Mary Magdalene, frame Judas and deceive Peter? Did Saul instigate the assassination of James, the brother of Jesus?

Was Mary Magdalene a well-respected leader among the early Jesus movement: Was she THE Migdal-Eder[7] "Tower of the Flock"? Was she THE principal Leader? Was the original Jesus Movement actually a Goddess sect derived from the ISIS Mystery Schools of Egypt, a movement that had every intention of undermining the male chauvinist YHWH cult that ruled UrSalem through intimidation, fear and guilt-ridden psychosis? What is the terrible secret that orthodox clergy, both ancient *and* modern, feared so much? Why were they compelled, for over two thousand years, to commit murder and wage a campaign of torture, terror and defamation in order to prevent the people from discovering the Truth? Was Mary Magdalene one the first great champions of religious freedom and philosophical thought in the modern world? Was she one of the early leaders of, what we today refer to as, the *feminist movement?*

Why do we, as a species, suffered so much pain, sorrow and frustration, when we attempt to reconcile our misunderstandings of the male~female principles[8] and the *creation/preservation/destruction* process[9]?

Was Mary Magdalene a Jewish or Egyptian Princess? Did she carry within her DNA structure the Blood Royal or *Sang Raal* of other equally (*or more* important) ancient cultures; an mt-DNA lineage, whose nano-data is critical to the future development of our Adamic Race and our long-term genetic goal-state?

Are we a food-crop being brought to maturity for eventual harvest and consumption by a hormone-addicted, alien blood-lust, *reptilian* society[10]? After all, the large majority of human societies breed turkeys, chicken, ducks, cows, pigs and sheep to satisfy their own blood-lust addictions. Is the harvest period near? The killing-fields are certainly over populated with humans. Whose life

7 Migdal-Eder ~ Later misunderstood as "Magdalene"
See: www. Migdal-Eder.com (or WWW.MIGDALEDER.COM)

8 Yin-yang / bagg-wa

9 /|\ Three rays of Goddehead: Creation~Preservation~Destruction

10 This hardly seems plausible considering the fact that the large majority of the world's populations are little more than skin and bones. A more likely scenario is that there are creatures hovering near our planet that feed on the radiant energy and *vibrations* of our emotional misery (psychic parasites); however when compared to the average chicken farm, *managed by humans,* our lot is not all that different from many animals today that we'll find subsisting in one of our various stock farms! They live mostly in squalor; and likewise, most of us live in squalor. Is this merely "bad management" on the part of both, the humans and/or the aliens?

is more sacred than another's? Are we to believe that our lives, as humans, are more important than the lives of our neighbors who inhabit the animal kingdoms of this planet? With humans being the most selfish and destructive creatures on earth today, it hardly seems fair. *If any creature should be culled from Earth's biosphere, the humans should be the first to go, at least, based on our performance to date.*

Was Mary Magdalene married to Jesus and if so, what did that mean in their lifetime? What might it mean to us today? Did they have children and were their descendents both persecuted *and* assassinated by the agents of a rogue faction operating within the Jesuit Orders? Who are the Jesuits really? Are they *dis*-intelligence-agents left over from a rogue faction of Zealots loyal[11] to Herod[12]and his hench*man*, Saul of Tarsus? Is the "Catholic" Church, after all, nothing more than a well disguised extension of the falsely acquired authority[13] associated with the original Temple of Jerusalem? And is it not run covertly, today, by the same families that once usurped control of the Temple of Jerusalem (with the assistance of Caesar) prior to the expulsion of all "Jewish" people from Jerusalem shortly after the so-called "crucifixion" of "Jesus Christ"?

Follow the money (see below 14C)...

When the Temple was destroyed and all the "Jews" (both genuine and *self-styled*) were sent into exile, what happened to all the money: Tithes & Taxes?[14]

---

11 ***Herod exiled to Gaul*** ~ remember that one particular "Herod" was exiled to Gaul (what is now Southern France) for a period, where he lived out his days with one of his many wives, the infamous Herodias, mother of Salome-the-Dancer, who was tricked by her (Salome's) own mother (Herodias) into demanding the head of one John the Baptist (for use in ***necromancy*** against the increasingly popular Mary Magdalene and her friends who constituted the main body of the Jesus Movement), while Saul (now Paul) went about touting a "new" version of what was essentially his own (Paul's) rendition of Judaic-Christology. In brief... Herod (and all "Jews") in exile who had been banned from living in Jerusalem (by the Roman Emperor after the destruction of the Temple by Titus in A.D. 70) needed a new "headquarters" for their religious banking operation. What better place than the "center of the known civilized world," where their funds would be well guarded and put to good use? (...All roads led to Rome, as did the trade routes for every conceivable commodity). Perhaps the rift between the original Jesus Movement and their archrival Paul (Saul of Tarsus) was more complicated that orthodox religion would have us believe. (More about *"follow the money"* after the definition of necromancy)

12 ***Necromancy*** ~ to conjure the spirits of the dead for purposes of magically influencing the course of events and destiny of living relatives and/or friends of the deceased, through BLACK MAGIC & SORCERY; a form of voodoo used in ancient times that exploited the severed body parts of a dead or living person.

13 ***HEROD*** ~ [there were many men named Herod of course (sons and grandsons), just as there were many Caesars] thus: Herod, the second son of Aristobulus' (Aristobulus' father was also "Herod" the Great {or the *Butcher*}), was king of Chalcis, and, after the death of his brother, he obtained permission from the Emperor of Rome to keep the ornaments belonging to the high priest of the Temple and to nominate whom he pleased (highest bidder?) to that office: *ref. Joseph. Antiq. l. xx. c. 1.* Thus the office of "high priest" had been reduced to a form of prostitution; that is to say that the office of high priest could be "bought and sold like a piece of meat."

About Aristobulus~ *Aristobulus,* who was son of Herod-the-Great {the *Butcher*} (~by Mariamne, she being a descendant of the Asmoneans {Hasmoneans}), *left two sons and a daughter, viz. Agrippa, Herod, and Herodias, (THE Herodias* so famous for her incestuous marriage with Antipas, in the life-time of his brother Philip.)

14 [A] ***King Aretas IV & Herod Antipas ~ {Aretas <=> Aretus}*** Herod Antipas married and then later "divorced" (or put aside), the Daughter of King Aretus IV (the Nabataean Princess Phasaelis) in order to marry Herodias, the daughter of Aristobulus (son of Herod the Great). ***Herodias' significance*** is best understood by the fact that her father, Aristobulus who was reared and educated

Will we ever know the answer to these, and other, related mysteries? Perhaps these questions are nothing more than decoys, designed to distract us from a Secret of much greater importance.[15] Perhaps a Greater Truth exists; a Truth that prefers to remain hidden from the eyes of the unworthy. Is there a Greater Truth that begs discovery by those who have paid the price? Who or what was, "ORMUS‡" and what is "The Secret Alchemy of Mary Magdalene"?

---

in Rome, was later executed by his own father Herod the (Great) "*Butcher*") Aristobulus was the son of Mariamne, the ***last of the Hasmonean (Maccabean) Royal family*** (*Maccabee, Simon*: the leader of the Maccabean Revolt; who lived a life that was similar to that of John the Baptist, in the wilderness, eating bitter herbs and *locust* [***locust*-carob beans**: the carob that is found in health food stores round the world today as a popular substitute for chocolate!] see also *Mandaeans*)

***King Aretus IV was undoubtedly put-off by this "betrayal" of confidence, however important Herod may have deemed the rearrangement of power at the time.* (See "[D]" immediately below)**

The importance of the Nabataean influence ~ cannot been emphasized strongly enough, when an investigation of Mary Magdalene is afoot! *"King Solomon reportedly wrote a book concerning the Philosophers' Stone called* haMa'pen *or* The Compass. *He wrote of how he had acquired the Philosophers' Stone from Bat-Shiva (House of Shiva) or the Queen of Sheba (descendents of Indra {SOMA}, who controlled a domain that stretched from eastern tip of the Oman/Yemen strip through to central Ethiopia [an ancient coastal sea-trade route), who had supposedly received it from her other husband Seman. Seman was reputedly a great sage who lived amongst either the Nabataeans or the Copts.*

[B] ***The distribution of silver*** coinage by Nabataean rulers is especially noteworthy. [To wit, those coins struck in times of Obodas II, 62 B.C. through Rabbel II, A.D. 106.] The political status of Judea under Roman rule, from 63 B.C. forward, was essentially equal to that of the Nabataeans, but curiously, from 63 B.C. onwards, the Nabataeans struck considerable amounts of silver coinage mainly under both, Obodas III (30-9 B.C.) *and* Aretas IV (9 B.C. -A.D.40), whereas none had been attributed to Herod. Then we also have the pure silver coinage of Mane Zori - a Tyrian currency.

[C] ***Follow the money~*** One of the most important Temple laws was a rule that demanded that every male, who reached a certain age (20 years old and onwards), was required to pay the Temple a yearly tithe of a half-shekel per person. These funds were supposedly used to cover the cost of Temple maintenance and its rituals. This religious statute, applied to the entire GLOBAL "Jewish" population regardless of their place of residence! Hence the annual cash income of the Temple amounted to a shocking sum totaling approximately half a million shekels ***per annum***! Thus, Herod's income from taxation alone was astounding! The Mishna is very clear about the form of payment: essentially, that it should be paid in the pure silver coinage of Mane-Zori, a Tyrian currency. Herod demanded payment from many geopolitical territories and might have enjoyed an annual income totaling 1,500,000 to 1,800,000 shekels from taxation alone, never mind all the monies garnered from the sale of sacrificial animals doomed to die for the sins of humans! This is considered to be a very conservative estimate in that Josephus' account detailing of the revenues of his (Herod's) grandson Herod Agrippa I, actually totaled nearly 3,000,000 shekels (Ant. XIX.352). The law remained in effect until the destruction of the Temple by Titus in A.D. 70 (so what happened to the tithes after that?)

[D] ***According to Josephus, Malichus II sent Emperor Titus 1000 cavalry and 5000 infantry in 70 AD, which took part in the destruction of Jerusalem.~*** tisk tisk, that's what you get when you mess around with a man's daughter: REMEMBER here* {Herod Antipas married and then later "divorced" (or put aside), the Daughter of King Aretus IV (the Nabataean Princess Phasaelis) }

15 ***Origins of the HEROD Family*** ~The Idumaeans were a tribe who had been forced by the Nabataean Arabs westwards into southern Judea, where they had been forcibly converted to Judaism by the Hasmonean rulers of Palestine. The Idumaeans were for this reason "Jews" of a recent and suspect background. At the same time they were shrewd, and had no scruples about making political deals with the Romans for their own advantage. They married for political gain and their own convenience; thus Paul and Herod had much in common, although, technically speaking, they might be considered to be "Jews," in actual practice (and in spiritual conviction) they were loyal first and foremost to themselves and there own private, political agendas. Respect for religious convention had little or nothing to do with their actions.

~ THE ONE WHO CEASED TO EXIST ~

We are all creating our own reality, within realities, and these realities either clash and or resonate with the realities of others, in many different ways... the result being this present moment.

One has the option of removing oneself from this dynamic chaotic exchange, but few choose that road less traveled.

There is a place, an island of stillness where a moment of serene bliss exists~ a unique occasion and right juncture. It "floats" in the midst of the conditions, but few there be that find it.

So long as you are striving with others, yours is a world of strife; but, when you retreat into the holy of holies, your life becomes a reflection of your own deepest Sacred Nature.

Either you flounder in the Seas of Samsara, or you rest serene beyond its waves, as a mere hint of existence, among the Mists of Avalon.

Fear nothing, such as possession by an evil-spirit, except that you create it for yourself: Certainly, there is an enormous amount of superstitious ignorance in this world!
If you would know the real, you must begin with "nothing" and cling wholeheartedly to interior peace and utmost emptiness.
Only she who has emptied both heart & mind can hope to embrace the Eternal.

When you have rid your mind and heart of all dross, you can begin to understand. But, so long as your mind is filled with thoughts of chasing your unwarranted desires, you cannot see the Light clearly, nor will you hear the Sound (Uni~Verse~All AUM). Desire is not a bad thing. Desire is an instrument to be used sparingly and in a focused manner. In Tantra we embrace the All while clinging wholeheartedly and single-mindedly to utmost emptiness; sexuality is to be revered and cherished; it is not treated as a dirty little secret.

Try to watch your breath, focus your heart and mind on your breath and the breath alone... you will discover the mind chasing away after illusions, time after time, like a wild horse. Call it back to the breath. When you can watch your breath with your minds eye continuously for an hour, without wandering, you will know the truth. All your fear and illusion will melt away. This is more easily said than done. If you can't watch your breath for an hour, you are not the master of the moment; and you have no idea what karma IS or what karma DOES- you have only glimpsed the hint of its existence.

Peace be with you friends
William Hearth

INTRODUCTION

A carefully constructed set of half-truths creates the perfect lie.

Regarding Alchemy and the Mystic Arts, there is nothing more dangerous than partial knowledge, which is passed-off as complete and thorough knowledge; and there is nothing more deceitful and beguiling than a carefully constructed set of half-truths, which have been presented as the whole truth and the *only* truth.

Any well-read scholar or spiritual adept will attest to the fact that:

> "***A carefully constructed set of half-truths creates the perfect lie,***" ~as it becomes nearly impossible to refute such a paradigm without serious loss of precious time and energy.

This then constitutes the essence of the mystery of **.666** and we shall return to this later and explain, once, and for all time, the Truth that is obscured by this most perfect lie. It has to do with its fractal proximity to .618: The Golden Mean[16].

Mary, Mary quite contrary, how does your garden grow?

There is a ***priesthood*** (hasn't there always been a priesthood?) which, preys upon the innocence, sincerity and naiveté of young men, women and their children- all those spiritually inclined individuals, who seek wisdom, hoping to find purpose and meaning within their immediate lifetime. These good children are the victims of the ***priesthood***.

The children naturally long for freedom and search for an ideal state, one that exists beyond the mundane drudgery of economic, psychological and religious slavery. They are fulfilling DNA's agenda as they seek the goal-state of joy and perfection. Then along come the manipulative intimidators with their priestly constructs, half-truths and partial knowledge, this being their stock-in-trade. The priesthood then proceeds to drive wedges into our social order. The priesthood fragments our families, creating unwanted divisions between brothers and sisters, family and friends, and then they teach us all manner of nonsense, causing us to feel guilty about our natural bodily functions.

If they fail at first to convince us to accept willingly, through clever discussion and cunning persuasion, the priesthood will then resort to "intimidation programming," attempting to instill the "fear of hell" and the associated "fear of damnation," with "guilt related to original sin," or "inherent karma" (as in reincarnation and the threat of being reborn time and again into a countless

16 .618 being the number associated with healthy DNA replication and .666 being the number associated with viral replication (counterfeit DNA)

lifetimes of pain, sorrow and suffering). *These are the consequences,* we are told, *of refusing to accept the yoke of blind-servitude to a god, gods or goddesses.* But these are consequences that can only exist in the imagination of the poor victim/ slave who has been beguiled by the priesthood; for the existence of vicious gods and vindictive goddesses, are nothing more than mere fantasy, the memes[17] that are engendered and embedded by greedy, insatiable, power-hungry and tyrannical individuals (who masquerade as priests *and priestesses*).

There is of course a Godde,[18] but Godde does not engage in the commerce of souls. Godde does not delight in the shedding of innocent blood, nor does Godde delight in the idea of revenge, per se. One's loss of freedom, which results from wrongful thoughts and actions, or negligent inaction, cannot be bought and sold, as the priesthood would have us believe.

Nether does Godde require that we perform rituals and rites such as those found in various superstitious mainstream religions and other sinister cults, nor that we should have need of casting spells, or that we should pray to heavenly bodies such as planets, moons or stars.

Neither does Godde require that we pray to Godde, for Godde exists in a pristine state that supersedes the need for such frivolous and trivial activity. Godde does not seek the young fool; the young fool seeks Godde.

If and when we finally recognize Godde and in so doing, eventually find our way to Goddehead, we contribute to the sum of all joy and bliss, which is ever-increasing in the heart-mind-body of Goddehead. Goddehead is a state of ever-expanding and ever-increasing bliss, or nirvana... but the size of Goddehead is a "relative" state (in Einsteinian terms). In an infinite and eternal space-time continuum, *size or volume,* when measured against infinity and eternity, is relative to the point of view of the beholder. It is a matter of perspective, or a lack thereof. Although ellusive and mysterious, Goddehead is a state of being that is available to some but, it defies description.

Indeed, ultimately, the enlightened individual enjoys a freedom that is unfettered by such frivolous comparative nonsense. The enlightened individual does not pray to trees or mountains, stars or invisible giants, nor to other men and women. One becomes the prayer. *One's very existence is prayer.*

Godde, although distant and aloof, is simultaneously warm and compassionate. Godde would have us commune consciously with certain Benevolent aspects of Creation so that we might experience, first hand, the joys, bliss and benefits of a personal relationship with the Sacred.

The Great Freedom knows no boundaries; Complete Liberation from ignorant superstition is all that is required of those who hope to attain the Final Emancipation. This is what Mary Magdalene and her Beloved *Friend* envisioned for those of us who would place loving kindness above all else. How one might

---

17 **Meme:** Etymology~ alteration of *mimeme,* from *mim-* (as in *mimesis*) + -eme. Date: circa 1976

meaning: an idea, mannerism, behavior, style, or usage that spreads (often insidiously) in a viral manner from person to person within a culture; usually in a subliminal manner and without the conscientious consent of the host.

18 **Godde:** An expanded concept of God as existing beyond a male or female aspect, wherein God is neither He nor She: more at the Chinese (Taoist) explanation of the **bagwa:** *"In motion they separate, In stillness they fuse."*

achieve this Liberation is the principal subject of this discourse: ORMUS‡~ The Secret Alchemy of Mary Magdalene Revealed.

Although it may be true that a small sacrifice will be required, it is not a sacrifice of blood, nor is it a sacrifice of our virginity, sexual or otherwise, (as many priests would have us believe). It is the sacrifice of our own greedy nature and the inner-beast, which is required, not the sacrifice of some poor animal at an altar, nor is it a sacrifice of the proverbial prenuptial virgin who has been seduced or beguiled into the bed of a so-called "tantric master" or some scheming S&M coven obsessed with Wiccan rituals.

We must fight the Holy War within ourselves, for the true Jihad is waged within. It is not an external battle, as some fanatics would have us believe. We face the enemy within and make a friend of our enemy; thus, neutralizing the beast~within, we *turn the lead into gold* and we achieve liberation from illusion and dismantle the programming of the *false-desires that are triggered by insidious* (.666) memes & virus.[19]

We must perform an exorcism; the "exorcism of the worm," (not snake or serpent, but *worm: as in mucoid plaque*) and we must transmute the "lead" into "gold," in a very real and tangible manner.

Make no mistake, the transformation is not allegorical, it is both, real and physical, as well as ætheric. When once you have tasted the BREATH of GODDE you will never be the same again.

The "transfiguration" is not a mere figure-of-speech, nor should the term be misconstrued in this instance as a symbolic gesture; it is a tangible, "what you see is what you get" reality, one that you can quite literally hold in your hand (not that you would want to: "mucoid plaque" is very ugly, stinky stuff!) But you will want to hold and keep forever the BREATH of GODDE that fills your entire existence and the golden flower that will blossom in your innermost being.

19 In one report found in ***Nature Magazine*** it was revealed that the DNA sequence of a virus that infects and replicates inside Synechococcus strains, eventually kills them. The research team discovered that this particular phage contains two genes for proteins required by the Synechococcus' photosynthetic process.

Under "normal" circumstances, these two proteins are damaged by sunlight, thus the bacteria are constantly building copies as replacements. However the supposition is that as a virus attacks a Synechococcus, the phage performs a shutdown of the majority of the native genes. Therefore, in order to support the continued production and transmission of energy essential to its own reproductive cycles, the phage supplies replications of the photosynthetic genes. Mann the team-leader surmises that, "It's not an act of altruism on the part of the phage. It's a cynical takeover of the cell."

Another concept that was developed as a result of such investigations of cyanobacteria, is that the cyanobacteria are not equipped, as many other bacteria are, with genes dedicated to perception of and reaction to, the environment. Since the ocean is such a vast and consistent (naturally homogenized) environment, the admixture of the overall ocean-space as a macro-environment is relatively stable, hence there's was no pressing need to sense change, to date. However, now that humankind have interfered so dramatically with the natural balance, one might say that "all bets are off," at least within the foreseeable future.

Man made interjection aside, iron concentrations within the ocean do vary considerably and there is sometimes a scarcity of that metal, depending upon volcanic plume activity and related issues. This phenomenon is therefore the most likely reason why cyanobacteria developed an additional, and very rare, genetic structure that enables enzyme activity, which requires nickel and copper, as opposed to iron, to carry out their metabolic activities.

The BREATH of GODDE exists in an intra-dimensional time-space continuum, and its presence is governed by a subtlety that, so long as an aspirant is subject to the "normal" mode of consciousness (which the majority of human beings operate under), defies logical explanation.[20] However, when the transfiguration occurs~

You can feel it in your heart.
You can touch it with your hands.
You can taste it with your mouth.
You can see it with your eyes.
You can smell it with your nose.
You can hear it with your ears.
And finally you will know the Truth.

But you might not be able to *explain it to those who are still living under the spell induced by modern technocracy or its more ancient theological dogmatic brainwashing systems which stem from (outdated and immoral) religious programming techniques.*

The Light of Godde, the physical world and our physical bodies, are not opposites working-at-odds with one another. The Light of Godde and Your Body are two aspects of a greater being, which must be brought into harmony. When Your Body and The Light of Godde are made resonant, the potential for transfiguration is created on an individual basis.

It is best likened to the tuning of a series of pianos~ certainly not quite as simple as tuning the strings of a violin or guitar; it is considerably more complex, and yet, it is a reasonable goal and an acceptable expectation for a sincere aspirant. Of course, tuning a piano requires a complex skill-set. Nevertheless, the serious and sincere aspirant will achieve the goal-state if they persevere. The stress between the highest notes, mid-tones and the lower octaves of the heart stings located in the subtle body, must be brought into balance. Once attuned, an opportunity will arise~ an opportunity to intone the "Lost Chord". This is a specific sound (resonance) that you will sing to the heavens at the appropriate moment.

Think of tuning a set of pianos. There are seven pianos (chakras) each ranging in size and pitch, each one an octave higher than the one previous. Think of each separate piano as one of your chakras[21]. The chakras must be tuned and they must each learn to recognize one another, and to differentiate between commands issued by the *conductor,* the "Master Architect (.618), as oppossed to those counterfeit commands issued by virus and other parasitic entities that exist at microscopic and subatomic levels (.666).

We will explain all this in greater detail to those who have completed certain

20 The inability to provide a logical, academic or intellectual explanation for paranormal phenomena does not preclude the continued persistent existence of said phenomena.

21 **Chakras:** The seven nexus within the human body where the subtle nervous systems interface.

prerequisite processes.

This immutable, indelible Truth is the original and everlasting Good News. It is the Word of Reason and It Lives and Breathes within each and every one of us for a limited period of time. During that limited period of time we are all given the opportunity to act consciously, and of our own free will, to implement the necessary activities that will liberate us from our larval existence and thereafter attain to a state of transfiguration (or metamorphosis if you prefer) at which time Goddehead[22] may be realized.

Mary Magdalene, also known as "Maria Prophetissima", or Prophetissa; a.k.a. "The Lady of the Lake" in Arthurian Legend, and Notre Dame [Our Lady] in Masonic and Templar Tradition, was one of the great teachers of mankind, a troubadour and messenger, who sought to bring this Truth and Light into the world of men. Both she and her Beloved Family of Friends, along with her descendents and her ancestors, kept this simple truth and method alive for generations dating back to times immemorial.

In keeping with those ancient traditions, we present here once again, for them that have ears to hear and for those who have eyes to see, the original Gospel of Peace and the Good News as it is written in the Book of Life~ the very DNA Itself and the Emerald Tablets of Thoth, the mighty chlorophyll, wherein all of Life's Wisdom resides. These two are the door and lock, through which we are admitted to the Tantric Wedding Chamber, where the Light, Power and Majesty of the Mitochondria are made manifest.

It was truly written that, *"The Greatest, Wisest and Strongest, resides in the smallest."* (Psychedelic Prayers by Tim Leary) It is on this premise that this discourse has been written. We pray that this work will help you choose the blessed path and Way of Life that will bring you all the joy, peace, bliss and prosperity that you so richly deserve.

With my sincere affectionate regards and a warm, heartfelt welcome-back to Goddehead!

Peace be with you friends,

William Hearth
Japan March 11, 2007

22 **Goddehead ~** The unified (field) state of enlightenment where male and female resolve into One; the Omniverse™.

PREFACE

Before the Bible was contrived, the Truth prevailed

Christology(1) and Pauline Christianity(2)[23] should not be confused with the original Jesus Movement(3)[24].

These three, although originating from the same root, should in nowise be regarded as one and the same thing, at least in so far as a genuine quest for truth is concerned.

While the **first** *(Christology)* precedes the Jesus Movement by several centuries as a mystical attempt at reflecting the truth, the **second** *(Pauline Christianity)* is an outright lie, malicious attempt at counterfeit *(.666)* and theft of resources; and both *(Christology and Pauline Christianity)* are mere sets of half-truths which only serve to beguile the unwary pilgrim, one being the result of benign error and the other a loathsome, cancerous growth.

The **third** above mentioned *original Jesus Movement* (and least popular we might add), ***is the genuine article***, but most wouldn't recognize the Absolute Truth even if it walked right up to them and kissed them between the eyes (or "on the mouth" as the Gnostics might say!).

A **fourth** offshoot from the vine, namely, Gnostic Christianity, which offers a threefold path to confusion, is no more rewarding than these first two. (Three classic versions[25] of Gnostic theology are proffered) The sincere aspirant must learn to "see through" *all* falsehoods if they would know the Absolute Truth about ORMUS, Mary Magdalene and her Secret Alchemy. One must research diligently the wisdom of the original Jesus Movement and its source.

---

23 ***Pauline Christianity~*** (.666)

24 ***Original Jesus Movement~*** (.618)

25 ***4th version of Gnostic assumption appears on the horizon ~***

We now have a fourth version of Gnostic thought emerging (for example www.essene.net: which in our opinion is a well constructed vegan website with a very rare and interesting online historical library, whose teaching comes quite close to the truth *[except that reincarnation is still touted as being an acceptable explanation for the human condition].*)

This concept (*reincarnation*) is yet another misunderstanding of how RNA-DNA operates as a *superconductive memory storage and processing apparatus*. Remember please, that *gnosis* is meant to describe *knowing* (*not guessing*). When one truly *knows* the Truth, such nonsense fades in comparison. If you feel the need to join an order or group of some description, you must be prepared to negotiate a labyrinth of rituals and rules (because legalists abound where genuine gnosis and understanding are absent).

The urge to join a tribe, sect or group is a natural human instinct, since human beings are essentially social creatures. However, the final liberation is a personal experience and the *journey within* is a sacred experience that is unique for each individual.

When you finally discover who and what you really are, the *false sense of separation disappears* along with the *illusion of a need to join a group* or a membership body. ***The unified field (state of enlightenment) is complete unto itself.*** When you finally become One with the Omniverse and attain unity, you ***are*** *the group* ***and the*** *individual* ***simultaneously***. Your sense of separation will disappear, and you will rest at ease in a state of pure enlightenment. There is no beginning and no end to your *self* (*selves*).

The "Spirit of Discernment" must be correctly activated, lest one remain lost in a labyrinth of benign fallacy, malicious deceit, lies or insidious half-truths.

"Take no man's word for it!" [26]

This having been clearly stated, we proceed.

Discussions of Mary Magdalene are very much in vogue of late, thanks to the writers of books like "Holy Blood Holy Grail," "The DaVinci Code," "Bloodline Of The Holy Grail," "Genesis of the Grail Kings," "Realm of the Ring Lords ," "Lost Secrets of the Sacred Ark," and "The Magdalene Legacy."

Dan Brown, Sir Lawrence Gardener, Margaret Starbird, Michael Baigent, Richard Leigh and Henry Lincoln, who are all best selling authors, all share a common thought. (Can you imagine what that might be?)

Thus, most recently, Mary Magdalene's role in the dispensation of the Truth has enjoyed much fanfare as well as scrutiny and ridicule. *The usual mudslinging prevails as well of course; and yet, fortunately for all of us, her detractors are rapidly losing ground.*

However, so long as scholars, cynics and historians continue to pour over dead and decaying scriptures, no Truth will ever come to light, for this is not The Way of Life; it never has been and it never will be. With all due respect, these all make for interesting stories, best selling novels and scholarly presumption, but it will never lead the sincere aspirant to a complete understanding of the final emancipation.

What we enter into here is a discussion concerning the LIVING Word. We are not preoccupied with the scriptures, which are dead. Like our ancestors before us, following in the footsteps of Mary Magdalene and Jesus, we declare ourselves to be heretics and we question authority with audacious impunity.

When we are born, our "names" are "written" into the Book of Life[27], generation after generation. Thereafter, when we die, with few exceptions, our "names" are in turn "removed" from the Book of Life[28],

---

26 "Take no man's word for it!" ~ an ancient alchemical axiom; also attributed to **ancient** *Freemason* reasoning. The reader will want to research the difference between an ***ancient*** *freemason* and other aspects of the modern (occassionally nonsensical?) Masonic orders; i.e.: ask yourself this question, "What is a Freemason as opposed to a Mason (in the sense of ancient and mystical fraternities)?" We refer here to the ***original and ancient freemasons and NOT to the modern (often, but not always, nonsensical?) Masonic orders.*** We however intend no disrespect to the individual members of modern Masonic orders whatsoever! To the contrary, any sincere seeker deserves the respect of his or her fellows, however misinformed they may be.

27 RNA-DNA: ~As processes of constructive protein routines that result in the formation of a conscious living organism.

28 RNA-DNA ~ observing the rules of data storage, filtration and processing of the lifelong experiences of a conscious living organism, which are used in turn for the construction routines of future generations. An organism's data is passed along for use by future generations essentially by three means;

1. through the standard (hard-wired) reproductive processes

2. through *subconscious* intuitive processes (wireless & *super*conscious!), which utilize the superconductive resources of ORMUS (ORMEs) nano-particles that are to be found naturally

generation after generation. At this point, when removal from the Book of Life occurs, only a small collection our more significant memories are retained. In this discourse we shall concern ourselves with the exceptions to this norm, for it is these exceptional people, who remain of interest to us. But please, make no mistake; one need not be exceptional at the onset of the journey. We are not elitists. One may of course become exceptional along the way, if they prefer, providing of course that they are willing to pay the price as they endeavor to perform the Great Work.

The offer is available to the rich and the poor alike. Whether you are a recognized graduate of an august University, a political refugee or a high-school dropout is of little or no import. Your present station in life doesn't matter either. All that is required is an absolute conviction and will to be of service to your neighbors both here on Earth and otherwise. This includes, not only humanity and your neighbors on all sides, the conviction must be extended to *all living creatures*, fauna and flora alike. Your willingness to serve others however may not always be returned in kind, and therefore, a spirit of discernment must prevail at all times. You are called and you are forewarned; "Cast not your pearls before swine, lest they turn and rend you."

"Inter ye in at the straight and narrow gate."

When we look around us, in all that we see, mixed in amongst all the beauty, bliss and joy that life has to offer, there is decay, corruption and oxidization; there is rot and misery ...a curious balance prevails.

Mixed in amongst all this birth, death, & rebirth, there are those few exceptions

occurring in nature.

3. through the production of a genetic-mutant, fruit-bearing limb, called a *"scion"*. A **scion** is a genetically altered branching limb ~ commonly found among *grafted fruit trees,* which are propagated generation after generation by merging a rootstock with a fruit-stock. After decades of sexual frustration (in the natural cross pollination process), brought on by human intervention, a fruit or nut tree will disregard the natural order of male-female hybridization. The fruitwood makes calculations based on its accumulated data and sends out a ***scion***. *The scion is a branch of the fruit tree that contains (internally simulated) inordinately evolved genetic data, wherein adjustments have been made to compensate for changing weather patters, soil conditions and/or other life sustaining or threatening issues. That particular branch* or **scion** *will bear fruit that is quite different from all the rest of the fruit on the tree. This is how many new and interesting fruit varieties are developed in modern horticultural nurseries and orchards.* **Now, reconsider the meaning of the "Priory of Scion."** Are royal families frustrated by the constant inbreeding and utter disregard for the natural selection process? Consider the similarities of Suleiman the Magnificent and Solomon, (King of UrSalem?); they were both polygamists, who insured that future generations had a substantial gene pool to sustain a varied and interesting (royal society) population. We are not making a case either for or against polygamy; we are simply drawing attention to historical facts. In our opinion polygamy is neither male chauvinistic or immoral; it is a matter of personal taste to be decided among consenting adults. Monogamists most certainly are not shining examples of moral fortitude; neither are polygamists to be regarded as immoral or indecent. In a polygamist society, it is crucial that the civil rights of all females be carefully guarded and that they enjoy equal representation in all aspects of government and all other areas where authority is asserted. We may even go so far as to suggest that women should have the right to have several husbands if they are collectively amenable to the proposition. Marital laws should be extended to protect the RIGHTS of CHILDREN over and above every other consideration; if several people agree to protect a clan collectively and they can manage their affairs without violence and bloodshed, that is their prerogative.

to the rules which have fascinated inquiring minds for countless generations. We refer to those elements that do *not* corrode and those elements, which can withstand the test of time. They also appear to be immune to the assault of naturally occurring chemicals and other naturally occurring elements, as well as daily weather and *solar storms.* We refer to the elements of gold, platinum, diamonds and such like.

To the eye of the unenlightened observer, even light itself appears to eventually fade as it dissipates into the void, becoming lost, seemingly forever. Only the gold and diamonds remain steadfast in this ever changing world. What then is the secret of their durability?

Our goal is to attain to a state of consciousness and a living presence, which reflects the qualities of those same said noble elements *and* to be able to shine a light from an unlimited source that resides within our inner core; a radiant light that does *not* fade...

Since ancient times, human-kind has reasoned, "If there be elements that are immortal, then why can't we be long lived as well? Can we not discover the noble element's secret of success and thereby extend our lives indefinitely?"

Then there are those ignorant creatures that would discount this notion, implying that there is something untoward or unnatural about entertaining such lofty ideals and visions of immortality (or if not immortality then, at least longevity), and they would prefer that we all simply accept our fate and die a so-called "natural death."

However, there is good cause to investigate this avenue of reasoning. If our lives were not so short, children would be able to enjoy their childhood and need not be rushed to premature ripening. It would not be necessary to "force-feed" them information in an effort to have them graduate with a PhD early enough to insure that they have sufficient time to payback all their student loans and educational expenses (a process that is unnecessarily expensive in the first place! Scoundrels!).

Our lives would be unhurried and the pace of life on earth would return to its intended gentle flow and subtle mood. Our aggression would subside and indeed we could, beat our swords into plowshares.

Children should be given ample time to enjoy their childhood, to frolic and play, enjoying the sweet dew, sunshine and rainbow-light of their youth. If we lived to be two, three or even five hundred years of age, we could play until sated. A childhood might last a hundred years, or more. Our caregivers will have become wise enough to allow us to partake of these privileges for an indefinite period of time, as they too will have shared in the same joys and compassionate fulfillment.

Our inner child might even become immortal, as we learn to live and breathe in the delicate Realm of the Blessed, in the Realms of the Enlightened. We would not thirst, nor would we hunger. We would not make war on one another. We would be patient, kind and tolerant of our humanity. We would no longer be so obsessed with the rapid and ruthless accumulation of wealth and power. Our desire to procreate would be reduced enormously by default, becoming much more subdued and overpopulation could be controlled naturally as the threat of premature death would be removed.

We should bear in mind, that when individuals feel threatened, they are prone to procreate at an accelerated pace. A wise, spiritually rich and materially wealthy individual is relaxed and moves through life like a Magnificent River; we rest serene like the Great Mountain, our compassion vast and shinning, like the stars that inhabit the great dark expanse of an endless cosmos. Our source of satisfaction is ever flowing, we are never left wanting; we can all drink deeply from the wellsprings and the soul of our Great and Benevolent Mother Earth.

If there were a secret method or a Way, to convert the dross of our corrupt and aging bodies into a more vigorous and healthy paradigm of incorruptible and ethically minded spirit, who would refuse the gift?

Would you not give, or do, whatever it takes to achieve that goal, when thereafter, you would have all the time in the universe to achieve your other objectives?

Then imagine, if you had found a path to "immortality," wouldn't you want to share your discovery with other good people like yourself? The only problem would be convincing others that your method works. Of course this is bad for business where slave traders and authoritarian rulers are concerned. From their corrupt point of view, better that you should die "young" and leave a new collection of slaves to take your place (namely your children), before you had lived long enough to figure it all out~ And rebel!

Is this the story that the books of Moses were trying to tell us, except that its original meaning has become lost in translation over the ages? Was the account intentionally garbled and relegated to obscurity? Did Moses attempt to feed those recently liberated slaves of Egypt the Royal Jelly, or manna, that would have set them free? And did he return with the ORMUS from the Temple of Hathor only to discover that the majority of those people had unwittingly rendered themselves unworthy of the sacrament? And if so, what was it that they had done wrong? Did it have something to do with worshipping idols, or was there something more subtle that concerned him?

Why did Moses die just before they reached Jericho after such an illustrious career of miracles and acts of wonder? After all, the man had supposedly parted the Red Sea itself! Makes you wonder doesn't it?

Was Moses assassinated by Aaron, or had one of Aaron's constituents launched a plot, unbeknownst to Aaron?

Did Moses & Aaron really *"Bring Joseph's bones out of Egypt?" or* did someone conveniently tag those few lines on to an "ancient" text or a copy thereof? Or was the phrase "*Joseph's bones"* indicative of a code-word that stands for something much more significant than the mere skeletal remains of a legendary man? -Particularly if we view the term Joseph as a man's *Title,* rather than a man's *Name.* There were many "Josephs."

"It is not the strongest species that survive, nor the most intelligent, but the ones most responsive to change."

~ Charles Darwin

The Secret Alchemy of
Mary Magdalene
Revealed
(Part "A")

Being the first book of a series in five parts:

~ The Theory of Absolute Nothing and Zero-Point Energy ~

A brief introduction to Ancient Disciplines pertaining to Subatomic Physics, Nano-Technology and their subsequent effects on ancient and modern society.

Part "A" of a Scandalous and Heretical Introduction to the critically acclaimed William Hearth and his much anticipated novel~
ORMUS ‡ The Secret Alchemy of Mary Magdalene
~ Parts I, II and III ~

It has taken all of 2,000 years for the true message of our Beloved Family of Friends to resurface: So **please, since you've come this far, if you skipped the first 40 pages of this book, you'd best go back now and read the book from the beginning...**

Excerpt from "THE HOLY STREAMS"
(Jesus is speaking to his disciples)

"I tell you truly, your body was made not only to breathe, and eat, and think, but it was also made to enter the Holy Stream of Life. And your ears were made not only to hear the words of men, the song of birds, and the music of falling rain, but they were also made to hear the Holy Stream of Sound. And your eyes were made not only to see the rising and setting of the sun, the ripple of sheaves of grain, and the words of the Holy Scrolls, but they were also made to see the Holy Stream of Light. One day your body will return to the Earthly Mother; even also your ears and your eyes. But the Holy Stream of Life, the Holy Stream of Sound, and the Holy Stream of Light, these were never born, and can never die. Enter the Holy Streams, even that Life, that Sound, and that Light which gave you birth; that you may reach the kingdom of the Heavenly Father and become one with him, even as the river empties into the far-distant sea.

More than this cannot be told, for the Holy Streams will take you to that place where words are no more, and even the Holy Scrolls cannot record the mysteries therein."

Original Hebrew and Aramaic Texts Translated
and edited by Edmond Bordeaux Szekely

SECTION ONE ~ THE POLITICS OF ECSTASY

A Welcome Heresy for the 21st Century

How can we begin to breakdown the walls of ignorance created by an endless barrage of misconceptions that have become crystallized in the hearts and minds of the unsuspecting masses over the past four thousand years?

Now that the day has finally arrived and at long last we have an opportunity to rid ourselves of the lies, deceit and illusions, once and for all, will it be the painless, joyful process of liberation that it should be?

Will we have the wisdom, fortitude and courage to dispel these myths that have been ingrained into our collective subconscious through a process of intimidation, wherein fear, guilt, violence and hatred prevail: myths that have been forced upon us century after century?

Will we be able to forgive ourselves and others for all the wrongdoings and acts of injustice that have been perpetrated in the name of God, gods and Goddesses? Or will it become a painfully belabored process of letting-go, shock and stupefaction? Will the process of uncovering the Truth elicit a combination of emotions almost impossible for some of us to stomach?

The procedure of removing the many fat, bloodsucking ticks and leeches that plague us will not be an especially pleasant experience, but the results are undeniably preferable to a blind, intentional ignorance of the Truth. To deny that these microscopic parasites exist and that they aren't slowly sapping our lifeblood is suicidal at best, and sociopathic in the worst instance.

Neither the Gnostic nor Pistic suppositions will suffice, neither Buddhist nor Muslim, nor will any other commonly accepted presumption of any organized dogmatic religion~ "Take no man's word for it!" Though there is an element of Truth in all of these, The Great Truth and the Final Liberation is a phenomenon that cannot be boxed, wrapped, labeled and sold.

In the best of spiritual encounters,
One does not realize that the Master is present.
In the next best spiritual encounter,
One thanks a teacher.
In the worst of spiritual encounters,
One pays the charlatans.

Although much maligned and misunderstood, Mary Magdalene (MarYam HaMelah ~ Lady of the Lake) and Jesus (Mar Yeshua the Maitreya[29] [messiah]) have an important tale to tell.

It is a tale that has endured much adversity. Their story has been told, retold, hacked, rehashed and twisted into a series of myths that are all but unrecognizable as compared to the true and original story. However, their message has survived

29 ***Reverence to the Maitreya***. "Thus, over the face of the Earth, She has laid the particles of the *One Stone*. This new miracle will bind the nations together in cooperation, and that cooperation in the Alatir-Stone, will either resurrect or consume." www.roerich.org www.roerich.net

and it remains with us today. Although those who know it and would tell it, have been forced to remain veiled and secretive for generations, they are coming forward recently in droves, in order that our Earth and its inhabitants might be saved in these troubled times.

Herein follows an account of the true message and Good News of Our Beloved Family of Friends ~ this is but a fragment of the genuine "Secret" Gospel of Peace: offered as an introduction to a novel, in three parts, entitled "ORMUS ‡ The Secret Alchemy of Mary Magdalene."

"Them that hath an ear let them hear; Them that hath an eye let them see."

In spite of the violent practices and horrific intimidator-tactics employed by those, who would deny the masses the knowledge that saves and heals, the "Secret" Gospel of Peace has survived against all odds.

As the masses become increasingly disillusioned with mainstream orthodox religion (and well they should!) many individuals have found themselves (much like Our Lady of the Lake) adrift in a "boat without oars." (so learn the ropes and use the sails!)

Recently, "The Boat Without Oars" story is fast becoming a well know mystical icon among diligent seekers and here's your second serious clue: It was indeed a boat without oars, but it had sails! This is a critical point that all, but a few, have failed to recognize.[30] Yes it was a boat without oars; but that doesn't mean that they were adrift on the Mediterranean at the mercy of the tides and the fates. It makes for a great "miracle story" but that simply isn't the way it happened. They did have sails and most likely a rudimentary rudder![31] "...without oars," yes, but

30 During and well before Mary Magdalene's era, a vast network of interlinked, well known and well traveled maritime trade routes reached all the way from the Japans to Britain and ran down along the east coast of Africa as well. These maritime trade routes augmented the overland routes considerably. Although Arab, and eventually Roman, ships were predominant in control of the (later) India to Egypt trade, most of the exchange between China and India was performed by ships owned or piloted by Indian, Malaysian and Indonesian entrepreneurs. However, it should be noted that historical records indicate that Chinese or Roman citizens rarely made the entire return journey between Egypt and China.

31 **Antikythera mechanism** ~ A mechanism, know as the Antikythera mechanism, is an ancient mechanical device employed to perform analog calculations. It was designed to compute the positions of stars and other celestial bodies. Discovered in the wreck of the Antikythera near the island of Antikythera in Greece, which is located near Kythera and Crete, the earliest evidence of its existence is dated around 80 BC, however, this is not to say that it might not have been around for hundreds of years prior to this date. It may well have been a device that was kept secret from competitors.

Discovery by archaeologist Spyridon Stais reportedly occurred in the year 1900-1902 at a depth of approximately 42 meters in proximity to numerous other statues and artifacts which were also retrieved by Greek sponge divers. Originally mounted in a wooden frame, the reconstructed bronze mechanism is surprisingly thin, at approximately 33 cm high, 17 cm wide and 9 cm thick. It was inscribed with over 2,000 characters, but the full text of the inscription has not yet been published despite the fact that about 95% of it has been deciphered. Why?

The device is displayed in the Bronze Collection of the National Archaeological Museum of Athens, accompanied by a reconstruction. Another reconstruction is on display at the American Computer Museum in Bozeman, Montana.

The ship was Roman, although the mechanism was apparently crafted in Greece.

Being one of the world's oldest known geared devices, a major article in Scientific American entitled "An ancient Greek computer," [June 1959] the theory that the Antikythera mechanism is a device specifically designed for calculating sidereal time, the positions and motion of stars and the

what does that mean? See how easily misconceptions arise? So, "How can we escape the quagmire of deceit and misunderstanding that surrounds us?"

What we need today is a spiritual compass and theological chart that will guide us safely through these troubled waters; a stable method that will insure our smooth and steady return to a safe harbor. In order to achieve this, we need to understand how to steer our boat with sails, a very special art indeed that was known to the ancients and in particular, the Phoenicians and Minoans:

There was a time, when sailors had not yet discovered the use of built-in rudders. They steered their boats with sails and sculling alone; sails and oars. Large galleys had many oarsmen, as they could not depend on winds alone, in the likely event they were attacked by pirates or enemy fleets.

Smaller, faster boats didn't employ a team of oarsmen however, as they relied on sails and their intimate knowledge of the winds. There were also times, when smaller boats lost their oars for one reason or another and they had to rely solely on their knowledge of ropes and rigging for steerage; i.e. they used the stress derived from the angle of sails juxtaposed to the stress of the keel as it pressed against the water. Thus their steerage was based on the manner in which the sails were set against the wind. At times the winds were adverse and a crew was challenged by the need to sail into the wind. Then they tacked from port to starboard and vice-versa, as they zigzagged their way across the oceans of the world. It took great strength, a subtlety of mind and great determination to sail into the wind without the use of a rudder.

To embark on a journey in a "boat without oars" meant that the spring winds were steady and the use of sails was the fastest, quietest and most dependable method of transport. It did not mean that they were cast adrift due to some cruelty on the part of others. The family of HaRamaTheo were all expert sailors, and quite skilled in the arts of seamanship and celestial navigation.

Mary Magdalene and her Beloved Family of Friends were faced with the challenge of sailing across an inland sea, a task that they were well prepared for, having successfully navigated the dark nights of human indifference for *countless* generations. They were not the helpless creatures that some would have us believe. They were very capable and shrewd, wise and experienced leaders. Though challenged on all sides, they had no problem surmounting their obstacles. Today we face similar challenges, though perhaps on a much grander scale, as we now prepare to suffer the consequences of (six thousand years of) criminal neglect and gross mismanagement of our natural resources.

---

planets.

The **Antikythera** device utilizes a differential gear ~ the principles of such having been previously attributed to a 16th century invention date. Known for its complexity and miniaturization, the differential gear arrangement allows for addition and subtraction of angular velocities. Such differentials were used to calculate synodic lunar cycles. If indeed the **Antikythera** mechanism is based on heliocentric principles, rather than the geocentric view espoused by Aristotle, which was dominant during that era, it might suggest that a heliocentric perspective was more widely preferred in those days than was previously supposed.

It is unlikely that the Antikythera device was unique in its day. Cicero, writing in the 1st century BCE, describes a device that was built by Posidonius, "...which at each revolution reproduces the same motions of the sun, the moon and the five planets." It is noteworthy that Cicero was a student of Posidonius and as such this may lend support to the concept that an ancient Greek tradition of complex mechanical technology was later transmitted to the Nabataean and Coptic societies.

We ignored the Laws of Life and in so doing we have almost destroyed the delicate web of emerald-green velvet (that precious fabric) that once embraced this fair planet, Earth: Our Web of Life.

Can we find our way back to our ancient primordial Root? Can we restore the pristine balance that we have virtually destroyed during the past two hundred years?

We may not have oars, but we do have sails, as did Mary Magdalene and HaRamaTheo, when they made their famous passage to the Cote d'Azur of Gaul, then later Glastonbury[32] and eventually onward to the Isle of Iona.

They understood the tides and the prevailing winds. They followed carefully, obeying the Ways of Nature; they revered Cosmic Law and held sacred the Laws of Life. They kept the faith, stayed the course, and fought the good fight. They fought with ideas, compassion, forbearance, brilliantly conceived non-violent strategies and most importantly, tolerance.

So how do we get ourselves back on course? We emulate Them. All we need know now, is how to use that same set of sails to steer our boats as well. We can navigate by using the same set of rules that served them so well: "The Laws of Life". It's time, for those of us who would align our individual wills with the will of the Divine Paradigm and at long-last, to make our way Home.

Safe Harbor

32 The word "Tor" of course, is of Celtic origin meaning 'conical hill'. It is located in the midst of a great plain in the Somerset Levels. The area is in fact reclaimed fenland where, the Tor once rose above the waters like an island, but now, it is a peninsula surrounded on three sides by the Brue river. Ruins of a lake-village were found in 1892, indicating that there was a Celtic settlement about 300–200 BC on what was once an island in the fens. The Britons called it *Ynys yr Afalon*, and is now widely believed to be the original Avalon of Arthurian legend. Makes sense in that HaRamaTheo (Joseph of Arimathea), accompanied by Mary Magdalene, is said to have raised the first, "above ground" (not so secretive) Ebionite church there. Now known as (the once medieval church of) St. Michael's.

In 1539 the Tor was the place of execution by hanging of the last Abbot of Glastonbury Abbey. Glastonbury Abbey today in Glastonbury, Somerset, England, attests itself as being "traditionally the oldest above-ground Christian church in the World" situated "in the mystical land of Avalon" and dates the founding of its own community of monks around AD 63; when *HaRamaTheo (Joseph of Arimathea)*, and the *Holy Grail (Mary Magdalene the Migdal-Eder)* planted the *Glastonbury Thorn.*

These Somerset Levels & Moors are a wetland area located in central Somerset, England which consist mostly of marine clay "levels" along the coast, and the inland peat-moors. The nearby Severn Estuary used to cause marine flooding due to its very high tidal range, but now is preserved by various sea defences.

Various scholars have observed geological evidence which suggests that, during Mary Magdalene's era, sea levels were as much as 50 meters higher than they are today. This would have allowed for a rather different approach to Glastonbury, i.e. aboard a ship, borne on the ocean-water.

Likewise this rise in sea level accounts for the flooding of the Celtic Salt flats of Britannia in southern France and the salt famines that ensued as a result of that flooding. This would also be a telling feature of the location of the caves at Qumran near the Dead Sea, i.e they were placed at that altitude to preserve them from the rising sea level. It is also interesting to note that many islands in the Ryukyu Islands chain in southern Japan have no snakes, whereas neighboring islands (only a few hundred meters away) are filled with many species of venomous vipers. Thus, at a certain moment in history, it might have been quite simple to rid Ireland of its snakes!

"Nobody's right, if everybody's wrong..."

"Young people speaking them minds,
Getting so much resistance from behind."

~ Buffalo Springfield

"Remember, ***your body is so much more than a temple, it is an alchemical laboratory*** designed to transmute "lead into gold."[33]

CAUTION! (this is, in part, a symbolic statement, **don't eat lead; it will cause serious illness and might even kill you.** All heavy metals are poisonous, even gold and any other heavy metal consumed, even in tiny quantities, can cause permanent injury or death)."

33 Alchemical terms, phrases and sayings can be both symbolic, allegorical as well as literal. Esoterically speaking, common metallic terms were often substituted for one another based on the **context** and specific placement of the terms within the discourse. Sun could mean Gold, or a chemical solution, or a period of time. Mercury also took on many meanings depending on the exact manner in which the term was employed, it didn't always refer to a silver-colored liquid metal. Lead too, was a word used in many different ways and its meaning varied widely according to the encoding process utilized by the author of the treatise.

CHAPTER ONE ~ MARY MAGDALENE MOTHER & MIDWIFE

Physician & Philosopher; Priestess, Princess & Prophet

If you skipped the first 44 pages of this book you'd best go back now and read the book from the beginning!

In order to explain Mary Magdalene's remarkable achievements and widespread popularity as a human being, covert and otherwise, we must understand, firstly, who she really was. But, in order to understand ***who*** she really was, we must also ascertain ***what*** she really was. When pursuing this line of reasoning, many theoretical dependencies arise.

If ***who*** then, ***what***? If ***why***, then ***how***? ***Is*** she a myth or ***was*** she a real person?

In this introduction to "ORMUS‡ The Secret Alchemy of Mary Magdalene," we will explore many possibilities and pose various hypotheses. More importantly we will offer various scientific discoveries and produce "evidence" as to what Mary Magdalene and her Beloved Family of Friends were really up to as an organized institution.

Certainly, Mary Magdalene and Jesus were not a pair of uneducated simpletons (carpenters and shepherds), as most modern Christian dogma would have us believe! [34]

---

34 ATOMIC THEORY dates back to the 400's B.C. era ~

The philosophy of atomism, that is to say, the idea that the universe is made up of a few simple parts, is thought to have originated sometime during the 400 B.C. period. Atomism was attributed to a Greek philosopher named Leucippus, and his protégé Democritus augmented the concept. It is thought that Democritus coined the term "atom," which literally translated means "that which can not be cut down to smaller fragment."

Leucippus, and his protégé Democritus hypothesized that the small, stable particles, which they called atoms, were all born of a universal substance but took on various shapes, sizes and characteristics. Later on in the 300's B.C., Epicurus, a Greek philosopher presented Democritus's theory of atomic science into his considerations.

ATOMISM~ During the so-called "modern" period known as the Middle Ages, the atomic theorem was not only ignored, but was often repudiated by superstitious church officials and other political leaders. Since atomism had been rejected by Aristotle, the predominant intellectuals of that renaissance period were thrown off-course. Fortunately, the theorem that atoms are formed from a basic unit native to all matter did survive. During the 1500's and 1600's, such founders of modern science, who were also reputedly grand masters of the Free Masons, such as Francis Bacon, Isaac Newton of England and Galileo of Italy continued to believe in the atomic theorem. But those scientists could add little more to the atomic theory as their research was stifled by obstinate politicians and church leaders, and in turn, they were sure to suffer religious and political persecution had they discussed such research and concepts openly.

It was during the Renaissance period that atomism enjoyed a popular return, though it's "rebirth" was accompanied by some unusually severe "labor pains". The word Renaissance is derived from the Latin word *"rinascere"* and alludes to the state of *being resurrected* and/or *reborn*.

It was during the Renaissance period, that many European scholars and artists, particularly those in Italy, were preoccupied with the philosophies and artistic works of ancient Greece, Troy, Rome, Egypt and the earlier cultures of Babylon, China and India. Atomism was one such concept that was under review and fortunately it was resuscitated and eventually *"resurrected from the dead,"* so to speak. They hoped to resurrect other such ancient wisdom and ideas pertinent to these cultures and thereby resuscitate the soul of that cultural beauty; thus, by adapting, adopting and rendering them

When we consider carefully, ***what*** she was, we should begin by reflecting on the context of Mary Magdalene's micro and macro environmental concerns, including both her mundane and philosophical agendas. Furthermore, if we wish to arrive at a realistic and in-depth understanding of her life and times, we should also include in our studies (but not limit them to), the context of her ecological, domestic, socioeconomic, sociopolitical and geopolitical environments.

Whether she was a real or an imaginary person is of great concern to some, whereas for others it is the significance of the ***message*** that she, as a symbolic or mythical heroine brings forth in present times. In this discourse it is her message that concerns us primarily, regardless of arguments pro and con as to her historicity, and this is what we will focus on, as opposed to the issue of whether or not she was a living heroine.

If a heroine is real in the imagination of the aspirant, then that aspirant might make the virtues of a heroine *real* within their own life and times. In this regard, a mythical heroine becomes real, and she takes-on *a life of her own,* by way of our interaction with the ideals that such a heroine represents.

Therefore in this instance we shall speak of Mary Magdalene as if she is a real person. For us, her ideals and aspirations reflect our own and in this regard she lives in us, as we give life to the teachings that she is an expression of. Additionally we shall remain ever mindful and respectful of the fact that the very real possibility exists, that she did in fact live and breathe; and that her descendents do live and breathe as well; and that they do walk among us today, right here, right now, on this very earth, even as we read this book. So...

Let's make Mary Magdalene's issues our own. Let's make Mary Magdalene's humanity our own. After all, people haven't changed all that much in two thousand years. Or have we?

We are affected by the weather, as she was. We are affected by trade embargoes, as she was. We, as good parents, brothers, sisters, teachers, aunts and uncles *and as good neighbors,* we are all concerned for the safety and welfare

---

into their own "modern" artistic, literary, and philosophic endeavors, it was envision that an integrated and holistic age of reason might be born. The Renaissance thus represented a process of independent thought, and quite literally bespoke the advent and rebirth of free-will expression during a period that had been otherwise extremely repressive from a religious and political standpoint.

The Middle Ages theoretically began in the 400's.

The Renaissance overlapped the end of that period (400's) and ran into late 1500's and 1600's. Many of the outdated and immoral attitudes and ideas of the Middle Ages were put to rest by the intellectual leaders of the Renaissance period.

One of the principal differences was the fact that the leaders of the Middle Ages, considered theology to be the most important aspect of education (the study of that which does *not* change: i.e. God and other such immutable concepts). But, the leaders of the Renaissance considered the study of humanity to be more significant and as such, the great accomplishments of other cultures were carefully examined for alternative views as to how and why the Universe operates as it does.

Church dogma and church policy had dominated the earlier medieval thinkers (who had been forced to believe that people's chief responsibility was to sacrifice to God and save wayward souls), the church endeavored to convince the world that all people and natural creatures are dominated by original sin (*and that sex is inherently evil);* including almost everyone except for the pope and his immediate circle of infallible bedbugs). Renaissance thinkers, to the contrary, focused on society's responsibilities and duties to the world in which they lived. They believed that through educational procedures, a civilized society could improve upon the lot of its people rather than trying to convince them that they are all wicked and must buy their way out of hell or purgatory.

of our children *as she would have been.* We are concerned, especially as mothers, for the safety and welfare of our children, as she very likely might have been.

Crop failures, vicious gossip, jealous neighbors, male chauvinism, priesthoods compromised by pedophilia, incest and rape; all the issues that vex humankind today and more, these, as always, are our problems as a species! *Some* of us even have stinky feet![35] [Don't neglect to read the ***foot***notes!]

Are we on the same page yet? Can you smell the earth, the flowers and the barn-carpet underfoot, where the cows and pigs are all so inadequately housed?

Mary Magdalene's issues are our issues, but did she enjoy a more evolved manner of dealing with these issues? Sophistication, diplomacy and charm; were these talents only recently developed, during the past few hundred years? Unlikely! Let's move in for a closer look.

Perhaps the most important and sorely neglected aspect of these issues, *as it likewise remains a sorely neglected issue today*, is the subject of our Natural Ecology: and in more specific terms~ *the environmental sciences and the attendant study of the mismanagement of natural resources and the inherent consequences of such neglect.*

Although indifference to our natural habitat has only become a major political issue during the past few decades, it should be noted that *mismanagement of resources has always been a problem, but we simply didn't realize it until it was all-of-a-sudden almost-too-late.*

Think about it: **Pollution** *and* **Deforestation.**

Did Mary Magdalene's friends and family worry about such issues? As you might be aware, many of today's researchers and scholars are often living under the false assumption that these concerns are limited to "modern" societies. However, this most certainly was not the case. There were very real and serious shortages of natural resources during Mary Magdalene's lifetime. Great wars were inevitably waged to assure acquisition of these limited resources and to extend control over their associated trade routes.

For example there were salt famines and shortages of timber; A severe shortage of medical supplies was an everyday affair. Exotic herbs and essential oils were extremely rare and always in short supply. Some were imported from eastern China and the islands of Japan. Soap and shampoo, dish liquid and bathroom disinfectants certainly weren't available at your friendly, neighborhood convenience store. There were no supermarkets or drugstores. Roads were dirty, pitted and rocky at best.

Additionally, we would surely hope to clarify another sorely neglected aspect of her upbringing; namely, the historical and philosophical issues inherent to Mary Magdalene's life and times.

Did she, and other women like her, read books, ***and if they did, was it necessary for them to do so in secret?***

Were women allowed to read and write and perform research in libraries? Who among them would have had access to the very few libraries that were maintained in her era? Good books were cherished as treasure, being extremely

35 Stinky ***feet*** ~ although having said this, it might surprise you to learn that her feet probably didn't stink. How's that? Well, simply put, her body was not composed of the same materials as are found in the average human being today... sound a bit far fetched? Read on!

rare and valuable, they would have been both guarded and coveted.

In particular, we should also look into the attendant contextual influences, in which her earliest ideals were shaped along with the philosophical environment from which her very thought processes would have emerged.

Did Mary Magdalene have an opportunity to read the works of Lao Tzu, Pythagoras, Zarathustra, and the Rig Veda? Did the Enuma Elish, the Gilgamesh Epic and the Egyptian Book of the Dead influence her thought processes? Had she and other women like her been allowed to read the works contained in the Libraries of Alexandria along with other important books, such as the collections of China's Yellow Emperor, Huang-Ti[36] who, remains one of the world's most celebrated pioneers of medical science and research, due to his landmark introduction of socialized medicine. And how about the I-Ching, which detailed the structure of human chromosomes long before the advent of what we have come to think of as modern medicine?

Had she read Plato, Confucius and the Mahabharata? And was she familiar with the legends of "Indra Who Ate The SOMA" and Siddhartha, the Prince who later became known as Gaotama Buddha; and was her understanding of Buddha at all similar to the twisted and revised versions of Buddhism that survive today?

Would she have been aware that Buddha was originally described as a blue-eyed long nosed Aryan born in the eastern regions of what we now call Nepal?

Did she have contact with the matriarchal society known as the HUNZA who used dried apricots and apricot seed as currency? Was she, in fact, descended from them and therefore a vegetarian or vegan, who abstained from eating animal products of all kinds, as a prerequisite to achieving an alchemical transfiguration within her lifetime? Herod's friend Cleopatra VII (died~44BC) could have been her grandmother!

The average person generally fails to understand the context of her era, her time-line and in general, we also fail to take into account the sort of books and stories that were in circulation at the time of Mary Magdalene's birth, during her youth, her adolescence and her post-puberty years; not to mention the fact that the documented history of those times was constantly undergoing enforced revision and was being, quite literally, rewritten generation after generation, on-the-fly as it were, to suit the needs and whims of whichever ruler was in power at any given moment in history. Her people's ***his***tory[37] was being rewritten two,

36 ***Yellow Emperor's Classic of Internal Medicine*** ~

Approximately five thousand years ago, three celebrated emperors made their appearance on the world stage. They laid the foundation for the empire-wide administration of Chinese medicine intended as an aid to the general populace. The Emperor Fu Hsi is credited with having conceived the system; He was followed by Emperor Shun Nung, who introduced a system for the classification of herbs known to contain aromatic and medicinal properties; Thereafter Huang-Ti, known as the Yellow Emperor, dispatched "doctors" throughout the empire to care for the populace. His treatise, and its later additions comprise the "Yellow Emperor's Classic of Internal Medicine" which is a book expounding the early core principles of Chinese medicine. It is required reading in most contemporary academies of traditional Oriental medicine and acupuncture.

37 ***HIS***tory vs. ***HER***story ~ has become a common expression employed by feminists who advocate a new era of ethical archeology and ethical academia.

The terms ***her***story and ***his***tory used in tandem are designed to draw attention to the possible variances in how ***his***tory may have been viewed, played-out and recorded had women been allowed a more prominent (fair-minded) role in the conception, execution and recording of the major events, which contributed to the development of the so-called civilized world.

three or four times during a single lifetime!

Alas: History is contrived at best; and Mary Magdalene's history was not immune to corruption, as it has also been rewritten, time and again, to suit the whims and private agendas of countless despot rulers, even centuries after her tenure in the Levant. Even to this very day authors manufacture stories, offering unruly and absurd assumptions concerning her history and her person.

Certainly, over the past few thousand years the regal authorities should have employed some sort of extensive, well-rounded, investigative process and a complementary record keeping system; but, as-we-all-should-know-by-now, and much to our chagrin, this was not the case! Neither are such just and ethical methods employed in modern times, when, even today as we read, write and speak, many of our governmental and theosophical institutions insist that we continue to endure a most biased and prejudiced "state of denial," wherein censorship prevails as the accepted norm, particularly among those, who care to possess the coveted "PhD".

Indeed the much overrated PhD, for many, has become little more than a certificate attesting the fact that, in essence, the bearer has agreed to avoid controversy. They agree to make every effort to relegate their public discussions to a "politically correct" turn-of-phrase; and one that has been approved by the church fathers as being "appropriate" (or at least stick to ideas that are appropriate according their financial patrons). Pronounce ideas that are outdated, immoral and simply ridiculous; promote ideas that often exist in absolute defiance of logic and in complete disregard for contemporary evidence that leads us in an altogether different direction! Indeed, the world remains flat for many a professor, confessor and their departmental deans!

As regards biblical history, indeed this sort of well-rounded investigation and complementary record keeping should have become the norm, whereas much to the contrary, the vast majority of people in the world, who are familiar with the name Mary Magdalene know only too well of the malicious myth that was spawned by certain members of the Catholic Church. They proceeded to lead us

---

Indeed ***her***story *(a greater respect for Nature and the Feminine Principle)* might have left the world in a better situation as compared to our current predicament (global **meltdown** ["global *warming"* hardly fits the bill any longer!]). Although this point of view may be embraced as contemporaneously and politically correct (and fashionable), it may also be argued that women are just as greedy and irascible as their counterparts. The real issue is, "would they have expressed their territorial imperatives in a more humane manner?" One is inclined to hope that the equal rights movements will provide evidence as regards these issues in the very near future, but we may never know unless men are prepared to make some major changes in the very near future, and behave in a more civilized manner in the majority. (We are running out of time, and on a global scale the clock is at about five minutes before midnight.)

After all, wasn't it the *mothers of the world,* who, *as the primary caregivers,* gathered the knowledge and wisdom associated with medicinal herbs and minerals, generation after generation, as they nursed their children and their husbandmen (their own little boys grown-up)? Why then is that we see mostly the names of men, when we look at the ***his***torical records?

Certainly Mary Magdalene and her female contemporaries would have asked these same questions at least privately, if not publicly. The problems would have occurred when they asked openly and any such outspoken person would have been denounced as having a "forward mouth." Speak once too often, about such matters of women's equality and no doubt a stoning was soon to follow; unless of course the Lady was from a wealthy and powerful family; then, perhaps after several warnings, if the outspoken woman did not heeded the admonitions, an assassination might be in invoked (against one or all of her family members, since it was they, who had failed to reign her in).

to believe that Mary Magdalene was a prostitute, or at the very least, a woman of ill repute. Then, to make matters worse, even those who sought to defy the teachings of the Catholic Church unwittingly perpetuated the myth, becoming conspirators with their archrivals. *Now they all continue to lead us to believe that Mary Magdalene was a prostitute and a whore, or, at the very least, a woman of ill repute.* **Fortunately, at long last, this rumor has now been exposed for what it really is~ vicious gossip, and an intentional attempt to slander womanhood and motherhood in general.**

Fast-forward to the present, to a time, when a plethora of recent studies, biased and otherwise concerning the sociopolitical agendas of Mary Magdalene have without a doubt, almost thoroughly exhausted the general public's patience!

"What is Truth!" *Bless it all!*

Are you angry too? Well... read on.

What, with there being so many theories and hypotheses surrounding her ministries, it is to be expected that, quite naturally, arguments and rebuttals abound, but, most unfortunately, few or none of them are being based on her original teachings and activities! More's the pity; her original teachings have been almost completely erased from the face of the earth! Her constituency have all suffered a similar fate: *vis-à-vis* The Global Inquisition (YHWH intimidation tactics), its trials and witch-hunts, the continental executions of the Knights Templar, the massacre of hundreds of thousands (some accounts say millions!) of vegetarian mountain people known as the Waldenses[38] as well as another group called the Cathars, along with many others like them, the list goes on and on.

Therefore, in order to avoid the usual confusion that generally prevails, when discussions of her person are taken up, we shall focus on certain issues which will, when viewed with an open mind and improved perspective, eventually bring the diligent inquirer to a rational understanding of her not-so-mysterious nature and the true message that she and her colleagues sought to distribute among the essentially well-intended, but sadly, ignorant, masses.

We shall focus primarily on her use of ORMUS and her remarkable skills and abilities, which allowed her to heal so many people during her tenure in the Levant, Southern Gaul and the Western Isles.

We will also devote considerable attention to her ancestry, in an effort to relieve the general population of their present fascination, *or should we say obsession,* with her genealogy; because *her existence and her message was of universal import,* ***and it implies something altogether, much more spectacular, than the mere reestablishment of a so-called Royal Dynastic Lineage!***

38 ***Waldenses vs. Cathars*** ~ A segment of medieval history, wherein the slaughter of the Cathars occurred, also gave rise to the emergence of another unique and altogether different religious community known as the Waldenses. These Waldenses were a reformist movement that began within the Roman Catholic Church. Unlike the Cathars, who viewed life in a dualistic manner (which set them in extreme opposition to Coptic and Pistic Christianity), the Waldenses didn't find the Manichaean teachings at all appealing. Instead they set about recreating (a restoration of) the church in the spirit of its original pacifist and vegetarian movement: that being an emulation of the original Ebionites (in the same vein as James, Mary Magdalene and their constituency).

CHAPTER TWO ~ MARY MAGDALENE IN PERSPECTIVE- A CHRONOLOGY

Mary Magdalene - Origins of Her Lifestyle & Philosophy

We provide herewith, at the close of this book, an abridged time-line for the past 700,000 years; a time-line generally accepted by mainstream (non-creationist) academia as being more or less correct. If creationists were to have their way, then we would be lead to believe that the Jomon people of Japan didn't exist and neither did their lovely pottery. This is significant from the point of view that the Jomon pottery is the earliest known evidence of pottery. It (the pottery) is dated at around 10,000 BC: a time that predates, by several thousand years, the Sumerian, Egyptian and Mesopotamian cultures. Also, the Jomon were spreading outwards from Japan and not from the middle east towards Asia as some might imagine. There is a gap of about 2000-5000 years in most modern high school texts: i.e. the gap between 10,000 BC and 5,000 BC. But why?

The insertion (and study) of the time-line at this juncture is imperative in order that the layperson become familiar with (and remind academics of) the philosophical background of the period in which the Jesus Movement is said to have emerged[39] and in turn, to aid the reader in placing Mary Magdalene into a more historically and philosophically accurate context (~in glaring contradiction to the scenarios that have been promulgated by the Catholic Political Institution, the Hebrew belief system, Buddhist theories, Hindu concepts, modern Islamic interpretations and Gnostic texts, etc. etc.[40]). For example: The Jomon were likely among the first sailors in known history and began sailing at least as early as 35,000 BC. But, there again, "History," you say? Who's history?

Most people fail to realize just how many important advances had already been made in civilized behavior and cosmopolitan mannerisms prior to the birth of the Jesus Movement.

Additionally people tend to believe that Jesus and Mary Magdalene were reading nothing but Mosaic Law and the Torah, but this is more likely a very serious misconception, and one which has been promulgated especially by organizations with private ends to serve; in particular, by political and religious organizations that were driven by underhanded political agendas and extremely sinister ulterior motives. Just follow the money! (as described in the FOREWORD

39 Emphasis is placed here on the word ***emerged*** rather than *commenced* because their movement, or more appropriately, *lifestyle*, had been around since truly ancient times; however, they (the pacifists) had been all but wiped-out by primitive, intimidator societies and their ignorant successors as wave after wave of their ilk marched across the face of the earth, slashing and burning everything in sight. It was all about rape pillage and plunder. Thereafter, *Might is right* and the rule of fear and hate became the norm. .

40 ***Catholic, Gnostic & Buddhist [etc.] Political Institutions*** ~ Just because two or more groups oppose one another's ideas, is no guarantee that either side is correct: They might very well be wrong in every instance. On the other hand, we may also discover an element of truth in each facet of an argument. In this instance we remind the reader that there exists a third or "middle path" (and we do not refer here to Buddhism, nor to any other commonly known [commercial] religious institution!). This is the *road less traveled*, and it doesn't lead to Rome; nor does it lead to the camp of the Zionist, neither does it wind, round and round, lost in cycles and theories of reincarnation. We are not hamsters racing inside wire-wheeled cages; neither are we ignorant monkeys who look to the skies for aliens, gods and super-heroes. We are not political puppets, who mistakenly believe that just because something is "ancient" that it is better than something futuristic. There is something timeless that exists beyond the realm of our present limited understanding.

of this book)

Certainly, two thousand years ago, there were individuals born of superior intellect who engaged, as we do now, in rational thought process.

They preferred scientific methodology, over and above ignorant superstitious nonsense.

They would have questioned the veracity of Judaic dogma and they would have read other theosophical and philosophical works while questioning their veracity as well.

They would have made comparisons, drawn conclusions and in many instances they would have rejected much of the superstitious nonsense just as we do today.

They did not however enjoy the basic human rights and civil rights that we do today.

They did not enjoy our marginalized protection from the state, as regards freedom of speech; a right that many of us take for granted (a right that we are on the verge of losing *if* the teeming masses don't wake up and smell the rosy-cross).

Lodging opposing views and posing public contradiction to the ideologies of despot rulers, kings, governors, corrupt priesthoods and officially appointed religious soothsayers, were considered acts of treason, generally punishable by imprisonment, torture and, more often than not, resulted in public execution (by *stoning* etc. ouch!); and all this just to insure that the teeming masses remained fearful, docile and obedient. Imagine how many women might have been stoned to death during Mary Magdalene's lifetime due to a rumor set in motion by a husband who simply wanted a fresh piece of cow!

Slavery was the norm, not the exception. Women's rights? What the *hell* are you talking about? "*Stone that bitch!*" *(Woops, can we say that?)*

Human and animal sacrifice was a daily ritual designed to terrorize the common people and their children into submission. Passed off as Scared Ritual, the youth of the world witnessed such depravity, from early childhood. The threat of state-endorsed execution of people and their animals was an ever-present reality. Persons in positions of local leadership were expected to carryout these executions with much pomp and ceremony. These executions were cloaked in "sacred vestments" masquerading as so-called "offerings to the gods" (or goddesses and GOD). But who were these so-called gods after all? Were they not those very rulers and heads-of-state who merely proclaimed that they were gods and/or the servants and ministers of the Gods; i.e.: "The Priesthood"?

"But why waste a perfectly good slave," one clever priest mused, when his *bride-to-be* was scheduled for sacrificial execution, *"when killing several lambs and goat or two will suffice?"*

After all, the ruler could serve those very lambs and goats at the their bacchanal on the morrow with fresh red wine, and keep those pretty girls for himself! ~thus buying precious time *and* an opportunity to make good his escape into the desert with his beloved, well endowed (very sexy) fiancée. Wily priest!

Intimidation was good for business and provided the patriarchy with great sex to boot! *"That'll teach that bitch to tell me no. Humph!" Oh dear!*

But of course, in spite of the most horrific intimidation procedures, there were those slaves who remained rebellious nonetheless and preferred death over and above a life of servitude (and singing to the microphone night after night, to an audience of fat-assed pigs with grasping fingers). Hence, despite the many "efforts" made to "tame" them and *convince* them that they should obey, some of those slaves, quite simply, were not genetically disposed towards servitude (or enforced fellatio!); they were natural-born leaders, Alpha-females and their mates, the Alpha-males. So the occasional human sacrifice of Alpha-females and their mates, the Alpha-males, served keep the unruly remnant in tow and eliminated (permanently) the possibility of organized uprisings. Or so they thought.

In retrospect, clearly an individual classed as an obstinate and unruly slave by a despot ruler, would be more correctly described, in today's psychoanalytical environment, as a natural-born leader. Occasionally these natural born leaders would out-maneuver their handlers and gain direct access to the ruling family themselves. Thereafter, from time to time, whether by wit or by charm, or a combination thereof, they would actually manage to seduce, the controlling members of that ruling family. Even slaves, on the rare occasion, have been known to marry a ruler and having become the favorite, they ascended the throne; or at least they became prime minister, or as others have done, they become appointed as principal counsel. DNA works in mysterious Ways! And we should all thank Godde for that!

Undoubtedly, human beings are amazing creatures and they have been known to behave most unexpectedly when their freedom is threatened, especially the more comely females. Cunning creatures aren't they, and this certainly is a good thing! They adapt to change and fight for their rights. Right-On Sister!

Here comes a subtle point, so please follow closely: Fortunately, for these freedom-loving individuals, the symptoms of physical slavery are quite obvious, and the treatment and remedy for this social pathology are equally obvious. However, mental and emotional slavery are often manifest in a much more subtle manner, and these more subtle forms of slavery, might go undetected for generations.

The disease then spreads insidiously, often disguised as a sacred and reverential spiritual movement~ it proceeds, unnoticed and unchecked, like a pandemic HIV virus, until eventually the large majority of an entire world's population has succumbed to its insidious debilitating whims. This subtle method, of course, has become the preferred means, employed by despot rulers, of maintaining control over the masses. It may have many heads and many faces, but at the core they all belong to the same nasty *beast (.666 vs .618).*

Mental, emotional, and economic subversion is a much more convenient form of slavery, in so far as upper (ruling class) management is concerned. The memes[41] are passed down from mother and father slaves to their unsuspecting children-slaves, who in turn pass the memes down to their own children, thus creating generation upon generation of self-appointed slaves with their own "democratically elected" slave leadership, who lobby on behalf of their enslaved

41 **Meme**: Etymology~ alteration of *mimeme*, from *mim-* (as in *mimesis*) + -eme. Date: circa 1976

meaning: an idea, mannerism, behavior, style, or usage that spreads (often insidiously) in a viral manner from person to person within a culture; usually in a subliminal manner and without the conscientious consent of the host.

electorate. They "intercede" on behalf of their collective slave body, and petition the gods-of-commerce by way of their slave-intermediaries for more frequently scheduled periods of rest and relief from suffering (videos, DVD's, computer games and brief holiday periods where they are fleeced for the little money that they were able to save from their meager "salaries" economic-slavery[42]).

Suffice it say that Mary Magdalene and her family come from a long line of freedom-loving individuals. Please take a moment to reconsider the time-line[43] and how Mary Magdalene's world might have been different from the world we live in today. Imagine which literature and ideologies might have appealed to their rational mind-set and which dogma would have been offensive to those individuals who placed the freedom of mind, heart, body and spirit above all else.

Remember also please, *how very quite* life would have been during her era and how very, very tranquil their lives were on a day to day basis, without the constant intrusions of televisions, radios, magazines and newspapers, soap commercials, used car advertisements, neon signs, DVD and video stores, Hollywood movies and hundreds of millions of automobiles, trains and trucks and factories belching poison and white-noise globally.

Their lives were quite different and it's actually rather difficult to imagine, except of course for those who have lived (at least part of their lives), surrounded by nature, in an electricity-free environment for several years. A few days or weeks are nice, but one can't really appreciate the difference until months or even years have passed; the city dwellers' nervous systems are that disoriented. Some never fully recover from the damage unless they begin a serious routine to insure complete DNA repair and related systemic repair of the subtle nervous system.

Just imagine if you can, turning your main breaker (house fuses) off every night, for several days or weeks in a row. Try it sometime; just switch ALL the power off in your house one evening and go to sleep without any electrical current running through your home. You might be in for the surprise of your life! That constant electromagnetic grid, flowing all around your body, takes its toll.

Light some candles as you peruse this time-line and see if you can put yourself in her sandals; following in her footsteps.

42 Remember that the word "Salary" is derived from "an allotment of SALT" at a time when salt was virtually worth its weight in gold.

43 (provided in the final pages of this book)

CHAPTER THREE ~ MARY MAGDALENE'S MOTIVE

CHAPTER THREE PART ONE - IF IT BLEEDS IT LEADS

The Semantics of Motive

When we hear the word motive, for many, the first topic that usually springs to mind is murder. And why is this, one wonders? We need look no further than our own living rooms and bedrooms for the answer.

In the first instance, as you are probably already painfully aware, we all live, as did Mary Magdalene, in a media-driven society. The delivery system was different but all the same "media-driven". We were and remain a society that subsists under the watchful eye of a Mass-Media-Marketing-Machine [and Churchianity], which, we are assured, was created *By* the people and *For* the people (if you live in America that is)[44]. The only problem however is that it feeds upon the lifeblood and misery of those very people whom it purportedly serves. Elections of officials belong to those private interest groups who can afford the advertising. We are "sold" on a candidate's issues and their promises, like the next wonder widgets from USA American Co. Inc. Our ***DEMO***cracy has turned into a ***ADVERT***ocracy. News is ***SENS***ational, rather than ***EDUC***ational. We are sold the myths of religeous giants and historical superheros and their ***sacrifices.***

When after all, what's the golden rule of the colossus media-machine with its time-tested and well-proven guideline for defining our prime-time news headlines?

If it bleeds it leads.

As we all know, "We The People" are the focus of that daily news and, like it or not, If ***We Bleed*** then ***We*** are sure to ***Lead*** in the front-page headlines of the daily news. No doubt the folks who started the rumors regarding the death and crucifixion of Jesus Christ must have shared a similar business philosophy. A good sympathy pitch can take you places you've never imagined possible; anyone in the marketing and advertising industry will tell you that. Elicit money, sex and violence, why it's the perfect formulae for a best selling novel or mindless Hollywood action movie or prime-time cosmetic, tobacco or liquor commercial.

Yes that's right! If it bleeds it leads; and just like the life-stories of our ancestors, whether biblical or otherwise, essentially this formula sums up the vicious downward spiraling cycle in which we live today.

Things haven't really changed all that much in the past two thousand years have they? Like caged hamsters running circles inside wire wheels, going nowhere fast! Politically speaking, there are wheels within wheels; the wheels of industry and commerce; the wheels of democracy; the wheels of free-enterprise, communism and religious dogma; and of course the voracious wheels of corporate interests

44 For those of you who are born in another part of the world, don't you worry! A group of US marines are probably on their way at this very moment to kick your ass into shape and teach your leaders how to rig your own underhanded democratic elections. (But don't hold your breath if you live in a country where there's no oil; you're probably still safe, at least until the oil runs out and the poles melt. After that, who knows what the weatherman has in store for us all?) But don't blame the marines; they are just following orders with nothing but the best of intentions.

that daily, grind the earth's women and children to death, sending them en mass, one and all, to an early, poverty stricken, grave.

We live in a spiritually bankrupt society where "might is right" very much the same as Mary Magdalene and her contemporaries did. Superficially we are quite different, but internally we remain the same. We live in denial of a Truth that is ever present. It is there right under our nose every moment of ever hour of every day. And yet, we consciously choose to ignore it.

The Truth. What is Truth? Is it the rubbish we see on television everyday? Hardly.

We hear hourly of violence in our email, we see violence on our televisions; we witness violence in our streets and office buildings, with minute-by-minute coverage. We live and breathe violence. We seek it aggressively in our romantic, thriller novels (reading-for-recreation), all the while paying the Hollywood movie industry billions of dollars annually to deliver, globally, ever increasingly violent content to our DVD screens and movie theatres. And sadly, of late, even heinous-war-crime has become a spectator sport delivered daily right into our living-rooms by mainstream journalists who are IN-bed-*dead* with the latest arms-dealers and crooked politicians; yes, even *duly elected* government officials who, have insidiously assumed control of the world's parliaments, congressional houses, senate committees along with the global military-industrial complex. ~Motive~

But is this the only definition of the word *motive*? Aren't there a few good men and women among us, who are motivated by love, compassion, and a willingness to serve one another? Of course there are, but what are the statistics? What percentage of your daily life is consumed with violent intent and what portion is devoted to peace keeping? The peacemakers today are clearly, desperately outnumbered, as were Mary Magdalene and her constituents.

Motive is an important issue to take into consideration when we delve into the lives of famous historical figures (or infamous as the case may be!) and particularly in the instance of our illustrious Lady of the Lake, the much-maligned Lady Mary Magdalene.

We will return for a closer look, at the issue of *motive* later in this treatment, but for now, let's just allow it to remain in-the-dark a while longer; in the back rows of the theatre, where the shadows are deep. We'll just keep it in a corner of our mind for the time being; as if it were lurking in a nearby alcove or as if it were hidden behind a stand of dark, twisted, gnarly, old oak-trees huddled together, just around the bend of a slippery forest trail at midnight. After all, that's where *insidious motive* is generally most comfortable. No? In the shadows of discontent.

Where do you suppose Mary Magdalene's motive lay? Did it rest serene in the grassy fields of a spring-green meadow amongst thousands of tiny little flowers, or under some dark dank rock, amongst slithering slimy worms?

More importantly, have you studied your own hidden agenda lately; where does your motive reside?

continued...

CHAPTER THREE PART TWO - MARYAM'S MOTIVE IN PERSPECTIVE

By Human Hands and Feet, the New World shall be built

Let us consider briefly, MarYam's[45] deepest fears and motivation, as a woman of childbearing-age, a wife, and more importantly, a mother and a grandmother.

Contrary to the majority of contemporary, pro-Magdalene opinion, the Jesus Movement, in which Mary Magdalene figured so prominently, was not concerned with territorial claims and geopolitical kingdoms. Again, "...her existence and her message was much more spectacular, than the mere reestablishment of a so-called Royal Dynastic Lineage."

Their aspirations and raison d'etat, or reason to exist, was much more sublime *and ethereal* in essence, perhaps even intra-dimensional; and yet, all the while, it remained a very practical, humane and *down-to-earth* mission. Their heads may have been *in the sky*, but they kept their feet *firmly on the ground.* However paradoxical this might appear at first sight, let us assure you that it isn't.

Certainly our Mary Magdalene, recently vindicated of being falsely accused of being a whore and a prostitute, should not in turn be relegated to the status of having been nothing more than a good woman who loved her man deeply, spiritually and passionately. That's simply isn't enough for our movie-going mentality, *is it?*

In a society where hero worship is the norm, it is not enough to have been, quite simply -*a good woman.* She *must have been a heroine of some description*; Right? A princess or a sorceress, or both! The first woman to promote feminism; or something, anything special! But isn't it enough, to have been quite simply nothing more than a good woman? Oh no- we need something *spectacular*!

After all, we *are* from a generation whose *modus operandi* reads: "IF IT BLEEDS IT LEADS!" If it's not on television and in the news it can't be true. Right? Only heroes and heroines are allowed to be in the limelight! Right? Wrong...?

It *IS* enough to simply be a good woman, to be a good mother, a good friend, a good nurse or physician and a good neighbor. It is enough! And it's OK if you want to become the prime minister as well. Women must be allowed to realize their full potential, each according to their own individual capacity, earthly volition and divinely inspired will. But none should be made to feel ashamed of simply being a good mother or a good wife and a good neighbor. People should not be pushed beyond their means as individuals. Our greatness lies in our collective harmony.

---

45 ***Mar*** *Master, Teacher, Wisdom,*
a wizened master-craftsman
(especially metallurgy), master-alchemist,
Yam *Ocean, Sea,* Yam HaMelah (the Dead Sea)
MarYam *An Ocean of Wisdom*
Magdal *Tower, Lighthouse,* Beacon in the Night
Migdal-Eder *Tower of the flock*
MarYam *the* **Migdal-Eder**
Tower or Lighthouse amidst an Ocean of Wisdom
The Lady of the Lake *[great salt lake ~ Dead Sea]*

Motive... Perhaps saving her people was much more appealing than ruling over them. Perhaps she was much more interested in the management of the Temples, as a High Priestess who, was willing to put herself beneath her people. Should women be allowed to rule the church? Is there a man living today who was not born of a woman? *Even Paul's "Christ" was born of a woman.* What a sick trick that he/they later played on the children, *telling them that we are all conceived in evil and sin.*

But the church and its leadership of course, will demand an explanation based on the outdated and asinine assumption that, "women are unclean and unfit to be entrusted with a nation's Temples and soil-shrines."

The male-dominated clergy will ask, "How can one be Heavenly minded and remain respectful of Natural Order and motherhood at the same time?" Isn't Tantric yoga *the work of the devil?* Hah! Isn't there a treatment or antidote for Ostrich syndrome yet? Get your heads out of that hole (-in-the-ground) boys!

For some the answer is painfully obvious, but for those others who still live under the gloom and ingrained mind-control routines of shame, guilt and fear, (that have been implemented by varied religious institutions for millennia), the answers are muddled and stand aloof, often lacking in distinction. For there are hundreds of millions of people today who still believe in that nonsense which says, that women, and especially Eve, are responsible for all the evils of the world. Whereas, in the most ancient of texts it is said that she was in fact responsible for bringing the gifts of civilization *to the people.*

Most modern religions are polarized and are either male chauvinist or female chauvinist and neither one is correct in denying the other.

Mary Magdalene and her constituency were attempting to relieve the misguided people of their era of their burden by dispelling the myths that kept them in a state of mental and emotional slavery. As simple as it may seem: A noble motive indeed, but a Herculean task in every instance, to say the least.

So, how can a person, and especially a High Priestess or an Empress, be both heavenly-minded and well-disposed towards sexuality, while remaining respectful of a human's predisposition towards fallibility, frailty and mortality?

Perhaps the ill-founded attitudes of her era towards women and other superstitious ignorance can explain this disparity. If the clergy had not held women and childbirth in such contempt, social environments would have been different then, as they would be today. Is menstrual blood something to be held in disdain, as the later Judaic laws prescribed? Certainly not! Menstruation is a condition to be respected and celebrated as the precursor to life. Women are to be loved and cherished, not scorned and abused by men with serious psychological issues; an ideal that Mary Magdalene and her constituency would have proffered.

So now, we shouldn't be surprised to find, that despite two thousand years of persecution, assassination, and in the aftermath of many campaigns of terror, people still prefer to champion the very ideals that Mary Magdalene and her following chose to espouse. These ideals are timeless and constitute the foundation of any reasonable attempt at implementing a civilized and sophisticated social order.

This understanding will help us to divine the true reason for Mary Magdalene's popularity as a potential Priestess~Princess in that her agenda did not include acquiring territories through force of arms (like a Queen/King); neither did she harbor ambitions aimed at overwhelming populations through religious intimidation (Like a Priest/Priestess). These are testosterone-driven, male-intimidator methods and motives.

To the contrary, theirs was a mission that revolved around the dispensation of medicinal wisdom and the Art of Ethical Healing Practices.

More importantly theirs was a mission of distributing the know-how associated with preventive health-care, environmental education (an economy-of-resources) as well as *preparation for the future*, both immediate, long-term *and perhaps encompassing even a time frame that many today will fail to comprehend!* Certainly it may be said that they were among the first ecologists, human rights activists and egalitarians.

Yes, Mary Magdalene's popularity arose from the public's appreciation of her constituency's collective compassionate nature, and not from the point of view, that she and her consort might rise to power at any given moment, to seize the throne of UrSalem as king and queen of a disputed territory; they were not intent on deposing the Pharisees, or Herod and his Sadducees, or the Caesars of Rome. This was far too petty for yogic adepts, who had experienced quite literally, a physically binding process of alchemical transfiguration.

Imagine if you will, being a butterfly and trying to explain to an earthworm how it feels to fly above the treetops and to live on an exclusive diet of pristine ambrosia derived from the sweet dew of flowers, and the *nectar of the gods!*

Dear earthworm, indeed we love you and have compassion for your lot in life, but you don't even have eyes to see! How can we possibly explain the colors of the rainbow to you? (Of course the situation was a wee bit more complex than this, but you, no doubt, get point?)

Truly, the fact that Mary and Jesus (*our butterflies*), were so outspokenly against violent insurrection, presented quite a problem for those Zealots (earthworms) who were intent on seizing control of UrSalem and the Levant, in order that they might acquire control and management of the salt, spice and silk caravans.

Again in brief: *the fact that they (the Ebionite congregation) were adamantly opposed to violent insurrection, presented serious problems (in terms of demographics) for certain Zealots factions, who were intent on seizing control of UrSalem, simply to the satisfy needs (and other mundane issues) related to the salt, spice and silk trade routes.* These same rogue Zealot factions were secretly prepared to commit murder, even amongst their own distant cousins and immediate family members, should any rival share a different or opposing political and philosophical point of view: Not unlike the present-day Zionist movements one might add.[46]

46 Race can play funny tricks on people who make that concept the basis for their likes and dislikes. Race-obsessed people can find themselves hating people who, in fact, may be their own racial kith and kin. This is certainly true of the so-called "Arabs and Jews" as well as many Celtic peoples. Go back far enough and, like it or not we are all one people. However, this does not discount the fact that genetic decrepitude and corruption has occurred among ALL races. "Chosen" is as "chosen" does... (As in *"the chosen people" according to Mosaic Law and the Law of Life*)

Tread carefully now at this juncture, remembering that not all Zionists are Jewish, and

Consider the fact that Merchants' Associations and Metallurgy Guilds, (intent on seizing control of UrSalem and the Levant) supported various Zealot factions, due primarily to issues of trade embargoes. The Zealots shared a mix of motives that ranged from the control and administration of trading alliances, to the control and management of local and foreign governments along with their political agendas, ***as well as the control of domestic and dynastic marriage arrangements***; all cloaked in the veils of religious and nationalistic pride and (jingoist) fervor.

"God and Country" was their rallying cry (as it is today), but a greed for money and other riches, the power over, and control of, trade routes and other financial issues were the real driving force behind many a deceptive leader or clandestine financier of the so-called Zealots.

They squabbled over such immoral issues, so mundane as, being able to control the local matrimonial arrangements: whose daughters would be allowed to marry another's other's son. The Zealots and their controllers were much more mundane and petty than most orthodox religious leaders would have us believe. After all, the Zealots were human; and they were subjected to all of the same mean-minded, greed-driven, lustful and lascivious desires; they were guilty of the same groveling, brown-nosing and clamoring that any other sniveling human being in any other part of the world is subject to. The Zealots were not all freedom fighters at heart. Of course there were a few genuine culture heroes mixed in amongst them, but for the most part their feet stank just as much as the feet of their rivals. Rest assured that the sun didn't shine out of their armpits either.

To be blunt, we, the modern media-driven humans, have a tendency to vilify or glorify historical organizations such as these, especially the most modern generations, who are all raised since childhood on daily doses of super-hero worship.

We must put and end to this oversimplification and set everything biblical into proper perspective. We must leave all the biblically inspired mythology (and it's attendant programming of hero worship) behind us when we enter the alchemist's laboratory. When we enter in, through the straight and narrow gate of alchemy, we must bring with us, as our only possessions, an open heart and an unsullied mind, empty hands, all untainted and refreshed: Remembering that there were many rival factions among the Zealots and knowing that they were not at all, a single unified force determined to defeat Rome. To the contrary:

They too had ulterior motives and some factions might be likened unto a mafia organization that hid behind the mask of "nationalistic unity" (like the Japanese Yakusa,[47] who were in fact setup by the CIA during the period immediately following the bombings of Nagasaki and Hiroshima) and other such jingoist notions. Some factions of the Zealots were little more than an invisible

---

not all Hebrews are Zionists. It was and is a complex world of stealth, deceit, cunning and treachery; political intrigue prevails. ***This is not about anti-Semitism.***

47 Have good look at the relationship between Nomura Securities and Solomon Bros during the 1970's and a character named Sasagawa Ryoichi (who has walked the White House lawns on numerous occasions with many a US president and US congressmen etc.). Check the LDP hardliners who still patrol the streets of Japan using loudspeakers that will put any North Korean dictatorial government to shame in terms of intimidator tactics.

group of gangsters mixed in among genuine freedom fighters who the Temple Priests used for "crowd control" in the Court of the Gentiles.

Tread carefully now at this juncture, remembering that not all Zionists are Jewish, and not all Hebrews are Zionists. It was and is a complex world of stealth, deceit, cunning and treachery; a political intrigue prevailed wherein fathers killed their own sons, wives, daughters and cousins if they suspected them of treachery. This is not about anti-Semitism. It's about brothers and sisters, who, having been misled by corrupt religious leaders, knowingly raised their heel against their own brothers and sisters, fathers and mothers, cousins and friends.

Rest assured that Mary Magdalene and her inner circles didn't fall for the ruse. She and her colleagues didn't resort to attacking their own kith and kin. She and her following held fast to the ancient concept that all people were stewards of the Earth and that the Earth in its entirety is the Holy Land; not only that small triangle of land situated near the northeast corner of the African continent or a spec of land near the Straits of Ormuz.

Indeed, the real reason that the Essenes and Therapeutae congregated around the Yam HaMelah (Dead Sea) had much more to do with the Salt-Roads[48], (often mistakenly referred to as the Silk-Roads or Spice-Roads) due to the medical supplies, cosmetics and spices that passed through there. We will return to this issue of Dead Sea Salt later as it is of major concern to us (it was used to make ORMUS!), *as it was to the ancient Babylonians, Egyptians, Alexander the Great, Cleopatra, Caesar and the rest of the world!*

Mary Magdalene expressed herself through a spirit of loving kindness, which was effectively enacted, not only towards the people that they encountered, but also towards their habitat, the very forests and its trees, the precious rivers and lakes, and most importantly the animals that were being so savagely abused on a daily basis throughout the so-called civilized world at that time. There were no animal rights organizations. There was no GreenPeace, no Body Shop, nor was there a PETA organization to act as advocate on behalf of those less fortunate.

---

48 Salt wars and Salt trade are much more important than the average person might realize~ the Amritsar Massacre, for example (also known as the Jallianwala Bagh massacre), occurred in the Punjab, India, in April 1919 at Amritsar. There had been riots earlier that year, in the Punjab, caused by the civil disobedience campaign led by Mohandas Gandhi (against British rule and monopolization of salt).

When British and Indian troops, led by General R. E. H. Dyer, arrived on April 11, a night curfew was imposed and all public meetings were banned. Two days later, a crowd of about 20,000 locals, rallied in the Jallianwala Bagh, inside a walled garden and were using the garden as a resting place (mostly villagers who had come to celebrate a religious festival). When a political speaker began speaking to them, Dyer, without warning the people to disperse, ordered 50 Indian soldiers, to fire on them. Within minutes, approximately 400 locals were dead and over 1,200 were injured and wounded. They received no medical attention until the next day. As a result of the massacre, Indians were convinced that the British were not interested in peace and justice.

Almost ten years later, in 1930, Gandhi joined hundreds of his kinsmen on a 386-kilometer peace-march to the ocean-side, where salt was manufactured from seawater in protest against the Salt Acts, which made it a criminal offense to possess salt not purchased from a government facility.

On Jan. 13, 1948, at the age of 78, Gandhi initiated what was to become his final fast. His intention was to encourage the Hindu, Muslim, and other religious groups to stop fighting. When their leaders pledged to stop fighting on January 18, Gandhi ended his fast. But just twelve days later, Gandhi was assassinated by Nathuram Godse. He was apparently opposed Gandhi's (FreeMasonic) standards of tolerance for all creeds and religions. ***"I like your Christ; But I do not like your Christians" ~ Gandhi***

There was no body of membership intent on joining and supporting a Women's League or Sierra Club, and none who concerned themselves with the deforestation of the Atlas mountains (Cedars) of Lebanon. One shouldn't doubt for a moment that there surely existed a widespread disregard among the rulers towards all natural resources during Mary Magdalene's lifetime.

The Egyptian, Babylonian and Phoenician cultures, along with the Judean, Greek and finally Alexandrian armies, followed by the Roman conquest, not to mention scores of other wood-burning and shipbuilding cultures, had *all taken their toll*, generation after generation, never giving anything back to their Great Mother, the Earth. By the time Jesus and Mary were born, the local forests (comparatively speaking) had been all but stripped bare and thousands of animals were being sacrificed to the "gods" as either, offerings-of-thanks, or to "atone" for each individual family member's so-called *sins*. Hardly seems fair, a multitude of senseless and abusive killing based on superstitious fear and ignorance? "Humans, uggh! What a sanctimonious lot of idiots!" said the spider to the fly. The lizards and beetles were in complete agreement, no doubt.

Suffice it to say that superstitious ignorance was rampant among the masses, as were the debilitating effects of disease, hunger and royal-religiously sanctioned *eco-villainy;* the innumerable priesthoods that preyed upon this superstitious ignorance were on the rise. Among them, one of the worst priesthoods to make its appearance was the one that actually dared to prohibit healing on a certain day of the week, as if such a practice should be prohibited at any time or place!

Thus it shouldn't surprise us that, among all this chaos, there was one commodity that was in great demand and highly valued above all else: Health and the ability to heal. For as we all know, both the rich and the poor alike suffer from the effects of a life, lived in ignorance of the Laws of Nature, good hygiene and common-sense biophysics. When the Temple priests had failed miserably to heal anyone of anything on occasions too numerous to count, it is no wonder they would have been threatened by anyone who, was repeatedly successful at healing the impoverished masses. But that wasn't all. The Essenes (Ebionites) were also skilled at causing gardens to flourish in the deserts! Whereas fields blessed by Temple Priests had failed time and again, the Essenes were able to bring forth fruits and vegetation in plentiful amounts and that was miracle enough for people on the verge of starvation.

Hence in an era when, purportedly, very little was known about agricultural science, medicines and human anatomy, Mary Magdalene's knowledge of medicinal and aromatic essential oils, associated wild-crafting skills and other assorted esoteric oriental medicine, would have lead inevitably to her considerable fame and relative good fortune. However, and to the regret of many, these remarkable and precious skill-sets would later become identified with those very skills infamously (and quite stupidly) attributed to witchcraft. Damn! ...those foolish men who were responsible for the implementation of the Spanish Inquisition and other similar atrocities: *despicable witch-hunts wherein those women, who had been fortunate enough to inherit her wisdom, were ruthlessly exterminated and the genocide of entire villages and rural communities was enacted.*

Of course modern renditions of history would have us all believe that it was her group's ability to achieve resurrection from the dead that provided them with such universal appeal and widespread acclaim. But, in reality it was more likely her ability to facilitate, as a teacher and practitioner of midwifery that ultimately lead to their long enduring reputations as miracle workers, along with certain other related skills that allowed her to literally manipulate and effect repair of the RNA-DNA routines of her acolytes, patients and followers.

Bear in mind that the importance of simple, day-to-day hygiene was all but unheard of among the general population; the cause of infection was virtually unknown. The medical practices of her era, generously speaking, were barbarous and consisted mostly of superstitious nonsense. So as she and her friends brought hope and relief from the pain and suffering caused by superstitious ignorance, they were well received and their reputation as healers inevitably grew, all out of proportion.

They healed and "performed miracles," using predictable and systematic scientific methods, whereas the organized religious institutions had repeatedly failed quite *miserably*. Simply put, *this was bad for business*. Although Mary Magdalene and her friends were causing a serious erosion of the people's faith in the Temple and its ministers in Judea due to many successful healings, that uproar represented only a small fraction of the damage that her people were inflicting upon the temple coffers. *And that was what it all boiled down to for the Priesthood and their quisling leaders. If you want to understand why the Temple priests were so adamantly opposed to Mary Magdalene and the Jesus Movement, just* ***follow the money*** *(see page xxiv~xxv). Compare the motives of the various political and religious parties to that of Mary Magdalene, Jesus and their principal constituency, the Ebionites.*

Among the Greek speaking aristocracy and erudite of her era, Mary Magdalene and her following were most frequently referred to as the *Therapeutae*,[49] the root from which we derive the modern terms therapy, therapeutic and therapist. They were also referred to as the Essene Order, and later as the Thebaid Federation, the Sages of Light and perhaps most interestingly, of late, as "The Society of ORMUS," another name associated with the Priory of Scion.

But, in truth, the original core group was essentially a very sophisticated family who, although descended from many Royal and Nobles Lineages, preferred to steer clear of assigning such names or titles to their own immediate family, organizations and following. "Why is this?" one might ask?

Naming and labeling in this instance ultimately creates limitations and attracts unwanted negative-attention, jealousy and in certain cases usurpers and thieves. The Desposyni[50] preferred quite seclusion, and self-imposed obscurity, but in

---

49 Note also the name *"Thera" the Volcanic Greek Island*, which was one of the strongholds of the Great Minoan Maritime Civilization. Look into the history of those people and the destruction of that island, along with its Neolithic architecture and artifacts; trace the trails from Stonehenge through Malta and on towards the Levant and to Ormuz up the Indus Valley into the Hunza and onwards to the far reaches of the Siberian forests into the Japans, and onwards to the ancient well of the Hopi Indians... why stop there? Continue along the Sierra Madre until you reach the mountaintops of Costa Rica and later Lake Titicaca in Peru. Flip the earth on its side and view what used to be our equator. Follow the pyramid building civilizations around the world and imagine a time when Atlantis might have been a reality rather than mere mythology.

50 Ebionites clearly revered the Desposyni (the sacred name reserved only for Jesus' blood relatives), especially James the Just (Yakov or Jacob), as the legitimate apostolic successors of Jesus, rather than Peter. This claim is supported by passages in the Pauline epistles (Galatians 2), and

order to achieve their objectives in the Levant, they were, eventually, resigned to forego the cloistered lifestyles which they indubitably preferred, along with their privacy and anonymity. This is not to say that they were dullards, introverted and boring. They loved a good drum-circle and joyful dance and singing as much as the next person. They laughed and told jokes, loved a good story. Of course they abstained from drinking alcohol and smoking but not for the standard accepted reasons. What set them apart was something entirely different. *(They weren't at all concerned with "sin" in the typical sense of the word as it is used by the misguided Christian churches today. Not at all![51])*

The names and labels that emerged at first (and that later ensued) such as "Desposyni," "Essenes," "Sages of Light" etc., were coined and employed by others in their various attempts to identify, describe and classify her family along with their close circle of Friends. Among themselves of course, when addressing one another in public or referring to one another, they employed the usual honorifics and titles of respect that are to be found in all refined civilizations, cultures, and language groups; *but when referring to themselves as a group*, they would have avoided such acclamations, being possessed of a humble and self-effacing nature. Again, theirs was not a message of "claims to territories" based on bloodlines and lineages of Royal Descent. This is not to say that they weren't concerned with the preservation of a bloodline, but it was not preserved for the purpose establishing a kingship, dynasty or governance over any given population, much less the conquest of local territories or the world, as some would have us believe today.

One should be very cautious with those individuals who, in recent times, claim succession from the descendents of Jesus and Mary Magdalene. This is not to say that Jesus and Mary Magdalene do not have descendents, for in all likelihood they do. But the true descendents of Mary Magdalene will not be the sort of people who set about to rule over others or lay claim to thrones and castles. We are much more likely to find them pioneering efficient techniques in the management of organic bio-dynamic farming communities, sustainable energy programs and eco-friendly societies that seek to protect the rights of animals, rainforests and thousand-year-old oaks, cedars and redwood trees.

Beware of those who say that they are the heirs to the Dragon Court's throne and other such nonsense. Mary Magdalene and her kind, to the contrary, were intent on delivering a message of community service and egalitarianism.

Their message was one of cooperation with their fellow human beings, nature's fauna and flora. To serve and be served: "The first shall be last and the last shall be first," and, "Ye shall be greater than I!" Their message was not one of guilt, fear and mistrust of the natural order. Women were to be cherished and loved, not treated as the source of sin and as unclean creatures that were not allowed to enter the Holy of Holies.[52]

---

portions of the Book of Acts (e.g. Acts 15) that supposedly present James as outranking Peter.

51 ***Sin (an ancient god)~*** This is explained in greater detail in the novel, "ORMUS‡ The Secret Alchemy of Mary Magdalene" by William Hearth (Volumes I, II & III)

52 ***Desposyni*** ~ those true descendents of Mary and her family are not roaming around declaring themselves. If you meet people declaring themselves to be descended from Mary, then you can rest assured that they are not. Those who are prefer to remain invisible, until such time as you, an enlightened individual, can "see" them for who they really are. *When you have eyes to see, you will recognize them instantaneously by their brilliant countenance and they will likewise recognize you!*

A few notes on the *Waldenses*

Followed by a quote from the 1599 GENEVA BIBLE ~

Waldo & followers had a system in which they went from town to town meeting secretly in small groups (Waldensians). The traveling Waldensian minister known as a barba could be either man *or woman*! ***(The idea of a female preacher was novel, almost revolutionary in and of itself, for the era. See <http://www.Celtic-church.com>)*** The group would shelter and house the barba making secret arrangements for the next town.

Mainstream views contend that Waldensians started with one Peter Waldo, when began preaching in public in Lyon in 1173. Originally a wealthy man, he decided to forsake his possessions. He went through the towns sharing his wealth with the needy while was a migrant minister. As he attracted a following Waldo promoted a philosophy very similar to that of St. Francis of Assisi.

Preaching in those days required the official permission of the Catholic Church, which the Bishop in Lyon denied him, thus in 1179 gained an audience with Pope Alexander III who praised his ideals yet ordered him not to preach without permission of local clergy. Waldo continued undaunted and by the early 1180s both he and his followers were excommunicated and forced from Lyon. Later declared to be heretics - because of their "contempt for ecclesiastical power" - they continued to teach and minister outside of the clerical authority and "without divine inspiration". They were also the first to translate and distribute parts of the Bible outside of Catholic interpretation. So again they were accused as heretics because they were clearly a danger to "divinely sanctioned church hierarchy."

In 1207, Durand of Osca, claiming to be a long-time friend of Waldo, "converted" to Catholicism and later went to Rome, where he gained permission from Innocent III, to establish the Poor Catholics. They continued the Waldensian legacy in part and began by preaching ***against*** *the Cathars. The Poor Catholics were later known as the Franciscan and Dominican Orders. The Cathars and the Waldensians were both "exterminated" in later years during campaigns of mass genocide.*

1180: the Jewish philosopher Maimonides attempts to bridge the Talmud and Aristotle in the "Guide for the Perplexed"

1184: pope Lucius III excommunicates Peter Waldo, founder of the anti-Cluniac ascetic Waldensians ("poor men of Lyons")

1190: the Teutonic Knights are founded by German lords to fight in the crusade, establish their capital at Acre, and adopt the Templars' white mantle and the Hospitallers' rule

1198: Cardinal Lothario Conti is elected pope Innocent III

1200: the Jews are expelled from England

1204: the Crusaders, led by Venezia, sack Constantinople, a Christian city

1206: Francis of Assisi gives up his wealth and adopts a life of absolute poverty

1208: pope Innocent III launches a crusade against the Catharist/Albigensian and the Waldensian heretics

1210: the Pope recognizes the Franciscan order of mendicant friars

1212: the Jews of Toledo are massacred by the Crusaders

1215: the Dominican order of mendicant friars is founded in Languedoc

1215: the fourth Lateran council defines the seven sacraments (in particular marriage and confession) and prescribes that Jews be confined in ghettos

1314: Friday 13th ~ Jacques de Molay, the grand master of the Templars, is burned at the stake in Paris

1599: GENEVA BIBLE (Waldenses Bible) ~ "23 Then if any man shall say unto you, Lo, here is
Christ, or there, believe it not. 24 For there shall arise false Christs, and false prophets, and shall shew
great signs and wonders, so that if it were possible, they should deceive the very elect. 25 Behold,
I have told you before. 26 Wherefore if they shall say unto you, Behold, he is in the desert, go not
forth: Behold, he is in the secret places, believe it not. 27 For as the lightning cometh out of the East,
and is seen into the West, so shall also the coming of the Son of man be. 28 For wheresoever a dead
carcass is, thither will the Eagles be gathered together. 40 Then two shall be in the fields, the one
shall be received, and the other shall be refused. 41 Two women shall be grinding at the mill: the
one shall be received, and the other shall be refused. 42 Watch therefore: for ye know not what hour
your master will come. 43 Of this be sure, that if the good man of the house knew at what watch the

So, was Mary Magdalene a Jewish Benjamite Princess? Maybe, maybe not, but this was not the principal concern of Mary Magdalene, Jesus, their family and beloved community of friends.

Like Prince Siddhartha (Gaotama Buddha) and Lao Tzu, who lived hundreds of years before them, their Way of Life was not one of temporal dominance and rule by way of intimidation. She was certainly an advocate of human liberation. As a princess, if indeed she were, her preoccupation with the emancipation of the human heart and spirit would have overshadowed any desire to ascend to the throne of Israel. There was something much, much more important on her agenda. Nevertheless, her legacy begs the question, "What is a *Jewish* Princess?" What is a Jew? Was Mary Magdalene a Jew? Define Jew! Easier said than done.

Many people assume that they know what the word Jew means... but very few genuinely understand anything about who, or what a Jew *really is; this includes the large majority of the people who, in modern times, refer to themselves as being Jewish.* This is largely due to the fact that, in reality, there is no such thing as a Jew, however there are endless semantic interpretations of the word Jew, but there is no single tribe or culture of people, nor is there a single religious body, for that matter, that can appropriately *and correctly* be referred to as *"the Jews."* This therefore, is one of the principal causes of confusion in the world today, when it comes to discussions concerning historical and biblical events.

Take for example a child born of Russian, Chinese or Celtic *ancestry*, who was *born in geophysical area* of the United States or Australia saying, "I am American!" or "I am an Australian!" Well what is that? "Chinese" is a *genetic* reality, whereas "American" is a *geopolitical location.* What are all these borders and country names that were fabricated by intimidator societies and their warlords? They are nothing more than the naiveté and general lack of perspective of a child who has been deprived of a proper, unbiased education. It is nothing more than a Jingoist or nearsighted religious label. That child might have been born anywhere under a different set of jingoist or religious dogma. "It's all relative," Einstein might say.

In order to understand who the Magdalene was, one must also understand who and what a Nabataean was, who and what a Celt[53] really is, who the Hittites and Trojans were and what a Scot is; not to mention *who* and *what* the Sarmatians, Scythians, Assyrians, Huns, Hungarians are; and (rather more importantly) who were the Persians, Ethiopians, Taxilians, Tocharians, Hunza, Japanese[54] and Seminole/Iroquois "Indians" (as hybrid cultural phenomena is concerned).[55] What is a Nazorite, a Nazarite and a Nazori (one and the same perhaps)? Who are the Mandaeans? Are they, like the Hunza, an endangered species?[56]

---

thief would come, he would surely watch, and not suffer his house to be dug through. 44 Therefore be ye also ready: for in the hour that ye think not, will the Son of man come." ~ GENEVA BIBLE 1599 (Waldenses Bible) ~

53 Some of the oldest known evidence of the Celts comes from Hallstatt, Austria, near Salzburg (ancient salt mines). Excavations there revealed hundreds of Celtic graves dating from about 700 B.C.

54 **Iroquois**~ whose tribal constitution was used to form the US Constitution... The Constitution of the Iroquois Nations/The Great Binding Law, Gayanashagowa wherein women were allowed to vote on an equal par with men!

see: http://www.yale.edu/lawweb/avalon/amerdoc/iroquois.htm

55 "**Jomon**" see index entries for the "**Jomon**" people of 10,000 BC

56 It was in **Nazara** that the ancient Nazoria or Nazireates held their *"Mysteries*

Did you know that almost all Japanese are descended from Russian/Scythian and Georgian, Uyghur [57] ancestry and that many others are descended from the (red-headed and blue-eyed) Hungarians and Babylonians?[58] The history that was foisted upon us in the past 200 years is at least eighty percent myth if not more so, and much of the so-called science that we were taught in school is naïve at best. We have so much to ***un***learn in order to understand what actually occurred in the ancient days. But the simple truth of the matter is that most seekers are not prepared to pay the price of embarking upon (and completing!) a massive genetic, cultural and comparative-religion research project.

So what we really need today is a course entitled, "the short path to enlightenment." And it does exist, as it always has. Mary Magdalene and her friends were trying to explain it to the world and this was the original, genuine and authentic good news, but years of suppression have prevented her message from surfacing. Fortunately this Dark Age of repression is finally coming to an end and the Truth is emerging at long last.

To make a long story short, consider carefully as you read along, that, among many other genetic haplotypes, Cleopatra VII, the high priestess of ISIS at the Temple of Hathor (famous "consort" of Marc Antony) was very likely just as much a Greek, Phoenician, and Minoan Princess as she was an Egyptian. In fact, most of the historical heroes and heroines with whom we are all familiar, are not the simple, black and white creatures (*caricatures*?) that we, as children, have been lead to believe they are. Indeed, what exactly was an Egyptian person like during Magdalene's epoch? What was an Egyptian in Abraham's epoch? Were the personages who lived and breathed among the halls of the Pharaonic Royal Houses of Egypt composed of the same genetic material as the present population of Egypt today? They most certainly were not. No more than we, are the same person as, well, say- our own parents and grandparents are. *People change! And that's the beauty of it!*

Likewise, Mary Magdalene belonged to no specific racial identity known to modern man. Some will argue that she was a Jewess, but even if that were so, then she represents a collage of ethnic peoples who had been intermingled for

of Life baptismal assemblies," a people whose baptismal customs existed long before the Laws of Moses were "coined."

57 See also ARMENIA; AZERBAIJAN; GEORGIA and the areas located to the north of the Caucasus Mountains; THE ***Caucasians (as in INDRA who ate the SOMA) as you follow the trails*** connecting Georgia, Azerbaijan, Kazakhstan, Kyrgyzstan, Mongolia, Korea, Tajikistan, Afghanistan, Pakistan and Nepal/Tibet: ***consider the proximity of Kyrgyzstan to Sweden and Norway*** if you go "over the top", double back and continue across the top to Mongolia and to the Japans.

58 The Chinese described "Factions of the Khazars" as tall, white-skinned, and green-eyed and were known as White Ugrians. These White Ugrians from the area of Scythia ascribed to "Hugie" who in fact were the Franks that later settled in France. They ruled the "Black" Ugrians a mixed Turkish and Mongolian group. The White Huns who another group, also known as "Nephtali," cooperated with the Khazars and were descend from a Tribe of Israel known as the Nephtali.

A group in East Scythia (the Juan-juan) who dominated the Khazars, White Ugrians, and Nephtalite Huns at one time. When the Khazars, White Ugrians, and Nephtalite Huns revolted, a majority of the Nephtalites moved to Scandinavia and settled in Norway. The Khazars and White Ugrians later defeated the Juan-juan ("Avars") killing the majority of them. Remnant Avars became leaders of the Black Ugrians (previously vassals of the "White Ugrian"). Black Ugrians later taking the title of "Avar" migrated to Central Europe. In the years that followed between 550-769 CE, they were thought to have dominated parts of Austria, and parts of Germany and all of Hungary. The Frankish Emperor Charlemagne later destroyed that group.

hundreds if not thousands of generations. If she wasn't a Hebrew at all and in fact of Egyptian descent, as others will argue *(as if such a thing were even possible!)*, then, that too would only serve to assure us that she is a cosmopolitan figure. She is a complex, genetic composite of noble and royal personages as well as those simple people whose feats of survival have separated them out, as unique and unusually strong, intelligent and most importantly sensitive individuals; people who were better equipped than their piers at expressing themselves in the art of adaptation. As much as it is becoming politically correct, or not, to think of her as a "Jewish" princess, she was oh so very much more than that. She is a cosmopolitan figure and as such she is not to be compared to a mere princess. *Let that sink in for a moment, **"not to be compared to a mere princess!"***

If anything, Mary Magdalene and her circle of friends were among the foremost in championing the idea of a world that would no longer be separated into the extremes that plague our class-structured hierarchal world of rich and poor, Royal and common, master and slave. They were working towards the establishment of a world free from mental, emotional and economic slavery; a society wherein intellectual chauvinism and jingoist concepts would be replaced by a zest for life, love, compassion and sharing. But the opposition's roots (talons?) were deep.

When we take a careful look around us we find that people haven't changed all that much in the past two thousand years. Most modern Christian, Gnostic, Islamic, Buddhist, Taoist, Shinto, Wiccan, Pagan, Heathen dogma and all the other religious-philosophical mind-sets are based on little more than a mere cursory glance at the surface of history, with its collage of myths and stories, intermingled with a few real facts. After all, even the observations and surmising of the greatest recognized modern scholars, is nothing more than sets of imposed hypotheses passed off as wisdom or so-called truth; for who knows how factual any of the so-called great writers of ancient times really were? We quote Josephus, Pliny, Plato, Clement, Augustine, Julius Caesar, Saul of Tarsus, etc. etc. etc. and, for better or for worse, we draw our conclusions. The list goes on and on.

These *modern* scholars of ours... they surmise, they suppose, they presume. They insist and persist. And through a detailed process of deductive reasoning and denial, they form myriad labyrinths of complex or deceptively simple and or complex hypotheses. Inevitably they extol, command and reprimand in haughty fashion. They contend. They argue. In worst-case situations they counsel improperly, political leaders who, in turn, make war on one another. And the women and children suffer. Arguably, eventually they *must* compromise, at least temporarily. After all, at the end of the day the universities and theological institutions have to make-a-buck and if they can't agree on something, they can't print a textbook. If they can't print the textbooks then, in turn, they can't presume to continually impose their hypotheses upon us and heaven forbid, expect that we should actually pay them for all the pandering that insures the receipt of grant-money. Then there are those pieces of paper they award to those, who bow down to these contrived realities, however tenuous and ill fated they be... PhD?

But Mary Magdalene was not one of these, neither professing nor bowing to pressure, she and her friends decided to "rock the boat." They tickled the status quo in its private places. And thank goodness for that. But what was her motive and what was her true, and so-called "secret" goal?

As we draw aside the curtains of religious dogma and politically instilled jingoism that we have been force-fed for generations; and as we discover that the magic act at the altar is mostly smoke and mirrors, we are justifiably dissatisfied... a righteous anger sets in. Then we dig deeper; and we look behind the curtains, where the wizards of academia reside, with all their little knobs, stops and whistles, only to discover that it's all *slight of hand.*

It is then that we want to look past their fabricated realities, but we inevitably come up against the same manufactured obstacles and impenetrable paper-walls of intentionally convoluted (and missing) historical documents. We are repeatedly denied the fruit of our intended labors, no matter how many times we pay the price of admission. "I give up...!" most will say at this point.

But what of those diehards, who refuse to stop and, in complete disregard of repeated warnings, delve too deep? Hellfire and damnation! Executions and assassinations! Well… the consequences for questioning authority can be quite grave: as Mary Magdalene and her associates might well attest.

We the courageous and willful pilgrims, who persevere and continue to dig ever deeper and wider for the truth against all odds, will soon discover that names and places become muddled and oh, so many documents have mysteriously gone missing! Entire libraries have been burned along with the occasional group of witches, not to mention the near complete eradication of their original champions, the genuine Templar Knights, Arabian Knights and Troubadours of later years.

In the end, the written history seems to contradict itself at every turn; all depending on who wrote the history. Did they "have an axe to grind"? Or worse still, did the scribe have an axe hanging over his or her head when *he wrote it* or when *she "confessed" to it*? In whom or what can we believe then?

Hence, all too often, even the most persistent and tenacious pilgrim will become confused and eventually exhausted and understandably so. Because, "That's the idea!" Confuse, confound and control. But there is a simple answer that has eluded the seekers for generations because it was hidden right under our collective nose. And this was Mary Magdalene's deepest heartfelt desire, that one day we might all be introduced to the short path to enlightenment.

Just remember one thing as you enter into the Secret World of Mary Magdalene's Alchemy: that "Hope Remains" and a chemical reaction will perform repeatedly in the same manner for a German as it will for a "Native" American Indian or a Watusi Tribesman in Africa.

Mix baking soda with vinegar and it will produce white, frothy foam. Drop dry ice in water and it will give off white billowy smoky trails. Reproduce the proper alchemical manipulations and you will end up with the Philosopher's Stone, regardless of your racial or religious convictions.

So it really doesn't matter whether you are a Druid or a Jew, a Muslim or a Buddhist, a Nepalese or a Norwegian. Chemical reactions don't care if you are a sinner or a saint. Hence, there is Justice to found in this world: you just have to know where to look for it.

Be forewarned nonetheless, that not everyone who approaches the "Avalon of Alchemical Science" will be able to pull the sword from the stone. "To them that hath shall be given, and from them that have not, it shall be taken away." This is the Law; the meaning of which, you shall soon be given the opportunity to understand.

In the following short work we will endeavor to touch upon only the highlights and mountain peaks of the journey, and as often as possible we will stick to the high road, avoiding the detailed relief of the valleys, gorges and thickets, where so many a pilgrim has been irretrievably and forever lost in a quagmire of misinterpretations, lies and intentional deceits.

Initially, although we may not have the advantage of the eagle, (She who soars above the mountains) at least you will enjoy the vantage of the Hermit, (One who sees from on high and from afar).

For those of you who persevere, not only will you see with the eyes of the eagle, you will have the opportunity to view the universe from the magical point of view of the *Almighty Phoenix. You will see the universe anew with the all-seeing, relentless diamond eye of an ascended master.*

Neither ancient religious models, nor modern New Age nonsense will suffice. However well intended the parents and guardians may have been, the truth of the matter, is that they have inflicted an almost irreparable damage to our virgin nervous systems through exposure to . So, you must be very determined and steadfast when the time comes to transcend your base nature and thereby transform your own personal "lead" into "gold." Mind you this is not merely a figure of speech. ***There will be an actual metallic, elemental and superconductive metamorphosis that exceeds the speed of light.***

We can supply the Key Words and Key Concepts, a treasure map if you will, that will lead you to this awakening, or what some might genuinely refer to as a state of "Enlightenment," but, ultimately you will have to make that innermost journey into Your Self alone, for as the Freemasons of old have warned us, we should "take no man's word for it."

You must take the road less traveled and turn your eyes inward.

But where is *within*? Anyone who has searched within will tell you that, *within* is a very illusive place, if it is a place at all. By the time you finish this book you will have a very good idea where and *when* within really is! But no guru or saint or religious organization can take you there. It is a journey that only you can take. And ultimately you will have to make that journey on your own. But once you arrive there, *or here, shall we say,* you will never feel or be alone again. A blessed union of souls awaits the sincere and tenacious pilgrim.

"There is no substitute for one's own personal interaction with sacred and the experience that follows." We can only guide and direct.

These time-honored questions remain, "Who or what is the Sacred- and where or when might it be found?" and, "What is the Holy Grail- and where and when is it to be found?"

Herein follows a brief description of the method that will lead you back to the Garden; herein is given: The Map and the Key of the Magdalene.

It's up to you whether or not your set your feet upon the path, or The Way as she called it in her day, and walk into the final freedom, into the Light and Sound of Godde.

This is your birthright and inheritance; it is nothing less than The Holy Grail itself. But the Holy Grail is not what most people think it is, however it is a very real and tangible thing. If you can conceive it, then believe in it; perform the necessary tasks, and *live-forever* in peace, bliss and harmony!

In conclusion to this chapter regarding Mary Magdalene's motive, we know what some of you might still be thinking, "Was she a Jew after all?" because if she were, this might have some bearing on understanding her motive.

Was she a Benjamite Princess or something along those lines? Or was she an Egyptian Priestess from the cult of ISIS perhaps, a Prophetic Alchemist perhaps?

And was she married to the man whom we, today, mistakenly call Jesus? After all, if Jesus was not his true given name, was it not something similar perhaps?

What was Mary Magdalene's real name?

They said she was a whore and now everyone has learned that this was a vicious lie spread by, ...whom? Who started that rumor anyway, and why?

Words, Translations, LEXICONS and semantics, our innumerable, distorted histories and hidden or "lost" manuscripts; most clues lead to a dead end...

We have all become Lost in the Translation.

Friends, for those of you who persevere and complete this little journey, you may discover that it really doesn't matter after all if she was a Jewish Princess or not... a Rose by any other name would smell as sweet. But since so many people seem to be preoccupied with this issue, it's better that we make short work of it once and for all and put it behind us.

What matters most is that Mary Magdalene's alchemy is color-blind and is indifferent to race, status and class; Mary Magdalene's alchemical stone will answer truthfully to any one who inquires skillfully.

If anything, she left us with a metaphysical point of view that promises justice for all who inquire skillfully and diligently. Godde's Laws and Godde's Love remains the same and works for all sincere pilgrims regardless or their race, creed, skin-color and political or religious orientation.

Her secret alchemy is an unfailing compass that will help us navigate the chaos of superstitious ignorance. It guarantees us a place is "heaven". It guides us home in our hour of need and greatest peril.

Her motive was and is the exorcism of the "worm" and the emancipation of humankind (*hu*-man).

In a phrase: The fulfillment of *Cosmic Justice.*

If you have managed to come this far in the reading of this work, then it's time to welcome you into a new dimension of thought, consciousness and awareness, Welcome to the omnicompetent realm of "ORMUS & The Secret Alchemy of Mary Magdalene - Revealed."

Here's your third clue:

Think along these lines if you please... What if Mary Magdalene was a very, very rare instance of a woman, born of a woman, who was born of a woman, who was born of a woman, etc etc, and so on, going back, back, back, for thousands and thousands of years. That is to say, what if she represents an uninterrupted line of mt-DNA[59] that leads back to another very special woman, who lived long, long before any of our existing records were inscribed? Some couples only have sons, others mixed, and still others, *only daughters.*[60]

What *would* her motive have been in this instance? Would her motive have included keeping that ***matriarchal*** lineage alive and intact?

Welcome to the OMNIVERSE
of
The Lady of the Lake
and
MarYam ***the*** Migdal-Eder.

59 ***mt-DNA ~ "Mitochondrial DNA"*** is passed only from mother to daughter, generation after generation. (See: http:// mt-DNA.com)

Mitochondria are considered to be independent living organisms that share a symbiotic relationship with human beings; although they live in our bodies, they contain their own DNA (deoxyribonucleic acid) which is entirely separate from each person's individual DNA that resides in own our cells' nucleus. Although our personal DNA (found in the nucleus of our cells) contains hereditary material from both parents, mitochondrial DNA in human beings is inherited only from the mother.

Mitochondria use energy released by the breakdown of carbohydrates and fats to make a compound called adenosine triphosphate (ATP)

60 Couples with the best overall mix and pairing of inherent DNA tend to have female offspring; at least this is what clinical tests indicate at present. Imagine that! Violent intimidator societies tend to wish for male offspring, but in the best of all possible worlds we might want to have a preponderance of very good females and just a few very high-grade males. Just a thought? It's certainly a change form the usual, "Hope it's a boy!" attitude. We have a lot to learn about women, the miracle of life itself and the mating habits of a peace-loving society; something we have little experience with, yes? It's not that a man has so may wives. It's more toward the fact that many women prefer to mate with that particular man.

CHAPTER FOUR ~ MARYAM MAGDALENE'S ICONS

The White Dove of Peace and the Great NinAnna

For thousands of years, The White Dove of Peace, descending from heaven, has been a standard icon featured in the symbol systems of religious circles and cults. She (White Dove of Peace) has been associated with the Holy Spirit, the Holy Ghost, the Host, the Sophia, the Egyptian Goddess ISIS and Hathor, the Shekinah of the Hebrews, Asherah, Astarte of the Phoenicians, Ishtar, the Migdal-Eder (Tower of the Flock), Inanna (or NinAnna), NinHursag (or NinKhursag), The Lady of the Lake, Manna from Heaven (of Moses); the list, quite literally, goes on and on and on! Often depicted flying earthward with a small white, shining disk in her beak she brings us a token from heaven. What is this gift that she brings and who is SHE?

In truth, although many Christians remain unaware of it, even long before the advent of so-called Christianity, the White Dove of Peace has always been a symbol associated with the goddess, with ISIS, and with a baptismal cult. Baptismal practice has been around for thousands of years prior to the advent of the Jesus movement. Never the less, it is to be found throughout all Christendom and it is pervasive, in the extreme, in its representation of the Holy Spirit, also known as the Paraclete.

In short Paraclete refers to the "One Who Intercedes," or the one who begs pardon on our behalf, when we transgress the Law of Life; a "go between." This Law of Life should not be confused with the laws of men nor with the laws of religious institutions, Judaic, Christian, Muslim, Buddhist or otherwise. Most importantly perhaps, the White Dove of Peace is the symbol of the compassion and forgiveness of the Mother (the behavioral tendencies exclusive to those individuals that carry the sacred data of mt-DNA).

The assignation of the White Dove of Peace as the primary symbol within Christian mysticism represents an attempt by the Sages of Light,[61] along with other similar religious institutions, to harmonize the many divergent cults and belief systems that existed during the post crucifixion era. Remember that there was no single compiled set of written accounts regarding the lives of Mary Magdalene and Mar Yeshua (Jesus), ***there most certainly wasn't a Bible per say***. There were various compilations of the Hebrew Torah, but there was no Bible as we think of it today. There was an **Oral Tradition.** What we now commonly refer to as the Kabbalah or Qabbalah, and an esoteric mystery school.[62]

There were, hundreds, if not thousands of rumors, tall tales and written accounts of various individuals', but few or none of those written accounts survived the slash and burn campaigns of Saul of Tarsus, the anti-Christian Roman Officials and later the Catholic Church and its Inquisitions. Except for the gallant efforts of a small inner circle of the Friends and Family of Mary Magdalene

---

61 http://SAGES-OF-LIGHT.COM

62 **Hebrew** הַלָּבָק (Israeli: Kabala) transliterated as Cabala, Kabbala, Qabalah; an oral tradition easily remembered through the use of a **TAROT** deck (which acted as a portable encyclopedia of ancient wisdom and alchemical procedures). Naturally the Catholic and other uneducated christian sects foolishly pronounced the TAROT as an instrument of evil, whereas it is a system of gematria (mathematical genius).

and Mar Yeshua, the truth and message of the original gospel might have been lost forever.

The near successful destruction and annihilation of the early Jesus Movement is rarely considered outside the context of Judaic and Roman history, however, the events that occurred during the lifetimes of Mar Yeshua and Mary Magdalene were much more complex than these modern-day children's stories of Moses and the Bible would has us believe. The events that came to pass, both during and prior to Mary Magdalene's appearance in the Levant, involved many other significant players, in particular, the subjugated governments of Egypt, which included those descendents born of marriages between Egypt's Royal House and General Ptolemy who was a commander in the army of Alexander the Great; a Dynasty whose extended family in Alexandria included numerous female descendants entitled to bear the name of Cleopatra[63] (*offspring from the campaigns of Alexander the Great).*

There were also the defending Parthian states at that time, which represent military mergers, leftover from Alexander's campaigns, as well as the Nabataeans (or Arabs if you prefer), who were remnants of the ancient and magnificent Indus Valley and Taxilan civilizations. We must also consider the Royal mergers of the Babylonian regions and its influences (which had also been under the control of Alexander the Great and his generals).

In addition to all those, who came before Jesus and Mary Magdalene, there are those who came after *and during their lifetime, and they must be recounted as well. Take for example:* the so-called attempts at a harmonization of Christian

63 ***The Ptolemies*** ~ In 323 B.C. Alexander died leaving his generals to divide his empire. One of the generals, Ptolemy managed to retain control of Egypt. Around 305 B.C., taking the title of king he sired the dynasty now known as the Ptolemies. Thereafter Alexandria became the capital Egypt's, where Ptolemy founded a magnificent library and museum. His rule later extended to include ***Judea (in the southern part of ancient Palestine),*** along with the island of Cyprus, and Cyrene, the Greek colony in northern Africa.

Almost 300 years later, ***just 60~70 odd years before the birth of Mary Magdalene,*** Cleopatra became queen in 51 B.C. after her father's demise (Ptolemy XII).

Her 10-year-old brother, Ptolemy XIII, became her husband and co-ruler. Incest and marriage between siblings was a common practice in Egyptian royal families.

In 48 B.C., young Ptolemy's guardians seized power for him and drove Cleopatra from the throne.

At that time, Julius Caesar, who came in pursuit of Pompey (the Roman general who was a principal rival in Caesar's attempts to become the sovereign ruler of Rome), arrived in Alexandria. Cleopatra then attempted to persuade Caesar, with some success, to reinstate her as a sovereign Queen of Egypt, and later claimed to have birthed a son sired by Caesar. In 46 B.C., at Caesar's invitation, she took both, Caesarian and Ptolemy XIV, to Rome where she remained until 44 B.C., when Roman aristocrats assassinated Caesar. Upon her return to Egypt, Cleopatra's brother Ptolemy was killed, so that Caesarion would reign as Ptolemy XV.

Thereafter, in 37 B.C., Cleopatra, *correctly known as* ***Cleopatra VII because she was the seventh Egyptian queen of Macedonian descent with that name,*** married Mark Antony, a co-ruler of Rome.

Antony gave his sons and daughter by Cleopatra much of the land once ruled by Alexander the Great. The Romans later executed Caesarion, after the tragic death of his mother and Antony, because they assumed he would lay claim, as Caesar's heir, to Rome's empire. The death of Cleopatra and Caesarion terminated the ***overt*** rule of the Ptolemies dynasty.

The various mystery schools that remained, both corrupt, ethical and otherwise, are worth considering, when any attempt is made to understand who and what Mary Magdalene was and who her ancestors really were.

and Egyptian Mystery schools, which followed in approximately 46 A.D. when a Serapic[64] priest, reputedly named ORMESIUS or St. Ormus, was (according to biased reports) "converted" to Christianity at Alexandria by St. Mark. This was not, however, so much about the Egyptian schools accepting and incorporating the Christian concepts, or the reverse, as it was about the misguided and deluded priests in general *on both sides* having been set back upon the correct course; or a return to the roots and methods of The Way if you will.

Also, let us consider the so-called early Christians who, after the period of the so-called crucifixion, were essentially divided into two exoteric (not esoteric) schools of thought, *A and B respectively* (and in turn, into hundreds of additional variations and subsets).

Group~A a very small but correct-minded minority, included those individuals, who understood and believed in the essential, alchemical message of Mary Magdalene and Mar Yeshua (the alchemical wedding), a group more appropriately referred to as the ***Ebionites*** (rather than Christians).

Then we have the other greater majority, Group B, being those individuals who were successfully deceived and subverted by Saul of Tarsus (Paul). Consider carefully this fellow Saul (that later styled himself Paul) who, after his *cunning self-professed conversion,* (wherein he had *seen a vision!)* consequently *claimed to be appointed by Jesus himself to the Priesthood no less!* He then named his own (Paul's) newly convened following, after the Greek word *Christos,* hence today we have the *Christians.*

Essentially, during Mary and Jesus' absence, Paul had patiently and dramatically purloined leadership by simply insinuated himself into the inner circles of distant enclaves of the enormous following that Mary Magdalene and Mar Yeshua (Jesus) had worked so diligently over the span of many years to develop. That group is estimated by some historians to have surpassed in numbers [by tens of thousands] all those, who still attended Jehovah's Temple (the Temple based on guilt-ridden, fear-bound, blood-sacrifice-oriented superstition[65]). Thereby, Paul seduced a large following whereby he created Group B.

James, the brother of Jesus, and others, were constantly at odds with Paul and his insidious efforts directed at subverting the early Ebionite congregation. The Ebionites were aware of his scam, and didn't succumb to the ruse, but the newly evangelized congregations who lived at great distances far away from the guidance of the core group ran like sheep to the slaughter, completely blind to Paul's political scheming, those crowds having been quite naive where the intricate politics, which governed that critical period of history are concerned.

Because the Ebionites baptized and forgave one another's transgressions without demanding sacrifices and tithes (much to Herod and Paul's dismay), *absolution* in essence, *was free for the asking.* So long as one made a sincere effort to follow The Way and return no more to the vulgar and ignorant superstitious

64 The name Serapis is likely a combination of Osiris and Apis, two well known gods of that period (and most probably created by Ptolemy I in an attempt to harmonize Greek gods with Egyptian gods)

65 Remember... that nasty god of the high-priest Aaron (YHWH) who, "is a jealous god" full of wrath, brimstone and threatening hellfire at every opportunity? No wonder a priesthood that healed and fed the poor, counseled love and compassion, and required no blood sacrifices at their altars became very popular over a very short period time.

methods (never again like dogs to their own vomit) that had enslaved them for the past few thousand years, they were free. Freedom was free! Just follow the The Way and respect the dharma. Makes sense doesn't it? Thus, as literally thousands flocked to join this new cult of emancipation, (to Group A) , they flowed en masse *away* from the Judaic Temple, where moneylenders sold animals on credit to the impoverished masses at wickedly usurious interest rates.

The people were leaving the old (usurious) ways of the Temple behind (in *droves)* and they were bringing their tithes and offerings and resources with them. Following that, a political conflict arose, which revolved largely around the fact that the Temple coffers and associated rivers of silver (blood-money: a sacrificial slush-fund) were rapidly drying up, alnog with the river of silver[66] that eventually made its way to Rome (by way of the corrupt and decadent Herod family).

Ultimately, when Jesus, Mary Magdalene and their core group were made to disappear *perforce*, all factions of their following were understandably confused at having lost their true and legitimate leadership to acts of genocidal butchery, (much of which had occurred thanks to Paul's concerted efforts both before and after his so-called "conversion").

Eventually the surviving groups in their near entirety, would fall prey to the insidious Saul of Tarsus (or Paul as he is referred to today). In their naivete they'd swallowed, hook, line and sinker, Paul's completely revised *and twisted* version of the message of Mary Magdalene and Mar Yeshua, (the seeds of the antichrist had been sown and were quickly geminating).

Whereas the other smaller (Ebionite) enclave made its way back to the great learning center of Alexandria in Egypt and to a mentor named Ormesius (reputedly a Serapic priest), the remainder of the following (Pistic~majority) were spoon-fed secondhand (and *third*-hand) half~truths and other scraps-of-wisdom *"in the name of Jesus Christ,"* by Paul (Saul) and all those other Pistics etc, whom he had duped into following him (all of whom subsequently remain in darkness unto this very day).

circa: 46 AD~

It was in Egypt, where an underground Ebionite fellowship was reconvened and the "lost lambs" were reunited (harmonized) with other vegan mentors and advocates; many of whom were in turn forwarded to Mystery Schools that had long been established in the lands of Gaul and further still in the Western Isles: the now renown areas of Glastonbury Tor and the Isles near of Iona[67] Others still were sent as far away as Tibet and the Japans: All well out of reach of the Roman Military-Industrial Complex. 300-400 years later their slightly confused descendents even made their appearance on the North American continents and were known as the Michigan Mound Builders.[68] But

---

66 See FOREWORD to this book & its notes re: *"silver shekels" and "Heord's massive annual income."*

67 archaic strata of Iona among oldest on Earth, generally believed *1,500 million years old*

68 see Appendix for Sumerian glyphs that were phonetically Japanese in origin. Also see :The Mystic Symbol: Mark of the Michigan Mound Builders *by Hariette MertzThe Mystic Symbol describes thousands of inscribed tablets, found in Michigan. 10,000 ~ 30,000 artifacts of The Michigan Mound Builders have been discovered in North America. Mound burials have yielded evidence of a pre-Columbian culture. Controversy has rages because they were here before Columbus in1492 a fact that is strangely disturbing to our academics today. Nevertheless, the Michigan artifacts continue to surface in the state of Michigan even until today. Henriette Mertz championed the authenticity of these tablets, tools and weapons of these mysterious people. During World War II, Henriette Mertz worked as a code-breaker for the U.S. government's cryptography department. She published several controversial books during the 1960s &'70s, including Pale Ink, The Wine Dark Sea, and Atlantis. Mertz died in 1982, at the age of 73.*

these groups (churches?) had more layers than a large onion, and only a few inner circle adepts knew the core truths and secret alchemy in the final days before being driven completely underground.

The harmonization, as defined by the Therapeutae, had reputedly occurred in Egypt, when the *so-called Secret* Gospel of Mark was conceived in cooperation with one individual Magi, who as previously mentioned went by the title Ormesius. Thus, according to legend, Ormesius, later know as St. Ormus, was instrumental in the creation and governance of the, understandably secretive and clandestine, Society of ORMUS. But they too were eventually subverted and, in the large majority, inevitably led astray. The charlatans were mixed in like weeds among the wheat. The weeds became so numerous that the wheat was lost in obscurity.

circa: 313~325 AD~

Thereafter, prior to the consensus reached at the Council of Nicea, which was convened by the Roman Emperor Constantine at a time when he decided to adopt Christianity as the Religion of the Empire (although he never converted to Christianity himself), there were countless cults and religious orders, each claiming to be the singular source and means of access to the true God or Goddess of Heaven. It was at this meeting of bishops who had come from all parts of the Roman Empire (and beyond) that a vote was counted, as to whether or not women even had souls! They also determined which books should be incorporated into the heretofore nonexistent Christian Bible. Those bishops who assembled there were already more than a little compromised in that they were only allowed to attend if they had agreed well in advance to certain rules of order and concepts that Constantine and his associates had already "written in brass;" Brass that was to be sold off as "gold" to the unsuspecting masses for centuries to come. These many "Christian" groups and, otherwise veiled, cabals and covens (diocese) all vied for supremacy and dominance over the people of the land, as well as control over their rulers... all and everything associated with wealth, power and cash flow (tithes and taxation), etc. The art of ORMUS perforce remained veiled and esoteric.

At this point our White Dove of Peace, poor dear, has a little metal band clamped around her ankle and her snow-white wings are somewhat sullied by the soot of chimneys that are filled with burning books and the ashes of ancient alchemical manuscripts. She chokes on the smoke of bones and seared flesh that smolder in vile places where public executions are carried out to delighted howls of demented humans. Therefore, in stark contrast to these anti-christ activities, The Society of ORMUS along with its Secrets of the Alchemical Arts has cloaked itself and taken refuge in Arabic mystery schools, bidding farewell to the ever increasing number of antichrist communities.

300 years later (570-632 AD), those Arabic mystery schools still followed an oral (Kabbalistic) tradition: the Koran being written by others, and not as many errantly believe, by Muhammad himself. All or most of the Qur'an was apparently written down by Muhammad's exoteric (not esoteric [inner circle]) followers while he was alive, *but* it was then, as it is now, *primarily* an account documenting an essentially *oral* teaching. The written compilation of the whole Qur'an in its present definite form was completed early after the death of Muhammad. Islam and the Koran soon went the way of Christianity and its "Bible," both having had

their version of a "Paul" and a "fanatical male chauvinist following" who have conveniently forgotten the original message of peace and compassion.

Meanwhile the knowing ones continued to long for a day when justice would be restored and women would once again walk the streets safely at night without fear and trepidation. Hadn't they waited long enough? Perhaps one day the moneylender's tables will once again be overturned and our white doves will be set free once more?

* Lest we forget, we recall to mind *once again*, that the White Dove of Peace was once representative of a Goddess who brings the gifts of civilization to mankind, and perhaps more specifically to the Adamic Race.

ISIS was *and is* a Goddess best known for her ability to heal and for the raising of one rather famous fellow, OSIRIS, from the dead. She is also known for her baptismal rites, wherein submersion into water was representative of the washing away of karmic stains from the soul of the applicant (again, an especially relevant bit of history, of which modern Christians today remain largely unaware).

Her belief system revolved primarily around the core elements that were associated with the promotion, sustenance and preservation of Life Itself, to wit, Earth, Air, Solar-fire and Water. The same is indicative of John the Baptist's true religious affections and political affiliations. Remember that John the Baptist was not a Christian. There were no Christians during the lifetime of John the Baptist. The term Christian came into use long after he was decapitated, when the naïve following of Saul of Tarsus later embraced what they had been erroneously led to believe were the teachings of one Teacher whom we today call Jesus "the Christ".

Although the symbolic term "Christian" did not exist during the lifetime of John the Baptist, another symbol did exist and it was in use among almost all of the popular cults at that time, The White Dove of Peace. The White Dove of Peace carries the Manna of Heaven, Sophia or Wisdom of the Ages, and descends into the dark world of ignorance and suffering.

This White Dove of Peace is associated with a long list of benevolent female characters, goddesses and other female rulers. There are as many names as there are cultures and languages, but they all have one issue in common and share the same basic precept that, "Forgiveness is the Way of the Divine."

The White Dove of Peace bespeaks a civilized sentiment and manner of behavior; this is the Way of the Mother, a compassionate and forgiving Matron who brings the gifts of wisdom along with the mannerisms of civilization to the Adamic race.

The White Dove of Peace is representative of a code of conduct, of decent behavior and is directly linked to the DNA.

DNA morphs and DNA mutates.

Our decisions and associated behavior directly shapes the structure of our DNA and the memories that are encoded there for future reference. The very character of our offspring is determined by our own behavior and decisions.

When we behave properly (or poorly), our DNA is affected. Over a very short period of time, our DNA morphs[69] and mutates intelligently, preparing the seed

69 ***morph*** *verb* ~ change or cause to change by small gradual steps, smoothly from one architectural consideration to another

for future generations.

This is truly a miraculous process.

Our experiences, being the direct results of our decisions and actions are encoded into our sperm and ovaries. This data in turn is carried forward to our offspring, who in turn do the same. Occasionally, a culture might become misinformed and thereby develop superstitious beliefs and behavior patterns that are unhealthy. Although the negative side-effects of the behavior may not become noticeable for several generations, the DNA nonetheless continues to record the patterns and results.

After a period of time the DNA makes changes to the brains, minds, hormonal balances and bodies of those individuals who unwittingly participate in that unhealthy behavior. Receptors in our brains are created and/or removed. Mood causes alterations of the DNA code itself; and in turn our DNA is altered "on the fly" (instantly). In time an entire ethnic culture may become seriously deformed as a result of their superstitious behavior patterns, in that the DNA is dependent on the brains and minds that it builds to gather sustenance and information about the environments that it inhabits.

In effect, our bodies and brains are bionic machines created by DNA to act as information gathering equipment, as well as transportation vehicles and as energy harvesting and processing devices.

Think about it for a moment.

The DNA carries all the data that we need to form our bodies, our brains, as well as our skeletal and muscular systems; it carries a fantastic amount of other vital statistics and memories along with other information critical to our survival such as reflexes and instincts!

It tells us how to keep time and maintain a constant body temperature that is universal to the entire human race! Did you ever pause to wonder, by what method does the human body keep time? Where is that clock located? How do the heart and lungs maintain that perfect rhythmic harmony, which results in what we call life? (We take an awful lot for granted on a daily basis don't we?)

DNA lives in cooperation with mitochondria.

They enjoy a symbiotic relationship. The mitochondria provide our vehicles with a power supply technology and the DNA provides us with the blueprints for the construction of so many useful organs, navigation equipment, memory storage and recall capacity, as well as repair and regeneration capabilities.

Most importantly DNA allows us to have feelings; and these feelings of pleasure/pain, happy/sadness and joyful/sorrow represent the primary binary survival mechanism with which we make decisions and learn to change and evolve.

The general idea of course is to avoid crashing into other objects or vehicles, while we search for and consume items that we need to assist the mitochondria in its efforts at energy conversion. Ultimately we search for joy, pleasure, happiness, fun and generally that overall good feeling.

Enter another creature.

It has no arms or legs to speak of and it has "crawled" on its belly during its entire existence for countless eons. It is destined to live a life without ever being able to manipulate its environment like most other creatures it encounters. It is extremely destructive for the most part in that it has to kill its neighbors in order to survive. It is similar to DNA in that is has a spiral structure. It attempts to mimic DNA but it cannot. It doesn't have the knowledge and power to reproduce itself without killing its neighbors and cannot exist on its own. Most of you are probably thinking of a snake right about now because throughout human history it has been compared symbolically to a snake. But it is far more deadly than a snake however and much more insidious. Did you guess what it is? Some people mistakenly refer to it as Beelzebub or the Devil. It is all but invisible to the naked eye. Can you guess what it is? It is the virus and its slave-partner: mucoid plaque.

Virus has been a source of pain and suffering for the human race since times immemorial. Even today we wrestle with its ill effects on a daily basis and it usually outsmarts all of us. It has killed and crippled millions and caused horrendous pain to almost everyone alive at one time or another during their lifetime.

Virus has stolen our vehicles. It hijacks our body and takes control of our senses, our desire body, and eventually commandeers our logical thought process to the extent that we lose our very own will to the will of virus. If left unchecked it will take over.

Do you think this example is a bit to extreme? You had better think again. *Virus is much more intelligent than you can possibly imagine. It masquerades as DNA. It takes over the architectural activities of DNA. It sends false signals and redirects proteins, the builders of the body. Cancer and HIV are born. Do you think you can stop them with so-called "modern" medicine?* Reconsider!

Did you know that the HIV-AIDS virus is quite capable of capturing dead bacteria in your blood stream? It has little "arms" that grab the dead bacteria as it's passing by, and it studies the DNA of the bacteria, compares it to your immune system and your DNA. It (virus) then makes adjustments to itself so that it won't die by the same method as the bacteria it has just captured, studied and discarded like yesterday's news. Virus is smart, clever and capable. It lives in you and preys upon your ignorance even as you read these very words. HIV & Herpes formed a new kind of virus by sharing data in the early seventies, but you never knew it did you? It didn't bleed so it didn't lead the headlines. It just keeps on goin'.

"An' der ain't notin' you kin do 'bout it!" it quips sheepishly in a condescending New York accent, as you consider in vain how to remove them from your bodily tissues.

This is where the White Dove of Peace and Her Wisdom (or Manna) comes into play~

After so many generations of living in ignorance,[70] the DNA mutates and becomes decrepit, leaving both itself and the bodies that it built, vulnerable to the devices of its arch rival VIRUS. As mentioned previously, when people do not behave properly, the DNA mutates. When people eat junk food, filled with artificial flavors and fragrances, their DNA mutates. When people sit in chairs, looking at computer screens, in buildings lit with artificial lights for 50-60% of their waking daylight hours, and then watch television for the remaining 15-30%

70 Note* the use of the word *ignorance* as opposed to *sin!*

of their waking hours, all the while surrounded by white noise, breathing pollution from factories and cars, their DNA quite literally mutates!

We can all stop worrying about the aliens arriving, because we have become aliens.

But these are all just tremendously advanced disturbances, which are the results of our abject failure to listen to and obey the Laws of Life.

Although we may be correct in assuming that we are much further from the truth than those who lived during the life and times of Mary Magdalene, Hope yet remains for those of us who will turn back and seek our deepest roots, unlearn our learning and "...walk the path of the Great Spirit," as the Hopi Indians might say. The sad thing though, is that we have been living in ignorance of the Law of Life for so many generations. We aren't talking about a few thousand years. The human race has been unwittingly wallowing in the "vice of virus" for eons.

So what is The White Dove of Peace exactly and what is this "Sophia" or "Bread of Heaven" that she brings from heaven only to the faithful? And to whom, or to what must we be faithful, in order that we receive the benefits and blessings?

In order to understand how the Manna works, you must first understand how the virus works. But don't worry; we aren't going to bore-you-to-tears with medical phrases and Latin terms. You don't need to know how all the gears of the watch are assembled on the inside of the clock casing, in order to know what time it is. However, you will need to understand how to decode the mysterious meaning of the two little hands that point at the base-twelve numbers. Rest assured, at this juncture, that the only thing we will attempt to do is to decode the face of the clock and to understand in no uncertain terms just, exactly, what time it is. We will explain in Part B of this series how the clock works. We will try to help you understand how to read the universal clock and how to decode the sacred message that is embedded in your own DNA, (look within and hear) a message that was encoded into your DNA several hundred thousand years ago.

This *inward looking* process bespeaks the beginning of our complete metamorphosis as a species. Be forewarned however, as it has been written in your DNA (your own personal, custom-tailored Book of Life) that it is not sufficient to simply make inquiries and to merely *know* the theories and history of theories of enlightenment; for gnosis alone will not transport you into the Land of The Blessed. You must choose the path of Dharma- The Path of Right Action, (and we do *NOT* refer here to the modern and corrupted Hindu/Buddhist theory of reincarnation, which is one of those half-truths that we carefully avoid!). If we're trying to understand where we're supposed to be going as a species, we *must first* learn how to *look within.*

"By the fruits of their labor (in heart, mind and body) ye shall know them!"

***A note on where we're coming from-** *i.e. we have lost our way and we are off the path. How do we return to the path?*

Buddha is known to have come from the western reaches of Nepal, near to what we now refer to, in modern geographical terms, as northern Pakistan, near Kashmir, where we find the sources of the Hunza River, The Darya River, The Indus River, The Ganges River and the ancient remains of the Sarasvati. River.

The Sarasvati River (whence we derive the name Sarah~ *Princess: as in*

Abraham and Sarah) also had its source there.[71] These rivers, and principally the Hunza River, were the source of longevity and livelihood of, what's left of, the gentle and magnificent Hunza People.

Contrary to popular misconceptions, the Prince, Siddhartha, later know as the Gaotama Buddha and founder of Buddhism, was originally depicted as a blue-eyed, man with Aryan features and was ***not*** of Chinese origins. He was more likely genetically akin to the Great Indra, *who ate the SOMA*. The SOMA was a kind of rock or metallic substance. INDRA[72] was a man who "held lightning bolts in his hand" (like Odin and Thor of Scandinavian fame, or Zeus of the Greeks).

Legends tell us that the Hunza people used dried apricots and apricot seed as their primary form of currency. It was their staple food, like rice is the staple to most Asian people, as wheat is the staple for Europeans and as corn was to Native American Indians. Only women were allowed to actually ***own*** apricot trees, and a consensus among female elders was required when a young man wished to betroth a Hunza girl.He had to prove that he was favored among a sufficient number of women, as he could not marry unless he was able to offer a reasonable number of apricot trees to his beloved bride-to-be (in effect, an orchard whose annual yield would be sufficient to sustain the new family). Since men could not own the trees, the women passed the trees "down", *through* him, to the bride-to-be, which represented their approval and consent to the wedding. The bridegroom became the *STEWARD* of the land and its trees and its people. Land was not owned by people. The people belonged to the land, much like the Native American Indians (if not the same).

Today the Hunza people along with their Way of Life are quite literally an "endangered species," much like their counterparts in the Levant, who formed the basis of the early Ebionite Church; what we call in this discourse,

---

71 see also "Serapis" as in Serapic Priests; in the Mystery Schools of Alexandria, Serapis was represented as a serpentine (En.Ki) god of Healing. The Greeks called him Aesculapius, and later Asklepios. In Egypt, Asklepius was Imouthis, or I-m-Hetep, son of Ptah and Sekhet, a component of the Memphis triad. To Phoenicians Asklepios, was Eshmun, wise in the Way of Taaut, also known as Thoth. In the Hermetica, Hermes Trismegistus was Asclepius' teacher. Agathodaimon and Hermes are the two primary prophets in the Sabians of Harran, . Agathodaimon as Hermes' teacher, parallel to Seth & Enoch. Ormus is said to have been a Seraphic priest when Saint Mark made his appearance. The Egyptian Mysteries & Ebionite practices merged, harmonizing the two, thereby establishing a peripheral (initiate level) school of so-called Solomonic Wisdom, thus perpetuating the Rose-Croix (inner war or Jihad of self-sacrifice: process of conqoring the beast within).

72 INDRA- learns how to pursue spiritual wisdom while still fulfilling his kingly duties (Tantric methodology: warrior/monk/king: a Malkuth-zadok [Melchizedek~Priest-King]). Indra is attested a god of the Mitanni. Mitanni (Hittite cuneiform KUR URUMi-ta-an-ni, also Mittani Mi-it-ta-ni) or Hanigalbat (Assyrian Hanigalbat, Khanigalbat cuneiform □a-ni-gal-bat) was a Hurrian kingdom in northern Mesopotamia from ca. 1500 BC. At the height of its power, during the 14th century BC, encompassing what is today southeastern Turkey, northern Syria and northern Iraq (roughly corresponding to Kurdistan), centered around the capital Washukanni whose precise location has not yet been determined by archaeologists. (Generally north of the area now known as Damascus, east of Tarsus and north east of the biblical Galilee etc.) The Mitanni kingdom believed to have been a feudal state led by warrior nobility of Indo-Aryan descent who invaded the Levant region at some point during the 17th century BC.

INDRA of the Vedic~ The Vedas (Sanskrit véda "knowledge") are a large corpus of texts originating in Ancient India which form the oldest portion of Sanskrit literature & the oldest sacred texts of Hinduism. According to Hindu tradition, the Vedas are *Apaurusheyatva* "not human compositions", supposedly having been directly revealed, and thus are called *Sruti* ("what is heard" *Kaballistic*?). Vedic mantras are recited as sacred sounds designed to activate the subtle nervous system.

the Jesus Movement (and what most people erroneously refer to as the *early Christian church*). Both are vegetarian societies that have been wiped-out by war, superstitious ignorance, ignorant political campaigns and religious prejudice. The Hunza are a persecuted society, just as the Ebionites were during the first few generations after the emergence of the Jesus Movement (also known as the Ebionite community or Therapeutae).

The earlier Mandaean followers of John-the-Baptist and later, the Manichean movement, along with their ancestors, reaching all the way back to and beyond Abraham (a name stemming from the Sanskrit referring to "father of Brahmin[73]" or "*great* grand father") and Sarah (a title meaning princess- as in SaraSvati) are a remnant that barely survive in remote areas of Iraq and Iran. What remains of their people and culture, which is next to nothing, is a ragtag band of refugees. They are such a small minority that their plight doesn't make the news and so they are passing into the halls of history virtually unnoticed by the global village. As self-effacing pacifists and vegetarians, they do not rattle sabers and beat the drums of revolution.

Let's not forget these people. From now on, when you think of early Christians, remember the Hunza and think *vegetarian*; remember please the Ebionites and recall to mind those noble personages whose migration began in the Hunza Valley long before the birth of Abraham~ A people who traveled down the Hunza River, towards what we call, the "Cradle of Civilization," where the Indus Valley Culture flourished. Eventually they crossed the Straits of Ormuz (Hormuz), near a place where a great Neolithic city now lies submerged under the sea[74] and made their way along the Oman/Yemen coast, where the frankincense trees flourish, and onward towards the to the Levant, bringing with them the knowledge of the SOMA, and the man known as the Melchizedek[75] (Malcuth, Malkuth, or Malkus Zadok~ *kingly priest).*

Remember too that ABRAHAM[76] (father of Brahmins) struck a deal with the

73 ***Etymology*** ~ from the Latin Bracmanus, from the Greek Brachman, *from Sanskrit...* ***br-Uhma-a*** *...of the Brahman caste: from brahman meaning* ~of the highest caste assigned by tradition to the priesthood

74 Ruins of a civilization carbon dated at around 7500 BCE discovered in January 2002 are there for all to see, 160 feet below the surface of the ocean.

Imagine! A city that is 9,500 years old, one that parallels (or is older than) the Sumerian civilization by several thousand years; older than the Egyptian civilization; older than the Chinese civilization. This will naturally affect our present understanding of the development of urban civilization on this earth tremendously, and necessitation of a complete rethink in so far as archeology is concerned! ***February 16, 2002 Surat, India -*** in mid-January, marine scientists in India announced they had sonar images of square and rectangular shapes about 130 feet down off the northwestern coast of India in the Gulf of Khambhat (Cambay). According to the news releases, they have done a radiocarbon testing on a piece of wood from the underwater site that is now yielding an age of 9,500 years which would place it near the end of the last Ice Age.

75 Melchizedek was a title, the title of a master craftsman and alchemist of biblical legend, one who possessed secret, mystical and magical powers. It was also the title of Abraham's teacher.

76 "Northern Afghanistan was called Uttara Kuru and was a great center of learning. An Indian woman went there to study and received the title of Vak, i.e. SaraSvati or Saraisvati (Lady Sarah). It is believed that Brahm (Abraham), her teacher (and half brother), was so impressed by her beauty, education, and powerful intellect, that he married her." (The Hindu History; p. 48, in passim.)

A holy society in Southern Afghanistan gave birth to a diaspora of similar communities which

Melchizedek upon entering the Levant. The knowledge that they shared later became incorrectly known as King Solomon's Key or The Solomon Key (and it is also referred to in recent works by Dan Brown and Lawrence Gardner).

The reason for this misnomer is detailed in the three-part volume, ~ORMUS ‡ The Secret Alchemy of Mary Magdalene~ by William Hearth.

*FINAL NOTE [to Chapter 3] Briefly, contrary to recent conjecture, Hiram H'Abif was NOT an invention of the "Modern" Masonic Lodge. Hiram was the King of Tyre. His name in so far as King Solomon was concerned was Hiram Haviv (stemming from Habibi or *beloved,* as in beloved spiritual brother, more at cousin). Habibi was later mispronounced as H'Abif and later Abiff.

When the King of Tyre (Hiram), upon completion of The Great Temple in UrSalem, accepts "bread for my (Hiram's) family" as payment from King Solomon, he is NOT negotiating from a position of weakness, nor is he in an inferior or subordinate position to Solomon; he is the equal (or even Superior) who yet remains humble and "shows favor" to Solomon by giving him (Solomon) an easy way to say, "thank you" to his mentor (Hiram).

When the King of Tyre (who was one of THE master craftsmen in his day) says that Solomon should "make bread for my family," he includes Solomon and all their cousins and relatives collectively speaking. The King of Tyre and King Solomon were cousins, genetically enjoined by noble marriage, generations earlier, as were the kings and queens of Egypt, Babylon, Nepal and India before them. "Make bread for my family" is more correctly interpreted as meaning, "Take care of our Great Seafaring Nation my brother!"

And where did this "manna" or "bread" come from that fed Moses and the family of Hiram Ha'viv (Hiram *Abif= Haviv= Habibi*)? Was this "manna" the SOMA ~ which The White Dove of Peace brings (to us) *from heaven*; Was this "manna" the SOMA, which was stored in the Temple of Hathor long before the days and generations of Moses? Mary Magdalene knew all about it, as did her Beloved Friend and companion. If you persevere, then so shall you.

"And ye shall be greater than I."

---

spread around the world: including the Asian, African, European continents and spread even as far as, what we today call, the Americas. Linguistic evidence of Brahm's presence in throughout the world evident: In the Persian: Braghman (Holy); In the Latin: Bragmani (Holy); In the Russian: Rachmany (Holy); In the Ukranian Rachmanya (Priest; Holy); In the Hebrew: Ram (Supreme Leader). The mystic syllable AUM is a sacred word among the Hindus and is representative of the earth, sky, and heaven, the Triple Universe. It is also one of the names of Brahm. The Aztecs also chanted the syllable AUM recalling the dual principal of all creation: OMeticuhlti (Male Principle) and OMelcihuatl (Female Principle). The Mayan priestly caste was called Balam or Baal-Am (pronounced B'lahm). There was no "R" consonant in Mayan, but if there had been the word might have been sounded out as Brahm. The Peruvian Incas worshiped the sun as Inti Raymi (Ram).

"Names that derive from Rama are pervasive in Native-American cultures, particularly among those tribes that extend from the American Southwest, through Mexico and beyond Peru. Compare the Durga religious ceremonies to those of the aforementioned cultures. The Tarahumara Indians of Chihuahua are an ideal example. Their real name is Ra-Ram-Uri. As in Sumeria and Northern India, the Ra-Ram-Uri "Uri" = "People." Because the Spanish "R" is trilled, this "Uri" could also be Udi or Yuddhi, the Sanskrit name for "Warrior; Conqueror." Many Mexican tribes mention that a foreign race of Yuri once invaded their part of the world. Many other astonishing Kashmiri/Sanskrit correspondences appear in the Ra-Ram-Uri language. Their relation to ancient Phoenicia, Sumeria, and Northern India is beyond question." Gene D. Matlock, B.A., M.A. discusses this issue extensively and we strongly recommend that the reader research the article entitled "Who Was Abraham?" by Gene D. Matlock.

CHAPTER FIVE ~ MARYAM THE MIGDAL-EDER'S OBJECTIVE

"Natural Order vs The Invisible God"

The best-kept secret of course is a secret that is hidden right under your nose; it was there all along but you just don't notice it.

The primary message of this book is this, "There is a secret code concealed right under your nose. It is concealed in every cell of your body, and within the very cells of your nose! Not only is it under your nose, it is *in* your nose and *it built your nose.* It resides in every cell of your body and it built your body. It constantly rebuilds your body as well. All the answers to all the great questions are right there, encoded into you DNA. This method, *this secret alchemy,* which allows the Living Word, *the code,* to be read and in turn be written into your Book of Life and into your Personal Temple (your body) will work for anyone, regardless of your race, religion, nationality, skin color or gender. The Secret Alchemy of Mary Magdalene and her Beloved Family of Friends is based on a universal, heavenly code of justice. If you decide, of your own free will, to perform the alchemical process, it will work for you, *if you are willing to keep the faith, to fight the good fight*[77] *and stay the course.*"

Look within! Isn't that what all the great spiritual leaders, since ancient times, have always told us, *time and again, world without end amen?* It is TRUE!

But there are unnatural forces and a few greedy bastards that are hell-bent on convincing us that the Secrets of Life are not to be found within our own bodies. They want us to believe that there are no answers to be found IN Life Itself.

They want to sell you a piece of yourself after they have stolen it from you.

Pretty sick scenario,wouldn't you agree? "Pie in the sky *after you die~* and you *can* have it but *only* IF you *pay our price.* Do what we tell you when we tell you. Play the game the way we tell you to and if you're *good* you might see god and go to heaven. But make no mistake! While you're on Earth *we own your ass!*" ~ Sound familiar? Well! Don't you believe it! *Not a word of it!*

One "priesthood" would have us believe in an invisible and omnipresent entity, who pervades all things, and yet is not accessible through Nature Itself; and that the only way we can access this God is through a book called the Bible; so long as we think of ourselves as filthy retched creatures. This "priesthood" would have us believe that Nature is inferior to a so-called "God the Father".

Yet another "priesthood" would have us believe that Nature is the Goddess and that the Mother of God is the Almighty Queen of Heaven, and that the male principle is subordinate to the female principle.

There is yet another group that would have us believe that there is no God at all, or gods and neither a Goddess. Others worship only money and they pray daily, on their way to and from the bank. Others say you must serve the state and

77 The Holy War (Jihad) that is waged *within. The Jihad is a war that an individual wages within one's own self. It is not an external war. It does of course require that certain actions be performed, but it does not require that we judge the actions of others, nor does it require that we urge or police our neighbors. Look within and conquer the beast that lives with you. Turn the lead to gold: you must achieve the transfiguration within this lifetime.*

surrender to servitude your entire life to pay off the debts of your past lives. Hah! The list goes on and on.

Who is right and who is wrong? Is there an invisible Father-God, as some would have us believe? Or is God neither male nor female, or both? Or is there a Godde that is representative of something beyond even these limited points of view?

Perhaps there is a Godde, but one that is none and all of these, a Godde that defies description?

A Godde that is androgynous as well as dialectic; a Godde who exists in an intra-dimensional space-time that we are unable to perceive and understand so long as we are bound by our limited state of mind at the present time.

Man wants to fit Godde into a convenient little box, with convenient little handles and convenient little labels. Let's call it what it is, "Convenience Store Religion"; or how about a TV-Dinner Salvation package that they will deliver right to your doorstep by courier, no need to even leave the comfort and security your living-room sofa. Pop it in the microwave oven and eat your share of god without missing a single minute of your favorite TV commercial. soap-opera or evangelical gala..

But Godde is so much more than that, thus man may never be able to tame Godde. If man could tame Godde in such a fashion, then Godde would not be Godde. So man may have to come to grips with the reality that Godde cannot be explained with words and will never fit the mould that man has devised to explain Godde. Godde exists beyond our vain attempts at limiting, defining and *confining* Godde. You can't put a lease or handle on Godde.

So why pretend that we can control or tame Life Itself? We can however, learn to follow well. We can transform our independent will into a will aligned with the Divine Paradigm; we should look around us and seek Truth in Nature and learn from the examples set forth by the UniVerse.

Isn't Nature, or the Mother-Godde, in fact, simply one aspect of The Body and Mind of the Godde-Eternal? Or is Mother Nature, as some philosophers would have us believe, merely the handiwork of an unapproachable Father-God, who exists beyond this physical realm, a God who, is disinterested in the natural world, with which we are daily acquainted? *Is this world, after all, a world of sin, lust and illusion? Is sex a dirty thing to be shunned, or is it a sacred act to be revered and glorified?*

Can we find Godde in a leaf or in the ocean waves; is Godde found in starlight and might we not discover Godde in the stamen and pistil of a honeysuckle flower? Isn't Godde simply waiting there in a dewdrop? Longing to be discovered in the wee hours of the morning, after an erotic, Wesak full-moon tryst in the meadows?

The Great Controversy rages… is there no convenient and easy-to-understand answer? Is there no means whereby we can know the ineffable Truth immediately-without any further adieu; or at least, hopefully, prior to our demise?

Do we really have to wait *until we die,* in order to learn that consciousness can exist outside of a typical, physical, living organism such as those that inhabit the mountains, forests and oceans of Earth?

Take it a step further~ Isn't our Earth indeed an organism as well, with parts and members, as are we, except that She lives breathes, feels and thinks on a much grander scale than we can possibly comprehend within our present, self-imposed, limitations? Does She have brother and sister planets that populate the Universe? Doe She have a Mother and a Father? Or do planets reproduce through an androgynous process? Are planets the result of an inexplicable orgy of experiences that accumulated over billions of "years"? Hmmmm?

Is the answer hidden from our eyes by a God who is intent on frustrating us at every turn? Or has the answer been right there under our nose all along?

Or is the answer ***in*** our nose, or embedded ***in*** our fingernails and could it be ***coursing through our veins at this very moment*** even as we read these words? Is the answer ***in*** our blood?

Does the answer go sailing out into the breeze in our urine every time we relive our bladder? Is it ***in*** the acorn, or ***in*** a grain of MUSTARD SEED? The answer could be ***yes to all of the above!*** The answer lies in the Faith of a grain of mustard seed! Does a mustard seed have faith? Is a mustard seed conscious? Does it calculate and devise plans and make decisions? Does a mustard seed have soul? Does it prefer Mozart to Bob Dylan or Puff Daddy?

Indeed the best-kept secrets are those that remain hidden right under our collective nose. Take, for example, the ears and nose of our neighbors:

A dog, horse, dolphin or cat can hear, smell and taste tactile stimuli that remains invisible to the average human's sensory organs. Many animals intuit psychic stimuli as well, in a manner far superior to that of the average human being. Dogs hear sounds that are thought to be inaudible to the human ear. Does this mean that dogs, cats and our other companions are more intelligent than we are? Or do we simply fall short in making adequate use of our equipment? Perhaps our antennae are in need of a tune-up?

Huh? Antennae? Do we have antennae; and if so, how do we *tune* our antennae? Have we lost the operator's manual? Have we received inadequate instructions from our mentors? Were we misled as children?

There is little or no disagreement with the idea that we use only a small fraction of our brain's capacity and abilities. But this is only the tip of an iceberg. We only scratch the surface when we say that we use only a small fraction of our brain. If the Truth be told, we utilize an even smaller fraction of our BEING. We live-out our lives under the false impression, that we are nothing more than this earth-bound creature that we see in our mirrors every day, whereas, we are oh-so-much-more-than-this!

There are areas of our being
that we do not see.
There are areas of our being
that we do not hear.
There are areas of our being
that we do not feel.
There are areas of our being
that we do not smell.
There are areas of our being
that we do not taste.

And, there are areas of our being, that require us to use sensual faculties of which we are not yet even aware!

We must activate these dormant senses and we must fine-tune those senses already made available to us. But how do we do this? The activation of new senses and attunement (a-tone-ment/at-one-ment) of our present senses is a critical aspect of our awakening, metamorphosis, transfiguration, resurrection and ascension.

There is a Divine Paradigm. It is a manifestation of the Divine Architect. It bespeaks a perfection that existed for all time and throughout all space. It was not created. Is has no beginning and no end. It is infinite and eternal. It is simultaneously omnipotent and mundane.

The question remains: How do we access the codices and holographic patterns of Perfect Wisdom and Pristine Cognition that reside in the Divine Paradigm located in our DNA? Once we access them, how do we implement them in our daily lives? The answer to these questions *is* the Good News. The answer to these questions *is* the true and original Gospel of Peace that MarYam *the* Migdal-Eder and her Beloved Family of Friends brought to the people of the world.

Here, in the midst of the conditions,
Find repose.
Here, in the midst of the conditions,
Rest serene.
Here, in the midst of the conditions,
Pristine cognition.
Here, in the midst of the conditions,
Truth endures.
Here, in the midst of the conditions
The Invincible awaits you.
Here, in the midst of the conditions
Compassion reigns supreme.

Now ask yourself this all-important question,
"Where does consciousness reside?"

INTRODUCTION TO SECTION TWO ~ POLITICS OF ALCHEMY

Preservation of Alchemical Wisdom: Birth & Assassination of Islam

Imagine yourself a young woman of childbearing age. During the month of December, in the very recent past, you enjoyed sexual intercourse with your loving husband, a kind and gentle man, to whom you were married in a secret ceremony. Your marriage service was convened in confidence and only the inner circle of a group of master initiates, high priests and priestesses were in attendance to bear witness to that sacred union.

As a married couple your combined lineages go back much further than any known written history, into the lands of the Hunza and Taxila, The Middle Kingdom, into ancient China and even the Japans; also to the west as far as the Rock of Iona[78] in the Western Isles, the Gateway to the Lands of Ancients, which predates the Neolithic Civilizations by millennia. Your ancestors have walked and ***sailed*** the Americas for hundreds if not thousands of generations long before the name *America* and Christopher Columbus was ever conceived!

Your ancestors have survived earth's cataclysmic changes for eons and your family members have been the stewards of a knowledge, which has the power to both save the world or to destroy it. Knowledge of a material that has more explosive power than several nuclear bombs combined!

The understanding of that material and the know-how associated with its manufacture has been the key to your family's survival for countless generations. But if that know-how were to fall into the wrong hands, into the possession of the primitive and greedy intimidator societies, they might destroy, not only themselves; they might also destroy the entire planet, in their haste to subjugate their neighbors. It has happed before and it could surely happen again.

The last time the know-how fell into the wrong hands, the explosions caused to earth to flip on its axis, there was a great flood, which had all but wiped out every last remnant of the human race, then it rained for an interminable amount of time, and an ice-age ensued, followed by even greater flooding, which had all but wiped out every last remnant of the human race. In fact less than three percent of life on earth remained after that first holocaust.

The survivors began teaching the remaining ignorant masses how to build great stone monuments that were aligned with the sun and stars in order to tell time and to be able to predict then seasons. This was critical to the establishment of civilization and agricultural. As the culture grew and spread round the world, they built new monuments to tell time.

Eventually the primitives had repopulated the earth, but few had developed intellectually and emotionally to the extent that they might be entrusted with the sacred knowledge. *In time they might be given access to the Manna, but only in carefully control instances.*

Thus for an indefinite period of time only a few pacifist priests and priestesses would be entrusted with the use of the Manna for healing and restoration of the forests and deserts.

So long as the Manna was used as a fertilizer and food supplement, and no

78 archaic strata of Iona among oldest on Earth, generally believed 1,500 million years old

one suspected its potential use as the most powerful weapon on Earth, the world would be safe from harm; at least for a few hundred generations. The Arc of the Covenant had been used only on rare occasions, but even then, the priesthood had never suspected that its unbridled power, if unleashed, could obliterate an entire planet as well as neighboring solar systems!

Thus it was only the privileged few who had access to the power of the Almighty, the Living Stone, which breathed and spoke through those few, whose personal vibration had been carefully attuned and synchronized to match that of the Arc. The Holy of Holies. (see explanation of "Meisner Field" in Part B of this work)

Imagine now if you will, that the young maiden is with child, and that her due date is somewhere near the first week of September. Like her ancestors before her, she will stay ahead of the game and fly away from danger- like a gentle butterfly, following in the footsteps of her great-great-grandmothers. She and her kind, who had been vegans for thousands and thousands of years, had chosen wisely to avoid conflict whenever possible. She would move west by northwest, taking her precious child and sacred knowledge with her, to a land that was still beyond the reach of Rome, Herod-the-Butcher, and others like them.

Can you feel her? Can you smell the wildflowers in her neatly combed hair and on her freshly oiled skin?

Can you imagine her hand resting lightly on thin Egyptian cotton, caressing her slightly swollen belly?

Her scent is rich, warm and delicious, a heady perfume created by all the hormones that course through her veins.

Her skin soft and full, rosy, glowing with life! Delicate and vulnerable, she needs security, shelter and a quite, snuggly place to lay her head at night.

Almost 1,400-1,700 years before Mary Magdalene was born, an Egyptian boat had made its way to what later became known as Scotland, to a place where her ancestors founded an alliance based mainly on salt, mineral and metals trade.[79]

One warrior-monk of great renown, an erudite man of Scythian descent[80]

---

79 ***B.C. 1400*** **~** an Egyptian Galley sailed to Scotland, the remains of which were discovered near Glastonbury. ***And before that:***

B.C. 1600. ~ The Egyptian Galley, using oars and a single square sail. Entire fleets of ships are sculptured on the walls of Deir el Bahari near Thebes. ***And before that:***

B.C. 1700 **~** *rumors have it that an Egyptian Princess entitled "Scota" was said to have married a warrior-monk [master craftsman] from Scythia [a Sarmatian, like King Arthur?] from the Russian steps named Mil or Niel.*

Concerning the origins of the so-called "Gaels" In Egypt we find that:

The Scoti were named after daughter of Pharaoh King of Egypt, the princess "Scota". Scota became the wife of Nelius [*Mil*]. It was a man named Nel, son {*nelson*} of Fenius Farsaid [*pharsee= pharisee=pharaoh*], that the Pharaoh Cincris [the King of Egypt] invited due to his renown skills, knowledge and learning. ~Called Feni from Fenius Farsaid. The Scots being the same as the Picts."

Such legends, {of the origin of the Irish race abound as the descendents of an Egyptian Princess called 'Scota'} are found throughout Scotland and Scottish legend. In Ireland Scota is revered as well - her burial mound honored - she being their maternal ancestor.

In the Lebor Gabala two distinct accounts of this Princess are recorded and have proven most useful in corroborating external sources in Egyptian history. **In the Lebor Gabala,** {concerning the identity of Pharaoh Nechtinebus, as King of Egypt at that time} it is sung that- *"Pharoa had a daughter named Scota whom Mil asked for in marriage, thus Pharoa gave her to be wed to him; when thereafter Scota bore him two sons, named Amorgen Glungel and Eber."*

80 **Sarmatian of Scythian descent ~** the same lands where, in years to come, the

named Niel (some say *Mil*), was wed to an Egyptian Princess later entitled "Scota." Together they made their way to the Western Isles some 1,400 years in advance of MarYam *the* Migdal-Eder. "Scota" referred to their complexion as a people, it was not likely a name per se, hence *The Scottish.* (...consider the biblical tribe of *Dan, the Danish & the Danube*)

Their genealogy helps us to understand the true origins of MarYam and it brings us once again to the foothills of the Himalayan mountains, where Indra ate the SOMA, and the vegetarian Hunza tribes have survived since ancient times, where the blue-eyed Buddha was born... in the ancestral home of the families of Abraham and "Sarah".

Now, in the footsteps of her ancestors, MarYam *the* Migdal-Eder (Mary Magdalene) will be escorted by one HaRamaTheo (Joseph of Arimathea), to the shores of the Isle of Iona.

Can you begin to connect the dots yet... from the land of the Hunza to the Isle of Iona? Take the northern route following along the snow line, where the sweet snow-waters melt and trickle down, forming the mountain streams in late spring. It's not so far as the crow flies... *Get out a map right now and look at it! Go across the top!* Next, alternatively, ***study the sea routes as well, from the Hyderabad of India, on along to the coastline of Oman and Yemen, continuing onward by way of Somalia, Djibouti, to the coasts attached to the lands of Ethiopia, and to the Red Sea, which is 3,040 meters deep!***[81] ***Sail all the way up to the local in Egypt where the Mediterranean Sea is less than a day's journey by horseback (and not by donkey)!*** *Use the well bred Nabataean Stallion that your cousin lends you!*

Remember here that Joseph of Arimathea, who was a metals trader, was the steward of a well-established ***network of trade routes running to and from the shores of Scotland and Ireland...*** where he traded in tin and gold, ***all the way to the Valleys of the Hunza.*** *Get out a map right now and look at it! Sail now from*

---

father of King Arthur would be born as well

81 Its companion, The Dead Sea, across the desert to the northwest, at 400 meters (1300 ft.) below sea level, is the lowest lying dry land on earth. As part of the 6000km Great African Rift Valley it is 55 km long by 17.5 km at its widest point. Interestingly, it also has a depth of up to 400m. It is, quite possibly, one of the single most concentrated sources or ORMEs and ORMUS on the entire planet. It is filled by rivers that start in both Jordan and Israel, along with the flash floods of winter and by freshwater springs, but no water flows out of the Dead Sea. Its waters are constantly evaporating in the dry desert winds and in the high temperatures. This creates one of the world's richest concentrations of natural mineral deposits, resulting in a vast collection of raw chemicals that are useful in agriculture, medicine and the sustainable energy industry. These resources are exported by the "Dead Sea Works" in Sedom to all parts of the world.

Renowned the world over for its health spas, beauty salons and excellent cosmetic products, the Dead Sea mineral deposits help to create a very healthy tourist industry as well, with customers coming from all over the world. The hot springs are famous for their healing powers, so it is no wonder that the Essenes chose to spend much of their lives there. Dead Sea water was even sent to Rome for the aristocracy and Imperial household. Herod and Cleopatra shared the rights to the Dead Sea at one point in history.

Its water is 10 times saltier than that of the Mediterranean and it is this high concentration of salts and minerals that draw toxins from the body. Magnesium concentrations are 15 times higher than that of the Mediterranean. This counteracts skin allergies and clears the bronchial passages. Bromine concentrations are 20 times higher than that of the Mediterranean and this has a soothing effect on the nervous system. Hot sulfur springs found along the shores and other deposits of medicinal mud, provide treatment for many other illness such as vitiligo, rheumatism, arthritis, neurodermatitis, dermatitis, eczema, and psoriasis. ORMUS and ORMEs abound.

the safety of an Egyptian port and head for a place at the far western end of the Mediterranean Sea, a place where the outbound currents, approaching low tide, are some of the swiftest moving waters on earth; as the waters pour out into the Atlantic Ocean over underwater cliffs they are compressed and agitated where the Mediterranean bottlenecks between the African and European continents; a place where many an unwary sailor lost his life to the massive power of the sea; a place where we find some of the largest waves on earth; the place called the Pillars of Hercules.[82]

Move on a bit to the north now, till you see the emerald green of the Western Isles.

A short distance inland from Glastonbury Tor, there is a township called Goulceby (pronounced *goolsbee)*, which in Old Norse meant the "Place of Gold" or "Town of Gold." The Vikings had many people who were intermarried and dwelling in that area; some remain, are redheaded like their ancestors. Is it named after their golden haired appearance, or was there some secret tradition of goldsmiths known only to the Vikings (and Scots)? Or perhaps they were merely fond of the golden honeybees?

Quite an adventure for our young female alchemist in a boat without oars! But not to worry, she came from a long line of expert sailors and their esteemed ladies. Earth, wind, stars, water~ wood, minerals and metals. It was an interesting time to be alive, to say the least! They had little computers to calculate the exact positions of the stars (see also index entry for: "Antikythera mechanism").[83] They knew how to blow glass and make, for the first time, distillation equipment from that glass. Tin was important to them as well, as it was used in the manufacture of glass. The tin was kept hot, molten in an iron "bath," where molten glass was in turn poured over the molten tin. This was how they manufactured plate-glass. It was during the days of MarYam *the* Migdal-Eder that techniques for manufacturing blown glass and stained glass windows were first revealed.

---

82 Complete control of the Strait of Gibraltar insured the Phoenician's control of trade going to and from the lands along the coasts of the Atlantic Ocean. Their trading monopolies along the coasts of Africa and Europe were renown. Many historians believe that the Phoenicians probably sailed to Cornwall, and worked those tin mines. They certainly sailed around Africa in the 600's B.C., approximately 2,000 years prior to the Portuguese in 1497. Herodotus, the Greek historian tells us of their prowess.

83 ***The Metonic cycle or Enneadecaeteris*** ~ in astronomy and calendar studies, ***The Metonic cycle or Enneadecaeteris*** is a particular approximate common multiple of the tropical year and the synodic month. 19 tropical years differ from 235 synodic months by about 2 hours. The Metonic cycle's error is one full day every 219 years, or 12.4 parts per million.

19 tropical years = 6939.602 days

235 synodic months = 6939.688 days

This, however, is merely a general mathematical approximation and an over-simplification of the physical reality. It is assumed by some that "the period of the Moon's orbit around the Earth and the Earth's orbit around the Sun are independent and have no known physical resonance." But it is difficult to prove such a theory.

None the less, the approximation is utilized to construct many ancient calendars, including the Hebrew calendar. It was described by the Greek astronomer Meton, who popularized the concept around 432 BC, as well as the Chaldean astronomer Kidinnu, who lived in the 4 BC. It is used to calculate of the date of Easter, thus connecting the Metonic cycle symbolically to the egg which Mary Magdalene is often depicted holding. However there is more to the egg in her hand than meets the eye.

The egg is intimately connected to the ancient manufacture of ORMUS. (see end of Chapter 9)

This helps to explain how MarYam *the* Migdal-Eder, was one of the first to introduce the use of glass as a tool for distillation. A wise and wily witch *par excellence, whose arts were passed on and preserved by the "Arabic" and Sufi mystery schools!*

So...

Why is Mary Magdalene often depicted as a woman with red hair?

Was she a witch? Are the red haired, green-eyed people borne of an people *evil* seed?

Were the Scythians red haired people?

How about the Hittite (rulers of Egypt) who, also inhabited an area we now call Turkey (home of the Anatolian rose)? The borders of Egypt were very different during the dynastic periods than they are today, extending all the way to Turkey and into Iran/Iraq and south to Ethiopia.

Was Saul of Tarsus a red headed man? Where is Tarsus? What is the connection between Tarsus, the Hittites, the Trojans and the Egyptians? Who are the Tocharians and why are there thousands of Tocharian mummies to be found in the western deserts of China near Taxila?

Was the UrSalem area originally populated by a society of red headed people; was Troy, Greece and even Persia originally a race of red headed people? Who are the Patricians of Rome and what is their connection to the Royal family of Troy (Paris and Helen)? If Alexander the Great and Achilles had reddish blond hair, as did the Hittites, was there a connection between Tarsus and what we now call Sophia in Bulgaria? Was Mohammed assassinated as some believe due to his son-in-law's (Fatima's husband's) knowledge of alchemical arts and distillation procedures? Did Fatima have green eyes and red hair?

The Secret of the Harmonic Scales of the Living Word of the Living Godde that is given to Living Prophets for the benefit of Living Men and Women; is nothing less than the Song of Heaven and Earth. It is the Uni~Verse.

Those who have heard the Stars Sing will understand.

They alone, who know the secrets of these harmonics hold the Keys to all Creation; the power to create or destroy entire planetary and sidereal systems: *"The Light & Sound within."*

Our lament~ Those who manufacture and sell ORMEs and ORMUS to the ill prepared, as a commercial product, do great damage to Us and to many others; they inflict harm much greater than they can ever know, wounding the human race in ways that are difficult to explain, as it is beyond their present limited scope and faculties-of-reason to understand.

ORMUS [ORMEs] can repair DNA and accelerate evolution, while conversely, it can also accelerate the growth of the counterfeit (virus), and its agent, the "worm "(mucoid plaque).

"Sometimes we know not what we pray for."
~Merle Haggard

Remember the Sabbath Day (the law of octave; the law of twelve; and the law of PHI [the pentagram, the phive]) and keep it Holy.

SECTION TWO ~ OVERVIEW

ORMUS, the precursor to life itself:
We are the Holy Grail.

Many modern researchers believe that ORMUS is the precursor to life itself.

In a nutshell, DNA utilizes the superconductive nature of ORMUS as a wireless communication network to run its simulations and confirm its next phase in programming the architecture of future generations and the texture of its collective consciousness. Those of us who cleanup our private laboratories (our physical body) have an opportunity to cooperate fully with DNA as we come closer and closer to achieving the goal state (divine paradigm) of this particular planet's individual evolutionary process.

In effect, we *are* the Holy Grail. We are a living, breathing network of individuals, who are capable of communicating, at hyper-light speeds, through a wireless quantum-dot nano-particle network; As a single complex organism composed of many individual wills that are aligned as One Will in a specialized hive-consciousness, we *are the Holy Grail.*

We, as a living breathing social organism, are the Holy Grail.

ORMEs are the "body and mind of Godde" to use a rather crude poetic analysis. A place where the light resides and moves at the speed of sound when it is "contained/static." When certain harmonics are intoned, communication ensues and the light "moves" between *and among* the ORMEs at speeds that are (*relatively* speaking) exceeding the so-called speed of light. That Light has the potential to move between all the individual ORMEs that exist throughout the cosmos.

This Holy Grail is the place where consciousness itself resides.

"There is no greater evil than the evil born of superstitious ignorance, an evil that parades itself, cloaked in the finery and veils of Half-Truths."

CHAPTER SIX ~ ORMUS ‡ WHAT IS IT?

The Egyptians and our Ancient ~ Future

We are told that the Egyptians knew of a place, which they referred to as "The Land of The Blessed," and that they used the "MFKTZ," or as we call it today, "ORMUS," to speed them along their way, when they journeyed to that mysterious land; a land also known as Al-Khemet.[84] At least that's what some individuals today would have us believe. But the passage isn't cheap. It's made from pure gold, platinum and other precious metals. One must know the secrets of making and have access to a very sophisticated lab with extremely expensive equipment. Sacred Alchemy- Was it such an expensive exercise for Mary Magdalene and her colleagues? Or did they know a shortcut to "The Land of The Blessed?"

The Egyptians, among others, had been struggling for generations to understand it, but it had defied all logical explanation. They knew what the ancients had passed down to them of course and how they were supposed to use it, but beyond that, no one had ever been able to penetrate the Heart of the Mystery. It had always remained just beyond their grasp and understanding. Even today it is very difficult to measure, despite all the sophisticated equipment we have available to us at the time of the writing of this discourse in 2007.

We can make it, we can melt it, we can shape it, we can mold it and we can hold it in our hands. We produce lovely artwork from it in the form of stained glass windows and otherwise. We can use it in magical and wondrous ways. ***When exposed to an arc, in sufficient quantities and under certain conditions, it is as powerful as a nuclear weapon.***

It can heal, it can kill, it can build and levitate, it can devastate and obliterate. We can train others and ourselves how to use it, but we cannot tame it. It is not dependent on us; and yet we remain dependent on It.

Perhaps one day we will know the final secret, but for now we remain humbled in It's presence. It is neither God nor Goddess as it has proven to us, as many would prefer to deny, that "Godde" exists, in a state beyond duality. Neither he nor she.

Excerpt: from "The Myth Magic and Murder of ORMUS"

~Begin quote~

> *"According to reports, a gentleman named David Hudson spent (appx) USD$8,000,000 to discover the process of converting ORMUS into precious metals and vice versa. He also attempted to patent the processes*

84 ***Al Khemit~***

Al: *great; almighty, lord;* also *place, seat or source of power*

Khemit (*Vast Darkness*)

The ancient "Egyptians" referred to their "country" as KMT, which is styled in a variety of phonetic renderings: Kemet, Kemit, Khemet, Khem, Al Khem—and the form we prefer, Khemit. **Literally** it translates as "the Black Land," referring to the dark, rich, alluvial soil found along the Nile River. However, in a mystical interpretation it also refers to the Infinite Darkness and the presence of Infinite Light, which complements the Great Darkness: see: haThor (Hathor - as the Milky Way). The ancient tradition of Egypt tells us that the civilization was known as Khemit, while the people and their native language were called Khemitian. Hence: Al-Khemy-> Alchemy-> Chemistry

of turning gold into ORMUS and ORMUS into gold, as well as other precious and semi-precious metals (but as previously mentioned earlier in this article, there is a dispute over the US patents due to National Security interests!).

It is further reported that at very high temperatures, the ORMUS "melts" and when properly cooled, becomes a Golden-Rose colored glass; This Golden-Rose Glass is, in-and-of-itself, a very high-powered superconductive material. Superconductive material is so important in military applications that whenever a patent application, which includes the word superconductor, is filled in the United States, it is immediately forwarded to the U.S. Department of Defense."

[truncated]

"During Hudson's earlier research, he tried to cause mono-atoms (a form of ORMUS/ORMEs) to assume a "low spin state." (This was before he understood the importance of the "high-spin state" in ORMUS materials). He used a water-cooled copper crucible with a tungsten electrode with argon gas and when he struck the arc on the ORMUS it totally decimated the tungsten electrode!

The resultant radiant heat (BTUs) generated was estimated to have surpassed any previously known chemical energy explosion thought possible. Understandably the researchers were extremely concerned and hence, since 1982, Hudson reportedly never attempted the procedure again. It is suspected that a nuclear level energy release had occurred. Go figure!

In 1991 Scientific American reported that Berkeley Brookhaven observed that super-deformed, high-spin atoms, when subjected to external magnetic fields sufficient to affect the nuclear quadripole moment, would cause the nucleus to emit gamma radiation without fissioning! The physicists doing the testing at Berkeley Brookhaven were mesmerized by their findings and had in fact confirmed Hudson's experiments regarding ORMUS."

~End quote~

As more and more people become acquainted with the ORMUS phenomena and its attendant repercussions, the demand for ORMUS materials will increase, as was the case in ancient times. Since most producers of ORMUS would have us believe that ORMUS can only be produced from precious metals through a convoluted (and in most cases secret) alchemical process, the medicinal and sustainable energy benefits (zero-point energy conversion) of ORMUS as a commodity might have remained in the hands of the rich and powerful, were it not for the courageous and compassionate efforts of a few wily visionaries.

Similarly, since ancient times a "priesthood" sought to control, for better or for worse, the mysterious properties of ORMUS. The reason for this is most easily explained by citing the effects of the Royal Jelly of honeybees, which the "workers" of the hive feed to their "larva" in order to create additional "queens". If a larva doesn't receive the Royal Jelly then they will grow up to become ordinary workers. However if they do receive the Royal Jelly then they will become a queen-bee. The key issue here is the queen's ability to bear offspring: a Royal privilege, the ability to sustain the colony through reproduction. Enter the morphing of DNA through a process of introducing a specialized food material.

Human beings likewise have the ability to control their DNA through the ingestion of specific food groups and related food supplements, although this has become, by and large, a lost and forgotten art. This know-how however was not lost to the inner circles of the Therapeutae. The Secret Alchemy of Mary Magdalene revolves around this arcane knowledge. The most curious aspect of her Art however is the fact that it has never been intended as secret or forbidden knowledge at all; however it was relegated to the status of heresy and blasphemy by the priesthood, and unfortunately, throughout the ages the slave-masters have sought to discredit her, along with the rank and file of her medical officers, in an effort to prevent the world from achieving emancipation. The same holds true even in modern times, although ***apparently*** for somewhat different reasons, the root of the problem remains the same. It simply expresses itself in a much more insidious manner.

The world today is suffering from an ancient addiction, an addiction that was introduced by "slave masters" thousands of years ago when the earth was young. It is this addiction that acts as a buffer, or measure of insurance, against a "worker" becoming a Royal without "permission;" in other words, if an individual were to acquire ORMUS and attempt to use it, and thereby promote themselves to leadership status among humankind, the presence of toxins that arise from the aforementioned addiction, which pollutes their bloodstream, will foil their plans by causing them to *"give birth to unhealthy and degenerate offspring"* and at the same time the contaminants in the bloodstream will trigger a condition commonly referred to as *"accelerated decrepitude.*[85]*"* They may at first experience what appears to be increased intelligence, along with increased powers of perception and physical strength, but this is only a temporary benefit. The condition will thereafter deteriorate into a dependency and eventually turn into a living nightmare.

Please understand:

The human body is a bio-computer that runs on sidereal energy.[86] It utilizes an array of parts comprised of both hardware and software, all of which require constant repair and upgrades. We consume, through various orifices and other vital processes, the ingredients necessary to sustain life. We breathe, we drink, we eat, we see, we hear, we smell, we feel. There are other subtle processes that are not so obvious, and yet, they are in many respects, much more important than those processes that readily come to mind, when we are discussing health related issues. We "eat" and "consume" in other subtle ways, but most individuals remain completely unaware of those processes.

Are you able to differentiate between those foods or consumable items, which we might think of as software, as opposed to those items that we would consider hardware in this instance? What do we eat that might be considered a floppy or CD? How is the data transferred to our system? How is the data in turn

---

85 Accelerated aging due to cellular decrepitude.

86 Starlight and other forms of radiant energy, both macrocosmic and microcosmic, which emanate from our sun and other distant suns (stars) and from the nucleus of atoms (tiny suns) as well as radiant energy emitted by black holes.

delivered to our extremities and how is it, that the proteins are enabled carry out those instructions and thereby establish the building and reconstruction routines essential to sentient life? Are the data-codes (protein blueprints) corrupted by viral activities that threaten to crash our system? Do we experience shortages of memory? Does our hard-drive fail at times? Do we need an update or an upgrade?

We know the names of cars and car parts. We know the names of computers and computer parts. We know the names of dishwasher and clothes-washing manufactures and parts makers for air-conditioners. We know the names of the latest DVD machines and videocams. But does it ever occur to you that all our inventions and contrivances are based on the human body and its most basic functions? And yet, observe how little we know and how little we bother to learn, about our bodies, on a day-to-day basis. More importantly, consider how little we know about ORMUS, the role it plays in our daily lives and the effect that engineered shortages of ORMUS is having on all of us, the human race.

Let's have a quick look at the concept of critical mass. The simplest explanation is this: Take a glass filled with only three centimeters of pure water and start adding small teaspoons of regular crystallized ocean salt. At first the water readily dissolves and combines with the salt crystals to form a clear liquid, but after consecutive additions of more and more salt crystals, the water eventually becomes saturated with salt and the salt crystals will begin to fall and gather at the bottom of the container instead of dissolving. The water (H2O) has become saturated with salt and cannot bond with (and thereby dissolve) any more salt. This is one instance of critical mass.

By one definition, the salt in the solution achieved critical mass; *critical* in that any further addition of salt will NOT result in dissolution of the salt crystals and therefore, salt crystals will gather at the bottom of the vessel rather than going into solution. This is but one of many different manners in which critical mass is employed in a chemical process.

Another good example would be that of adding NaOH[87] to distilled water. ***(CAUTION* NaOH is a dangerous caustic chemical!)*** When we add very small amounts of NaOH to the water, such as 1 or 2 grams per liter, the reaction is almost undetectable without the aid of equipment. But if we add a few hundred grams, it will create a chemical "explosion" releasing a "volcano" of frothy foaming poisonous spray, fumes and gasses accompanied by intense heat that will burn your skin, both chemically and through radiant heat. The fumes can blind and suffocate an unwary observer, resulting in death or permanent crippling injury.

These two examples of critical mass will pale in comparison to the critical mass definitions employed in the ignition of atomic bombs.[88] ~ When critical mass is achieved nuclear fission occurs.

87 ***NaOH*** ~ Sodium Hydroxide (Caustic Soda; common lye)

88 ***critical mass*** ~ "Nuclear fission occurs when a neutron (a subatomic particle with no electric charge) strikes the nucleus of a uranium or plutonium atom. Splitting the nucleus transforms a small amount of its matter into a large amount of energy. In addition, two or three additional neutrons are released. These neutrons may then split other nuclei. If this process continues, a self-sustaining chain reaction begins in which many nuclei split rapidly, and their combined energies produce a fission explosion. Generating a self-sustaining chain reaction requires a minimum amount of fissionable material known as the critical mass. A mass too small to support a self-sustaining chain reaction is called a subcritical mass."

Critical mass as applied to ORMUS, in conjunction with the human organism, refers to a state wherein the human body contains a sufficient percentage of ORMUS.

The most obvious, and we shall *note** ***incorrect,*** approach to accumulating a critical mass of ORMUS in the human body, is to consume it orally, ingesting it directly, in a synthetic or partially man-man form. This is what the various priesthoods propose; that is to say, they suggest that we buy their ORMUS made from gold, platinum, or silver or whichever noble metal they are using and in turn "eat it." Another method that they propose is that we eat it after it has been extracted from common ocean water. To date, neither of these methods have been proven to be both safe and effective. There have been clinical tests that indicate great benefits may arise from the correct use of ORMUS in medical applications, but a definitive prescription is yet to be confirmed. The exact use in synthetic environments is undetermined.

It is critical to note here that heavy metals are extremely toxic when ingested. ORMEs and ORMUS are all forms of heavy metals that have been broken down into their smallest particulate components: that is to say they are in their monatomic and diatomic nano-state.[89]

But there is a much better and more effective, long lasting manner that we should employ, when attempting to increase the total percentage of ORMUS in our bodies.

Although some small concentrations of ORMUS are to be found in all common fruits and vegetables, it is reportedly found in much greater quantities in others, more specifically, in grapes, carrots, Aloe Vera and some seaweeds, to name but a few. However, one would have to eat an awful lot of these foods in order to acquire a quantity of ORMUS (critical mass) sufficient to trigger a quantum leap in consciousness, in other words a state wherein an individual body would contain enough ORMUS to trigger the metamorphic transfiguration process (ascension process or enlightenment process) wherein "All things are made new."

A Taoist adept, who is well-informed concerning reductionist theorem, will have no problem in deducing the answer to the equation, thereby revealing the solution to the problem. The required action is simple and easy to understand: "Rid yourself of all unnecessary baggage."

Mary Magdalene and her Beloved Family of Friends were all expert in the execution of this process. They were known as The Poor (Ebionites and Rechabites), A vow of poverty was not to be interpreted as that of promising to be poor and miserable; it was a vow to reduce one's needs to a minimum by realizing the difference in what we *need* vs. what we *want.*

When we finally realize what it is that we really need, we then rid ourselves of what we incorrectly think we want. But in order to understand this process fully, we need to understand what it is that we are meant to become. So long as we buy into the story that we are born to slave-away and die as "wizened" old men and women at 50-90 years of age, then there is little hope for us. But if you would prefer, as we do, to believe that there *is a better way* to think, feel act and live, then you are in for a very pleasant surprise! Why not live to be a thousand

89 ***nano-,*** (combining form.) ~ a billionth (used in subminiature units of measurement). Ex. Nanosecond = a billionth of a second..

years young?

But, if we are to achieve this goal there are sacrifices to be made; personal sacrifices. But it is not an unpleasant business, because the object of the "sacrifices" to be made can also be considered "good riddance"!

Once you begin to understand what you really are and what you can become, you begin to understand what you really need and you can adjust your desire body to focus on what you really should be wanting. We empty the mind of all false doctrines, we empty the heart of all false desires, we empty our bellies of the bad foods that we have been lead to believe are "healthy" and we think of each and every one of ourselves as a HOLY GRAIL: a sacred vessel, waiting to be filled with the Light of Godde.

We no longer seek after those things that the uninitiated crave, such as fame, glamour, power over others, an excess of material possessions and other such worldly things. We love the world and our bodies, but we reduce the things we don't really need and replace those false values and items with the things that will truly benefit our communities and ourselves. Thereafter, from the point of view of the uninitiated, *we appear to be poor!* Whereas, in actual fact, nothing could be further from the truth!

Externally we are beginning to understand that what we really needed all along was solar technology as opposed to oil-based technologies. We are beginning to realize that what we really needed all along was clean-burning hydrogen fuel instead of dirty coal and diesel based engines. Hydrogen fuel "doesn't burn;" it combines and separates over and over in a closed circuit environment, and doesn't create any by-product other than the electricity that was stored in it.

Now, we need to begin to understand that our bodies, which are little microcosms of the Earth/Cosmos, deserve the same careful consideration as our planetary environment.

In all honesty, we're approaching the whole issue of sustainable energy in a rather ass-backwards manner. If we understood how our bodies were originally designed to function, we would readily understand how to manipulate our external environment properly. But because we, as a society, choose to completely ignore the Law of Life as regards the correct use of our physical body, nothing else makes sense. We stumble along in blind *ignore*-ance of the Truth that has been right there all along, under our collective nose, for thousands and thousands of years.

If you have managed to continue reading this far, then you are one of the luckiest people alive on this earth today. You have an opportunity to be a part of the solution to global warming and to bring and end to the problem. Becoming a part of the solution is much easier that you might imagine. The reversal of global warming is really very simple, if only the people of the world had the will to end their addiction to the blood-lust.

We are the lucky ones and we become wealthy beyond description when we receive our inheritance in the form of a Golden Light Body, a light-form that will no longer thirst or hunger. Henceforth we may draw our breath and sustenance from the Great Expanse of Infinity. You can start today to reverse all the damage that we as the human race have inflicted on this planet.

Isn't it time that we, as a society, stop defecating in our own nest?

"Blessed are the poor in spirit;
For they shall inherit the earth."
Why is this true?
Because she, who knows
When she has enough,
Will always have enough!"

CHAPTER SEVEN ~ THE MYTH, MAGIC & MURDER OF ORMUS

Introduction to The Society of ORMUS

The politics of a compassionate, benevolent and enlightened Empress presiding alongside her gentle, loving entourage, would certainly be a welcome relief to the present suffering and misery caused by today's so-called democratically elected officials who, propped-up by their gunrunning buddies from major oil companies, prance in and out of the halls of power, with their media-moguls in tow.

But can we look forward to such a scenario in the very near future, *"a compassionate, benevolent and enlightened Empress presiding alongside her gentle, loving entourage?"* Well, we may as well bring Santa Clause at gunpoint to a bar mitzvah on Christmas eve, at an Islamic Mosque, for a Hindu couple with Buddhist babies. And perhaps we shouldn't laugh to soon at the thought.

Considering mainstream Christianity's wanton and derelict behavior over the past two thousand years, it shouldn't surprise us if Mr. and Mrs. Claus decided to come along willingly, because they realized at long last to defect and abandon the violence of Christianity in favor of a more nonviolent Buddhist approach to life. Perhaps we'll all hear *Namaste!* [90] when he comes down the chimney, rather than the traditional *ho ho ho!*

Only problem is that he might be sorely disappointed by the history of the Buddhists, HIndu and Muslims as well, for although the Buddhists may have enjoyed a rather auspicious beginning, the sad truth is that they (like most of the others) ended their best days, much like the Catholic Church (and *other* religious sects), in violent hypocrisy. As Buddhism literally marched across China on a tirade of violent conquest, in their attempt to displace the Taoists, they employed Kung Fu to intimidate any Taoist monastery and attendant monks, who chose to stick with the Tao (rather than accept the new, ruling party's ideology, who were running under the banner of Buddhism).

Eventually the few remaining Taoists who hadn't been killed, developed T'ai Chi Ch'uan as a method of defending themselves against the aggressors. But their response, although superior to Kung Fu, came too-little, too-late and the violent conquerors, who had cloaked themselves in the veils of Buddhism, had already become deeply entrenched throughout Asia, taking over almost all of the monasteries and local government offices.

T'ai Chi Ch'uan was more in keeping with the original concepts of Siddhartha's ahimsa, being a soft (yet truly *deadly*) form of martial arts based on the feminine principles of yielding, and was much more Buddha-like in nature than the hard form employed by those who used Kung-Fu. The Taoists would have been able to overcome the Kung Fu of the false Buddhists, but the Taoists simply weren't willing to stoop to the same low levels of immorality that their rivals were willing to employ. Although superior in number, the monks who had adopted the spirit and lifestyle of the hard-form Kung Fu had failed miserably in a spiritual sense. Although they were Buddhists on the surface, they were nothing more than thieves internally (much like the Catholic Church is today as compared to the

90 ***Namaste*** ~ I salute the Deva within you.

original Jesus Movement).

The Buddha slowly lost his Aryan complexion and his features gradually gave way to those of a more Chinese countenance; he lost his blue eyes and long nose, and morphed into a chubby fellow with a thick-lipped dung-eating grin; as if to mock those, who continued to make offerings at the temples (previously Taoist) from there on out.

Does this sound similar to the Muslim and Christian morphology?

Eventually he became interposed and co-mingled with the Goddess Quan Yin, who was, in effect, a composite image between the Taoists' Universal Mother and the Buddha as Living Saint- Father-God image, the natives having need to consolidate him with NinKursag (Mother Eve) and the ancient of days Gaia, Mother of the Universe, NinAnna.[91] But, in fact Quan Yin had previously been venerated since earlier times as Avalokitesvara (Sanskrit), the most widely revered bodhisattva in Buddhism. In China, Avalokitesvara evolved into a female form known as Quan Yin, Kwan Yin or Guan Yin. The followers are vegetarian.

Interestingly, most people fail to realize that Buddhism is not of Chinese origins; just as Christianity is not originally Judaic, but most think that it is. They are both, of noble Vedic heredity, mixed with Taoist principles that decayed over a period of several centuries into many splinter groups, with a militant evangelical intimidator faction at the head.

Does this sound similar to the Muslim morphology?

Meanwhile for decades (even centuries) the last remnants of a Feminine Principled society quietly endured the ignorance that plagued the world at that time; known to us today as the founders of the Shinto culture, they lived in splendid fashion in the mountains of Japan, where they survived for a short while before other local intimidator societies swarmed in like locusts and eventually destroyed the seeds of that remnant culture as well. There in the forests of Japan, the original Shinto families lingered for a brief period, with only a hint of existence, but sadly, most of their remnant were either executed, or sold into slavery or forced to intermarry with vulgar warlord communities; hence, they too, lost hold of the threads that once allowed them to weave their lives into the fabric of consciousness known only to the immortals. Some few remain, scattered around the world, but they are extremely timid and understandably reclusive.

The faire have now, all but faded from view in our lives, and who can blame them? In self defense, they have retreated into the Land of The Blessed; a place where they have retired to safe havens, out of reach and immune to the grasping hands of greedy men and women. *"Elves don't die, they just fade."*

Today, on a global scale, only a very few remain of those gentle, loving societies that were originally cultivated and nurtured by the Therapeutae.

So, "Where *have* all the *flowers* gone?" The sweet, compassionate, gentle and playful young children and their mothers who no longer have a place to play. But, certainly, this situation will not last forever- *all things pass.*

---

91 The reader may want to investigate the legendary AMATERASU-OMIKAMI of Japanese legend at this juncture. http://AMATERASU-OMIKAMI.COM

One who knows how to guide the
leaders in the path of Tao
Will never try to subjugate the world
though force of arms.
Because it is the destiny of a military weapon
that it be turned against its wielder.

Wherever armies are stationed; deserts are born.
After a great war, bad years invariably follow.
What we want is to protect efficiently our own state,
While abstaining from arrogance.

After one has attained the goal,
One should not parade her success,
One should not boast of his ability,
One should not be proud,
One should regret rather
that she was unable to avoid the catastrophe.

One should never think of conquering others by force.
For to be over-developed is to hasten decay,
And this is against Tao,
And what ever is against Tao shall soon cease to exist.

Tao Te Ching verse 30

These immortal words come to us from the Tao Te Ching written by Lao Tzu hundreds of years in advance of the birth of Mary Magdalene and her contemporaries. And yet, when we research biblical records in search of hints or clues as to who and what Mary Magdalene was or is, we see little or no discussions whatsoever concerning the wit and wisdom of China. But this omission is certainly not due to any shortcomings on the part of the glorious Chinese, Korean and Japanese cultures.

Indeed, Roman and Greek citizens were importing silk along with many other treasures that originated in China and beyond. Silk, at that time, was very much *in vogue* in Rome, and blown-glass was just beginning to emerge on the market, along with many other medicines, tinctures, salves and ointments made from oriental herbs and flowers! And there were those people, as there are today, who were in the business of supplying those perfumes, incense, spices, medicinal herbs and silk at inflated prices to the nobility and members of a ruling class that was scattered throughout the Roman Empire; so why ne'er a mention in the Bible of those glorious empires of the east?

Recently, the discoveries of hundreds of Tocharian mummies have provided much "hard evidence," which attests to the fact that trading and other societal exchange existed between Western Europe and China for several thousands years before Mary Magdalene was born. Taxila was, in fact, a well-known trade center and seat of knowledge, wisdom and learning that was strategically situated near a nexus of trading routes that connected the east to the west. When we consider the fact that most trade involved bringing sophisticated goods FROM the east TO the west rather than from the west to the east, certain important questions arise:

Why then do all standard modern bibles appear to completely ignore the existence of the sophisticated civilizations and cultures in the Far East?

Why is there no mention whatsoever of the magnificent Chinese Civilization and their Indian neighbors to the south, who lived just across the Himalayan Mountain Range?

Alexander the Great made his way to Taxila hundreds of years before the birth of Mary Magdalene and it was near that ancient center that he finally met his match when, he attempted to conquer the ancient Mauryan Empire's society.[92]

One must admit that many important points and events are conspicuously absent from the Bible, which was compiled (and perhaps rewritten in many instances...) by Constantine and his cronies at the Council of Nicea (...as well as those who came before them!).[93] This likely has much to do with the fact that the fastest growing religion at that time was not Pauline Christianity, as many people today erroneously believe. In fact, the primary thorn in Constantine's heel was the ghost of a man named Mani[94], who was a vegetarian prophet, and it was he, who

---

92 ***Mauryan Empire,*** pronounced MOW ree uhn, was the first empire to provide a single government for almost all of India. Mauryan emperors ruled from about 324 to about 185 B.C. Their empire centered on Magadha, a rich kingdom in the Ganges Valley.

Chandragupta Maurya ruled from about 324 to about 298 B.C. He conquered much of what are now called northern India, Bangladesh, Pakistan, and Afghanistan. His son Bindusara held the throne from about 298 to 272 B.C., and Bindusara's son Ashoka (also spelled Asoka) governed from about 272 to 232 B.C. Both expanded the empire far into South India. Ashoka eventually gave up further conquest and outlawed war. The empire broke up into smaller units after Ashoka's death.

93 ***Nicea ~*** ***313 CE:*** The years of Christian persecution came to an end. Emperor Constantine (289-337 CE) issued the Edict of Milan, which formally established freedom and tolerance for all religions, including Christianity. Contrary to many people's beliefs, Christianity was not made the official religion of the Roman Empire at this time. That happened later in that century. ***325 CE:*** The period of time from 325 to about 590 CE is often referred to as the "post-Nicene" era. This interval takes its name from the church Council of Nicea that was held in 325 CE.

94 ***Mani and Manichaeism~*** Mani, born in Babylonia April 14, 216 was told at the age of twelve, in a vision, to stop attending a baptizing sect associated with Elkhasai. Near to his 24th birthday Mani proclaimed himself a prophet. His teaching of celibacy was too severe for most Hindus; later he enjoyed more success in Khorasan, and there converted the governor Feroz. Feroz introduced Mani to his brother the King Shapur and reassured the King that Mani had no political agenda and he wanted simply to the reunite the empire with his new universal religion.

Mani died a vegetarian sixty years later while imprisoned. Mani's decapitated body was fed to carrion while his head was placed at a significant city gate as an example to others; the persecution of all Manichaeans followed throughout the Persian Empire and continued for centuries until they became one of the greatest threats to Rome's theological dominion. Mani's success may have been one of Constantine's principal inspirations for the creation of the Catholic Church.

Manichaeism spread rapidly throughout the Roman Empire during the fourth century. Manichaeanism was treated as a Christian heresy rather than a new religion, due to the fact that Mani accepted Jesus as the Vegetarian Christ. But Valentinian I prohibited all meetings from 372 onwards. Even Augustine had adopted Manichaeanism for nine or ten years until Pistic Christians urged Theodosius I to deny Manichaeans all civil rights in 381: within months all Manichaean elders were killed and all Manichaeans were banished. Valentinian II concurred; in 389 all property in Rome

had created a religious system wherein a collage of various belief systems were harmonized and introduced to the people of the world, as one integrated whole. It was this Manichean religious order, (that also embraced the Hindu principle of reincarnation along with a blend of Mandaean [Johannite] Rights of Baptism) and Buddhism, which posed the greatest threat to the Pagan Emperor Constantine and what was later to become his state imposed version of Pauline Christianity.

It might be argued that it was the Manichean model of *catholic* (*universal*) religion and its approach to harmonization that inspired the Counsel of Nicea. If it had worked so well for Mani, why not use the same method for creating a new catholic[95] religion? They would embrace the world; why stop at harmonizing the Druidic, Judaic (Pauline Christology) and Pagan mythos alone, when they could go ahead and secretly include the icons and symbol systems of the Buddhist, Hindu and Durgee beliefs, along with the rites of the Johannite Baptists (Cult of ISIS) as well? Enter the numerous Black Madonna cults and statues, and a mystical Gypsy culture that seems to puzzle so many scholars; but why the Black Madonna should puzzle anyone is a curiosity in and of itself. It is so obvious where the Black Madonna cults are born. All one need do is look to the east at Yemen's (and Oman's) nearest neighbor.[96]

Yes, a Catholic Church that "embraced all religions"; a religion to end all religious fragmentation and a war to end all wars... There would be an secret, elite, esoteric (*internal and secret*) tradition for the elect, complemented by an exoteric (external *dumb-down the slaves*) tradition for the ignorant masses, and then- *All roads (and streams of money) would lead to Rome; World without end, Amen.*

So, fast forward to the present: Armed with this (heretofore "suppressed" knowledge) it should be easy for the seeker to understand why it was in fact, the vegetarians, (Manicheans and Ebionites) who were rounded up en mass and literally thrown to the lions alongside their other vegetarian friends, factions of the true Buddhists, Ebionites, Essenes and Therapeutae."

Vegetarians had been the number one threat to the Pharisees and Sadducees of the Temple in UrSalem *(even as they are today! Just look at how much Kosher Food Law Certifications add to the cost of our foods today! We don't need that nonsense in the 21st century!); and* it was that same growing mass of vegetarians who again posed the greatest threat to the Roman Empire *(even as they do today! What would happen to the global Catholic economy if everyone stopped smoking tobacco and drinking wine and started buying organic apple juice and Amsterdam-spliff instead?).*

It was the vegetarian culture that had captured the hearts and imagination of the Ladies of the Empire and in turn had swept the Roman Empire by storm, just as it had during Mary Magdalene's tenure in the Levant.

---

confiscated.

95 ***catholic*** ~ *universal*

Etymology: Middle English catholik, from Middle French and Late Latin; Middle French catholique, from Late Latin catholicus, from Greek *katholikos* ***universal, general***, from *katholou* ***in general***, from kata ***by*** + holos ***whole*** or more at *CATA-*, ***SAFE*** (circa 14th century)

96 This issue is far too interesting to treat briefly; it is discussed in great detail in William Hearth's novel "ORMUS‡ The Secret Alchemy of Mary Magdalene." Parts I, II & III available at http://WWW.ORMUS.NET

According to the Pistics, "*the Essenes and Ebionites were enticing the wise and noble women into a life of sin and degradation!*"

But nothing could be further from the truth. Just imagine what a stir it would have caused when Saul of Tarsus came along, speaking openly to the male population concerning *the evils of the malignant spread of vegetarianism and all that talk of women's liberation.* All the while he was secretly plotting to relieve those same-said women of their silver and gold by "confiding" in them that his true mission concerned their imminent emancipation from a male-chauvinist regime that denied women their civil rights. A silver-tongued devil, who was burning the candle at both ends, had set wheels in motion that would turn long after his own decline in popularity and even centuries after his demise. While in the company of men he spoke of "a place for women and women in their place" all the while promising the women "a place in heaven and eternal youth" *if they would obey both his God and his God's representatives on earth (namely Paul himself!)*

As for Paul's greatest (posthumous) student, a man named Constantine? A man, an Emperor no less, who lived many decades after Paul's death[97] (the one who supposedly "rescued" Christianity, and like Paul, had conveniently been visited by a *vision of Christ)!* Well, that "great man" never knowingly or willfully converted to Christianity, as so many erroneously believe. In fact, Constantine was as much a Christian, as Mary Magdalene was a whore and a prostitute! (Two bits of wicked gossip and rumors that still circulate among the *illiterate* masses even unto this very day!)

Truth be told, Constantine remained a devout and clever Pagan ruler till the bitter end, being "baptized and consecrated" only at the last possible moment, on his deathbed by a sneaky Bishop.

Concerning his formation of the so-called state-sponsored (enforced by further bloodshed) "Christian" religion, the following brief explanation may come as a surprise to many a devout bible thumper...

> "It is said by some, that the earliest recorded conflicts that occurred within the ranks of the Jesus Movement, originally broke out between the Pistic and Gnostic factions (while the true inner circle of the Jesus Movement, of course remained quietly and secretly undeterred in their core mission).
>
> To the delight of the opponents of the Jesus Movement, this seed of unrest, having been well-placed in the fertile soil of discontent, was then cultivated and promoted by the "antichrist;" thus allowing for the "Divide and conquer" method to successfully play itself out; much to the delight and satisfaction of Mary Magdalene's detractors and rivals. Then and now they argue and debate unceasingly to the general annoyance of the remnant of the true and original Jesus Movement.
>
> The Gnostics of course, would have us believe that numerous Gospels are clearly Gnostic in orientation, including the Gospels of

97 ***Constantine*** ~ in this discourse, we assert that, "There is a grain of Truth to be found somewhere in all popular religions (however deep it may be buried under the heavy stones of superstitious ignorance); and that this partial truth of course, is not the Truth in its entirety. Half-truths, conceived as intentionally constructed deceptions, constitute the most insidious and worst manifestation of a lie; this type of deception has always been a principal cause of unrest, war and disease." This having been reiterated, we continue...

John, Thomas, Philip, and Mary (perhaps because they were written by Gnostics tens and even hundreds of years after the fact?).

According to these and certain other suppressed versions of history, it was the Pistics (whom most people today, refer to incorrectly as, "the Early Christians") who were called heretics by other members of the Jesus Movement. These Pistics, like many of their rival sects, factions and counterparts, were fanatics, being over zealous and prone to extremes. They too were often hated by their "colleagues," just as much, if not more so, than they hated the others, because it was (and still is) those Pistics, and later their descendents, who would burn both the writings and leaders of rival cults (such as the Gnostics, Mandaeans, Manicheans and Cathars), wherever and wherever they could find them."

Both sides held fast to their inaccurate, *partial~truths* version of the Gospel and *together* they created a world of chaos for the original inner circle; each one claiming that the others were heretics, while the inner circle did there best to fade into obscurity in hopes of surviving the fallout of the theosophical war that the others had unwitting launched.

There was a great deal of finger pointing and mudslinging. Meanwhile, the remnant of that true inner circle of the Jesus Movement were left with the unsavory task of trying to "pick up the pieces" of a torn and essentially "broken alliance" that had been most carefully and painstakingly forged by Mary Magdalene, Jesus and their "underground" networks.

When the original Church of Antioch, in Asia Minor, (located in the extreme south of what is today known as Turkey and *not that far from Tarsus*) was founded a few years later around 38 AD,[98] it was situated only a few hundred miles north of the Sea of Galilee where Jesus and Mary had first established their political base in the Levant.[99] Three men purportedly founded it; two of which were ostensibly the brothers of Jesus: i.e. James and Peter,[100] and a third man known today as Thomas.

But it was not long thereafter, in AD 64, that Pistic (Pauline) Christianity (fanatical and cultish) began expanding by leaps and bounds. In response, the Roman Emperor, Nero, began throwing those Pistic Christians to the lions. Paul had angered many a Roman husband, and not necessarily for the usual reasons touted by the Catholic Church![101]

---

98 A tragic blow to the infant church occurred just nine years after the disappearance of Jesus and Mary. An officially sanctioned "assassination" took place during the fifth major persecution~ to wit: James the First Bishop of Jerusalem was killed, some say, in AD 44. The reader will want to discover for themselves, the truth of the matter; where was Saul of Tarsus at this time? And where was Saul of Tarsus at the time of the so-called stoning of Stephen?

99 The Hebrew who were situated in the north were not the best of friends with the Hebrews in the south, *to say the very least! All Temples in the north had been "banned" by the central Temple in UrSalem. Thereafter ALL TITHING and live animal sacrifices (all religious cash-flow in general) had to be made, BY LAW, at the one and only central Temple in UrSalem. Go figure! Follow the money!*

The average fellow couldn't drive his animals all the way across the desert once a year to UrSalem, so they bought their sacrificial animals upon arrival in that very place where Jesus is rumored to have tied a cord and "turned the tables of the money lenders" and "liberated the animals and birds". Ask yourself this question, "What happened to all that blood, urine and excrement which were expelled daily at the Temple?"

100 Explained and discussed in great detail in William Hearth's novel "ORMUS‡ The Secret Alchemy of Mary Magdalene." Parts I, II & III available at http://WWW.ORMUS.NET

101 Apparently Saul of Tarsus, masquerading as Paul, had beguiled one Roman Lady after another, enticing them with promises of heaven; then came the day, when he had crooned

Fortunately for those willing to capitulate, the Roman courts had offered the Pauline (and other) Christians a way out: *if they denounced their religion publicly, they were set free.*

But the Pistics (the Pauline suicide bombers of their day) refused to do so and thus died in a most unflattering manner (assuming they would "all meet again in heaven!"). The Gnostics, and other sensible people, were understandably nauseated by such a scenario. Their brainwashed friends and neighbors however were committing group-suicide in a very public and high profile manner by walking willingly into the Roman arena and into the mouths of voracious lions. While the inner circle of the Jesus Movement (as well as the Gnostics) attempted to maintain a profound respect for honesty, they were much more concerned with staying alive and protecting their young from growing up as slaves and sexual toys among their oppressors. They wisely chose life; knowing that *"he who fight and run away, live to fight another day." They fought with ideas, words and a gradual change in lifestyle: a living example to others.*

Thus, since the original Jesus Movement consisted exclusively of pacifists and vegans, staying alive was the primary objective: "Feel good and do no harm~ walk away from trouble when you can..." Theirs was a war of ideas and words, a war that was waged inside, not at all an external war of swords and bloodshed. *"My kingdom is not of this world."* If they, forced at the point of a sword, had denounced their faith publicly one day, and lived by so doing, their families endured. They lived to sow new seeds of wisdom for years to come, spreading their teachings to others for a few more decades. Their path was obvious.

Yet, they were hated by the fanatical and "heaven-bound" cults, who interpreted suffering and mortification as the path to redemption. The Ebionites, who revered Life, were scorned by the Pauline Pistics (revering blood sacrifice) for refusing to die a senseless death alongside the other Pistics (who thought that self-mortification opened the gates to heaven).

A better marketing scheme has never been devised. It was a great sympathy pitch! No other belief system has ever been more impressive to a vulgar audience than one which thrives on gossip and dirty laundry. ***If it bleeds it leads!***

Meanwhile the inner circle of the Jesus Movement (those in the know) were trying to be as quiet, invisible and innocuous as humanly possible.[102]

The atrocities committed in the arena captured converts by the hundreds, and it was the Pistic Pauline Christianity that they sought out, in order to learn more about this powerful religion that was supposedly headed up by none other than "GOD" himself, a man made of flesh who had literally risen from the dead! Saul of Tarsus was on a roll and *James was rolling over in his grave (in disgust);*

---

one tune too many, and thus he had incurred the wrath of more than a few jealous husbands. He had enjoyed the favors and finances of his patronesses to excess. Like all habitual gamblers he didn't know how to walk away from the casino after a big win. The leaders of the various hypocritical churches that he inspired (*spawned*) have done well to maintain the tradition! ...Vis-à-vis, the Pedophilia, witch-hunts, dumbing-down of the masses etc. etc.

102 5 And when thou prayest, be not as the hypocrites: for they love to stand and pray in the Synagogues, and in the corners of the streets, because they would be seen of men. Verily I say unto you, they have their reward.

6 But when thou prayest, enter into thy chamber: and when thou hast shut thy door, pray unto thy Godde, which is in secret, and thy Godde, which seeth in secret, shall reward thee openly.

and it appeared as if nothing would ever stand in the way of Paul's "poor me, pity my friends and I" approach to religion; even long after he was gone. If only he had been able to exploit the benefits of live Television Evangelism during his own lifetime, perhaps the world would have remained mesmerized for another five to eight thousand years. But he didn't even have the benefit of a printing press. All he had to work with was a bunch of poor sops who couldn't keep their stories straight, much like folks today tend to twist the gossip, rumors and tall-tales. Heard any good fish stories lately?

Here's a good one: The so-called Gospel of Mary has been reported as having said that a certain *famous guy* kissed a certain *naughty girl* on the mouth; but truth be told, that particular part of the crumbling document has a hole in it and folks just assume that this is what it *must* have said, "on the mouth"! Even if it did, well that's ok too, after all it's only natural. Right? But what if it said forehead? Or cheek? (Or some other delicious location? heh heh!)

So, anyway, a few hundred years later, in AD 325, the seed of the Roman Catholic Church, which was planted by Paul, was nurtured and cultivated by the pagan emperor, **Constantine**. He decided it was time to weed the garden, and get rid of the competition!

Superficially it was a Pauline Pistic Christian Church. He and his cronies had convened the ***First Nicene Council,*** where only those church leaders who had publicly and permanently agreed to acquiesce to the Emperor's whims were allowed to assemble, to work out the subtleties of the ruse and its nefarious details. The thesis? ***Armies are expensive and have their limitations, whereas an all-seeing all-knowing GOD can be anywhere and everywhere watching your guilt-ridden ass! Like Santa Claus, GOD knows if you've been good or bad! This approach would certainly save on personnel, equipment, training and it might even work better than butchery (especially after a few generations of wives and children had been slapped around and introduced to painfully inflicted brainwashing)!*** Willy Constantine! Who needs an army so long as the masses are convinced that a vengeful and wrathful GOD is watching~ eternal punishment and hell await those who defy Rome.

The counsel was comprised of all the brown-nosed elders from all the major Pagan religions of Rome, as well the groveling Bishops from the cults of Mithras, Tammuz, Oannes (Dagon), Ceres, Janus, Bacchus, Apollo, ISIS, Osiris, Jupiter, not to mention those fellows from Constantine's own religion: Sol Invictus. Of course those Christian elders from five major Christian centers (Rome, Athens, Alexandria, Jerusalem and Antioch) were invited as well, so long as they had agreed in advance to play along. "The nail that sticks up will be hammered down!"

It was Constantine's strategy to quell the Pauline Christian's expansion by "harmonizing" their Judaic teachings with that of all the other Pagan religions (whose constant bickering with one another, was creating a barrage of unprofitable and otherwise troublesome conflicts). He had envisioned a unified "Catholic" church, with emphasis on "Catholic" *meaning universal,* and as such *a universal subservience was to be expected,* along with the usual mental, emotional and economic slavery.

Constantine ruled the proceedings of that council with an iron prod, and the primary provision that he insisted upon, was to make the Pauline Pistis doctrine the foundation of the "new church." He needed plenty of self-sacrificing sadomasochists who were willing to kill and die for *his* (whose?) cause.

Gnosticism, the Manicheans, Buddhists, Druidic Groves and even his own beloved Paganism would not be tolerated as such, because they all encouraged their members, in one way or another to think for themselves and to question authority. Pistis to the contrary was politically expedient, because it encouraged its following to be willing to die for a cause, and most importantly to never question the authority of "*God*" and *his representatives on earth* (much like that wrathful God, YHWH who, had successfully presided over the citizens of UrSalem for generations: hellfire and brimstone for all who dared blaspheme against the YHWH's priesthood and question the Temple Authorities). One had to admit that the Hebrew population had been successfully cowed for hundreds of generations and this guy Paul, *well*, what a cunning fellow he had turned out to be! If the masses had fallen for his ruse and his rather convenient vision of Jesus, then it would work just as well for Constantine and his bankers; especially if the vision were backed-up by a few thousand swordsmen and a healthy dose of religious persecution and torture... heh heh heh!

And the rest is history-according-to-Garp, *but now*, history (the *unofficial* version) is repeating itself, *again*. The vegetarians are on the rise and they have returned in numbers that promise major changes in a world filled with very destructive people; a world that is nearing its final hour.

Will we self-destruct? Or will we rise to the challenge and hear the wake-up call that has been ringing so very long and loud in our collective ears?

And you might well ask, "So how do we incorporate the wisdom of Mary Magdalene and her colleagues into our daily life? What the devil does all this have to do with ORMUS? How do we achieve a state of grace within our lifetime?

The answer has been right under our collective nose for generations, but we continue to ignore the signs.

Who or what is the "Society of ORMUS"? Does it still exist? Have they been infiltrated and subverted, like the originally well-intended Buddhists, Christians and Muslims?

Well someone has to tell the truth and ring the bells of freedom! Who do you think the original members of the Society of ORMUS might have been, now that you have a few more clues to work with? What kind of people would they have been? Were they drug addicts and parasites, who thrived on the misery of others? Or were they vegans, alchemists and master craftsmen who knew the healing arts and lived only to serve Mother Nature and the Earth along with all Her children?

ORMUS~ WHAT IS IT?

~ THE MYTH, MAGIC AND MURDER OF ORMUS ~

By H. Alfred Goolsbee

The following excerpt is reprinted with permission of the Author.

(As described at http://www.ormus.org)

AUTHOR'S NOTE

Important Notice*

This pocketbook, entitled "ORMUS~What Is It? The Myth, Magic and Murder of ORMUS" by H. Alfred Goolsbee, made available through ORMUS Publications International, is the first book in a series of "ORMUS How-To Pocketbooks."

Notice* "ORMUS~What Is It? The Myth, Magic and Murder of ORMUS" ***is not intended to be an exhaustive study of ORMEs and ORMUS. Rather, it is intended only as a brief introduction to the subject. Therefore, no attempt has been made to provide academic references and bibliographies;*** however, the author asserts that wherever facts have been presented, references and bibliographies are available, upon request, to the serious enquirer. Additionally, most topics covered will be addressed in future publications by the Author wherein, the topics are discussed in greater detail and in those instances, references and bibliographies will be included in the respective works.

PREFACE

A word about religious discussion and ORMUS

The phenomenon that surrounds the ORMUS elements is not a modern fiction. Although, it may be true that we have certain difficulties in quantifying and qualifying the ORMEs/ORMUS elements, due to deficiencies in our modern equipment, the fact is that ORMUS is a reality. It is a tangible element that you can hold in your hand and is an eminent force that demands our attention. The ORMUS elements are as real as rain, sunshine, the rocks in the rivers and the leaves on trees. However, in order to understand the elusive nature of ORMUS in a modern context it also becomes us to investigate its effect on humanities historical and religious development.

When viewed in this light, we must be aware that humanities broad spectrum of both historical experience and interpretation of religion can leave us bewildered, even in the best of times. When we attempt to discuss these histories and the endless varieties of religious interpretation, no matter how carefully we tiptoe around the issues, there will inevitably be those, whose religious or dogmatic sensibilities are offended. In the worst of cases there will be a call to arms, wars will break out in diverse places and acts of genocide all-to-often ensue soon thereafter.

Therefore dear reader, we implore you, as you read through this Book of ORMUS, please, bear in mind that whatever your predisposition to religious or spiritual issues might be- fear and hatred can only lead to suffering and therefore it is the writers humble request that we all agree, well in advance, that if this book should lead to a difference of opinions among us, that we will all make a sincere effort to *"~disagree, in an agreeable manner."* In short: *"Pray for Peace; feel good and do no harm."*

This writer remains humbled, open minded, is interested in hearing everyone's opinion and does not presume to be an authority on anything other than knowing to seek shelter in a storm, as well as having a very deep and extremely profound willingness to accept good advice and make changes whenever and wherever it becomes necessary, in order to keep the peace.

We genuinely hope that this work helps us all to achieve a better understanding of one another and the universe we live in *and* that we may all one day live together in peace and harmony on this Earth.

CHAPTER EIGHT: PART ONE~ ORMUS / ORMES

The World's Best Kept Secret

ORMUS (or ORMEs) is, perhaps, THE single-most interesting and coveted material found in both, the modern and ancient world.

Also referred to as The Philosophers' Stone, Shew~bread, Manna, Holy Communion, Bread (Biblical), White Powder Gold, ORMES and a variety of other names, ORMUS is directly related to the Quest for the Holy Grail, The Last Supper of Jesus Christ (Mar Yeshua) and the Ark of the Covenant[103]. One of the easiest ways to begin an attempt at understanding what ORMUS is really all about, is to think of it as "The Church of ORMUS" vs. "The Church of ROME." Although there was no known church by that name, for the sake of argument we will use it ("The Church of ORMUS") figuratively as an aid to understanding.

The "Church of ROME" of course, did exist and it was created approximately 400 years after the so-called crucifixion of Mar~Yeshua (herein after referred to as the Master Jesus or Jesus [the Christ]). The "Church of ROME" was an institution intent on controlling and subduing *(subjugating?)* the rapidly expanding following of Jesus, Mary Magdalene and their Beloved Family of Friends around the world.

By means of a campaign of intimidation, terror and indoctrination, the vast majority of the good people who had embraced the teachings of Jesus Christ and Mary Magdalene, were made slaves to a reign of fear, guilt, terror and political coercion, whereby the Royal Houses of Europe were ultimately brought to heel as well, by "The Church of ROME."

On the other hand and very much to the contrary, "The Church of ORMUS," (*figuratively speaking*) or perhaps, more appropriately, the ABBEY of ORMUS, was expanding at a rapid pace, in very much the opposite direction, philosophically speaking, than that of "The Church of ROME."

"The Church of ORMUS," proffered a lifestyle free of economic, mental, emotional and physical slavery. Indeed "The Church of ORMUS" espoused forgiveness and tolerance, living in peace with one's enemies and perhaps most importantly an abstinence from killing on all levels. "The Church of ORMUS" promoted a "*vegetarian and agrarian lifestyle*" as opposed to the "*might is right; invade and conquer, dog-eat-dog lifestyles,*" which had previously dominated the Earth and it's so-called civilizations.

During the previous few thousand years, as a direct result of a tragic campaign of terror and intimidation that was carried-out, not only by "The Church of ROME", but by other dynastic rulers from other earlier so-called "civilizations," millions of people have been enslaved, tortured, murdered and assassinated in an effort to force them to either reveal the secrets of the Orders of ORMUS or to reveal the paths that led to the encampments of those who endorsed the Way of Life as taught by the Society of ORMUS and the Family of Friends; and sadly, hundreds of thousands of people have subsequently been slaughtered in attempts to *control* the distribution of secrets of ORMUS.

Even now, as you read this book, wars rage around the planet due to

---

103 Ark of the Covenant~ used as a source of power in the field of battle by the Israelites and as a cornerstone of religious worship in the Temple of King Solomon (a Master Mason) and his predecessors.

the confiscation and deliberate concealment of the knowledge of ORMUS materials and associated ORMUS technologies.

ORMUS has inspired the creation of countless Secret and Occult Societies and has given birth to Royal lineages, Empires and Dynasties. It was the subtle driving force behind the creation of the UNITED STATES of AMERICA and was considered a sacred material by the ancient Egyptian Priestesses and Pharaohs, Phoenician Goddess Societies, Babylonian and Biblical Kings, as well as the Druids' High Priestesses, to mention only a few. The Knights Templar and subsequent Masonic Society of Free Masons were created in an effort to preserve the knowledge and applications of ORMUS.

Evidence of mankind's knowledge of ORMUS predates typical human history, while our written accounts and archeological records of ORMUS take us back in time well over 6,000 years. The "Holy Roman Empire" and the "Holy Roman Inquisitions" have successfully suppressed this information for over two thousand years. The majority of witch-hunts wherein people were actually tortured and burned alive at the stake were all, in one way or another, connected to the ORMUS phenomenon; and the assassinations of *so-called* heretical thinkers and many scientists were clearly related in one way or another to the ORMUS phenomena.

Fortunately, due to the unwavering perseverance of a few groups of dedicated individuals throughout history, the Truth about ORMUS has finally resurfaced and has been revealed. Additionally, thanks to modern scientific equipment and a better understanding of "how things work," we are now sufficiently equipped to accept the paranormal realities that ORMUS presents and indeed the message and activities of ORMUS are truly mystical, to say the least. ORMUS forces us to reconsider and redefine what we think of as *normal.*

Many modern researchers today, both in Universities and otherwise, believe that ORMUS is the precursor to life itself and their views are reflected in ancient writings that date back over 4,000 years.

The Sumerian Tablets describe an alien race of super-beings (not necessarily aliens) who came (back?) to Earth to harvest ORMUS and subsequently created (made improvements on) the *hu*-man race, as well as having genetically engineered most of the domestic grains and fruits we all take for granted and consume on a daily basis. There is considerable evidence, which suggests that a "Mother Eve" did actually exist, but not at all in the manner that the Catholic Church and other fundamental Christians would have us believe. Similarly, Mary Magdalene was *not, as we were all lead to believe* a whore and prostitute; Mary Magdalene was, in fact, a revered Lady descended from a Royal family whose mitochondrial DNA might be traced back to a "Mother Eve" who manipulated the ancient populations of earth with ORMUS materials and thereby affected immensely the RNA-DNA paradigms of all sentient life on this planet. (More on Mary Magdalene and the Holy Grail follows.)

But, "*What* Is It?" *exactly* and why has it dominated the development of mankind throughout all known history- and *why* was it one of the world's best kept secrets of all time?

CHAPTER EIGHT: PART TWO ORMUS- FOOD OF THE GODDESS
A Scientific Explanation

Hitler was obsessed with his search for ORMUS alchemical technology, as were the ancient Chinese, Mayans, Israelites and all the Royal Courts of Europe. Its potential use as a military weapon is phenomenal.

King Solomon manufactured it, as did Moses before him and the Egyptians and Sumerians before them. But from whom did Moses and Solomon learn the Sacred Art; where and *why* did those secrets remain hidden from modern man? Did Indra know the secrets and was SOMA another name for ORMUS? These questions give rise to many interesting topics of investigation. Hence we have the Quest for the Holy Grail and The Search for the Lost Ark (Ark of the Covenant) and stories concerning a Philosophers' Stone (turning lead into gold).

There is a scientific explanation for all of this.

During the past twenty-five years a great deal of research and studies have commenced in universities around the world and entire laboratories have been dedicated to the study of ORMUS materials. As a result of these studies some researchers have coined the name *superatoms* to describe the ORMUS particles and consequently new positions on the Periodic Table of Elements have been assigned to accommodate the *re*-discovery of ORMUS.

The material has created such a stir that the United States Government has reportedly entered into the affair, due to so-called national security interests, and the "US Patent and Trademark Office" recently denied approval for various patents pending concerning the manufacture of ORMUS. The reason for this is astounding when viewed from a scientific standpoint. ORMUS, it appears, is a superconductor that operates (unlike other superconductors) at room temperature. ORMUS has the potential to completely revolutionize the energy industries and may prove to be the actual warp-drive (Star Gate) factor featured in so many episodes of Star Trek and Star Wars movies and other science fiction stories.

Irrespective of it's potential as a drive for spacecraft; there are various other significant reasons why an ancient super-race would have wanted to harvest ORMUS on Earth.

One of the principal uses of ORMUS is the actual eating of the "*manna*" *(in the Biblical texts: food provided miraculously to feed the Israelites in the wilderness)*; literally eating the "*bread*" or "*white powder*" that is now known as ORMUS. It has been reported that many unusual and positive results have been obtained through the ingestion of ORMUS.

It is reported that the protégée's of the ancient Sumerian mystery schools (and later of Egypt, Babylon, Phoenicia and Druidic, etc.) prepared for years in order to be permitted to consume the "*shew*-bread" or "*Holy Communion,*" especially as in "*the Last Supper of Jesus Christ.*"

Consider the two following factors

A ORMUS levitates and

B ORMUS disappears & reappears

CHAPTER EIGHT: PART TWO (a) **ORMUS levitates**

Does ORMUS really levitate?

It has been reported by researchers that under certain laboratory conditions, at certain temperatures, ORMUS will quite literally levitate. It has also been reported by researchers that, when in contact with certain materials, ORMUS *brings those materials along with it when it levitates.* This is a noteworthy point to bear in mind. (Generally speaking, levitation has been achieved through various types of resonance-induced conditions and electromagnetic repulsion *and* levitation is a common occurrence these days. However, ORMUS *as a room temperature superconductor,* combines other unique and valuable states and functions that other simple electromagnetic or resonance levitation procedure can not offer.)

CHAPTER EIGHT: PART TWO (b) **ORMUS disappears & reappears**

Is ORMUS a building block for Stargates?

It has also been reported by researchers that ORMUS disappears completely, apparently into another dimension, at certain temperatures and mysteriously returns from the other realm when temperature is raised or lowered! It has also been reported by researchers that, when in contact with certain materials, *ORMUS brings those materials along with it when it disappears and reappears.*

Note* ORMUS (nano-particle) materials, unlike all other known elements, cannot be "seen" by most spectroscopic equipment. In fact the only way to prove that it is, what we say it is, is to convert it from a superconductive nano-particle into it's other forms, ie: Precious Metals. (And again according to reports by researchers and David Hudson's Patents, this has been accomplished.

CHAPTER EIGHT: PART THREE~ NATIONAL SECURITY ISSUES

The Impending Doom of the Energy Cartels?
"(ORMUS 1982)...surpassed any previously known chemical energy explosion thought possible!"

According to reports it has been scientifically demonstrated that ORMUS can be valence bonded to other ORMUS atoms. The resulting materials are Platinum, Gold, Rhodium, Iridium, etc. This has become a major concern to governments and banking institutions worldwide for obvious reasons. Since ORMUS can be produced from common purified ocean water and the subsequent conversion to gold and platinum has become a scientifically proven reality, enormous fortunes can and would be gained and lost.

According to other reports, David Hudson spent over USD$8,000,000 to *discover the process of converting ORMUS into precious metals (he called it ORMES [and some say ORMUS] but ORMUS has become the most popular term describing the phenomena in general). He also attempted to patent the processes of turning gold into ORMUS and ORMUS into gold, as well as other precious and semi-precious metals (but as previously mentioned above, there is a dispute over the patents due to National Security interests; hmmm?).*

It is further reported that at temperatures of C 1,160 (Celsius), the ORMUS "melts" and when properly cooled, becomes a Golden-Rose colored glass-like material; This Golden-Rose Glass *is*, in-and-of-itself, a very high-powered superconductive material. Superconductive material is so important that whenever a patent application, which includes the word *superconductor*, is filled in the United States, it is immediately forwarded to the U.S. Department of Defense.

During Hudson's earlier research, he tried to cause mono-atoms (a form of ORMUS) to assume a "low spin state." (This was before he understood the importance of the "high-spin state" in ORMUS materials). He used a water-cooled copper crucible with a tungsten electrode with argon gas and when he struck the arc on the ORMUS it totally decimated the tungsten electrode!

The resultant radiant heat (BTUs) generated was estimated to have surpassed any previously known chemical energy explosion thought possible. Understandably the researchers were extremely concerned and hence, since 1982, Hudson reportedly never attempted the procedure again. It is suspected that a nuclear level energy release had occurred. Go figure!

In 1991 Scientific American reported that Berkeley Brookhaven observed that super-deformed, high-spin atoms, when subjected to external magnetic fields sufficient to affect the nuclear quadripole moment, would cause the nucleus to emit gamma radiation without fissioning! The physicists doing the testing at Berkeley Brookhaven were mesmerized by their findings and had in fact confirmed Hudson's experiments regarding ORMUS.

CHAPTER EIGHT: PART FOUR~ CONTROVERSY AND MYSTERY

ORMUS: Is it just an old wive's tale?

All of the Indiana Jones movies are concerned with ORMUS although it is never actually named as such. ORMUS is directly correlated to the Ark of the Covenant, the Philosophers' Stone and even the Holy Sacrament shared at the Last Supper between Jesus Christ and His disciples.

Many of the Dan Brown novels (DaVinci Code) are concerned with ORMUS (and the Priory of Scion) although it is never actually named as such.

The Catholic Inquisitions had *much* to do with (*the suppression of*) ORMUS and the associated knowledge surrounding it and even the BIBLE itself (especially including the missing portions) is a historical allegory of the story of ORMUS itself throughout the ages.

The Buddha can also be linked directly to the migration of ORMUS culture;

and in particular, ORMUS also helps to explain much about the thousands of red-haired, blue and green and blue-eyed (*sometimes 7 foot tall*) Tocharian Mummies found in Chinese desserts near *Taxila* (an ancient seat of learning) located to the north of the land of the long-lived Hunza Society and west of the Tibet and Himalayan Mountains. Hence, the sacred Tibetan cultures can also be directly linked to ORMUS.

In Muslim history "The Prince of Bees"[104] *and his colleague were very much concerned with ORMUS (whether their descendents and followers knew it or not is uncertain) but there definitely appears to be an Arabic connection in the preservation of the knowledge.*

CHAPTER EIGHT: PART FOUR~ (a) cure for cancer and disease

DNA repair by ORMUS

It has been reportedly been proven in laboratory tests that ORMUS appears to be a cure for various forms of cancer and many other diseases related to RNA-DNA malfunction. It has also been reported by researchers that ORMUS can repair corrupted DNA data and may be able to reverse or suspend the aging process in certain instances.

(see: http://www.rnadna.com)

104 **Prince of Bees ~ *an honorific title*** Most likely in memory of ***Milarepa*** – An ancient Tibetan Teacher...

Prince of Bees ~ *Ali Ibn Abi Taleb*: The Commander of Faithful (The Prophet's cousin and the Prophet's son in Law) ~ Many believe that he was assassinated and that the true legacy of Islam was thereby usurped; leading the followers into war and fanatical superstitious ignorance from that time onwards.

Considered to be the First Muslim, an intimate associate of the Holy Prophet of Islam in the life and Holy Islamic mission, the Greatest Guardian of Islam, as husband to the Prophet's daughter the Immediate Successor to the Holy Prophet of Islam *(except that he was assassinated).*

Prince of Bees ~ *Napoleon*: In 1804 Napoleon took the Coronation Crown from the Pope into his own hands and made himself Emperor; when he performed this act he had affixed to his coronation robes hundreds of tiny golden bees that had been previously discovered at an important Merovingian tomb in 1653. They were found in the Ardennes in the tomb of King Childeric I, son of Merovee who was father of Clovis, they being the most famous and influential of all Merovingian rulers. It was in this royal tomb, along with armaments, regalia and treasures, that a bull's head made of gold and a crystal ball were found, as well as a severed horses head (no one is sure who placed these items there), ***and no less than three hundred miniature bees made of solid gold were discovered. This was probably the single most sacred of all Merovingian symbols (honey bee).*** *The honey bees are vegan, eating no animals or their products, are harmless when left to their own devices, work together in harmony, are industrious and smart workers, steal nothing from other creatures, assist other plants to pollinate and insure the continued procreation and natural hybridization of flora on all continents.*

<<<*>>>

Austria suffered many defeats in the Napoleonic Wars of the late 1700's and early 1800's. In these wars, Napoleon I of France fought an alliance of European states that included-in addition to Austria- the United Kingdom, Prussia, and Russia. ***Napoleon conquered large parts of the Holy Roman Empire, and in 1806 he forced Emperor Francis II to dissolve the empire.***

CHAPTER EIGHT: PART FOUR~ (b) health laws

Human Consumption of ORMUS

During the past 10 to 15 years (although ORMUS is not officially sanctioned by the Food and Drug Administration, either one way or the other) thousands of people around the world have begun consuming ORMUS and are reporting many beneficial effects. Unfortunately most of the claims are not substantiated by scientific process; however, the first medical data taken from a live human subject is being collected and studied in Japan at the time of the writing of the booklet. The writer is performing an ORMUS~OCEAN~FAST™ in Okinawa Prefecture. The associated metabolic processes and DNA data is being collected and recorded by qualified medical doctors who specialize in anti-aging, life-extension and related sciences.

(see: http://www.ormus-ocean-fast.com)

CHAPTER EIGHT: PART FOUR~ (c) agriculture and reforestation

Sustainable and Bio~Dynamic Applications of ORMUS

It has also been reported by researchers that ORMUS can increase agricultural production enormously. Photos showing ORMUS crops include corn plants that are twice the height of an average American (male) farmer, as well as walnuts and oranges that are huge in comparison to those grown without ORMUS. Fruit trees usually requiring 5-6 years to show commercial quantities of fruit are showing fruit in as little as three-plus years. Potatoes and other vegetables are showing almost TWICE the yield in only 60-70% of the average growing-time due to both an increase in overall size and rapid growth.

(see: http://ormus-reforestation.com)

CHAPTER EIGHT: PART FIVE~ SOME ORMUS HISTORY

ORMUS Through the Eyes of Popular Culture

CHAPTER EIGHT: PART FIVE~ (a) ormus history introduction

Leaves faithfully report their memories to Tree

If mankind's history tells us anything, it is that mankind's written records of history are, for the most part, unreliable. Man's misunderstandings, gossip and so-called ***his***tories are innumerable, like the myriad leaves in a dark forest of uncertainty.

Every Leaf is different, gathering light and enduring darkness and shadow, each in its own unique way.

Leaves faithfully report their memories to Tree on a daily basis, year after year: How and when the wind blew coldest; In which days the spring was warmest; When the rains refreshed and the sun scorched; When the snow came and the late and early frosts burned the buds; and then Tree calculates, synthesizes, extrapolates and compresses the averages, saving the histories to Seed for the sake of progeny.

Every Leaf tells the Truth according to its individual experiences, but not a single story matches another. They are all correct of course; Leaves don't lie. If only we could say the same of Men.

And of Virus? Well, that's another story altogether... those Masters of Deception.

For the most part, human beings are like Leaf. They record faithfully for future generations the data that they believe will help their children's, children's children. Every single story is different. To the best of each Man's knowledge, they are all correct, at least according to that individual's experiences, but not a single story matches another; they are similar in many respects, but none are ever identical.

When two or more stories match perfectly, one should suspect the possibility of a falsehood or deceit in the making. Enter the Virus-like people: Masters of Deception. Virus-like people are the *few among the many*, the *minority* and yet, they (the Masters of Deception) are responsible for the *majority* of the damage; especially those destructive and elusive *memes*[105]. What are memes? It is well you might ask.

Memes are intangible, neural-nested holographic virus, which are known to propagate in the psychic realms, across and within the minds of men (even dogs and cats are not immune). Memes are highly contagious as well. You can catch them from many sources such as video games, TV Commercials, laundry room gossip, soap operas, Hollywood movies, the sounds in a casino, *books* on History and, perhaps the worst of all, the *Books and Rituals of Religion* (to name but a few). There are good memes and bad memes. Some seduce us into a world of self-centered consumerism and desire, while others bring us ever closer to the Truth. But what is Truth and what do memes have to do with anything esoteric, especially where ORMUS is concerned?

When it came to ancient civilizations, scribes, popular citizens, playwrights and historians remained popular *only so long as they said and wrote little or nothing of the Truth*, especially with regard to discussions concerning the local tyrants and rulers in power during the corresponding times. Words that subtly flattered the elite insured not only publication, the writers were also often rewarded with continued support and occasionally generous favors trickled down from above courtesy of the Royal Family, Nobility and Ruling class (not to mention that "the right to live" for another week or two was insured to some

105 some references on memes
<http://www.memecentral.com/>
<http://memes.org/>
<http://www.iampariah.com/memeslist/index.php>
<http://en.wikipedia.org/wiki/Meme>
<http://pespmc1.vub.ac.be/MEMIN.HTML>
<http://www.drmenlo.com/abuddha/bookmark.htm>
<http://www.yale.edu/lawweb/jbalkin/cs.htm>

small extent).

Consequently for humans, the Truth has always been held at bay by the deceitful and kept at a considerable disadvantage. The Truth has always been a "hard sell," and in turn, books and *people* who espoused certain concepts that alluded to the Truth were often, quite literally, *burned along with their books after being tortured to extract confessions that they were agents of one demon or another and that their ideas and teachings were not truthful.* This paved the way for history to be rewritten and the current dictators' vision and version of history could then be, more effectively, *imposed* upon the unsuspecting population. Thus the history of ORMUS comes to us, somewhat marred, indeed scarred and the book-cover is both tired and aged, worn and foxed, as a result of neglect and abuse. A few crucial pages are missing as well, due to malicious and deliberate intent.

Nevertheless, like Seed, the stories and histories of ORMUS have endured many trials and tribulations throughout the ages and weathered many a tempestuous ruler, conqueror or pretender to the throne. Unfortunately during that process the line between truth and fiction has become somewhat muddled and obscured, as neither a written, nor an oral tradition has survived outside of esoteric societies and secret circles of learned men and women. Those who knew the Truth passed silently, incognito, through the ravenous crowd and have perforce kept their peace, generation after generation throughout the millennia; not so much that they were trying to keep ORMUS a secret or to withhold something from the *others*- it was more to do, then as it is now, with surviving the unpredictable behavior and superstitious times in which they lived and the all-to-often vulgar mind-set of those who assume control through violence of the heart, body and mind. It was dangerous for Truth to "walk the streets at night" alone and things haven't changed all that much in the past 2000 years.

But, Seed perseveres, never gives up,
Nor does She give in and
She does bide her time well.

Look all around you, if you live near a park or in the country... Seed is an expert gambler; Seed takes a calculated risk. She takes a spread on the odds, across the green velvet boards of Earth's landscapes, millennia after millennia, and with great success! Her legacy is one of admirable accomplishment. One win after another, heaped upon previous sets of successes, win after win, again and again, for billions of years! And then came MAN... Eons of work undone; "*in the blink of an eye*" as Earth and Seed count time.

Man's short history has been that of unbridled greed and one rude, selfish obsession after another. In less than 100 years Man has managed to utterly destroy the last vestiges of Mother Nature's delicate fabric of life and He has all but hacked down the Tree of Life itself; in fact He probably would have, if the sacred Tree of Life weren't so cleverly concealed from His vain, insatiable and voracious eyes.

Fortunately for all of us, She is forgiving and patient. She is waiting for the little boy to become a man. Her hopes for Him are like that of any great and good Queen. She wants only the best for Him: to become a KNIGHT, to don the sacred robes of chivalric orders and champion Her just cause. Alas, even at this late hour the Virus prevails and histories are twisted to suit the needs of the Masters of Deception~ And yet, admittedly Virus is not truly to blame. For Virus can only enter in, where it is invited, through neglect and untoward behavior. To arms then! Let's set the stage aright! But where shall we begin? Is it dragons that need slaying? Is it a Devil that hounds us? Or is it our own greed and avarice that plagues us first and foremost? Perhaps a magic mirror will do the trick, one that will allow us to see ourselves for what we truly are. Perhaps then we may begin to face the enemy within.

Which mythical demon will you attempt to defeat first? With which mythical sword or mystical incantation will you strike them down? In the name of which nation state or god will you conquer? "Which belief system is right for me?" you may well ask.

Myriad philosophical perspectives and their histories were abundant in ancient times just as they are today, and most histories were written by scribes or priests in the "employ" of self-proclaimed rulers; rulers who ascended the throne through violence and bloodshed. Or in the case of so-called modern-day democracies, by way of a plethora of lies and deceit, embedded in the delusions of mass-media-junkies. They were not "the friends of Truth;" And ORMUS knew them not.

Pacific (non-violent) societies and individuals throughout history didn't stand a chance, they were repeatedly overrun by other, less scrupulous, hoards and gangs throughout the ages; and the good people, since the dawn of time were, more often than not, outnumbered by charlatan priests and hooligan rulers. This is the norm even in today's so-called democratic fictions.

Is it not a wonder that the Story of ORMUS survives at all?

Here then consider well the hidden truths that wait within, "The Myth Magic and Murder of ORMUS"~

"Blessed are the meek, for they shall inherit the Earth."

CHAPTER EIGHT: PART FIVE~ (b) the double edged sword

In water we may quench our thirst~
And in water we may surely drown.!

In order to achieve a better understanding of the socio-political effects of ORMUS in our daily lives (as so-called *modern people*) it is important to understand its effects on our ancestors. For those of you who wish to skip ahead and bypass the history, the following ancient saying was designed for people such as yourselves:

"In Water we may quench our thirst, and in water we may surely drown."

And if that's not enough to get your attention~

REMEMBER: "...there is an alchemical myth about a poison which for most men is extremely deadly, while for the elect it confers mastership and absolute power..."

Throughout the millennia, many legends and myths sprang up around the ORMUS phenomena. Whether or not they were true or false (*or a blend thereof, which, of course is most often the case, as that is* the *time-tested formulae for the most powerful of all lies,)* people in general, especially those in power, wanted (*needed?*) to believe in those myths and legends. The reason for this is that the legends and myths surrounding ORMUS promised marvelous benefits, including: immortality, telepathy, prophecy, teleportation, co-location and multiple-location of a single person's body (or bodies), the power to heal, the power to destroy or vanquish one's enemies, power over death in general and the power to raise people from the dead, and perhaps most importantly "Enlightenment," to name but a few.

But, for every benefit there is a danger, a caution and *a price to pay*.

There were then, *as there are today*, many charlatans and soothsayers who attached themselves to the Alchemical trades. Fortunes were lost and made on the premise that, the process of distilling the Philosophers' Stone, was known to many a self-styled "adept," "Master-Craftsman," or *Wizard*[106] if you prefer.

That being said, let's throw caution to the wind and assume that the modern day scientists are not lying to us, and accept blindly, for the moment that they (scientists) really have proven the existence of the Philosophers' Stone; *the fact that the ancients knew about ORMUS thousands of years ago is extremely important to both modern researchers and ourselves (we the people).* If you value your freedom, there are important lessons to be learned from the past. It is also very important to remember that ORMUS has been RE-discovered. Then this leaves one to wonder, "Why has the knowledge been "lost" for so long; or has it? Has it been intentionally kept secret from the masses and if so, *why*?"

The answers for these and other important questions will soon be made clear.

"For them that have eyes, let them see.
For them that have ears, let them hear."
~From the Ancient Essene Codices.

CHAPTER EIGHT: PART FIVE~(c) a scientific basis for ormus

25 Years Later: After Millions of Dollars of Research

David Hudson was not interested in Alchemy when introduced by his uncle to the concept of the "Occult Gold or Philosopher's Stone." Initially, it is reported that he began reading a Time-Life book, called Secrets of the Alchemists. The book presented ideas about the "Alchemists of Olde" and their goal of distilling a "miraculous white powder (from pure metallic gold)" for the purpose of creating a "container of the light-of-life;" when he read that those who "stand in its presence don't age," and that those who "partake of it, will live forever!" he began to wonder, after further reading, about the similarities he had observed between the Philosophers' Stone and the strange and inexplicable behavior of the material that he was investigating.

Unintentionally, Hudson found himself on a treasure hunt, that took him

106 Wizard ~ c.1440, "philosopher, sage," from M.E. wys "wise" (see wise (adj.)) + -ard. Cf. Lith. zynyste "magic," zynys "sorcerer," zyne "witch," all from zinoti "to know." The ground sense is perhaps "to know the future." The meaning "one with magical power" did not emerge distinctly until c.1550, the distinction between philosophy and magic being blurred in the Middle Ages. As a slang word meaning "excellent" it is recorded from 1922. <www.etymonline.com>

on a journey beyond most peoples' wildest imaginations; he continued reading hundreds of books on alchemy, biblical history, the occult, esoteric and Masonic Lore, and perhaps most importantly Grail History and the Chivalric Orders. After considerable investigations he decided that perhaps his ORMUS concepts were not so far-fetched after all. He basked in the warmth and comfort found in the additional support and confirmation derived, most unexpectedly, from a world of ancient and modern scholarship.

Hudson's QUEST lead him down an ancient trial that took him back over 400,000 years into some of the earliest known periods of "*hu*-man" mythology and history. The big difference between Hudson and Indiana Jones though is that Hudson had actually found the treasure and was quite literally holding it in his hands! If only he could understand how to use it? And of course, as with the Egyptians and others before him the question remained:

"What Is It?"

CHAPTER EIGHT: PART FIVE~ (d) they nu'ked the establishment

The age of censorship and half~truths

The last century has been one of amazing discovery and astounding fascination; and during this period one of our most significant collective achievements pertinent to the understanding of ORMUS was the deciphering of countless Sumerian and Essene texts from our ancient past (2,000 and 4,000 years ago, respectively).

Fortunately for all of us, as part of the process of unearthing everything from the *Dead Sea* scrolls and (Nag Hammadi) *Daj Hammeraji* libraries to literally thousands of ancient Sumerian cuneiform-engraved earthen tablets, the eventual translation and (belated) publication of these documents has successfully undermined our entire established view of Christian and Judaic history, the history of man, creation and otherwise! In fact, the documents created such controversy that the translation of the Dead Sea scrolls, discovered in 1947 and 1952, were intentionally withheld and were not made available for study and comparative translation until 1990. Thereafter, it was not until 1992 that other portions were finally made available to the general public, a delay of almost half a century!

Meanwhile a veritable trove of ancient Babylonian and Sumerian tablets were discovered and translated which, in tandem with the *Dead Sea* scrolls and (Nag Hammadi) *Daj Hammeraji* libraries, have cast serious shadows of doubt (even among staunch believers) on writings such as those concerning the Biblical Patriarch "Moses" and those who followed in his *footsteps.* It would appear that the heretofore infallible accounts of Moses and Genesis are nothing more than poorly condensed reconstructions of Essential Sumerian Chronicles (or myths?); These facts, coupled with the discovery of (thousands of...), the now famous, blue-eyed, red haired, 7-foot tall, "Tocharian Mummies" that were found in the desserts of what is now modern-day western China, has left many of the so-called historical authorities, religious leaders and uppity academics in a quagmire of intellectual, political and "gender-based religious" chauvinism.

We will return to the tale of the excavations of the blue-eyed mummies shortly~ *(An archeological dig, which was quickly shut down and heavily censored by the Chinese Central Government!).*

CHAPTER EIGHT: PART FIVE~ (e) a cast of stars

A hidden agenda among historical figures

The previous may all be better understood in due course when, in later chapters, we will also discuss the Key Players in greater detail; to wit- The *Mary* (Lady) Magdalene and her *husband* Jesus ["the Christ" in Pauline terms] and Their respective roles in the perpetuation of a noble and ancient order of Healers known as the *Essenes*: as well as Her (Mary's) historic champions, The Knights Templar, the Celtic Church, the Royal House of Stewart and the Free Masons of both ancient and modern-day lineages and *of course* the modern-day Essene Family of Friends.

Fragments of This Groups "*Essene* teachings" are to be found in Sumerian hieroglyphs and on tiles and stones dating back some eight or ten thousand years. Some of the symbols, such as those used for the sun, moon, air, water and other natural forces, are from an even earlier age preceding the cataclysm that *ended* the Pleistocene period. How many thousands of years previous to that the teaching existed is unknown at present. *(The Pleistocene epoch lasted from 1,640,000 to about 10,000 years ago. It was marked by great fluctuations in temperature that caused the ice ages, with glacial periods followed by warmer interglacial periods. Several extinct forms of human, forerunners of modern humans, appeared during this epoch.)*

Evidence of the Essene Way of Life has made its appearance in almost every country and religion on Earth. Fundamental principles of The Way were shared and recorded in ancient Persia, Egypt, India, Tibet, China, Japan, Palestine, Greece, ROME and many other countries. Without question however, The Way has been handed down in its most pristine form by way of the Essene Orders, a mysterious Family of Friends who, according to archeological evidence, have survived (at least since) the last two or three centuries B.C. on through the first century of the Christian era near the Dead Sea in Palestine at Qumran and at Lake Mareotis in Egypt. In Palestine and Syria the members of the Family of Friends were known as Essenes and in Egypt as Therapeutae, or healers.

Some exoteric parts of their teaching have been translated and are rendered in prose and poetically in the Tree of Life, the Essene Communions with the Angels, and the Sevenfold Peace, among others, by Edmund Bordeaux Szekely. Other exoteric or outer teachings appears in Book One of "The Essene Gospel of Peace" and the other "recently" discovered Dead Sea Scrolls.

Although it may be true that we cannot pinpoint their origin at present, the Essenes did exist under various names and veils since times immemorial and if there is any one teaching on Earth that genuinely points to an immortality of consciousness, the Essene Way of Life would be the One. It makes an early appearance in Zarathustra's "Zend Avesta" where it is translated into The Way of Life and was followed, ostensibly, for millennia. From that wellspring come most of the spiritual and yogic concepts later made popular in India, Nepal and Tibet. (The Buddha of the Bodhi Tree and the Tibetan Wheel of Life being prime examples.)

Essene principles have been incorporated into innumerable schools of thought in various forms. Consider the Pythagoreans and Stoics in ancient Greece, the Phoenicians and the Alexandrian School of Philosophy in Egypt where most branches of Western culture, Freemasonry, Gnosticism, the Cabala and Christianity find their origins.

The Essenes were communally oriented and always lived in natural, secluded areas near sources of clean clear waters, far from the cities and villages, spending most of their time interacting with Nature, while husbanding fields and orchards of a considerable variety of fruits and vegetables in arid lands. They were "headquartered" near the Dead Sea not far from UrSalem [Jerusalem] not necessarily because they were Jewish or Semitic; rather they were especially interested in the Qumran caves that overlooked the Dead Sea. The Romans became highly attracted to this area for the same reasons and eventually surrounded the area, putting it under martial law. The reasons for this specific geographical location will become clear in due course. They were the original *vitarians*; that is to say, vegetarians who eat only raw, uncooked foods; ie: fruits, salads and sun-baked breads (made from whole-grains, soaked and crushed into a sweet dough) and they were therefore the earliest known *earth-friendly,* sustainable farmers who introduced biodynamic and organic farming to this planet. It may also be said that they were the first to introduce the cooperative farming precepts that are so popular today. To bad no one would listen to them, *we would not be in the environmental predicament that we find ourselves in today!* Did you know that 2 out of every 3 people in the U.S.A. are members of one kind of cooperative or another? That's about 65% of the population! You are probably supporting several agricultural and energy cooperatives without even knowing it!

The Essenes of course, being a communal cooperative kept no servants and certainly there were never any slaves to be found among them. In fact the Essenes were the first to openly condemn slavery (including economic slavery) both in theory and practice and the most famous among them would be their champions of justice: John the Baptist, John the Beloved [an pen name or alias {code word for} Mary Magdalene and her writings?, James the Just, The Mary (*Lady*) Magdala (Magdalene) and Her *husband* the Great Essene Master Yeshua (*Jesus the Christ*).

The Way of Life according to the Essenes has been recorded in the writings of their later contemporaries- recounted and lovingly remembered as, "a race by themselves, more remarkable than any other in the world," "the oldest of the initiates, receiving their teaching from Central Asia," "a teaching perpetuated through an immense space of ages," "constant and unalterable holiness;"

They were revered by such noteworthy authors as Pliny the Roman, Philo the Alexandrian, as well as Josephus the Roman, Solanius and many others among the erudite, who obviously held the Essenes in the highest regard. It was only in the past 1600 years that the Essenes were virtually forgotten due to the concentrated efforts of the Emperor Constantine and his cronies, who had all attached themselves to Constantine's so-called Catholic (*Universal*) Church; A church whose early and latter inner-circle members endeavored to exterminate every vestige of the memory and progeny of Mary and Jesus *(a literal campaign of assassination and murder, which fortunately failed! [See especially the connections between Princess Diana and the Merovingian Legacy for more detailed information on the descendents of Mary and Jesus]).* Much evidence to this effect is well preserved and is now rapidly becoming public knowledge.

As to the prior knowledge of the Essenes in modern times, some translations of The Essene Way of Life in Slavic text* have been found, well preserved, in the possession of the Habsburgs in Austria. It is reported that Nestorian priests, fleeing the hordes of Genghis Khan, saved the manuscripts when they came out of Asia to the west during the thirteenth century. (*During the 800's, the Slavs established *the Great Moravian Empire, which united the peoples of central Europe for the first time.* In 907, the Great Moravian Empire was conquered by the Magyars, the *ancestors of the Hungarians.* The significance of this fact becomes apparent in the following chapter. Note* do not confuse *Merovingian* and *Moravian.*)

NOTE~ It might be prudent at this point to pause and reflect for a moment, in order to remind ourselves that we are talking about a scientifically sound process (of global significance) that results in the production of a set of elements that have been recently added to the periodic table of elements. It is the bridging of science and history that takes us into dangerous territory where the line between fact and fiction may become somewhat obscured by our present-day, media-driven "intentionally-engineered-state-ignorance."

CHAPTER EIGHT: PART FIVE~(f) setting the stage
Among the Ancients

(i) sumeria
Perhaps Not so Ancient as We Imagine?

Let's turn back the pages by a mere few-thousand years (just a few nano-seconds on the galactic clock)[107], to the days of the Sumerian Civilization, to the world's (purportedly) oldest, known civilization.

From circa 4,000 B.C.E.[108] to around 2,000 B.C.E., the Sumer civilization of Mesopotamia (now affectionately known as *southeastern Iraq,*) bloomed and flourished and most of its population made their living by growing crops or raising livestock.[109]

Their founders are credited with the design and construction of magnificent

107 ***nano-,*** (combining form.) ~ a billionth (used in subminiature units of measurement). Ex. Nanosecond = a billionth of a second..

108 ***B.C.E.***~ Before Common Era

109 ***Ubaidians*** ~ By the year 5000 B.C.E., a White Mediterranean and some early Nordic tribes (together known as Ubaidians) established settlements in the Tigris and Euphrates river basin.

palaces and temples. They built walls around their cities apparently for protection against invaders. This is an important point to remember when, later you may begin to wonder, *just exactly who those invaders might have been!*

They constructed canals to irrigate fields that boasted crops such as barley, wheat and dates, complimented by a sumptuous variety of fruits and vegetables. They also raised cattle, donkeys, sheep, and goats. Wool from the sheep was used to make textiles, and according to early theories, that wool constituted the main export of the area. As textile workers they wove fine cloth, but, once again, where and to whom were these exports destined?

Sumerians were accomplished craft-workers, and they were skilled in metalwork and stonework, although most of the stone and metal had to be imported. Other craft-workers made jewelry, earthenware, weapons and armor. Apparently traders carried their goods to nearby regions by land and by boat and their ships sailed to distant lands obtain ivory and other luxury items.

Around 3000 B.C.E. they[110] invented[?] cuneiform as a means of keeping written records. By pressing a tool with a wedge-shaped tip into wet clay tablets they thereby fashioned the cuneiform symbols. In turn the tablets were then baked in the sun. In turn, the Sumerians founded some of the earliest schools, mainly to train scribes who kept records for government offices, temples, and other institutions.

Hundreds of thousands of these tablets have survived to provide information concerning Sumerian politics, literature, economy, law, religion and more importantly, according to some scholars, a 400,000 year old record of THE ORIGINS OF THE "ADAMIC RACE" or the *Hu*-MAN (*hu*-manna) Beings. The tablets also indicate that the Sumerians had knowledge of astronomy, mathematics, medicine and a tradition that suggests that *Sumer people were descended from a Race of Super Beings (not necessarily aliens) capable of manipulating the genetic*

---

110 **Sumerians** ~That "original" Ubaidian culture was, in turn, overwhelmed by a new White Mediterranean tribe known as the Sumerians circa 3250 B.C.E. and they gave their name to the region: Sumer. During the next several hundred years that followed the immigration of the Sumerians, the country grew rich and powerful. Art, architecture, crafts, religious and ethical thought, flourished. Thereafter, the first large-scale Semitic invasion took place in 2335 B.C.E. when a Semitic group, called Akkadians overran Sumeria. It was shortly after the Akkadian invasion that the first "Jewish people" are recorded as entering Sumeria in greater and greater numbers. Eventually, after several generations, the Semitic tribes began to intermarry with the original Nordic and otherwise blue-eyed tribes, and although this process was not absolute, the distinctions between the various peoples became obscured. This mixing of the races in the region led to an increasingly hybrid population and was clearly on of the first cosmopolitan civilizations in recorded history while under the rule of Hammurabi's (The White King's) Code of Law. The original introduction on the Hammurabi Code, which was engraved in stone and is still existent, reads as follows : "Hammurabi, the exalted prince, who feared God, to bring about the rule of righteousness in the land, to destroy the wicked and the evil-doers; so that the strong should not harm the weak; so that I should rule over the black-headed people like Shamash, and enlighten the land, to further the well-being of mankind..."

"Hammurabi, the prince, called of Bel am I, making riches and increase,...who enriched Ur;... the white king,...the mighty, who again laid the foundations of Sippara...the lord who granted new life to Uruk, who brought plenteous water to its inhabitants...the White, Potent, who penetrated the secret cave of the bandits ..."

(Translated by L. W. King, The Eleventh Edition of the Encyclopedia Britannica, 1910. Further translations of Hammurabi's code can be found in The Code of Hammurabi, R.F. Harper, University of Chicago Press, 1904).

codes of Earths' more "primitive" creatures. ("Primitive," being a very relative term in this instance.)

Here it is important to note, that the process of deciphering and translating the ancient cuneiform tablets of Sumeria lead us to the discovery that the "nearest neighbor" to the Sumerian language in modern times, linguistically speaking, is the Hungarian Language!

(ii) babylon

Babylon, After the Fall of Sumeria

As *Babylon* rose to power after the fall of Sumeria, it naturally inherited much of its literature and therefore, additional historical accounts of the Sumerians were recorded (and perhaps altered, inadvertently or otherwise) by the Babylonians. These recent translations of the cuneiform tablets have provided a wealth of information on the very ancient world of Sumeria (predating ancient Rome, Greece, and even ancient Egypt, but the later only marginally[111]). In particular: the compression, reconstruction (retelling) and (in some cases) corruption of the original stories by the Babylonian historians, Hebrew Patriarchs and Catholic Church, have now become glaringly obvious. This hints strongly at why the ruling counsels in Jerusalem (the Sanhedrin, Pharisees and Sadducees) were very much discontent with Mary and Jesus' attempts to correct those same anomalies.

The Sumerian texts included everything from daily journals of the courts, ancient ledger sheets including the number of animals brought for blessing or sacrifice to the temples, even literary epic tales of their heroes, gods, and all their escapades; one of the more significant examples being the *Enuma Elish* (Epic of Creation). Reportedly, the original Sumerian description of the Manifestation of Heaven and Earth was retold, translated and dutifully recorded somewhere between of 2000 B.C.E. to 1500 B.C.E. by the Babylonian scribes and scholars.

Perhaps most significantly: The planets Uranus, Neptune and Pluto were not discovered by modern science until the 18th, 19th and 20th centuries *and* were apparently unknown to the ancients, yet, there they are, named (differently) and described in detail by the Sumerians thousands of years ago! More precisely, Uranus and Neptune in the cuneiform texts are described as twins; this fact was not known to N.A.S.A., until Voyager 2 took data from each of the two planets in 1986 and 1989!

The cuneiform texts also explained that the apparent age of our Earth is approximately 500 million years younger than our Moon.

The Sumerian texts are now recognized as being extremely accurate as regards various scientific and astrological facts. It has also been confirmed that the biblical story of Genesis is nothing more than a very condensed (and seriously

111 ***"Ginger" the mummy*** and other inhabitants of Early Egypt ~Racially speaking, the inhabitants of Egypt at this period in time were divided into three groups. Skeletal evidence from grave sites show that the original White Mediterraneans and Proto-Nordics were in a majority in the area - a well preserved body found in a sand grave in Egypt dating from approximately 3000 BCE, on display in the British Museum in London, has even been nicknamed "Ginger" because of his red hair - a racial trait only found in persons of Nordic ancestry.

altered!) version of an epic tale contained in the original cuneiform tablets. This is easily understood when one recognizes that the Biblical Genesis was actually penned, for the first time circa 600 B.C.E., at a time when the Hebrew people were being used as slaves in Babylonia (where the Sumerian records and stories were translated, preserved and retold). The point is however, to finally understand how all this history is both *peculiarly and critically* pertinent our understanding of ORMUS

(iii) the anunnaki

Controversy Surrounding Zechariah Sitchin

According to Zechariah Sitchin (who devoted decades to translating the cuneiform texts) and the Sumerian tablets, a group of super-beings arrived on *(or returned to? their ancient home?)* the Earth in ancient times, *in search of gold and other precious metals.* These extraterrestrials were reportedly called, in the Sumerian texts, the **Anunnaki**, which loosely translated means, "They who, from heaven to earth did come." By Zechariah Sitchin's reckoning, based on translations of the Sumerian texts, the Anunnaki arrived on (*or returned to*) Earth some 485,000 years ago. Of course around this time, as far as we know, the only "*hu*-man" types were a species we call *Homo erectus.*[112] Purportedly, the Anunnaki, under the leadership of the one named EN.KI ("Lord [of] Earth) and the first-born son of ANU the Elder (the localized High Command) was in charge of a gold-mining enterprise designed to retrieve *nano*-particles of precious metals from the Earth's ocean waters. In time (30,000 years later) it was decided that the operation was no longer yielding sufficient amounts of gold (apparently they had exhausted the primordial reserves, and as an alternative they began mining gold from an area then known as the ABZU, in, where else? South Africa!

Reportedly the cuneiform texts documented the change of method as well as a change in command. The new commander was EN.LIL a younger half-brother of Enki. Enki was still in command of the mining operations, and EN.LIL was promoted to principal commander of the Earth-mission overall.

---

112 Homo erectus fossils ~have been found at a site called Dmanisi in the country of Georgia (eastern end of the Black Sea and not far from northern Iraq [ancient Sumeria]). It is estimated that the fossils are about 1,800,000 years old. Fossil remains imply that Homo erectus wandered as far as the island of Java in Southeast Asia prior to migrations towards southern Europe and northern China.

Some anthropologists have suggested that the earliest Homo erectus fossils found in Africa should be renamed as, Homo ergaster. It has been observed that the earlier fossils have thinner skull bones than those of later Homo erectus fossils. It is thought that Homo ergaster migrated out of Africa to Asia and that Homo erectus may have then evolved from this earlier species. Experts disagree however on the fate of Homo erectus. Some say that Homo erectus was an ancestor of modern human beings, but others insist that the species became extinct!

The most complete skeleton of an early human ancestor ever found, in 1984 (1,600,000 years old), was that of a nearly complete fossil skeleton (an adolescent Homo erectus boy, 11-14 years old?). It was found near Lake Turkana in Kenya.

AN.TU (Antum) Great Mother of the Sky	AN.U (An) Great Father of the Sky	KI (Urash) Earth Mother

EN.KI	EN.LIL

Enlil, according to the Anunnaki laws of succession was the true heir-apparent, being the first-born son of Enki's father by his father's half-sister. The same arrangement is suggested in the *Book of Genesis'* in the story of Ishmael, Abraham, and Isaac (Abraham's first-born son by Abraham's half-sister, Sarah).

Consequently, a problem arose. Water based mining required a chemical and electromagnetic process to "extract" or "precipitate" the nano-particles from the salt-waters. It was essentially a much more elegant chemical process that required little equipment and almost no hands-on activities as opposed to the rugged and dirty tunneling and digging required by a land based operation. Therefore at one point it was decided that the Anunnaki would be better served by "creating" a group of slave-miners, rather than using there own kind to perform the labor-intensive and otherwise menial duties. By creating a "mixed worker" to perform the hard labor that resulted from the switch to land-based mining as opposed to water-based mining the Anunnaki would be spared the hassles of a 9-5 job routine; and so half-breed creature was to be created~ something similar to a modern-day mule (a donkey genetically crossed with a horse). Only one small difference... The creature should have two legs instead of four and would be wanting a pair of hands as well!

"But what big eyes you have grandmother," said Little Red Ridding Hood... "Ahhh, the better to seeeee you with my dear!" answered the Big Bad Wolf.

By engineering a hybrid mix using the genes of the Anunnaki and the genes of the *Homo erectus* the ideal (by Anunnaki standards) slave might be created. Once again it has been reported that the Sumerian texts explain in exquist detail the process of decision-making and processes of genetic modification and enhancement of the *Homo erectus* that later resulted in an Anunnaki-*Homo erectus* hybrid creature. Et Voila! They called him........ youuuu guessed it! AD. APA. (...later he was genetically modified and the new improved version was called AD.AM).

The Sumerian texts left us to wonder about the later versions retold in Genesis 1:26, when Jehovah, God, the Creator (in the Sumerian version, Enki) said, "Let us make man in our image, after our likeness..." thereafter the Sumerian version again says, as in Genesis 1:27: "And God created man in his own image, in the image of God created he him; male and female created he them."

However, in the Sumerian story it is the Sumerian Goddess Ninti who carries the first Adapa embryo to term.

"Let *us* make man in *our* image, after *our* likeness."

At this point it is important to note that mules can not procreate. The primary difference between the Adapa and the Adama is this; that in order keep the expenses down, it is far better to have a slave that can birth and feed and rear it's own kind that to be constantly cloning and or using Anunnaki "breeding mothers," as apparently was the case. (Talk about a need for some women's lib organizers!)

If you find this whole hybridized hu-man process a bit repulsive, as the saying goes, "You are not alone!" This is where the Essene Order eventually came into play long, long ago. The rebellion within the Anunnaki had begun almost the instant the idea of creating a slave system was conceived. But we will return to that later.

Consider the accounts in the biblical Genesis wherein Enoch, Methuselah and other biblical patriarchs were rather long lived as compared to hu-mans today.

According to the Bible, Methuselah lived 969 years (Gen. 5:25-27), making him the oldest Biblical person. Babylonians believed because of their Sumerian texts, that some of their ancestors lived to be as old as 36,000 years of age.

Now this is where ORMUS, the "Philosophers' Stone" and ancient history begin to cross paths. You will have noticed by now the constant use of the term "hu-man" throughout this document (as opposed to the usual noun human). Enter the terms "manna" and "hu" but not necessarily in that order. Those of you who were raised in a Christian, Muslim or Judaic country (or for those of you who watch enough television or Hollywood movies) you may be familiar with the MANNA that a certain "hero" fed to his "people" when they were crossing a desert and were nearly starving to death. The hero "feeds" the (so-called naughty) people (his wayward family and distant relatives who wouldn't do what he told them to do) a magical substance referred to repeatedly in the Bible, Koran and Torah as manna. This manna was reportedly made from a gold statue, an idol of a god, which the hero didn't want the wayward children to worship. So he melts the golden statue down and "burns" it into to a white powder. Ring any bells? Any alarms going off? A White Powder of Gold. The Philosophers' Stone!

So, the point here is, how did he learn to make it and what is it really supposed to do for us and most importantly, was he (Moses) like Prometheus who is known as the "too soon or too quick god" (quicksilver~ Mercury)[113]*, ...was he guilty of giving the "fire" to the people of Earth prematurely? Should Moses have given the manna to the children of Israel even though they were not well and truly prepared for it? Or did he perform the act of a desperate patriarch and give his family whatever it*

---

113 *Mercury~* also: *Hermes Trismegistus* – (Gr.). The generic name given to many ancient Greek writers and having its origin in the Egyptian God Thot, Thoth or Thos, associated with wisdom and knowledge. Most of the Hermetic writings have their origin deep in antiquity and represent true Ancient Wisdom upon which most of our present knowledge (esoteric and exoteric) has its basis. ***There are others who suggest however that, this was an appellation applied to writings of Maria Prophetissima (Mary Magdalene?) during an age, when females were generally regarded as "inferior to males" and thus were incapable of scientific and/or rational (deductive reason) thought process. (~similarly "John the Beloved" may also have been a code word for Mary Magdalene for the same reasons)***

Compare MIGDAL EDER (Tower of the Flock) and the Hermit card of the TAROT. The One who stands on the mountain and holds up a light (lantern) for others to see by, and hence pilgrims may find their Way home!

took to keep them alive at a time when they were in a life and death situation? Or was that simply his justification for playing god, like EN.KI and EN.LIL?

This is where it all starts to become really interesting.

Let's summon the Essenes once again. According to various reports and ancient documents membership in the Essene inner circles was attainable only after a probationary period of a year plus three years of initiatory work, followed there again by seven more years before being admitted to the edges of the inner circle of the "spiritual elite" and thereafter learning the occult sciences. However, now, dear reader, you will have the unique opportunity to take the short path to enlightenment. In the next chapter we will discuss: the importance of Ocean Water in relation to ORMUS (What EN.KI and EN.LIL were *really* collecting,) why the Essenes' Biblical "headquarters" were located over 50 meters above sea level in the caves at Qumran overlooking the Dead Sea and how you can acquire information that will enable you to repair and encode your own DNA and return to your own garden of Eden (or E.DIN if you now prefer the original Sumerian version!)

Before we leave this ancient era, in all fairness it should be mentioned that the City of Jericho had walls as early as 8000 B.C.E., and yet most scholars date the first real attributes of civilization to the Sumerians between 4000 and 3500 B.C.E. Huh? How did Joshua bring those walls down anyway?

The Ark of the Covenant, remember?
And a piercing sound~wave~~~~~

"Lofty Anu, lord of the gods who from Heaven came to Earth, and Enlil, lord of Heaven and Earth who determines the destinies of the land, determined for Marduk, the firstborn of Enki, the Enlil-functions over all mankind; made him great among the gods who watch and see, called Babylon by name to be exalted, made it supreme in the world; and established for Marduk, in its midst, an everlasting kingship." ~The Babylonian White King, Hammurabi

(iv) egypt~ mfktz "realm of the blessed"

The Great White Brotherhood

Although the histories and accomplishments of the Sumerian civilization are beyond the scope of the average high-school student's education, much of the histories and accomplishments of Egypt are known to virtually everyone. Egypt's wisdom and know-how have become legendary throughout the modern world. Yet, in truth, little is understood about their actual origins as a people and their intercourse with ORMUS remains a mystery to most of us. The fact that many of the ruling class were depicted as being blue-eyed is an interesting curiosity, considering the obvious genetic influences of the modern Egyptian peoples. Being one of the most culturally diverse and well informed of all the ancient civilizations Egypt was undoubtedly one of the greatest empires that the modern world is aware of. But, for all her knowledge of herbs and chemistry, medicine and mathematics, as well as her expertise in alchemy, architecture and engineering, Egypt was sufficiently baffled by the ORMUS phenomena that her philosophers and high priests resorted to calling it simply, 'MFKTZ' or "What is it?"

'MFKTZ' as does "manna" translates literally as "What is it?"

Among the learned Egyptian elite, 'MFKTZ' was discussed in reverential tones and praised as a wondrous substance; a substance which defied both description and analysis. Is there a connection between the ORMUS and another dimension? Was the Golden Glass of ORMUS merely a component of a Star Gate of an actual Star Gate in and of itself?

Bearing in mind that the Old or Middle Kingdom Egyptian pharaoh's have disappeared without a trace and that no mummies or bodies have ever been found, it certainly leads one to wonder! Out of 12 dynasties, more than 80 of the kings have gone missing!

(Here, it is important to remember, as mentioned earlier, that ORMUS has been proven to both levitate and phase shift into another dimension in clinical experiments and can be fashioned into a brick of gold glass that is a superconductor found to be operating at room temperature. Superconductors can be encouraged to transfer enormous amounts of photon (light) energy at velocities exceeding the speed of light, the energy transfer process being triggered (switched on and off) by specific sound frequencies, or harmonics if you will.)

Interestingly, it is in Egypt that we find the earliest specific archeological record of the 'MFKTZ' white-gold powder. In the 5th-dynasty pyramid tomb of King Unas at Saqqara, among the sacred writings found therein, an intra-dimensional location called the Realm of the Blessed, is mentioned in specific relationship to the substance they called 'MFKTZ'. It is in this Realm of the Blessed that the King is said to "live forever among the Gods" and it is also called the Field of 'MFKTZ'.

Additionally it is in ancient Egypt that we find further discussions relative to the 'MFKTZ' in numerous other sacred locations. One such example is found in records that are concerned with the metals that were numbered among the possessions and treasures of Pharaoh Tuthmosis III[114]*. Numerous cone-shaped objects are described as being made of gold but, curiously, are described as "white bread." It was in the year (approximately) 1450 BCE, that Tuthmosis III founded a brotherhood of metallurgical and alchemically inclined Master Craftsmen at Karnak, and it is in Karnak that the first instances of an Order named "The Great White Brotherhood" are to be found. They were so named due to their preoccupation with a miraculous white powder of transformation and projection.*

114 ***Tuthmosis*** note the similarity {thuth=thoth} {moisis-moses} thothmoses

CHAPTER EIGHT: PART SIX~ PREFACE TO PART SIX

"Harmony" ~ Our Ancient Future

As *an* Introduction to this section this "disclaimer" is offered:

"If mankind's history tells us anything, it is that mankind's written records of history are, for the most part, unreliable. Man's misunderstandings, gossip and misinterpretations of our so-called histories are innumerable. That superstitious ignorance spreads like a cancer, breeding hate, disease and unrest."

If this statement is true, then where does it leave us? How shall we proceed in the process of uncovering the truths and mysteries that surround the ORMUS legacy? Where, in these days and times can we find a sacred fountain whose living waters will quench our thirst? Were Wisdom, Truth and Justice set aside as an exclusive domain reserved only for the Wise Ones of Olde?

The Tree of Life stands in our midst, if only we had eyes to see it. The birds of paradise sing in it eternally if only we had ears to hear them. It stands in a garden filled with the fruits that will satisfy our yearning, if only our feet would follow the path and The Way that leads us through it. In the following chapter "The Book of Life" we will explore the Spirit of the Fountain That Dies Not, and the ever-unfolding blossoms of Joy and Bliss that are attended by the Ambrosia of the Gods.

She whispers~

Have you been imbued with
The fragrance of the rainbow?
Have you ever heard the stars sing?

We answer the Call~

"Sweet, morning dew of the Harvest Moon,
Nectar of the Queen of the Heavens,
Send your sweet Rain
Down to us in our time of need,
We, the humble servants
Of our gracious Mother,
Nature Herself~
We do implore Thee;
Do not abandon us
In the ignorance of our youth...

Tarry with us a while longer,
That we may yet
Discover your eternal peace
Nestled amidst the conditions,
And that we may know in its entirety
The Majesty of your Creation
And make it Our Own."

CHAPTER EIGHT: PART SIX~ ORMUS & MIRACULOUS SEA-SALTS

CHAPTER EIGHT: PART SIX~ (a) ormus-ocean-fast™

A Modern-day Enigma

For the past 17 years (prior to May of 2007) a man 60 years of age, by the name of PILA (his nickname), who now lives in Maui, Hawaii, has been performing a 40~50-day ORMUS-Ocean-Fast™ on an annual basis. He drinks pristine ocean water that has been collected from tide-pools. It is filtered and then exposed to the sun's UV rays for an extended period of time. During the ORMUS-Ocean-Fast™ he spends an average of 4-6 hours per day in the ocean, floating in his own homemade *thalassotherapy* pool.

His grey hair has returned to a shiny, lustrous brown.

His arthritis has disappeared- (at one point he had considered suicide, on several occasions, as the pain in his bones had become unbearable); He now sports like a young deer in spring!

What is the secret of his newfound youth and vigor? The "ORMUS Ocean Fast™"

Throughout the ages, generation after generation, wise men and women have retreated into the wilderness, away from the eyes of the teaming crowds and have found solace in meditation and fasting. They have found rest from their daily toil, but few have found the immortal truths.

You may ask, "Is there an Immortal Truth? Really?" and it well you should ask. It is good if you want to know. It is well that you seek. It is important that we should have Hope. When we lose Hope, we either fall into despair or into temporary (or worse, permanent) delusions of smug indifference.

Is despair is a better state of mind than indifference. And if yes, why?

When indifference builds a fortified wall around us; we become *spiritually nearsighted* and *sociologically hard-of-hearing.* Then when help and answers do come, we *neglect to listen* and *fail to see* the obvious solutions that were right in front of us all along. Despair can be rectified through exposure to Natural Elements, the company of loving friends and family, augmented by a complete retreat from cities and electronic equipment. A Smug-Indifference however, born of Pride and Egoistic thought process, is a "hard nut to crack." The *know-it-all* type of person is difficult to reach and as we can plainly see, their "inner-rooms" are filled to capacity, bursting with *all-they-know*, consequently there is no room available for new and important ideas. They cannot escape, trapped inside all that clutter of knowledge, thus there is no way out of that crowded-house.

But for the *meek*, that is to say, *a person with an open mind and a will to learn*, Hope remains. One of the most common misunderstandings among moderns is the confusion surrounding the word "meek." Meek does not mean stupid or gullible or foolish as many tend to believe.

Words that are more appropriately *associated* with *meek* would be: *gentle, courteous, kind, patient, even-tempered, mild, forbearing, not easily angered, compassionate* and *loving*; and dare we say *vegetarians*?

These are all excellent character traits and it is certainly a wonderful compliment for any civilized lady or gentleman, to be associated with the attributes of being "gentle, courteous, kind, soft, pliant"

If you are such a person then you will benefit greatly from the following pages. This having been said, let's have a stroll in the "Gardens of E.DIN"[115] together, shall we?

CHAPTER EIGHT: PART SIX~ (b) scientific investigations
The Manufacture of Monatomic White Powder Gold

There are those who claim to have made Gold and other precious metals from PPT.

However they are unwilling (or unable? to prove it in open laboratory experiments for various reasons (being bound to confidentiality agreements is the most common excuse).

HOWEVER~ Let us assume, for the sake of argument, that we will be able in near future (in an open, cooperative and sharing [public domain] environment) to prove that there is ORMUS inside the PPT made from ocean water):

Let's look at what would happen if we made a partially dried PPT and compressed it into a "wafer" similar to the small round disks that are commonly used for communion [116] *in modern day Christian churches. (The Last Supper Ritual employed by most Christians)*

The question is this, "Will the hydrochloric acid, intestinal flora and other enzymes in the human stomach be sufficient to allow the ORMUS to become 'liberated' from whatever it is that the ORMUS is bonding to, (or perhaps more appropriately: shelled within) while suspended in ocean water?"

What were the early Essenes actually eating and drinking when they celebrated communion?

Was it Essene-ORMUS™ perhaps?

What was actually served at the so-called Last Supper? And was that indeed the LAST Supper, or was it a ceremony that had been around long before that particular event transpired?

Does the juice of the fruit-of-the-vine have something to do with the breakdown of the "bread ~ (ORMUS)?"

For those who have been working with the PPT long enough, you will recognize instantly the similarities between the calcium/magnesium cakes made from PPT

115 E.DIN (Garden of Eden) according to the original Sumerian cuneiform tablets, the name originally ascribed to what is now referred to as the "Garden of Eden" in Biblical texts.

116 ***Eucharist see index: references to "White Dove of Peace"***

and the flavors of standard bread wafers (milky and a mild sweetness). A wafer made from high quality, pharmaceutical grade (clean) Deep Sea Ocean Water PPT, (also referred to in the ancient texts as "Manna") tastes very much like "bread" as we have come to think of it, and will mix very nicely into a wafer becoming almost an INVISIBLE and unrecognizable ingredient embedded within a wafer of sprouted-wheat bread cooked in the desert-sun on super hot and dry stones (as is the custom of the devout Essene Community even until this very day).

Is the "wine" somehow connected to the "shew-bread~(ORMUS)" as regards the stomach acids and the efficient digestion/absorption of the ORMUS (M-state materials)?

Let us assume for a moment that the various ORMEs or ORMUS particles enjoy either an affinity or "revulsion" for one another. When the m-state materials (found to be naturally occurring) in wine and the M-state materials (found to be naturally occurring) in ocean water are combined in the stomach (as a PPT condensate), will they all have an effect on one another? Will an atomic "tug-of-war" ensue? This is very likely the case.

Enter the Essene Community's preoccupation (some say obsession!) with fasting.

Certainly the greatest of care is employed when pharmacists, perfumers or alchemists are engaged in the preparation of medications, fragrance and esoteric formulae. The smallest infraction can lead to explosions and what might have been a medicine then becomes a poison; an otherwise lovely bouquet becomes a foul stinking mess. The chemical marriage[117] becomes a chemical disaster and the atomic and molecular structures all frantically attempting a massive divorce and abortive process wherein free radicals abound. Sounds like some peoples' stomach, doesn't it?

Many spiritually minded people today try to think of their body as a Temple of Light. It is also important to think of one's Temple as an Alchemical Laboratory. Your body is a Scared Vessel, or HOLY GRAIL if you wish. But "Whom does the GRAIL serve?" Does it serve "mammon" or does it serve "The Master Architect?"

If one truly desires enlightenment, one must put aside certain extraneous growths and focus the entire Will upon the goal.

Your stomach is your laboratory. It is the first stage in a process that leads to the transfiguration. It must be first cleared of all dross. When your stomach is clean and the "worm" has been ejected,[118] it will perform its task admirably and faithfully. The pH balance and the associated alchemical activity is a very delicate matter and it is not to be taken lightly!

CHAPTER EIGHT: PART SIX~ (C) MUTANT NINJA TURTLES

Dear Mutant Ninja Turtles,

We humans owe you, all fauna and flora, a collective apology. What we, with few exceptions, have done to Planet Earth is all but unforgivable.

As a species we humans have always been very culturally and genetically

117 al***chemical marriage*** ~ consider *bridal chamber* in the orthodox Christian sense.

118 ***The true exorcism~ process ejecting the mucoid plaque by means of saltwater (fresh ocean water only) fasting techniques.***

diverse; indeed since the "Times before Time."

What we have mutated into most recently, however, is not only novel but, often rather shocking, especially when compared to what Nature apparently had in mind for us; something which is arguably altogether different from what we have become~ To wit: The Number One Destructive Force on Planet Earth.

We have managed to destroy our natural environment in less than a few hundred years, with most of the destruction having occurred within the past 60 years! [119]

For example: We have albino crocodiles that live in cement sewage systems in various parts of the world. Albino gecko lizards populate the cement jungles of Japan and Malaysia. Globally we are witnessing exceedingly obese people who spend most of their waking hours glued to little boxes punching keyboards who, may one day become albinos as well, as they rarely and sometimes never see the sun (on a case by case basis)! Their children play, all~day~long, on asphalt and cement and steel contraptions and many of them don't know how to climb a tree or make a campfire. They (and their families) all think that the universe glides around their country or city and they live on food and energy resources literally stolen, by force, from other countries.

How ORMUS will affect those people who are consumed by urban jungle lifestyle as opposed to those who still run free in temperate rainforests will probably be different in the extreme. The final outcome is difficult to predict, however, intelligent assumptions may and have been made, similar to global warming patterns having been predicted and ignored decades earlier. Those who did heed the warnings, made the necessary sacrifices and changed, adapting themselves to a more sustainable approach and began living lightly on the land (in some cases as far back as the 1940's). Then there are those who remain stubbornly outside the will of nature. How does this scenario apply to ORMUS consumption and the bottle-necking of information? Go figure.

Clearly we are not all going to the same place (time-space continuum or dimension). It is not too late, for many, to reverse-course; for others, well, they have made their choices and unfortunately the survivors will be left to bear the consequences of our collective decisions.

REMEMBER that since ancient times it has been wisely counseled that: "...there is an alchemical myth about a poison which, for most men is extremely deadly, while for the elect, it confers mastership and absolute power..."

And "absolute power soon destroys, absolutely, those who do know how to wield it."

The meek (open-minded) shall inherit the Earth.

Seriously!

"ORMUS What is It? The Myth, Magic and Murder of ORMUS"
Ends here.

119 1950's ~ since the introduction of television especially

CHAPTER NINE~ ORMUS AND ORMES DEFINED

~ How to use ORMUS ~

The commonly known, present-day methods used to manufacture ORMUS (or *ORMEs* if you prefer) are best understood by referring to David Radius Hudson's patents registered in various countries (however: view his applications denied by the US Government!).

First let's define the words ORMUS and ORMEs.

David Hudson described the elements as:

"**O***rbitally* **R***earranged* **M***onatomic* **E***lement[***S***]."*
O.R.M.E. 's

ORME(s) is the word he used on his patents to describe the rare-earth minerals that he had stumbled upon [rediscovered] and researched at such great expense. The ORMEs elements are also described as having a "deformed" nucleus.

Sometime thereafter, either through a typographical error or as an intentional pun, the word ORMUS appeared on the scene among ORMEs enthusiasts and was substituted for reasons as yet undetermined (a heated debate ensues between a certain individual [who has created an extensive ORMUS archive along with many ORMUS forums] and certain others [who claim to have worked closely with David Hudson] as regards the definition and "appropriate use" of the two words). That having been said however, the word ORMUS is by far the most frequently used term, semantically speaking, when we refer, in general, to the subtle elements in question. Other scientists in university settings have called them "superatoms," or "stealth-atoms," but the term "superatoms" does not enjoy widespread use and is somewhat confusing (almost utterly devoid of any real meaning). "Stealth-atoms" is an interesting term in that the ORMUS elements are "non-spectroscopic" when typical equipment is employed for observation, quantification and quantification.

ORMUS, historically speaking, apparently comes to us by way of St. Ormesius or Saint ORMUS[120] who purportedly had interactions with St Mark, at a time

120 ***ORMUS*** ~ see also Ormuz and Hormuz: the area where modern-day Yemen/ Oman (Arabia) almost touches with the continental shores of India (an ancient crossing where the strategic Straits of Hormuz are located). At one point in history this land was probably connected as evidenced by massive artifacts, which depict a Neolithic civilization that is now covered by ocean water. (Where the migrants from Hunza crossed over to the (now) Arabian Peninsula; A land of great wealth and one of the principal nexus for ancient sea-trade and overland spice/salt routes).

more at **~** The Byzantine monk Eutychus, who lived from 387CE to 454CE, wrote that: *[in the] ...time of Abraham reigned Shabib (Sheba), wife of Sinn, priestess of the mountain, who built Nisib and Edessa* (Ur) *and surrounded them with walls. She founded also the sanctuary of Harran, and made on idol of gold, called Sinn.*

*The reader should investigate the SOMA and INDRA for interesting and enlightening adventures. Indra "swallowed" the SOMA (a mineral or metallic substance), which imparted the AGNI (spiritual fire, ie: fiery baptism).

INDRA ate the SOMA ~ (a mysterious metallic substance).

The Soma cult, coming from the northern realms, pervaded India from the mountains to the sea.

Did descendants of the Blessed INDRA family (of the SaraSvati~ Hunza River areas) cross

when Mark supposedly brought the so-called "Essene Gospel" to the (wayward?) Egyptian Priests. Certain researchers suspect that this Mark fellow and the ORMUS fellow then proceeded to "harmonize" the Egyptian Mystery Schools' teachings with representatives of a remnant of the Jesus Movement.

This merger, some suggest, gave birth (esoterically) to the Coptic Church (which was originally representative of the Thebaid School, or Sages of Light), an alchemical school and symbolical-mystically oriented church, whose esoteric belief system was extremely different from that of the Pauline (Saul of Tarsus) theological mind-set.

Thus the esoteric and alchemical teachings were to be preserved for future generations among the Egyptian-Arabic mystery schools, while the very *antithesis* was being promulgated by the Pistics (who were to become the victims of a scheme designed to subvert the true and original Jesus Movement for all time). One group pursued the mystery of communion through a vegan-pacifist lifestyle, fasting and meditation, while the other (Pistic) remained addicted to the "blood-lust" (carnivorous lifestyles), *animal sacrifice* and the *bloody~cross/ bloody~Christ*, and usually found themselves martyred and *bathing in their own blood*... Whereas, the original Jesus Movement preferred a quite, secluded, vegan lifestyle (Ebionites), were not contentious (as were the so-called Christians) and chose a more secretive and secluded (cloistered) methodology; that is to say, they were intent on surviving peacefully among the various societies of the world. This group (Family of Friends), later linked to the ***original*** Celtic Church~ ***original*** Freemasons and the ***original*** Templar Knights were well informed and intimately acquainted with the ***oral tradition*** (and were quickly attacked, infiltrated, subverted and subjugated by the Pistic Holy Roman Empire at the point of a sword and other means of intimidation such as rape, torture of young children, slave trafficking, witch-hunts, etc.).

All this rich and sordid history *and more* lay in wait for David Hudson as he began his quest for the Holy Grail.

As David Hudson was researching the mysterious materials he had discovered, he was also reading books both ancient and "modern" that foretold of an alchemical process, which had been known to the ancients; a process that started and ended with a substance that shared many similarities with the material he was testing: The Philosophers' Stone. At first he thought that it was all a lot of "New Age" nonsense, but reportedly at the gentle insistence of his father and friends he continued reading. Did he discover the connections between Mark and the master craftsman known as Ormus and their ancient connections to the Melchizedek lineage of priest-kings and the SOMA of Indra?

Upon further investigation, an ancient line of master craftsmen (and crafts-women!) who are intimately involved in metallurgy appear on the scene, along with magnetic stones that levitate and statues of Black Madonnas and the White Dove of Peace (ISIS), not to mention Alexander the Great's guild of metal-smiths which he had collected in what is now called Pakistan/Afghanistan and brought to Alexandria in Egypt (the Gypsies: "tinkers"); and lest we forget, a certain sword in a certain stone (extracting the Light of Truth from the Philosophers' Stone), Excalibur, the sword of Truth. "Only the true king can extract the "sword" from the "stone"!

---

at Hormuz (Ormuz OMUS) into Oman/Yemen (land of Frankincense; the [3] MAGI: Star of Bethlehem)?

Forming the ray from Heaven, you flow through all forms. Soma, as the ocean you overflow. Soma, beloved enter the ocean. RV IX.64.8, 17,27

The ocean-going angels have flowed to the wise Soma. RV IX.78.3

ORMUS and ORMEs as specific industry related terms define a GROUP of mysterious precious metals that are now known to exist in various states, which have not yet been fully understood or explained by modern science. When clustered, they assume a metallic state, but when in monatomic or diatomic mode they are *not* metallic. Some researchers say that they become superconductive. ORMUS is extremely stable and generally defies bonding with other elements; and when clustered as precious metal, of course, defy oxidization (they do not "rust").

ORMEs is a term coined by David Hudson for the materials that he patented; materials that are understood to the extent that, they can be identified by a scientific process which has been repeated under controlled laboratory conditions by unbiased third parties; to wit: a process that can be carried out under specific conditions according to specific protocols. Whereas, ORMUS might be better defined as those particles that remain aloof and are not, as yet, fully explained or understood.

ORMUS are those mysterious materials IN GENERAL, whereas ORMEs are a specific set of those materials that have been successfully manipulated, repeatedly, in a predictable manner, under conditions and in terms that are acceptable to empirical science.

With ORMEs there is some evidence, with ORMUS there is little evidence but, a reasonable assumption can be made (in terms of deductive reasoning and scientific hypotheses).

ORMUS represents those aspects of ORMEs that remain, as yet, undefined and are as yet "undiscovered" or defy the labeling process of quantification and qualification. An example of this would be where ocean water is used to make an extract wherein nano-particle gold, platinum and other precious metals are known to exist in a non-spectroscopic state. If we make such an extract (or "precipitation" derived from pH swings, to be more precise: abbreviated as "PPT") we have a white slurry that settles at the bottom of a glass container which very likely contains ORMEs, BUT, until we can confirm the exact content, we might prefer to refer to it as having some quantity and various qualities of ORMUS in it. "The ocean-water PPT contains ORMUS which, in turn, likely has some ORMEs in it."

ORMUS, is/are the *mysterious elements in general*; whereas ORMEs are *those that have been isolated by one scientific means or another*; especially where they are "synthesized" by reducing precious metals to their monatomic or diatomic forms.

The issue of whether ORMUS and ORMEs are monatomic or diatomic is still under investigation (and much heated debate rages in the inner circles of ORMUS pioneers and researchers). The theory is that there are S-State (high-spin, superconductive [non-spectroscopic]) forms of ORMUS; and that there are M-State (monatomic [non-spectroscopic]) forms or ORMUS.[121]

We might conclude that there are ORMEs to be found in ORMUS, but ORMUS

121 The spectroscopic [non-spectroscopic] aspects of ORMUS are very complex and exceed the scope of this dissertation, however, one might wish to begin by searching the two terms "ORMUS" & "MEISNER FIELD" on google or yahoo to initiate a more serious and in-depth investigation into the ORMUS phenomena.

is not to be found in ORMEs. But even this may not be true. There is much that we do not know and much remains to be revealed at the appropriate time.

ORMUS in general refers to the entire family of precious metal "nano" particles that are no longer metallic due to their isolation as individual atoms (not clustered).

ORMEs are a few specific members of that family of precious metal "nano" particles that are no longer metallic due to their isolation as individual atoms (not clustered). ORMEs is a modern term, whereas ORMUS has a rich history steeped in alchemical mystery and a long line of illustrious personages, many heroic, who have preserved sacred knowledge at the peril of their own lives and those whom they loved and held dear: Persons such as Mary Magdalene and Maria Prophetissima (also: Prophetissa)[122] and *her* descendents.

The Essenes, Therapeutae, Sages of Light, Thebaid Brotherhood (Sisterhood?), Anunnaki, Ninhursag, DINGIR, NINANNA, NINTU, Melchizedek, and modern day Vegans all share a common denominator: ORMUS.

While the cultish priesthoods seek to control the manufacture and distribution of ORMUS, and thereby control the masses, there are those others, who would set the slaves free~

ORMEs are made exclusively from precious metals and require extensive laboratories and employ the use of extremely dangerous and caustic chemicals; and thus remain available only to the rich and powerful (intimidator types) and these very people are usually (but not always) the least worthy of consumption.

Mary Magdalene, Jesus and their Beloved Family of Friends taught an alternative route to enlightenment and "salvation" or *atonement* (at-one-ment and a-tune-ment). They teach us of a method whereby, anyone, regardless or financial prowess and political might, can partake of the "sacrament" of "holy communion". But this method has nothing whatsoever to do with blood sacrifice;

---

122 ***Mary Magdalene and her ancestors*** ~ In 1975 during an archeological expedition in the Indus Valley (which actually begins in the **Himalayan** rage near the **Hunza River** and Hunza Valley [**Darya** as well] and runs down through an area where the **SaraSvati** [homeland of **Sarah and Abraham**] once flowed, in regions of modern Afghanistan/Pakistan), Dr. Paolo Rovesti was surprised to discover a remarkable terra-cotta apparatus, which was on display along with other terra-cotta ***perfume*** vessels in a museum in **Taxila** *(an ancient trade nexus and seat of learning)*. It appeared to be a primitive ***distillation device,*** but the 3000 BCE date attributed to it would have placed it some 4,000 in advance of the date that most credible sources had previously attributed to the invention of distillation. Soon thereafter another device of similar design, dated around 2000 BCE, also undoubtedly a primitive ***distillation device***, was discovered in nearby Afghanistan.

Maria Prophetissima ~ The earliest known written description of a distillation device (in the modern western world) depicts the artifact attributed to one ***Maria Prophetissima,*** which is detailed in ***"The Gold-Making of Cleopatra,"*** an Alexandrian text, one reportedly written around the same time that ***Mary Magdalene*** would have been with child (or having delivered her child) while in Alexandria. The device was designed to distill aromatic and medicinal essential oils It was also used to capture the ***phenol-ethyl-alcohol from rose water and lavender water***; two ingredients essential to the preparation of skin ointments and unguents. Here we find evidence of the advanced knowledge of the medicine and science that existed among the Therapeutae and Essenes, along with other aspects of sacred teachings associated with *her* **Beloved Family of Friends**.

Mystical Egg ~ As Mary Magdalene is often depicted in mystical renderings bearing an egg, one can't help but make a connection with the Mesopotamian cuneiform tablets which, in the 13th century to the 12th century BCE described elaborate egg-shaped vessels that contained coils that are similar to those used for distillation. Many art historians and scholars have wondered at the "cosmic" egg in Mary's hand and its significance. They need wonder no more! Mary Magdalene and Maria Prophetissima are one and the same person.

neither the blood of innocent animals, doves or goats, neither the blood of virgins, nor the blood of menstruation (as some rather twisted individuals have suggested), neither the blood of martyrs (and most certainly it has nothing to do with the blood of the man we call Jesus as certain other twisted individuals have suggested throughout history).

Jesus and Mary Magdalene's message was all about intelligent society weaning itself from the blood-lust addiction; for that's exactly what it is: AN ADDICTION.

There is The Way that teaches us how to wean ourselves from the blood-lust and it then lends further guidance as to how we, as common, day-to-day people can gain access to the very finest ORMUS and ORMEs that exist in the universe!

There is an ancient mitochondrial lineage that has been passed down from mother to daughter for countless generations that is shared with the male offspring, but the males cannot impart the mt-DNA to their sons; hence a matriarchal lineage must be complimented by the correct male Y-chromosome lineages. This marriage creates the Malkus-Zadok (Malkut-Zadok or Malkuth-Zadok) or Melchizedek title that is bestowed upon the KING-PRIEST or PRIEST-KING.

The Melchizedek owes his very existence and title to his Ancient Mother (Mother Eve) and to his Ancient Father the ATMA (Adam).

As the pieces of the puzzle begin to fall into place one cannot help but wonder: "Where does ORMUS fit in to all of this?" "How can I, an average and simple person acquire pharmaceutical grade ORMEs and ORMUS for free?" "Is this really possible, even though the male chauvinist "priesthood" tells me that I must kiss their tutu if I want my share of the Tears of Horus?"[123]

Well friends, it is true and yes you can get ORMUS for free. ORMUS is available in great abundance on planet earth, but we ***DON'T need to "eat or drink it in a synthesized form"*** per se. There is a better way to embed ORMUS into our systems.

There is a better way to acquire it and that's what Jesus and Mary were really all about, and that's the know-how that the Catholic Church and some other nasties were trying to quash/control for the past 2,000 years!

123 ***Tears of Horus*** ~ Egyptian code for **ORMUS**

Chapter 9 ends here.

The following chapter is not "officially" entered in
The Table of Contents, neither was it indexed.
It is not a part of Chapter 9; it is simply nestled here,
Like Mary's famous egg, within
A secret chamber of this book.

MARY MAGDALENE'S SECRET ALCHEMY

Invisible particulates- stealth atoms- and an esoteric family

This chapter has no "official" entry in the Table of Contents as a Chapter, neither is it indexed, and yet, it includes the KEY to Her Alchemy. It is included here for those of you, who share our passion in the discovery and revelation of truth. It is included here for those of you who are willing to make a change for the better. Most of these words will fall on deaf ears; perhaps less than 0.05% of the world will want to understand these words. Fewer still will be able to understand them. In truth, the sacred alchemy is not meant for everyone, who, at a whim, may decide that they want to lay hold of it. But here its is...

"Cast not your pearls before swine, lest they turn and rend you!"

My words are very easy to comprehend, and it's easy to enact them:
But the world cannot comprehend them, nor portray them.
These words have an Ancestor.
My Dharma has a Lord.
Yet masses have no understanding of this.
Therefore, they have no recognition of me.
The fewer persons that recognize me,
The nobler are they that heed me.
Therefore, the Sage wears simple attire,
While secreting the jade in his innermost being.

There are those people who would skip the periods of preparation and run straight into the arms of disaster. As they say, "Fool's rush in where angels fear to tread." If only the damage were limited to the fools themselves, it wouldn't be a problem. The sad truth however, is that the fool usually brings harm to so many innocent bystanders. Thus strict precautions become a "necessary evil".

Know-how that should be made readily available and accessible to all of us is, perforce, "withheld" until a candidate's sincerity and determination can be confirmed; at least that's how it was in the past, when the Arts were passed along from priestess to protégée, after years of careful evaluation and a temperance of character had been assured.

In the orthodox and somewhat dubious modern "Christian" models, any individual who is willing to confess to so-called "sins" and mumble words in robotic fashion and pay tithes once a week, will be "saved." But this most certainly was not the case in the original Jesus Movement and it certainly isn't the case as regards the Secret Alchemy of Mary Magdalene.

In stark contrast to orthodox Judaeo~Christianity and other commonly known religious orders today, we are adamantly opposed to anyone having to "pay" for something that was, is and should be given freely. If we have inherited the sacred know-how freely, it should be passed on freely. In our carefully considered opinion, a ministry should be self-supporting and a minister should be gainfully employed. Thereafter if an individual chooses to share the wisdom of the ages that they have received freely, they should be prepared to impart that knowledge freely for the sake of future progeny. The Art and its attendant resources are not commodities to be bought or sold, nor are they quaintly eccentric curiosities to be auctioned the highest bidders.

That having been said, and all money related issues aside, we should be ever mindful that several aspects of the processes necessary to achieving the Great Work, if abused, represent a clear and present danger to the genetic wellbeing of the global population (both fauna and flora).

Individuals come and go, and many have fallen by the Wayside in their vain attempts to take what they have not earned. Thus a period of probation is required of those who would "drink" from the Grail Cup. But this probationary period is not a process that is administered by an organized "church" or priesthood. To the contrary, each individual must put himself or herself on probation and when you have completed the necessary procedures, "you" will initiate "yourself."

Here is a simple and easy to understand first step: you must liberate yourself from any addiction you may have to blood. You must resist the temptation to steal and consume the blood (minerals, elements and hormones) of other animals. Just because others do it, is no indication that it is healthy for us to follow their bad example. That blood contains subatomic instructions that are not compatible with your goal-state. This is the behavior of ignorant slaves. Set yourself free.

Here is a simple and easy to understand second step: Don't interrupt the cycle of Seed. Eat only live foods that taste good in their natural state. This is a little bit more complicated, but anyone, who has a sincere desire to achieve the transfiguration and metamorphosis can do it. Even a child can understand the procedure once explained in detail. (For "how-to" info see footnotes below: [124])

> "Remember, ***your body is so much more than a temple, it is an alchemical laboratory*** designed to transmute "lead into gold."[125]
>
> CAUTION! (The above is a symbolic statement, ***don't eat lead; it will cause serious illness and might even kill you.*** All heavy metals are poisonous, even gold and any other heavy metal consumed, even in tiny quantities, can cause permanent injury or death).

124 For "how to" info on "Uninterrupted Seed Cycle" diet see:
http://www.ORMUS-ESSENE.COM
http://www.ORMUS-VEGAN-CAVIAR.COM
http://www.ORMUS-NATURAL-FOODS.COM

125 Alchemical terms, phrases and sayings are both symbolic and allegorical, as well as literal. Esoterically speaking, common metallic terms were often substituted for one another based on the **context** and specific placement of the terms within the discourse. Sun could mean Gold, or a chemical solution, or a period of time. Mercury also took on many meanings depending on the exact manner in which the term was employed; it didn't always refer to a silver-colored liquid metal. Lead too, was a word used in many different ways and its meaning varied widely according to the encoding process utilized by the author of the treatise.

CAUTION!! Also please be advised that the manufacturers of many so-called ORMUS® products on the market today offer no evidence that their products actually contain ORMUS® or O.R.M.E.S.™.
Finally consider this quotation from a text penned in 1910 [note our comments in brackets]:

BEGIN QUOTE

"We entered into a circular hall in the form of a temple. It had no windows, but received its light from a cupola of clear glass. High over our heads, below the cupola, was a large interlaced double triangle made of gold and surrounded by a snake biting its tail. In the midst of the room, and directly under that symbol, stood a round table with white marble top, in the centre of which was a smaller representation of the figure above, executed in silver. The walls were ornamented with bookcases, in which were a great number of books on alchemy. At one side of the room there was a kind of altar upon which stood a burning lamp. A couple of crucibles, a few bottles upon a side-table, and some armchairs completed the furniture of the room.

I looked around, expecting to see some furnaces, stoves, retorts, and other implements, such as are described in books on alchemy, but could see none. My instructor, reading my thoughts, laughingly said: "Did you expect to find here an apothecary's shop? You mistake, my friend. All this array of bottles and pots, of furnaces, stoves, retorts, mortars, filters, strainers, distilling, purifying, and refining apparatus, etc., described in books on alchemy, ***is nothing but nonsense, written to mislead the selfish and vicious, and to prevent them from prying into mysteries which they are not fit to receive.*** *The true alchemist requires no ingredients for his processes; such as he could buy in a chemist's shop. He finds the materials, which he needs within his own organization* [organism]. *The highest processes of alchemy require no mechanical labour; they consist in the purification of the soul* [for lack of a better term?], *and in transforming animal man* [based nature] *into a divine being* [divine paradigm]." <text truncated>

The Adept smiled, and said: "Through your lips speaks the learned ignorance of your modern civilization, which cannot see the truth, because it has created a mountain of misconceptions and scientific prejudices which now stand between itself [the learned ignorance of your modern civilization] *and the truth. Let me then tell you once more that Nature is a Unity, and that consequently each particle of matter, even the smallest, is a part of nature in which the possibilities of the whole are hidden.* ***Each speck of dust may, under favourable conditions, develop into a universe in which all the elements existing in nature can be found. The reason why your scientists are unable to comprehend this truth is because their fundamental doctrines about the constitution of matter and energy are entirely wrong.***[126] ***Your Dualism in theology***

126 Again: see index for ATOMIC THEORY in case you missed it in Chapter One of this book.

has been the cause of untold misery, creating a continual quarrel between God and the Devil; your Polytheism in science blinds the eyes and obstructs the judgment of the learned, and keeps them in ignorance. *What do you know about the attributes of primordial matter? What do you know about the difference between matter and force? All the so-called "simple substances" known to your science are originally grown out of primordial matter. But this primordial matter is a Unity; it is only One. Consequently each particle of this primordial matter must be able to grow under certain conditions into gold, under other conditions to produce iron, under others mercury, [and so on...] This is what the ancient alchemists meant when they said that each of the seven metals contains the seeds of the other seven; and they also taught that, for the purpose of transmuting one body into another, the body to be transmuted would have to be reduced first into its Prima Materia.*

"But," he continued, "I see that you are anxious to have the truth of these doctrines demonstrated by an experiment; ***let us then see whether it is possible that we can make gold grow out of its seed."***

END QUOTE

So, if Mary Magdalene and Her Beloved Family of Friends knew the Secret of Seed and were, in turn, *very discerning* as regards those to whom they might choose to reveal it, would it not be reasonable to assume that they would have protected that knowledge at all costs? Would it not also be reasonable to assume that there were those who would stop at nothing in their attempts to force that knowledge from the sealed lips of those who knew?

So in truth there were martyrs and then *there were martyrs!* Now ask yourself these all-important questions: "Did such knowledge ever actually exist?" and if so, "Does it survive until this very day?" Indeed it does, but, "There are those who *profess to know*; and there are those *who know that they do not know.* And then, there are those who have *ceased to exist*!"

How does an individual cease to exist? By becoming whole and by achieving AtOneMent, through a splendid merger with the unified field.

We refer here to the transfiguration process:

A process wherein the Law of Abraham takes on an entirely new and different meaning!

"An eye for and eye, and a tooth for a tooth."

This is to say, "every eye will be replaced with a new eye, and every tooth will be replaced with a new tooth." This is very much in contrast to the commonly accepted, violent interpretation, of the Law of Abraham, wherein revenge is the predominant and recurring theme.

Remember this, that when Moses first returned from the Temple of Hathor (after he had lead the children "across" the Red Sea into the Sinai), he returned with a "set of rules of behavior," or perhaps more appropriately *"living standards,"* that would have insured the continued freedom of the previously enslaved children; only to discover that they were behaving, contrary to his advice, in a rather unruly manner. He then, sadly, returned that ORIGINAL set of laws (a Tablet? a Stone or THE Philosopher's Stone) to the primordial fire and brought back a MODIFIED (and very much lesser) version~ a simple set of mundane rules that might keep them directed, at least moderately, towards a healthy lifestyle.

This interpretation may be corrected in this light:

Moses had gone up into the Temple of Hathor to prepare the Philosopher's Stone (traditionally interpreted as "stone tablets that contained the Word of the Law").

The Temple of Hathor, had previously been included in his political domain (came with the "turf," as it were), as he was a High Priest in the Cult of ISIS; a cult of both *baptism* **and** *resurrection of the dead* (sound familiar?) a cult, which, from ancient times had also used as its icon the White Dove of Peace: a white cloud descending from heaven, which was later to be invoked by one John "the Baptist" [as in the Johannite tradition of the Free Masons[127]]). He (Moses) was in fact (presumably?) the genuine article: a Master Craftsman, *par excellence*, skilled in both ancient Egyptian *and* Babylonian Masonic arts (decidedly pre-European masonry) and chemistry (an alchemist, trained and actively involved in metallurgy, thaumaturgy, glass making, pharmacology, a goldsmith, etc.). Moses was a member of two "Royal" families, one of "Judaic" origin (Babylonian- *to wit:* the city of UrSalem [read Melchizedek of Salem who worked closely with Abraham and Sarah of "Ur[128]"]) and another of so-called "Egyptian" origins.

He was preparing to administer the sacrament to those leaders and their following, who were willing to listen to and act upon his advice (and in so doing would have become worthy to receive the sacrament).

However, upon his return he discovered that only a small number of people in the "inner circle" were keeping the Law. According to his (Moses') considerations the majority had been consumed by their own debauchery.[129] *Subsequently he was left with no other choice than to deny them the right to "drink from the Holy Grail". He perforce was unable to administer the Sacrament to them. A Sacrament, which later became associated with what modern Christians erroneously call "the Last Supper". The so-called last supper is anything but the "last" supper. It is THE first and last, the Alpha and Omega in a transfiguration process; it is THE institution of an existence that transcends time altogether.*

---

127 See also indexed references to **Mandaeans**

128 Consider also an investigation of the nouns "Ur" and "Ursvati".

129 And the Master Architect spoke to Moses, saying, *"Only the Children of Light can understand the Commandments, they alone are worthy to know the true Nature of the Law. As the Stone has been returned to the fire, so shall it remain, ever hidden, with its essence concealed in the Book of Life, distributed and revealed only among those, who are able to keep the Law, that is, the Law of Life."*

And thus the Law of Life lives ever hidden in the breast of those, who keep it as a sign to the Children of Light. Hence, only the written law of a dead scripture, designed for a wayward people, remains visible to the eyes of men; meanwhile, The Oral Tradition, which breathes and lives, shall be sealed up for a time, like a hidden sprout waiting for the long winter of Mankind to come to an end. Until it shall came to pass that the Children of Light appear in the desert and the angels walk the earth once again, the fragments of the Invisible Law will be laid up, as a treasure, in the breast of the Elect."

First let's examine the provision of the Manna by Moses to the recently liberated "children of Israel" and their subsequent "disobedience." As a prerequisite to this undertaking, let us consider, in the first instance, the "instructions" given by "Godde" to the Adamic Race: Whereas, since "the beginning" it was suggested that we should feed upon, *what is it,* exactly?

[From the Geneva Bible of 1599]

29 And God said, Behold, I have given unto you every herb bearing seed, which is upon all the earth, and every tree, wherein is the fruit of a tree bearing seed; ***that shall be to you for meat****;*

30 Likewise to every beast of the earth, and to every fowl of the heaven, and to everything that moveth upon the earth, which hath life in itself, ***every green herb shall be for meat****; and it was so.*

Here the children have a choice to make, will they feed upon the flesh of animals or upon the Manna...

[From the Geneva Bible of 1599]

10 Now as Aaron spake unto the whole Congregation of the children of Israel, they looked toward the wilderness, and behold, the glory of the LORD appeared in a cloud.

11 (For the LORD had spoken unto Moses, saying,

12 "I have heard the murmurings of the children of Israel; tell them therefore, and say, At even ye shall eat flesh, and in the morning ye shall be filled with bread; and ye shall know that I am the LORD your God.")

13 And so at even the quails came and covered the camp, and in the morning the dew lay round about the host.

14 And when the dew that was fallen was ascended, behold, a small round thing was upon the face of the wilderness, small as the hoar frost on the earth.

15 And when the children of Israel saw it, they said one to another, It is MANNA, for they wist not what it was. And Moses said unto them, This is the bread, which the LORD hath given you to eat.

16 ¶ This is the thing, which the LORD hath commanded: Gather of it every man according to his eating an Omer for a man according to the number of your persons; every man shall take for them, which are in his tent.

17 And the children of Israel did so, and gathered, some more, some less.

18 And when they did measure it with an Omer, he that had gathered much, had nothing over, and he that had gathered little, had no lack, so every man gathered according to his eating.

19 Moses then said unto them, Let no man reserve thereof till morning.

20 Notwithstanding they obeyed not Moses, but some of them reserved of it till morning, and it was full of worms, and stank; therefore Moses was angry with them.

What's this? What was filled with worms and what stank? It ***wasn't*** the Manna that stank. It was the dead bird carcasses retained by those who chose to feed upon the flesh of dead animals rather than follow the Law of Seed.

ORMUS (Manna, MFKTZ, the Stone) when properly prepared can be kept as a liquid paste, in an earthen or glass jar, for many months without refrigeration. We have personally prepared and kept ORMUS in a sub-tropical climate for over one year, without refrigeration and without being hermetically sealed (water-tight). It was exposed to various types of oral bacteria (human) and other air-born fungus. After one year it was as clean as the day we made it. Nothing had grown in it, it was odorless and colorless; it remained pure white with only the slightest hint of a cyan-blue hue that glowed like an aura around the material. This blue glow had been present since the first day we made it and the glow remained after one full year of no refrigeration and without the benefit of a hygienic seal.

But What Does It All Mean?

Most earthbound humans are addicted to drugs but don't realize it.

The simplest way to understand the human condition and Mary Magdalene's agenda is to review the warning signs of an addictive personality. Then add the warning signs of brainwashing and cultish behavior.

You may be surprised to discover that the large majority of the human race is addicted to drugs and other related elements such as natural hormones (i.e. "naturally" occurring in nature) and toxic environmental hormones (those that exist as a by-product of industrial waste~ i.e. man-made hormones).

You may also be surprised to learn that the large majority of the human race is addicted to religion and cultish behavior or one sort or another, but the former is the one that *HAUNTS* us.

Blood-lust is an ancient addiction. It is THE single most destructive force in the world today and it is this addiction that stands in the way of our enlightenment.

Do you recognize any of these traits in yourself (or in someone you love and hold dear[130])? Are you addicted to blood? Have you become a parasitic creature without even realizing it? Do you steal (as in *thievery*) and feed upon the blood of others (that which doesn't belong to you)?

Mother Nature in Her wisdom has offered you an array of beautifully perfumed delicacies; they are color coordinated and sweetly flavored, to insure that you can recognize them easily. Mother Nature wants you to eat these fruits and in so doing, help Her to spread Her seeds far and wide in the process. She has also given you both sweet smelling and pungent herbs, rich in alkaloids, enzymes and other elements essential to your wellbeing. These herbs can also be used for medications if and when you have accidents.

And yet, so many of us choose the path of bondage, and remain enslaved (at an elemental and sub-atomic level) to a diet of blood. If you steal and eat the blood of others, in essence you are addicted to hormones, elements, mineral salts and nano-particulate precious metals (superconductive precious metals).

There is a simple, scientific explanation, but it is not at all what you might expect. We will give you the KEY now, (we will also explain the origin of the much misunderstood Nephilim (the "giants" [131]), who were neither good nor bad; rather, they were ***confused***) but before we do, please take a moment and reflect upon these simple, self-evident truths (it's time for the human race to stop living in denial of its addiction; and it's time we all stop lying to ourselves and others):

First, take a moment to review these warning signs of addictive behavior:

1] An addict won't admit to themselves or others that he or she is addicted.

2] An addict becomes angry, belligerent and often violent towards people who care to and try and help the addict (to recognize that they are addicted).

3] Addicts group together to reassure one another that they are "in control" of their addiction.

4] A group of addicts support the illusion that they are in the right and that "the others" are wrong in their observations, opinions and assertions.

5] Addicts eventually steal and kill to get what they want.

Second, take a moment to review these warning signs of brainwashing (mind control) behavior patterns:

1] National Governments and their "health" departments have been quite successful in convincing the large majority of the population that eating animals is a necessity to maintaining good health.

2] Governments tend to cater to the commercial needs of pharmaceutical companies over and above the needs of the people themselves.

3] Governments are failing to protect the global population from companies that promote Genetically Modified Foods, companies that are introducing such GMO without regard to the possible unforeseen long-term and irreversible damage to our natural ecosystem. Seed is Sacred and not something to be owned and controlled by big-business through enforcement of DNA related patents.

---

130 Sometimes its easier to see the errors of others in the first instance; then later you may discover that you too, are not so very different from your "enemies" and/or those you love

131 ...Remember ORMUS makes things grow! At an amazing pace

4] Govenments have access to new and efficient forms of energy but refuse to pass laws that will enforce the use of sustainable energy technology because lobbyists are still too powerful. Governments dare not contravene the limits put in place by big oil and nuclear power companies.

5] Manufacturers and dealers of drugs, oil, nuclear power, arms, weaponry and blood, all stroll along hand-in-hand, laughing all the way to the bank. It is a deeply ingrained addiction that dates back hundreds of thousands of years. It's all about the true story of Cain and Able: but it is the version that has been hushed-up by intimidation tactics for thousands of years.

It's all about SALTWATER and the superconductors contained therein!

Most people are living under the mistaken impression that people eat meat in order to acquire proteins (and some carbohydrates). However, this is an inaccurate assumption borne of blind acceptance of the idea that the meat of animals is a necessity (prerequisite) to human health and excellence. This simply isn't true. In fact~

Nothing could be further from the truth!

When the craving to kill and eat another animal (or human) occurs, what our body really craves, wants and needs are the salts, minerals and elements found in that blood. Once we went down that path it became almost impossible to return to our intended pristine lifestyle; and the Garden of E.DIN scenario was removed from our conscious routines. Thereafter, over a period of time that spanned thousands of years, we developed a dependency on blood, as well as a chemical addiction to the panic, fight~flight hormones that are sent into the bloodstream of the dying animal.

What our body really craves, wants and needs are the salts, minerals and elements found in that blood. Not those hormones.

These salts, minerals and elements are essential to ***Human metabolism.***

The proteins are not. Human bodies can manufacture their own proteins if given the proper building blocks, i.e. the salts, minerals and elements!

To add insult to injury, the proteins of the dead animals then accumulate in our intestinal tract where they continue to send false signals to our brain and other organs instructing our bodies to build body-parts that are not native to our human organism. Pigs' protein routines instruct our human cells to build new pig-cells. Cows' protein routines instruct our human cells to build new cow-cells. Chickens' protein routines instruct our human cells to build new chicken-cells. Fishes' protein routines instruct our human cells to build new fish-cells. Pandemonium occurs at a cellular level, DNA becomes decrepit, and virus inevitably takes advantage of the human body's confusion and resultant weakness. You then age, grow old and die from any number of RNA~DNA related disorders. Consider the following facts:

Dr. Alexis Carrel reportedly kept a chicken heart alive for over 27 years by nesting the pulsing heart IN A SOLUTION OF DILUTED SEA SALT (isotonic ocean water). Dr. Carrel decided to terminate the experiment after almost three decades, since he had clearly proven that living tissues are capable of physical immortality.

Professor C. Louis Kervran, a candidate for the Noble Prize, links the mysteries of immortality to trace minerals derived from ocean water. Other physicians have confirmed (and additional research has proven) that salted sour plums, fermentations of briny salt pickles, and other salty fermentations are indeed both powerful and effective medicines.

According to an article in Scientific American, July 1972 edition: "The Chemical Elements of Life," by Earl Friden, it was revealed that ocean salt contains 92 essential minerals (24 of the elements found in unadulterated ocean salt are essential to human metabolism) whereas almost all refined common sea salts sold on the market today contain only 2 elements (Na and Cl).

One of the most important books you will ever read, entitled "Sea salt's Hidden Powers," by Dr. Jacques de Langre, Ph.D., states that properly preserved sea salt (sun-dried) may prove to be the single most important factor in preserving our social sanity as well as being a critical element in avoiding absolute planetary panic in the coming years.

The benefits of well made and properly administered sea salt are too numerous to list here, but we recommend a thorough investigation of the history and use of salt; in particular the disastrous effects of switching to common "refined" table salt as it is found in the open market today.

For example:

Saline solutions have proven effective in treating and preventing influenza and other chronic disorders of the respiratory system, lungs and sinus areas.

Ocean salt has been used effectively in the treatment of chronic depression.

Ocean salt has been used effectively in the treatment of chronic lethargy and despondency.

Cleopatra carried both, Dead Sea waters and Dead Sea mineral salts [132] to and from The Temple of Hathor on a regular basis.[133] "King" Herod and Cleopatra

132 The Temple of Hathor was the principal abode and Temple used by Cleopatra. It was a major repository for ORMUS powder. Tons of a mysterious white powder was discovered under the altar there but the records of the discovery and the powder have since been altered and or destroyed. It was also a favorite haunt of Moses and his wife (Akhenaten & Nefertiti)

133 See books by Sir Lawrence Gardener, author of numerous books on the subject of ORMUS and MFKTZ and MANNA or 'shem-an-na' (- denoting cone-shaped or 'highward fire-stone').

A theory originally proposed by Sir Laurence Gardner in his book, "Genesis of the Grail Kings" is that ORMUS substances were made and kept at the Temple of Hathor. It was this same temple that Moses visited when he lead the children "out of Egypt". There he received the "tablets of stone" or perhaps more accurately, the Philosopher's Stone. Sir Gardner has suggested that a white powder discovered and examined by Flinders Petrie in 1903 is THE white powder ORMUS that was made in this temple. (In effect "laboratory") Below included is a passage from Petrie's official record of this find:

"Of this period [Amenemhat IV] a very interesting result was found beneath the later temple. Over a large area a bed of white wood-ashes is spread, of a considerable thickness. In the chamber O

shared exclusive access to the resources of the Dead Sea; they shipped great quantities of very large earthenware containers of the Dead Sea waters to Caesar and other Roman nobility on a regular basis. These waters were used for both medicinal and cosmetic purposes as well as for use in sacred rituals and sacred food substances (ORMUS manufacture).

Finally, if nothing else, let's be clear about one thing; ingesting ***The Stone (ORMUS) is a serious matter and not one to be taken lightly.*** Without proper periods of preparation ingesting ORMUS can yield the most unexpected and detrimental results. ORMUS accelerates growth in most instances, for better or for worse... And although (temporary) "cures" for various illnesses have been reported, those repairs to the DNA are only a passing phenomena, unless of course, the proper lifestyle is invoked; a lifestyle that will insure consistent and sustained benefits of ORMUS~induced repair. The ORMUS~induced architecture is fragile. One cannot use ORMUS as a "crutch" to make constant repairs to disease that is the direct result of consciously (knowingly-willfully) self-inflicted damage.

Unless the prerequisite activities have been completed in advance of consumption, we create monsters both figuratively and literally, within both the gross physical body and subtle light-body (or so-called astral realm).

Inside of every human being there are several sets of seed. The seed that you cultivate and bring to maturity will determine your countenance and presence. You have a garden to tend. Will you fill it with hardy weeds and vermin; or will it be filled with divinely inspired fruits and flowers? Your body is a temple. It is also a garden. A Temple Garden must be cultivated and tended with loving care and wisdom.

So the only question that remains is, "Will you take the time to perform the necessary actions required to prepare your Temple~Garden for the transfiguration?"

Or will you become the misguided Nephilim of the new world? Though the Nephilim were not the evil creatures as we have been led to believe, there were those among them who abused power just as we do today.

So... Will you wean yourself of the ancient addiction to blood and in so doing pave the path to heaven's gate? Or will you rush ahead blindly, in search of power, glory, instant health and immortality?

[of the later temple] there is a mass, 18 in. in thickness, underlying the walls and pillars, and therefore before the time of Tahutmes III [of the 18th Dynasty]. In chamber N it varies from 4 to 15 in. thick; west of the pylon it is from 3 to 12 in.; and it is found extending as far as chamber E or F with a thickness of 18 in. Thus it extends for over a hundred feet in length. In breadth it was found wherever the surface was protected by the building over it. All along the edge of the hill, bordering on the road of the XIIth dynasty past the steles, the ashes were found, all across the temple breadth, and out as far as the building of stone walls of chambers extends on the south. In all fully fifty feet in breadth. That none are found outside the built-over area is to be explained by the great denudation due to strong winds and occasional rain. That large quantities of glazed pottery have been entirely destroyed by these causes is certain; and a bed of light wood-ashe would be swept away much more easily. We must, therefore, suppose a bed of ashes at least 100 X 50 ft., very probably much wider, and varying from 3 to 18 in. thick, in spite of all the denudation which took place before the XVIIIth dynasty. There must be now on the ground about fifty tons of ashes, and these are probably the residue of some hundreds of tons..."

The single most Inconvenient Truth

Perhaps the single most *inconvenient truth* is one that even vice-president Al Gore, will have trouble swallowing (as will most Americans), despite all the *excellent* work of his contingency to date (and we are ***most grateful*** for all of his dedicated work performed to date!), is the fact that the cattle industry is indirectly possibly THE number one cause of deforestation and global warming. People's criminal and immoral appetite for the blood of other creatures is the number one cause of global warming. But in order to understand this one must look into the *domino effect* of carnivorous behavior patterns. This is an *inconvenient truth* that was conveniently omitted in the DVD version of his work on Global Warming, "An Inconvenient Truth."

Addicts live in a perpetual state of denial.

Let's face it, if a worldwide addiction is accepted as the norm, who would dare to accuse the teaming masses of-the-world of being addicts, (blood-lust addiction)? Addicts react violently and viciously to those who point out the addiction. When the majority of the people of the world are addicted, the angry mob is the majority. The few who have liberated themselves from the addiction can see clearly and without prejudice the plight of their fellow human beings, but there is little that they can do about it.

Walk into a dark, urban, back-alley and try telling the twenty or thirty crack junkies that they are all very, very sick and need help. If they don't kick your ass from here to kingdom-come, then their pimps and dealers certainly will. And if all else fails the corrupt element of the DEA, FBI and local police will soon have your ass in the slammer on some bogus trumped-up charge. Your fingerprints will be on a "throw down" weapon and a bag of white powder will mysteriously appear in your luggage or in your clothes-pockets.

But these guys are pussycats compared to the cattle industry and their buddies in the oil and gas industries.

"Resist not evil," A phrase wisely spoken!

We, as pacifist vegans, cannot go head-to-head with such power. But, Mother Nature can, and She will, in due course. She has been waiting patiently like any good mother for her children to come of age and recognize the error of their ways. We are given free will. We are free to deviate from the path of truth and freedom. We are free to make mistakes and to hopefully learn from them. But we have run out of time. If we do not turn back now and, as the Hopi Prophecy says, "walk the path of the Great Spirit," an event of cataclysmic proportions awaits us all.

This event will occur in our lifetimes. It is not something that "future generations" will experience. WE ARE that "future generation." We are the very ones, the very people who will feel the sting and pain of our reckless abandon; and this is as it should be. We will live-out our remaining days among the rubble, horror and suffering; as a direct result and consequence of our abuse and neglect of our Mother's extended Family, the Earth and ALL Her Children, fauna and flora alike.

It is only natural that we crave salt and minerals. It is fitting that we should acquire them, but not at the expense of our fellow creatures.

Mother Nature provides us two basic paradigms of lifestyle: vegan and carnivorous. The illusion is that the carnivores excel while the "dumb vegetarian" animals are but prey to their vicious and destructive methods. However, mankind has a destiny that exceeds all this. We are given an opportunity to behave, of our own free will, in a sophisticated manner. If we do, we will have our reward.

"All the world is stage..." as Shakespeare correctly notes.

Which role will you choose to play? Those who behave themselves will be given the ultimate award: the KEYS TO THE KINGDOM. The rest? Well...

Mary Magdalene's Mysterious & Magical EGG

In the second half of "ORMUS‡ The Secret Alchemy of Mary Magdalene ~ Revealed" ("Part B" sold separately as a sequel to this book) we will explain how the ORMUS is manufactured by natural means (i.e. How to produce and consume ORMUS in the wild, on an organic farm without the use of machinery or modern lab equipment). We will also explain how to perform an ORMUS-Ocean-Fast® in a totally natural environment, free of electronic equipment and mechanical devices[134]. All you need is some flint-rock and a bit of ancient, earth-friendly know-how!

"Verily, they shall have their reward."

May we ***all*** receive exactly what we deserve...
Peace be with you.
Emanatize the eschaton!

your friend,
William Hearth[135]

The Living Word of Godde refers to: "Those who Live the Law" as opposed to those who merely read the Law and talk about it. Hence Mary Magdalene, Jesus and their apostles *are* the *Living WORD* as opposed to those who would have us worship a "book" written by men. In truth~ the DNA which contains all the architecture of, and design of Life Itself, might be referred to as The Living Word. It is the CODE, the SCRIPT, the executable file that drives the operating system of our bio-computer and all of its peripheral devices.

Thou shalt not kill. Love is the answer.

134 http://ormus-ocean-fast.com
135 http://williamhearth.com

Excerpt from "THE HOLY STREAMS"
(Jesus is speaking to his disciples)

"I tell you truly, your body was made not only to breathe, and eat, and think, but it was also made to enter the Holy Stream of Life. And your ears were made not only to hear the words of men, the song of birds, and the music of falling rain, but they were also made to hear the Holy Stream of Sound. And your eyes were made not only to see the rising and setting of the sun, the ripple of sheaves of grain, and the words of the Holy Scrolls, but they were also made to see the Holy Stream of Light. One day your body will return to the Earthly Mother; even also your ears and your eyes. But the Holy Stream of Life, the Holy Stream of Sound, and the Holy Stream of Light, these were never born, and can never die. Enter the Holy Streams, even that Life, that Sound, and that Light which gave you birth; that you may reach the kingdom of the Heavenly Father and become one with him, even as the river empties into the far-distant sea.

More than this cannot be told, for the Holy Streams will take you to that place where words are no more, and even the Holy Scrolls cannot record the mysteries therein."

Original Hebrew and Aramaic Texts Translated
and edited by Edmond Bordeaux Szekely

A FINAL NOTE FROM THE AUTHOR

Make no mistake, whether by error in translation, a mismatch of lexicons, or by way of semantic interpretation, be it explicit, implied or otherwise:

I insist emphatically that:

We are not racists;
Heretics yes, but not racists.
We abhor all two legged "parasites" equally!
Regardless of race, creed, color,
Religion or geopolitical origin:
We might love you all, but we don't
necessarily have to like what you do!
Now~ Let's all have a good laugh at
ourselves, and then, *let's get busy!*
We have our work cut out for us, yes?

~ And Life is Victorious!~

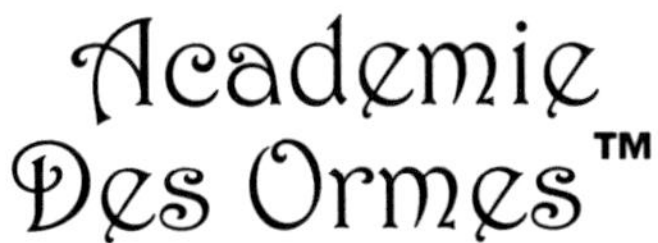

Index

Symbols

B

C

D

E

G

H

I

J

K

L

M

N

O

P

Q

S

T

Y

Z

TIMELINE OF ANCIENTS

700,000 B.C. - Earliest evidence for hominids in Egypt.

500,000 B.C. - Evidence for lower Paleolithic culture in Egypt.

250,000 - 90,000 B.C. - Earliest evidence found of buildings in Egypt -(Homo Erectus).

100,000 - 30,000 B.C. - Hunter and gatherer society (Homo-neathanderthalensis).

60,000 B.C. - The Nile defines present course.

30, 000 - 13,000 B.C. (?) - Humans enter the Americas.

15,000 B.C. - rising sea levels began to submerge coastal areas

15,000 - 10,000 B.C. - Cave paintings at Lascaux (France) created.

13,000 - 9,000 B.C. - Evidence of ritual burial in Egypt. Some evidence for agriculture in Egypt.

11,000 B.C. - first known evidence of domesticated dog (Middle East)

10,500 B.C. - first known pottery and beginnings of farming in Asia- (Jomon, Japan)

10,000 - c. 5,500 B.C. - Evidence for more consistent settlement along the banks of the Nile.

9,000 B.C. - beginnings of farming in the Middle East

8000 B.C.+ - Wheat and barley were cultivated in the Near East. This is a very important development in ancient civilization.

8,000 B.C. - evidence of grain storage and processing (Ain Mallaha, Mesopotamia)

7,800 B.C. - first evidence of domestication of emmer wheat (Tell Aswad, Mesopotamia)

7,500 B.C. - evidence of use of domesticated grains (Ali Kosh, Turkey)

7,000/8,000 B.C.

7,000/8,000 B.C. - use of wild rice (Southeast Asia, Southern China, Northern India)

7,000/8,000 B.C. - wild pigs and cattle were domesticated after sheep and goats (Middle East)

7,000 B.C.

7000 B.C.+ - Flax is cultivated is Syria and Turkey for fibers and seed. Agriculture in the Americas.

7,000 B.C. - early evidence of fishing communities (Southern Sahara, Africa)

7,000 B.C. - Chilies and avocados important along with squash, maize, and beans (Mesoamerica)

7,000 B.C. - small scale cultivation in New Guinea; taro becoming a dietary staple

7,000 B.C. - management of wild herds of goats (Beidha, Mesopotamia)

7,000 B.C. - domestication of goats (Jericho, Mesopotamia)

6,700 B.C. - permanent villages (Zagros Mountains, Turkey)

6,500 B.C.

6,500 B.C. - grain farming resulting from diffusion into Greece and Balkans (Europe)

6,500 B.C. - first use of metallurgy (Middle East)

6,500 B.C. - cultivation of wheat and barley along with use of sheep goats, and cattle (India)

6,000 B.C.

6,000 B.C. - millet farming (China)

6,000 B.C. - cattle domesticated (Sahara, Africa)

6,000 B.C. - wild African yam exploited through vegeculture (Africa)

6,000 B.C. - cultivation of millet in the Yellow River Valley (China)

6,000 B.C. - date palm important (southern Mesopotamia)

6,000 B.C. - villages with domesticated grains, sheep and goats and early pigs (Jarmo, Turkey)

6,000 B.C. - horse domesticated on the steppes of the Ukraine (Russia)

6,000 B.C. - domestication of chickens (China)

5,500 B.C. - first pottery (China)

5,000 B.C.

5,000 B.C. - farming continues to diffuse (Europe)

5,000 B.C. - cattle herding assumed great importance throughout the Sahara (Africa)

5,000 B.C. - grain farming (Egypt and eastern Sahara)

5,000 B.C. - wet rice farming (China)

4,500 B.C.

4,500 B.C. - copper (Europe)

4,500 B.C. - megalithic tombs in western Europe

4,500 B.C. - earliest evidence of maize cultivation (Mesoamerica)

4,500 B.C. - emmer wheat cross with local goatsface grass to produce bread wheat (India)

4,300 B.C. - cotton cultivation (Mesoamerica)

4,000 B.C.

4,000 B.C. - climate shift with Sahara becoming a desert

4,000 B.C. - first temple pyramids (South America)

4,000 B.C. - introduction of simple ox-drawn plow (Europe and Mesopotamia)

4,000 B.C. - pottery used and farming villages in the Indus Valley in India

4000 B.C. - 4-3 millennium B.C. - Ancient barrow (pit) archeological culture, formation of pra-Türks. Kurgans.

3,500 B.C. - copper metallurgy in southern Asia

3450 B.C. - World's first cities appear along banks of Tigris and Euphrates. They make up Uruk culture, with principal city Uruk, Biblical Erech. This culture invents writing and lunar calendar, uses metals, develops medicine, builds monumental architecture.

3450 B.C. - In Uruk culture no unified government evolves, and they remain independent for almost one thousand years

3,300 B.C. - first writing (Mesopotamia)

3,200 B.C. - second type of cotton domesticated in Americas (South America)

3200 B.C. - Sumerians are making use of wheeled transportation

3100 B.C. - Cuneiform writing emerges in Mesopotamia. This form of writing, involving wedge-shaped characters, is used to record first epics in world history, including Enmerkar and Lord of Aratta and first stories about Gilgamesh

3,100 B.C. - Narmer unites lower and upper Egypt, Reading on the unification of Egypt

3,000/4,000 B.C. - evidence for use of peaches, watermelons, water chestnuts and tubers (China)

3,000 B.C.

3,000 B.C. - first known pottery (South America)

3,000 B.C. - wild ass tamed in the Nile Valley (Egypt)

3,000 B.C. - llama and alpaca domesticated (South America)

3,000 B.C. - copper age in the Mediterranean area begins

2,700 B.C. - silkworms used in sericulture (China)

2700 B.C. - Sumerian King, Gilgamesh, rules city of Uruk, which has now grown to a population of more than 50,000. Gilgamesh is subject of many epics, including Sumerian "Gilgamesh and Enkidu in Nether World" and Babylonian "Epic of Gilgamesh"

2650 B.C. - step pyramid (Giza in Egypt)

2,500/3,000 B.C. - potatoes were domesticated in the Andes (South America)

2,500 B.C.

2,500 B.C. - cities of Mahenjo-Daro and Harappa (Indus Valley, India)

2,500 B.C. - bronze (Southeast Asia)

2,500 B.C. - coca was cultivated adding vitamin C and calcium (South America)

2,500 B.C. - breadfruit tended in plots (Southeast Asia and Philippines)

2,500 B.C. - cattle and goats raised for milk as well as meat (Mesopotamia)

2,500 B.C. - pull plows with oxen and wild asses (Mesopotamia)

2,500 B.C. - rise of Kush in Ethiopia

2,400 B.C.

2,400 B.C. - first temple-platforms (South America)

2,400 B.C. - collapse of the Old Kingdom in Egypt

2320 B.C. - Sargon conquers independent city-states of Sumer and institutes central government

2130 B.C. - Sumer regains its independence from Akkadian rule, though it does not revert back to independent city-states. At this time, Sumer is ruled from important city of Ur

2100 B.C. - Sumerian King List is written, recording all kings and dynasties ruling Sumer from earliest times. According to this list, Eridu is named as earliest settlement, a claim that seems to be confirmed by archeological evidence

2,100 B.C.

2,100 B.C. - Ziggurat built at Ur of the Chaldees (Mesopotamia)

2,100 B.C. - Stonehenge reaches its final form (Europe)

2,000 B.C.

2,000 B.C. - earliest Minoan palace constructed (Crete)

2,000 B.C. - first city-states in Anatolia (Turkey)

2,000 B.C. - guinea pigs a common domesticated animal (South America)

2,000 B.C. - chickens common in India as a result of diffusion (India)

2,000 B.C. - introduction of iron into southern Asia

2,000 B.C. - bronze usage in southeast Asia

2000 B.C. - 2000-1600 B.C. - Old Babylonian period begins after collapse of Sumer, probably due to increase in soil salt content thereby making farming difficult. Weakened by poor crops, lack of surplus goods, Sumerians are conquered by Amorites, situated in Babylon

2000 B.C. - Consequently, center of civility shifts north. Though they preserve most of Sumerian culture, Amorites introduce their Semitic language, an early ancestor to Hebrew, into region

1900 B.C. - Epic of Gilgamesh is redacted from Sumerian sources and written in Semitic language. Thus, though Gilgamesh was Sumerian, his Epic is Babylonian

1,900 B.C. - first true cities (China)

1,876 B.C. - first recorded eclipse (China), Reading on the first recordings of eclipses

1,800 B.C.

1,800 B.C. - earliest cities of the Indus Valley abandoned (India)

1,800 B.C. - rise of the Hittite Kingdom

1766 B.C. - Eventually recorded Chinese traditions tell of Kia, 17th member of old Chinese Hia dynasty, dethroned due to evil ways. His son Sunni went with 500 members of his Hia nationality to Hun relatives. Hia still has many common words with Altaic languages

1766 B.C. - Oldest Türkic words are in Chinese annual chronicles noting cultural and political events. Hsiung-nu words tanry, kut, byorü, ordu, tug, kylych etc are oldest monuments of Türkish language. State rulers' endoethnonym is Hun, Türkic "man, male, people"

1763 B.C. - Amorite King, Hammurabi, conquers Sumer. He writes Code of Laws containing 282 rules including principles of "an eye for an eye" and "let buyer beware". It is one of first codes of law in world history, predated only by Laws of Lipit-Ishta

1750 B.C. - Hammurabi empire lasts for another one hundred and fifty years, until 1600, when Kassites (Kas=Türk. 'mountain'), a non-Semitic people, conquer most of Mesopotamia with help of light chariot warfare

1750 B.C. - Semitic group of nomads migrate from Sumer to Canaan and then on to Egypt. They are led by a caravan trader, Patriarch Abraham, who will become father of Israel nation

1,700 B.C.

1,700 B.C. - destruction of earliest Minoan palaces (Crete)

1,700 B.C. - chenopods and sunflowers domesticated (eastern North America)

1,700 B.C. - imported cloves from India found in Mesopotamia

1,640 B.C. - Hyksos invaders occupy Nile delta (Egypt)

1,600 B.C.

1,600 B.C. - Shang Dynasty of kings begins (China)

1,600 B.C. - Hittites capture Babylan

1,550 B.C.

1,550 B.C. - New Kingdom begins (Egypt)

1,550 B.C. - Citadel founded at Mycenae (Greece)

1,500 B.C. - manioc wide spread root crop (Caribbean)

1500 B.C. - 15-9 centuries B.C. - Frame culture. Kurgans.

1500 B.C. - First evidence of widespread organized pastoral nomadic economy in Bronze Age Andronovo culture (mid-second to early first millennium B.C.), found throughout steppe. Settlements of up to forty rectangular, semi-subterranean dwellings found at Atasu, Karkaralinsk and Alekseevka in Kazakhstan. In Dzhezkazgan and Zyryanovskfound are mines from this period

1,450 B.C. - Minoan palaces destroyed (Crete)

1,400 B.C. - phonetic alphabet (Mesopotamia)

1390 B.C. - First elements of Hun state in highlands of Ordos

1,323 B.C. - death of Tutankhamen (Egypt)

1,300 B.C. - fall of Knossos in Crete

1,200 B.C.

1,200 B.C. - Olmec culture at San Lorenzo (Mexico)

1,200 B.C. - soybeans introduced throughout China (native Manchuria)

1,200 B.C. - age of the Mycenaean palaces

1200 B.C. - First Hun state in highlands of Ordos

1200 B.C. - Cimmerians (Turk. Kam-er, Kimer - "river man", akin to "Suv-ar", "Bulakar" ("Bolkar, Bulgar"), "Sub-ar", "Suv-ar", "Shum-er") begin to occupy Pontic Steppe

Chou Dynasty, 1050-256 BC Lao Tzu ~ Tao Te Ching father of Taoism

1,100 B.C.

1,100 B.C. - culturally distinct peoples in the Middle East have their own pantheon of deities

1,100 B.C. - feudalism in China

1,027 B.C. - Anyang falls in rebellion (China)

1,000 B.C.

1,000 B.C. - colonization of Samoa (Pacific)

1,000 B.C. - rise of Meroe/Aksum in Ethiopia

900 B.C.

900 B.C. - Olmec center of La Venta founded (Mexico)

900 B.C. - beans and squash along with maize diffuse north (North America)

800 B.C.

800 B.C. - use of an alphabet adopted (Greece)

800 B.C. - rise of the Greek city-states

800 B.C. - Assirian chronicles report about Cimmerian invasion to countries of Transcaucasus and Near East. Beginning of Scythian domination in East-European steppes. Assyrians called Cimmerians Gimirrai (Hebrew Gomer; Gen. XI)

800 B.C. - Plinius of Scythian origins: "Ultra sunt Scytharum populi, Persae illos Sacas in universum appellavere a proxima gente, antiqui Arameos"

800 B.C. - Hesiod, 7th Century B.C., writes: Inventors of bronze working were Scythians. Early Mesopotamian name of metal Zubur, indicates that northern Mesopotamian Subartuan's or a people of region were indeed inventors of process.

800 B.C. - Herodotus on origin of Scythians from area of eastern Anatolia: "nomad Scythians living in Asia (once only Near East) were attacked by Sarmatians and were forced to cross Araxes (modern Turkish Aras) and wander to land of Cimmerians."

800 B.C. - Greeks associated invention of iron working with northern Mesopotamian and Anatolian Scythian tribes like Kalybs tribe which gave steel its name in many early European languages. In time Sarmatians and Yazig absorb Kalybs.

800 B.C. - Kalybs are absorbed by Sarmatians and Yazig, via Yazig cavalry taken by Romans to Britain and were foundation of King Arthur myths of Ex-Calibur, and sword myths, which are all early Anatolian traditions.

800 B.C. - Sword myths traditions are all early Anatolian, are also found in Hun and Magyar traditions and mentioned by Herodotus amongst early Scythians.

770 B.C.

770 B.C. - fall of the Zhou Dynasty of Kings (China)

770 B.C. - beginning of the Spring and Autumn period in China

750 B.C.

750 B.C. - rise of Nubian Kingdom of Kush (East Africa)

750 B.C. - first gold working (South America)

750 B.C. - deteriorating climate in Europe

750 B.C. - cattle become increasingly important (Europe)

750 B.C. - Assyrian economy based on fertile, extensive agriculture (Middle East)

750 B.C. - trade through Mediterranean

722 B.C. - Pi-van moves capital to the East to Loi or Tsyaju, supposedly because capital with some Chjou territory was under "barbarians" because of disturbances. Later Tsin rulers Syan-gun and Ben-gun captured this territory. Only a part of land returned to Chjou

710 B.C. - In late 8th century B.C. - Cimmerian and Scythian troops fought against As-

syrian king Sargon II, and at end of 6th century B.C. - conflict arose between Scythians and Achaemenian King Darius I

700 B.C. - age of Homer

700 B.C. - Scythians replace Cimmerians in Steppe region

700 B.C. - Cimmerian tombs of their kings were shown on Tyras (Dniestr), and on south-east another group threatened Assyrians

700 B.C. - Scyths (Assyrian Ashguzai, Heb. Ashkenax, fr. Türk. As - "nomad", Güz, Kish, Kiji - "tribe, people") whom Assyrians welcomed as allies and used against Cimmerians, against Medes and even against Egypt. Hence references to Scyths in Hebrew prophet (Jer. IV.3, VI. 7).

685 B.C. - 685 - 643 B.C. - Rule in Tsi of Huan - hun

679 B.C. - Huan - hun organizes a congress of rulers inTsi, taking that right from Chjou

659 B.C. - 659 - 621 Rule of Mu-hun in Tsin

653 B.C. - Scythian interregnum in Median Dynasty history. Herodotus dating of this event remains uncertain but traditionally it is seen as falling between reigns of Phraortes and Cyaxares and as covering years 653 to 625 B.C..

633 B.C. - Scythian invasion to Transcaucasus and Fore-Asia.

612 B.C. - Assyrian Empire falls (Middle East)

604 B.C. - report birth of Lao-Tzu, founder of Taoism (China)

600/500 B.C.

600/500 B.C. - iron used to forge plows, hoes, spades, sickles (China)

600/500 B.C. - Greek colonies become major agricultural producers

600/500 B.C. - sorghum and millet certainly grown western Africa (Africa)

600/500 B.C. - Warring States period in China

600 B.C. - F. Altheim "Das Alte Iran" writes that Iranian Avesta's most archaic texts, Gathas, are still not understood by today's linguists.

600 B.C. - R. Stiehlel writes, it is quite obvious that language of old Avesta is closely tied to ancient Altaic languages. Since newcomers to Iran joined older settled inhabitants often associated with Scythians, Türks and Finno-Ugrians, and borrowed much

600 B.C. - Many of local people were Iranianized, today we call certain Scythian nations as Iraninan in origin. Much of Persian literature in Persepolis is not in Iranian but in aboriginals' Elamite language that up until last century was also called Scythian

600 B.C. - About 500-600 B.C. - Hungarians moved south to steppes, where, according to linguistic evidence, they took animal breeding from Chuvash people, as a high proportion of words specific to agriculture in Hungarian language are of Chuvash origin

599 B.C. - birth of Mahavira, founder of Jainism (India)

570 B.C. - birth of Siddhartha Gautma (the Buddha) founder of Buddhism (India)

551 B.C. - birth of Confucius (China)

539 B.C. - Babylon destroyed by Persians (Middle East)

521 B.C. - Darius I "the Great" succeeds Cambyses as emperor of Persia. He engages in many large building programs, including a system of roads. In addition, he institutes first postal system

520 B.C. - 6th cent. B.C. - Invasion of Transoxiana by Achaemenids of Persia under Darius I and Cyrus

516 B.C. - Darius' expedition (516 - 513 B.C.) against Scythians in N. Pontic is described in great detail by Herodotus, who provided first and perhaps most penetrating description of Europian great nomad empire

510 B.C. - Hecataeus (6th century B.C.) map showing Scyths

512 B.C. - Scythian war with army of Persian king Darius I Hystaspos invading Scythia

500 B.C.

500 B.C. - first iron (Sub-Saharan Africa)

500 B.C. - Bantu-speaking farmers begin moving southward (Africa)

500 B.C. - Monte Alban founded (Oaxaca, Mexico)

500 B.C. - Herodotus mentioned Sarmatians living to north of Scythians of N. Pontic regions and not close to their old homelands along Araxes, Sarmatians must have been a long time thorn in Scythian side.

500 B.C. - Herodotus: "Anyone who does business with Scyths (Sakae) needs seven interpreters speaking seven languages"

500 B.C. - Scythians who make this journey (via Budini (Beçen/Peçenek, Budun=Türk. "clan, nation, people"), Thyssagetae (Tis-Saka-it =Türk. outer Sakas), Iyrcae (Yürük=Türk. nomad), Argippaeans (Arik-bay=Türk. pure+ bay=rich man) communicate with inhabitants by means of seven interpreters and seven languages.

500 B.C. - Sarmate (Sauromatae, Sarmate=Türk. 'with sac') speak language of Scythia, live W of Palus Maeotis (Azov Sea). W of Tanais (Don) and fifteen days' journey N of Sarmate, dwell Budini, "blue-eyed and bright red-haired", whose territory is thickly wooded with trees of every kind

500 B.C. - Persepolis inscription text is "Darius Hystapes (522-486) rex popularum bonorum posui. Hi adorationem igni mihi attulere: Choana, Media, Babilon, Asyria, Guthrata, Armenia, Cappadocia, Sapardia [Sabir], Hunae."

499 B.C. - beginning of the Persian Wars involving the Greek city-states (lasts until 479)

499 B.C. - Athens and Eretria supported an Ionian revolt against Persian rule.

496 B.C. - 497 B.C. - Sophocles (d.406 B.C. - E), the 2nd Greek dramatist after Aeschylus, was born. He is considered by some as the greatest of the Greek dramatists. His works include: "Oedipus Rex" and "Antigone."

496 B.C. - 406 B.C. - Sophocles added valuable elements to the developing tragic drama. His work involved all men in the tragic elements of life. His work included the drama Philoctetes. It was about how the Greeks needed the aged Philoctetes and his magic bow to capture Troy, but had exiled him to a remote island. They send Neoptolemus, son of Achilles, to secure the bow by deceit and trickery. In 1990 the play was rewritten by Seamus Heaney, 1995 Nobel poet laureate, as "The Cure at Troy."

495 B.C. - 429 B.C. - Pericles, Athenian leader during the early years of the Peloponnesian Wars.

494 B.C. - In Rome the first victory of the plebeian class over the patricians resulted in an agreement between the two classes to allow the plebeians to elect officers, and tribunes with the power to veto any unlawful acts of the magistrates.

492 B.C. - Darius put his son-in-law, Mardonius, in charge of a Persian expedition against Athens and Eretria, but the loss of the fleet in a storm off Mount Athos forced him to abandon the operation.

490 B.C. - First Persian attack on Greece. Greeks led by Miltiades defeated the Persians at the Battle of Marathon. Pheidipiddes, a hemerodromi or long-distance foot messenger, was dispatched to run 26 miles from marathon to Athens to announce the victory. He reached Athens and proclaimed: "Rejoice! We conquer!" The he dropped dead. In the Battle of Marathon Darius the Great of Persia was defeated by the Greeks. The Greeks initiated the war when Persia, the strongest power in western Asia, established rule over Greek-speaking cities in Asia Minor. [see Sep 12]

490 B.C. - Phidippides of Athens set out on his 26-mile run that inspired the Marathon. Phidippides was sent to seek troops from Sparta to help against the invading Persian army. The Spartans were unwilling to help, until the next full moon, due to religious laws. On Sept. 4th, Phidippides returned the 26 miles Marathon without Spartan troops.

490 B.C. - A Persian force under Datis, a Mede, destroyed Eretria and enslaved its inhabitants but was defeated by the Athenians at Marathon.

490 B.C. - Athenian and Plataean Hoplites commanded by General Miltiades drove back a Persian invasion force under General Datis at Marathon.

490 B.C. - 479 B.C. - The Greco-Persian War is commonly regarded as one of the most significant wars in all of history. The Greeks emerged victorious and put an end to the possibility of Persian despotism.

c490 B.C. - 430 B.C. - The Greek philosopher Zeno of Elea proposed a number of paradoxes to support the claim of Parmenides that the world was a motionless, unchanging unity. The race between Achilles and the tortoise is one example.

487 B.C. - Greek dramatist Euripides, was born. He wrote "Medea" and "The Trojan Women." His plays used a device called "Deus ex Machina," literally "God from a machine." Today the term refers to sudden events that come from nowhere to advance the plot.

486 B.C. - Darius, ruler of Persia, died. His preparations for a 3rd expedition against

Greece were delayed by an insurrection in Egypt. He was succeeded by his son Xerxes.

486 B.C. - 465 B.C. - Xerxes the Great, king of Persia, ruled Egypt as the 3rd king of the 27th Dynasty. His ruled over extended from India to the lands below the Caspian and Black seas, to the east coast of the Mediterranean including Egypt and Thrace. Persia's great cities Sardis, Ninevah, Babylon, and Susa were joined by the Royal Road. East of Susa was Persopolis, a vast religious monument. To the north of Persia were the Scythians

c485 B.C. - Athenian democracy was accompanied by an intellectual revolution with beginnings in Sophism. Sophists situated ethics and politics within philosophical discourse, which before was limited to physics and metaphysics alone. Protagoras, the leading Sophist, stated: "Man is the measure of all things." For him all truth, goodness, and beauty are relative to man's necessities and inquiries. In opposition to the Sophists emerged Socrates, Plato and Aristotle, each of whom offered alternatives to the Sophist's relativism.

484 B.C. - 420 B.C. - Herodotus was the first historian to lay out a coherent story. He authored the 9-book history of the Graeco-Persian War: "Researches into the Causes and Events of the Persian Wars," and the "The Histories of Herodotus." He also wrote a book dedicated to his travels through Egypt.

484 B.C. - 420 B.C. - Herodotus claimed that the Etruscans were Lydians who had immigrated to Italy from Asia Minor. But modern scholars believe the Etruscans evolved from an indigenous population of Iron Age farmers of the Villanovan culture.

484 B.C. - 420 B.C. - The Greeks always called the Etruscans the Tyrrhenians, after the prince Tyrrhenus who, according to Herodotus, led them to the shores of Etruria.

484 B.C. - 420 B.C. - Herodotus mentioned gold-digging ants and that some were kept at the palace of the Persian king. It was later learned that the Persian word for marmot is equivalent to mountain ant, and that marmots in the Dansar plain of northern Pakistan bring up gold dust from their burrows.

484 B.C. - 406 B.C. - Euripides was an Athenian tragedian who brought the gods and heroes down to earth. He presented pictures of human life that were sometimes tragic, sometimes comic, but always and undeniably real.

481 B.C. - 221 B.C. - The Waring States period of the Chou Dynasty. The states of Ch'in and Ch'u emerged as the primary competitors in the struggle to found an empire. During this period a 4-tiered class structure emerged consisting of lesser nobility (including scholars), the peasant farmers, the artisans, and the merchants, who held the lowest position in society. This was also known as the period of the Hundred Schools of Thought with the emergence of several schools of political philosophy that included: Confucianism, Taoism, Mohism and Legalism.

c483 B.C. - Gautama Siddhartha Buddha, the founder of Buddhism, died.

481 B.C. - Warring States period begins, lasts until 221 B.C. (China)

480 B.C. - The Persian army defeated Leonidas and his Spartan army at the battle Thermopylae, Persia.

480 B.C. - Themistocles and his Greek fleet won one of history's first decisive naval victories over Xerxes' Persian force off Salamis. Persia under Xerxes attacked Greece. Athens got burned but the Athenian fleet under Themistocles trapped and destroyed the Persian navy at Salamis. Phoenician squadrons were at the heart of Xerxes' fleet; the king of Sidon was among his admirals. 31 states of the Hellenic League fought Xerxes.

480 B.C. - Greeks defeated the Persians in a naval battle at Salamis.

480 B.C. - Xerxes performed a sacrifice at the site of Troy on his way to battle the Greeks.

480 B.C. - The Acropolis temples were destroyed during the Persian invasion. The ruins lay untouched for 30 years until 447, when Pericles initiated a reconstruction program.

c480 B.C. - Vardhamana Mahavira, the semi-legendary teacher who reformed older doctrines and established Jainism, died. He is regarded as the 24th and latest Tirthankara, one of the people to have attained personal immortality through enlightenment. Jainism was founded as a dualistic, ascetic religion as a revolt against the caste system and the vague world spirit of Hinduism.

c480 B.C. - Herodotus said marijuana was cultivated in Scythia and Thrace, where inhabitants intoxicated themselves by breathing the vapors given off when the plant was roasted on white-hot stones.

480 B.C. - 406 B.C. - Euripides, Greek tragic dramatist. He authored "Medea," "Alcestis," "The Cyclops," "The Trojan Woman," and "The Bacchae." His drama dealt with situations that were analogous to human life. In 1997 Greek archeologists claimed to have discovered the island cave where he worked.

479 B.C. - Aug 27, A combined Greek army stopped the Persians at the battle at Plataea.

479 B.C. - In China the philosopher Mo-tzu (d.438 B.C. -), founder of Mohism, was born. He taught a message of universal love and compassion for the common plight of ordinary people.

478 B.C. - Athens joined with other Greek states in the formation of the Delian League. The League continued even after the end of the Greco-Persian War and transformed into a naval empire with Athens as its leader.

475-221 B.C. - The Waring States (Greek) period.

474 B.C. - The Etruscans were routed by the Greeks of Syracuse in a sea battle off Cumae near Naples.

c470 B.C. - Hanno the Navigator, Carthaginian sailor, described his encounters with "hairy, wild people" on the west coast of equatorial Africa.

c470 B.C. - 469 B.C. - Jun 5, Socrates (d.399 B.C. -) was born in Athens. He served as an infantryman during the Peloponnesian War between Athens and Sparta. A sophist (teacher of philosophy), he claimed not to know anything for certain and used the interrogatory method for teaching. He left no written works. He was a major critic of popular belief in Athens and was the protagonist of Plato's dialogues.

469 B.C. - Sophocles (d.406 B.C. -), the 2nd Greek dramatist after Aeschylus, was born. He is considered by some as the greatest of the Greek dramatists. His works include: "Oedipus Rex" and "Antigone."

467 B.C. - A meteorite crashed to earth and convinced Greek philosopher Anaxagoras that heavenly bodies were not divine beings. He became the world's earliest figure to be indicted for atheism.

465 B.C. - Xerxes the Great, king of Persia, was assassinated.

465 B.C. - 424 B.C. - Artaxerxes, son of Xerxes I, ruled Persia in the Achaemenis dynasty and Egypt as the 4th king of the 27th Dynasty. The books of Ezra and Nehemiah remember his warmly because he authorized their revival of Judaism.

461-429 B.C. - In Athens this was the "Age of Pericles." Athenian democracy reached perfection and the court systems were completed. A jury system was put in place with the jury serving as the absolute authority in judicial matters.

460 B.C. - Herodotus turned back in frustration at the first cataract at Aswan. He stated: "Of the source of the Nile no one can give any account."

460 B.C. - Democritus born in Abdera, SW Thrace. First proposed theory of atoms as the basic particle of all matter. Only bare fragments of his work survive.

460 B.C. - 400 B.C. - Thucydides lived about this time. As author of the History of the Peloponnesian Wars, he inserted into his history speeches by important war figures that he made up. He also wrote on the Athenian slaughter of the Melians. He is associated with the historical view that cycles of growth, expansion and decline are a natural part of international life.

455 B.C. - Artaxerxes, ruler of Persia, put down a revolt in Egypt.

c450 B.C. - The golden plate known as the "Phiale Mesomphalos" was made.

450 B.C. - Herodotus World Map (ca. 450 B.C.) shows Agathirsi (Agach-ir=Türk. forest+people), Scythians and Massagets, Malanchleni, Budini and Geloni, Thissagets and Jurcae

450 B.C. - In Issyk fifth-century B.C. - Sak's kurgan in town in Kazakhstan near Lake Issyk (Issiq), in a royal tomb, in 1970 is found a flat silver drinking cup jar with Türkic 'Issyk' Inscription in Türkic alphabet, attesting that Sak-Massagetan tribes spoke Türkic

450 B.C. - In Issyk kurgan all human skeletons found in graves showed race characteristics very similar to today's Anatolian Turks, with no trace of Mongoloid features at all (Larousse)

450 B.C. - Roman law was codified in the twelve tablets. The law allowed the plebeians to have knowledge of their relationship to the law. The plebeians were primar-

ily farmers, craftsmen and tradesmen with foreign backgrounds. The patricians made up the aristocracy.

450 B.C. - Herodotus journeyed to the Scythian lands north of the Black Sea and heard tales of women who were fierce killers of men. He named these women "Amazons," from a Greek word meaning without one breast. Legend had it that one breast was removed in order to carry quivers of arrows more conveniently.

447 B.C. - Athens under Pericles initiated a reconstruction program that included the construction of the Parthenon on the Acropolis.

438 B.C. - The Parthenon was built atop the Acropolis in Athens, Greece.

432 B.C. - Meton devised a 19-year "Metatonic cycle" to reconcile the lunar and solar years.

431 B.C. - Euripides wrote his tragedy "Medea," based on the legend of the sorceress Medea, daughter of Aeëtes, King of Colchis, and wife of Jason, whom she assisted in obtaining the Golden Fleece (ORMUS).

431-404 B.C. - The Peloponnesian war between Athens and Sparta. It was finally won by Sparta. Athenian trade was destroyed and democracy was overthrown as Athens surrendered to Sparta as a subject state. Sparta assumed dominance over the Greek world and replaced many democracies with oligarchies.

430 B.C. - Thucydides in his history of the Peloponnesian War tells how the Spartans attempted to destroy the city of Plataia with a flaming mixture of pitch and sulfur.

430 B.C. - 410 B.C. - A mysterious disease killed one-third of the Athenian population.

427 B.C. - Plato (d.347 B.C.) - Greek philosopher, was born. His work included the "Republic," and the dialogues "Critias" and "Timaeus" in which he mentioned the island empire of Atlantis. He claimed that an Egyptian priest confided information about Atlantis to Solon, the Athenian legislator, whose memoirs Plato claimed to have read.

424 B.C. - Thucydides in his history of the Peloponnesian War tells how the Spartans used pitch and sulfur against the Athenians at Delium. In this 7th year of the war unexpected Boeotian horsemen charged on the right flank of Athenian hoplite column causing many Athenians to flee. Socrates and Alcibiades retreated into the woods and survived.

410 B.C. - Darius II, ruler of Persia, quelled a revolt in Media but lost control of Egypt. He secured much influence in Greece in the Peloponnesian War through the diplomacy of Pharnabazus, Tissaphernes, and Cyrus the Younger.

407 B.C. - Euripides wrote "The Bacchae" while residing at the court of the king of Macedon. He had left Athens in the last years of its war against Sparta. The play dealt with the violent introduction of the cult of Dionysos into the city of Thebes.

405 B.C. - Persian rule of Egypt ended.

404 B.C. - 399 B.C. - Amyrtaios, believed to be a Libyan, ruled Egypt following the death of Darius II from Sais as the 1st and only ruler of the 28th Dynasty.

404-338 B.C. - Sparta is not able to persist in the rule of Greece. Power over Greece shifts from Sparta to Thebes and then to numerous other city-states, none able to maintain rule over such a large empire.

403-321 B.C. - During the Waring States period in China, the Pu people buried wedged wooden coffins into the cliffs a 1,000 feet above the Yangtze River in Jingzhu Gorge.

401 B.C. - In the Battle of Cunaxa Cyrus attempted to oust his brother Artaxerxes from rule over Babylon. Greek forces, hired to help Cyrus, were left stranded when Cyrus died. The Greek army elected Xenophon to lead them back home.

400 B.C. - 250CE - The Yayoi culture is identified by its pottery. Mongoloid people from Korea entered Japan and mixed with the older Jomon populations.

c400 B.C. - The first temple known to be dedicated to the "supreme" Zeus was constructed about this time. In 2003 a 2,400 B.C. - year-old headless marble statue was found along with 14 columns depicting eagles, one of the symbols of Hypsistos Zeus, the chief deity of ancient Greece.

400 B.C. - Sarmatians take leadership over Scythians.

400 B.C. - 300 - In China the Zhuangzi, the 2nd great Taoist text, was compiled.

400 B.C. - In India Panini's "Sutra," the earliest Sanskrit grammar, was written.

c400 B.C. - 300 B.C. - The Greeks founded Neopolis (Naples), their "New City" in the 4th century B.C. - They carved blocks of tufa stone to build the city structures and left behind cavernous quarries. Centuries later the Romans turned the quarries into cisterns and connected them with tunnels. Water was brought in from the Serino River in the hills of Avellino, 96 miles to the north. This provided the water supply until 1883.

400 B.C. - 300 B.C. - The Chinese began suffering from fierce attacks of nomadic herdsmen, the Hsiung-nu, from the north and west. They began to build parts of what came to be called the Great Wall for protection.

c400 B.C. - In a wave of Celtic expansion tribes poured through the Alps into Italy.

400 B.C. - By this time the Sarmatians were occupying outposts of the Roman empire in the Balkans.

c400 B.C. - A nomadic tribal chief was buried at Pazyryk in southern Siberia. This tomb in the Altay Mountains was later found and discovered to contain wool fabrics, a carpet, a saddle of felt and leather, felt figures of swans, a horse harness with carved wooden rams' heads. and a fleece in near perfect condition. The origin of the carpet with its 1,125,000 knots is under debate. It might have come from Assyria or Iran.

400 B.C. - 300 - Aeneas the Tactician in his siege craft manual advised generals defending city walls to throw burning bags of linen fibers treated with sulfur and pitch on the enemy.

400 B.C. - 300 B.C. - The Greek writer Ephorus referred to the Celts, Scythians, Persians and Libyans as the four great barbarian peoples in the known world.

c400 B.C. - 300 Praxiteles sculpted Aphrodite, the 1st known sculpture of a nude woman.

400 B.C. - 300 - Theophrastus, a natural historian, wrote a treatise on pyrophoric minerals.

c400 B.C. - 200 B.C. - The "creative" phase of classical Greek geometry.

399 B.C. - Socrates was condemned to death on charges of corrupting the youth and introducing new gods into Greek thought. A tribunal of 501 citizens found Socrates guilty of the charge of impiety and corruption of youth. Socrates (469-399 B.C. -) had been the teacher of two leaders who were held responsible for the Greek's loss to Sparta in the Peloponnesian War (431-404 B.C. -). Plato's Apology, Crito, and Phaedo describe Socrates' trial, imprisonment and death.

399 B.C. - 393 B.C. - Nepherites served as the 1st ruler of Egypt's 29th Dynasty. During his rule he entered into an alliance with Sparta against the Persians. A gift ship to Sparta was lost at Rhodes, which had defected to the Persians.

396 B.C. - Sacking of Veio (Etruscan city), after a ten-year siege, ended the city's long conflict with Rome.

395 B.C. - Agesilaos of Sparta ravaged northwestern Turkey.

387 B.C. - Rampaging bands of Celts captured Rome and then settled down to a life of agriculture in the Po Valley.

384 B.C. - Aristotle (d.322 B.C. -) was born in Stagira, Macedonia. He entered Plato's Academy at age 17. After several years as tutor to Alexander the Great he returned to Athens and founded the Lyceum Academy.

382 B.C. - 336 B.C. - Philip II of Macedon, king of Macedonia (359-336), and father of Alexander the Great.

380 B.C. - Academy at Athens founded by Plato (Greece)

373 B.C. - 288 B.C. - In China the Confucianist Meng-Tzu (Mencius) lived. He departed from the ideas of Confucius by positing a theory of just rebellion against immoral rulers.

371 B.C. - The ruling class of Sparta, dedicated to war, were decisively defeated in the Battle of Leuctra by the Thebans under Epaminondas.

371 B.C. - 289 B.C. - Mencius, Chinese philosopher

c369 B.C. - c286 B.C. - Chuang-tzu (Zhuang Zhou), Chinese philosopher and writer. His work included the spiritual masterpiece "Inner chapters." "Rewards and punishments are the lowest form of education."

367 B.C. - In Rome the first plebian consul was elected to the assembly. The Plebeians also became eligible to serve as lesser magistrates, formerly a position reserved for the aristocratic class. Because an ancient custom allowed promotion from the magistracy to the Senate, the patrician-dominated Senate was broken.

367 B.C. - 348 B.C. - Aristotle studied under Plato at the Academy in Athens. He left Athens to travel for 12 years and returned to Macedonia where he tutored Alexander, son of Philip for 3 years.

367 B.C. - 283 B.C. - Ptolemy I (Soter), founder of the Macedonian dynasty of Egypt. He ruled Egypt from 306-285.

364 B.C. - Gan De, noted Chinese astronomer, reported a viewing of Jupiter and one of its 16 moons.

363 B.C. - Artaxerxes III (Ochus), son of Artaxerxes II, became king of Persia.

359-336 Philip II ruled the Kingdom of Macedonia. He founded Plovdiv, Bulgaria.

355 B.C. - Alexander the Great (d.323 B.C. -) was born about this time. Alexander III later married a barbarian princess, Roxana, the daughter of the Bactrian chief Oxyartes. Alexander also married the daughter of Darius, whom he defeated in 333, and a Sogdian princess while staying firmly attached to his comrade, Hephaistion.

354 B.C. - Demosthenes wrote a series of speeches, later called the Philippics, which urged Athenians to defend the city against Philip of Macedon.

350 B.C. - First evidence of humans in southwest Colorado: corn pollen. Nomadic hunter-gatherers planted crops in the spring, then left to forage and hunt over the summer, returning in the fall to harvest and seek shelter in caves for the winter. They made baskets of yucca fibers, sometimes waterproofed with pitch from piñon pine.

350 B.C. - Babylonian tables of astronomical numbers regularly use zero.

c350 B.C. - The Anasazi were probably living in Colorado caves. Their present name comes from a Navajo word meaning "the ancient ones" or "the ancient enemy." They observed the Metonic cycles and their homes were all aligned to greet the Lamas Moon annually.

350 B.C. - Macedonian burials in kurgans

c350 B.C. - In Greece the new philosophy of the Cynics emerged led by Diogenes. He argued against conventional life and that people should live naturally and strive for self-sufficiency.

c350 B.C. - Temples in Greece began to be used by ill worshippers hoping for a cure from the gods. These were later considered as the first hospitals.

c350 B.C. - The kingdom of Illyria emerged in the region of Shkoder in what is now Albania.

350 B.C. - 338 B.C. - In China Shang Yang ruled the Ch'in Dynasty. He operated against the assumptions of a theory of absolute aggression justified by the "School of Law."

348-345 B.C. - Aristotle lived and taught in Assos, (later Behramkale), Turkey, before he was summoned to teach Alexander in Macedonia.

347 B.C. - Plato (b.427 B.C. -), the most distinguished student of Socrates, died. His real name was Aristocles. Plato meant broad and he was known to have broad shoulders. He was a prolific writer and considered by some as the most important of all Greek philosophers. His works were all in dialogue form and include: the "Apology," the "Symposium," the "Phaedo," the "Phaedrus," and the "Republic."

344 B.C. - Alexander the Great brought cultivated rice to the west after his invasion of India.

343 B.C. - Artaxerxes III of Persia led a successful campaign against Egypt and Nectanebo II fled to Ethiopia. Artaxerxes appointed Pherendares as satrap of Egypt and returned to Babylon laden with treasures.

343-332 B.C. - In Egypt the Persians ruled for a 2nd time.

341-270 B.C. - Epicurus, Greek philosopher born [342 B.C. ? - ?] in Samos, held that happiness is the supreme good. He had studied under Democritus and was a confirmed atomist. His happiness is interpreted to mean the avoidance of pain.

340 B.C. - Aristotle argued for the spherical shape of the Earth in his "On The Heavens."

339 B.C. - Macedonian raids to North in 339,335,331, 313 è 292 against Scythians and Celts. Celtic alliance with Scythians evidenced by Celtic artifacts in Scythian sites

339 B.C. - Defeat of Scythians led by king Ateios in battle with army of Philip of Macedonia. Death of Atheios.

338 B.C. - In Greece Philip of Macedon conquered the country and was succeeded by his son 2 years later. Athens ceased to be a major power from this point on. Philip's League of Corinth was composed of impotent Hellenic states that had lost their collective freedom at the battle of Chaeronea.

338 B.C. - Philip II erected Olympia's Philippeion in Athens following his victory at Chaeronea. The round marble building was completed by his son, Alexander.

338 B.C. - Artaxerxes III (Ochus), king of Persia, was murdered by his own commander Bagoas.

338 B.C. - Arses, the youngest son of Ochus, succeeded his father as king of Persia. He served as the 2nd ruler of Egypt's 31st Dynasty.

336 B.C. - Alexander inherited the throne of Macedonia and all of Greece. He went to see the Oracle of Delphi but was initially refused entry. He forced his way and dragged the seeress into the temple. Plutarch wrote: "As if conquered by his violence, she said, 'My son, thou art invincible.'" "That is all the answer I desire," replied Alexander. He began his campaign to acquire new territory in Asia at age 22. Within 4 years he conquered the entire Persian Empire.

336 B.C. - Arses, king of Persia and ruler of Egypt's 31st Dynasty, was murdered by his commander Bagoas.

338 B.C. - Macedonian barbarian Philip II defeated united Greek states at battle of Chaeronea in beginning of August 338 B.C. - and appointed himself "Commander of Greeks"

336 B.C. - Philip II of Macedonia (382-336 B.C.), king of Macedonia, is buried in kurgan per Macedonian custom. Greeks viewed Macedonians as barbarians (non-Greeks), and consequently treated them in same manner in which they treated all non-Greeks.

335 B.C. - Aristotle opened the Lyceum in Athens which was devoted to scientific work. He invented the science of logic, and divided the sciences into different fields distinguished by subject matter and methodology. He believed in the innate inferiority of slaves and females. He wrote the "Nicomachean Ethics," a book about virtue and its reward, happiness. He identified circularity in reasoning as the "fallacy of the consequent" i.e. A good man is one who makes the right choices.

335 B.C. - 332 B.C. - Darius III was raised to the throne of Persia by the eunuch Bagoas, who had killed the 2 previous rulers. Darius in turn had Bagoas murdered.

c335 B.C. - c263 B.C. - Zeno the Stoic set up a school in Athens at the Stoa Poikile (Painted Colonnade), and taught that happiness consists in conforming the will to the divine reason, which governs the universe. Thus a man is happy if he fully accepts what is and does not desire what cannot be. Zeno was a Phoenician from Kition on Cyprus. He taught that "events were destined to repeat themselves" in endless cycles.

334 B.C. - Alexander (22) left Pella, Greece, with 30,000 foot soldiers and 5,000 cavalry and proceeded to conquer western Asia including Miletus and Samos. His favorite horse was named Bucephalus. At Gordium, where King Midas is fabled to have held court, Alexander solved the puzzle of the Gordian knot by severing it with his sword.

333 B.C. - Alexander first confronted Darius, king of Persia, and defeated him at the battlefield of Issus.

333 B.C. - Alexander the Great (353 B.C. - 323 B.C. -), married a barbarian (Sogdian) princess, Roxana, the daughter of the Bactrian chief Oxyartes. Alexander also married the daughter of Darius, whom he defeated in 333, while staying firmly attached to his comrade, Hephaistion.

333 B.C. - Alexander's forces overcame the Pisidians of Sagalassos.

c333 B.C. - Hittite lands and the village known as Ancyra (later Angora, Ankora) was conquered by Macedonians led by Alexander the Great.

332 B.C. - Alexander the Great conquers Persian Empire

332 B.C. - Jul, In Phoenicia Alexander stormed the island of Tyre by building a causeway to the island. He then besieged the city of Gaza. He moved on to conquer Egypt and founded Alexandria.

332 B.C. - Alexander entered Egypt and founded Alexandria.

331 B.C. - Alexander's scouts encountered the camp of King Darius near Guagamela. The force numbered 25,000 horsemen, 50,000 foot soldiers, 200 chariots and 15 war elephants.

331 B.C. - In battle of Gaugamela with Alexander Macedonian, Darius had Scyths (35K Cavalry) and Bactrians in his army

331 B.C. - Alexander the Great shattered King Darius III's Persian army at Gaugamela (Arbela), in a tactical masterstroke that left him master of the Persian Empire.

331 B.C. - Alexander left Egypt and left Cleomenes of Naukratis in charge. This po-

sition was later claimed by Ptolemy. When Alexander died, Ptolemy's generals divided the kingdom.

331 B.C. - Alexander conquered the Persian Empire and made his way to India and conquered part of it.

331 B.C. - The Achaemenid King of Persia, Darius III, died in Bactria. Bessus, the satrap of Bactria had him murdered.

331 B.C. - Alexander reached Persopolis, the capital of Persia, and burned it.

330 B.C. - Alexandria became the capital of Egypt.

c330 B.C. - Euclid showed that an infinite number of Prime numbers exists, but occur in no logical pattern.

330 B.C. - 320 B.C. - A Temple of Zeus was built at Nemea, Greece, on the foundations of an earlier temple.

329 B.C. - Alexander the Great took Samarkand [in what is now Uzbekistan]. Its ancient name was Marakanda.

329 B.C. - 326 B.C. - After conquering Persia, Alexander the Great invaded Afghanistan. He conquered Afghanistan, but failed to really subdue its people. Constant revolts plagued Alexander.

327 B.C. - 326 B.C. - Alexander the Great passed through the Indus Valley and installed Greek officials in the area.

326 B.C. - Alexander crossed the Indus river at Hund and then the Jhelum river and defeated King Porus at the edge of India. This was his last great battle.

326 B.C. - The Charsadda site (aka Bala Hisar) in northern Pakistan was besieged by Alexander. It then passed from Mauryan to Indo-Greek, Parthian, Sassanian, and Kushan rule. The pagan Kalash of Pakistan later claimed to be descendants of Alexander's soldiers.

325 B.C. - Pytheas (c380 B.C. - 310 B.C. -), Greek merchant, geographer and explorer, made a voyage of exploration to northwestern Europe around this time. He traveled around Great Britain, circumnavigating it between 330 and 320 B.C. - He claimed to have sailed past Scotland and mentioned a land called Thule, where the surrounding ocean froze and the sun disappeared in winter.

325-300 B.C. - Flavius Josephus, historian of the first century, wrote that a Samaritan Temple was built (on Mt. Gerizim) that was a copy of the Second Temple of Jerusalem. Josephus dated it to the late part of the fourth century. The temple's first chief priest is said to have been Manasseh, a Jewish priest who married a Samaritan woman named Nikaso. The Jewish elders forced Manasseh to choose between the Jewish Temple or his wife. He chose his wife and her father, Sanballat, built for Manasseh a copy of the Jewish temple on Mt. Gerizim.

323 B.C. - Jun 10, Alexander died in Persia at Babylon at the age of 32. His general, Ptolemy, took possession of Egypt. Apelles was a painter in Alexander's court. He had been commissioned by Alexander to paint a portrait of Campaspe, Alexander's concubine. Apelles fell in love with Campaspe and Alexander granted her to him in marriage.

323 B.C. - The Temple of Artemis in Ephesus, a Graeco-Roman seaport (later in Turkey), was completed after 125 years of construction. It was acclaimed the most beautiful structure in the world and considered one of the 7 architectural wonders of the ancient world. Its ruins were discovered in 1869 by archeologist John T. Wood (d.1890).

323 B.C. - The Greeks ruled Bactria (Northern Afghanistan)

323 B.C. - The death of Alexander provided an opportunity for an independent state in India. Chandragupta Maurya founded the Maurya dynasty, the first Indian empire with its capital in Patna.

323 B.C. - 285 B.C. - Ptolemy I Soter, son of Lagus and commander under Alexander, ruled Egypt as the first king of the Ptolemaic Dynasty. Under his rule the library of Alexandria was commissioned.

323-30 B.C. - In Greece this period is called the Hellenistic Age, the time from Alexander's death to Roman rule.

323-30 B.C. - Ptolemy and his descendants ruled over Egypt. This era came to be known as the Ptolemaic period. At the ancient library of Alexandria, Callimachus of Cyrene was the first to catalog writings alphabetically.

323-30 B.C. - During the Hellenistic Age the Grand Theater of Ephesus was built into the side of Mt. Pion and could hold 24,000 spectators.

322 B.C. - Athens was brought under the control of the Macedonian empire. Demosthenes was sentenced to death, but he escaped and sought refuge on the island of

Calauria, where he committed suicide after troops followed him.

322 B.C. - Mar 7, Aristotle (d.322 B.C. -) died.

320 B.C. - c235 B.C. - In China the philosopher Hsun-tzu, the founder of Legalism, lived. He was an orthodox Confucianist and believed strongly in moral education. He repudiated any belief in a spiritual realm and believed that human beings are evil by nature.

318 B.C. - First historical document connected with Huns is Chinese-Hun treaty signed in 318 B.C. - 310 B.C. - Sirac(i), a Sarmatian tribe occupied Kuban region north of Caucasus shortly before 300 B.C. - (Tr. Sarig=yellow, blond, Sirs are ansestors of Cumans/Kipchaks)

316 B.C. - The Ba people on the Yangtze River were subjugated by the Qin.

316 B.C. - The Ch'in conquered Shu and Pa (modern-day Szechuan) and gained a serious advantage over the Ch'u.

312 B.C. - Appius Claudius, the Blind, as consul began the building of the Via Appia. The historian Procopius states that the road was completed at this time. It ran due south from Rome to Capua.

312 B.C. - King Glauk of Illyria expelled the Greeks from Durrës.

310 B.C. - Aristarchus of Samos founded Hellenistic astronomy. Contrary to Aristotle he said that the earth and all the other planets revolve around the sun.

310 B.C. - Pytheas (b.c380 B.C. -), Greek merchant, geographer and explorer, died about this time. He made a voyage of exploration to northwestern Europe around 325 B.C. - E. He traveled around a considerable part of Great Britain, circumnavigating it between 330 and 320 B.C. - E.

309-247 - Ptolemy II (Philadelphus). He ruled Egypt from 285-247?.

304 B.C. - Cnieus Flavius, a commoner, brought justice to Rome by stealing a calendar. He posted his purloined tablet in the Roman Forum. The letters A-H corresponded to an 8-day Roman market-day cycle.

304 B.C. - In India Chandragupta traded 500 war elephants to Seleucus in exchange for the Indus region and lands immediately to the West.

301 B.C. - The generals of Alexander fought the Battle of Ipsus in Phrygia that resulted in the division of the Greek Empire into 4 divisions ruled by Seleucus, Lysimachus, Cassander and Ptolemy. Greek cities revolted against Macedonian rule but to no avail.

300 B.C. - Türkic language splits into 2 branches, Oguz (Eastern) and Ogur (Kipchak) (Western). Oguz 'z', 'y,i', (Oguz, yilan, Yaik) Ogur 'r', 'd, dj', (Ogur, djulan, Djaik)

300 B.C. - From Chinese sources Alans are listed as one of four Hunnish tribes (Xula, Lan, Hiu-bu, Siu-lin) most favoured by kings of Eastern Huns (Mao-dun/Mete and his son Ki-ok/Kök) of 3rd century B.C. - 300 B.C. - In 300 B.C. - Neapolis Scythia In Crimea (Simpheropol area) was capital of Royal Scyths

300 B.C. - Earliest occurrence of Parthian name in form of Aparnoi or Parnoi in Turan. According to Armenian historians who served Armenian dynasty of Parthian origin, Parthian Arsac who founded dynasty was of white Hun (Ephtalite) origin

c300 B.C. - In 2005 a well-preserved and colorful mummy from the 30th pharaonic dynasty was unveiled at Egypt's Saqqara pyramid complex.

300 B.C. - Euclid compiled his "Elements of Geometry." Included was his demonstration for "regular partitioning."

c300 B.C. - In Greece Epicureanism and Stoicism originated in Athens. Both Epicurus and Zeno, the Stoic, believed in an individualistic and materialistic philosophy. Neither believed in spiritual substances. The soul was thought to be material. The Epicureans believed that pleasure is the highest good, and that only by abandoning the fear of the supernatural can one achieve tranquility of mind. The Stoics believed that tranquility of mind was only achieved by surrendering the self to the order of the cosmos.

300 B.C. - Kautilya (aka Chanakya), an Indian statesman and scholar, authored the Artha-Shastra (the Science of Material Gain) at the end of the 4th century B.C. - . This is the first known treatise on government and economy.

300 B.C. - In Ireland 2 men were murdered about this time. In 2005 their preserved remains were found in a peat bog. One dubbed Clonycavan Man was about 5 feet 2 inches and used hair gel. The other, dubbed Oldcroghan Man, stood 6 feet 6 inches. "Oldcroghan Man was stabbed

through the chest. He was then decapitated and his body cut in half while Clonycaven Man had his head split open with an axe before he was disemboweled.

300 B.C. - Carthago Nova (Cartagena, Spain) had coins minted in the Greek style. One face bears the image of Melqart, chief god of Tyre, the other face shows a horse and palm tree, emblems of Carthage.

c300 B.C. - As early as this time, travelers went to Petra in the northwest corner of the Arabian peninsula for its abundant spring water.

c300 B.C. - Palur in eastern India near Chilika Lake has yielded red-and-black-ware potsherds, one of which had the image of a boat.

c300 B.C. - By about this time iron-working had spread all along the savanna belt of West Africa.

c300 B.C. - Zeugma was founded by Seleucus I Nicator, one of Alexander's generals in southeastern Anatolia.

300 B.C. - 250CE - Late preclassic period of the Maya.

c300 B.C. - 200 B.C. - Aristarchus, Greek philosopher of the late 3rd cent., proposed the Sun as the center of the universe. [see 310 B.C. -]

c300 B.C. - 200 B.C. - Apollonius, Greek poet emigrant from Alexandria to Rhodes, and author of the "Argonautica."

c300 B.C. - 200 B.C. - In China an emperor dispatched the sailor Hsu Fu to search the Pacific Ocean for the "drug of immortality." He came back empty-handed after the first trip and set out again never to return.

c300 B.C. - 200 B.C. - In China Qu Wan, a poet and official, despaired on the possibility of justice in this world and threw himself into a river.

c300 B.C. - 200 B.C. - In Egypt scientists of the Univ. of Calif. Berkeley expedition of 1899 uncovered hundreds of crocodile mummies encased and stuffed with papyrus covered with writings from the ruins of the city of Tebtunis. The site dated from the 3rd century B.C. - when Ptolemy the Great ruled.

300 B.C. - 200 B.C. - In 2006 archaeologists at the San Bartolo site in Guatemala dated Mayan hieroglyphs painted on plaster and stone to this period.

300 B.C. - 200 B.C. - The city of Berenice on the Mediterranean coast (later in Libya) was named by the Greeks.

c300 B.C. - 200 B.C. - Andronicus Livius, a Roman actor of the 3rd cent. B.C. - improvised silently and originated pantomime.

300 B.C. - 200 B.C. - During the 3rd century B.C. - Mongolia became the center of the Hsiung-nu empire.

300 B.C. - 200 B.C. - In Thailand Ban Chaibadan on the Pasak River is one of several sites that has archaeological remains that show the development of a complex society.

300 B.C. - 64 B.C. - Antioch served as the capital of the kingdom of Syria.

300 B.C. - 68CE The Dead Sea Scrolls of Qumran, Jordan, date to this period. The scrolls are usually identified with the Jewish-monkish cult, the Essenes, know for their pathological aversion to stool. In 2004 Chicago Prof. Norman Golb authored "Who Wrote the Dead Sea Scrolls."

The Dead Sea Scrolls were discovered by Bedouin at the caves of Qumran in Jordan around 1947. The scrolls predated the Christian gospels, but contained many similarities. They also contained some differences from the traditional (Masoretic) text of the Hebrew Bible. In 1955 Edmund Wilson published "The Scrolls from the Dead Sea." In 1998 Hershel Shank published "The Mystery and meaning of the Dead Sea Scrolls." From 1978-1998 over 6,000 books were written about the scrolls. The discovery date was later contested as were many of the historic circumstances surrounding the scrolls.

295 B.C. - The Battle of Sentinum. Etruria was defeated by Rome and the Etruscan decline continued for more than 200 years.

290 B.C. - Hun state consists of 24 clans, some of them: Kuyan (Jack rabbit) Lan (Orchard) Suybu (West Tribe) Suylyanti Tsulin Taychi Uyti Tsetszuy...

290 B.C. - Hun state leader is titled Great Shanüy - "Chenli gydu shanüy" - "Son of endless sky" Succession is from father to eldest son.

290 B.C. - Ptolemy I of Egypt authorized the construction of the Pharos Lighthouse in Alexandria. It became one of the seven wonders of the ancient world.

290 B.C. - The 110-foot Colossus of Rhodes, one of the ancient seven wonders of the world, was built to the sun god Helios.

287 B.C. - In Rome the plebeians passed a law that allowed the decisions of the assembly to override the Senate.

287 B.C. - Theophrastus (b.c371 B.C. -), Greek philosopher, died. He produced the 1st known work on plant reproduction "De historia plantarum. He was a contemporary of Aristotle and succeeded him as head of the Lyceum.

287-212 B.C. - Archimedes, Greek mathematician, physicist and inventor. He discovered the principles of specific gravity and of the lever. His works included "Method of Mechanical Theorems" and "On Floating Bodies." He named the number, later known as pi, as the Archimedes Constant. Scientists in 2000 began translating the Floating Bodies treatisse from a single known parchment copy, dating to about 1000CE, that was scraped and reused for a prayer book.

285 B.C. - 246 B.C. - Ptolemy II (b.c309 B.C. - , Philadelphus) of Macedonia served as the 2nd king of Egypt's Ptolemaic Dynasty. During his reign (285-247) he founded the Cyprian port of Famagusta and built a canal to link the Nile to the gulf of Suez.

280 B.C. - The Achaean League was reformed along political lines. It had been a confederation of Achaean cities formed for religious observances and was broken up by the Macedonians.

280 B.C. - Li Ssu, Legalist scholar, was born in the kingdom of Ch'u, later a region of China.

279 B.C. - The Pharos at Alexandria was constructed. The lighthouse, one of the Seven Wonders of the World, was toppled by an earthquake in 1303CE. It was rediscovered by archeologists in the waters off Alexandria in 1996.

279 B.C. - The Celts plundered the shrine at Delphi and then retreated north to Thrace. The Thracians later routed the intruders.

273-232 Ashoka, the grandson of Chandragupta Maurya, ruled India, an area of a million sq. miles, and 50 million people. He was the most impressive ruler of the Maurya dynasty and was strongly disposed in favor of Buddhism, which orientation showed positively in his public policy.

269 B.C. - The Roman system of coinage was established.

265 B.C. - Rome completed its domination of the entire Italian peninsula and began its pursuit of a larger empire that resulted in a series of wars with other nations.

264 B.C. - Emperor Ashoka experiences spiritual crisis and converts to Buddhism (India)

264 B.C. - Rome initiated the Punic Wars with Carthage, an oligarchic empire that stretched from the northern coast of Africa to the Strait of Gibraltar. The primary cause was the Carthaginian expansion into the Greek cities of Sicily. Carthage was forced to surrender its control over the western region of Sicily and this marked the end of the first Punic War. The three Punic Wars: 264-241 B.C. - , 218-202 B.C. - , 149-146 B.C. - , also known as the Carthaginian Wars, finally resulted in the destruction of Carthage and Roman control of the western Mediterranean.

262 B.C. - War broke out between Carthage and Rome. Three long wars lasted till 146 B.C. - when Carthage was destroyed by Rome.

261 B.C. - Rome captured a Punic quinquereme. In two months they copied it plank by plank and built 100 like it and eventually the Roman fleet was able to defeat the Carthaginians.

260 B.C. - Ashoka, the 3rd ruler of the Mauryan empire (India), converted to Buddhism after defeating the Kalinga region. He began promoting Buddhist teaching throughout the subcontinent and beyond to Sri Lanka and even Greece.

256 B.C. - The Carthaginian city of Kerouane was sacked by the Romans.

251 B.C. - Aryan Hindus occupied Ceylon. [see Sri Lanka]

c250 B.C. - Eratosthenes ascribed the difference between the positions of the noon sun at Alexandria and at Styrene at the summer solstice as due to the curvature of the Earth and not due to the proximity of the sun. He thereby calculated the radius of the Earth to be about 4,000 miles. The modern value is 3963 miles.

250 B.C. - In India a general council of Buddhist monks was held in Patna, where the canon of Buddhist scripture was selected.

c250 B.C. - In Patan, Nepal, the 4 corners are marked by stupas said to be constructed on orders of Emperor Ashoka.

250 B.C. - In Persia about this time two brothers, Arashk (Arash Pers. Arsaces, Lat.) and Tirdat (Tiridates), with their forces under the command of five other chiefs, occupied the district of upper Tejen. Arashk (Arsaces) was to become the first king of the Ashkanian (Arsacid or Parthian) dynasty. In 2005 the Ashkali community in Kosovo claimed roots to this period.

250 B.C. - A finely burnished red pottery was introduced by the Parthians into northern Oman.

250 B.C. - 150 B.C. - Punic wars between Rome and Carthage. [see 264 B.C. - & 146 B.C. -]

250 B.C. - 1400CE The city of Jenne-jeno on the inland delta of the Niger River (Mali) was inhabited over this period. Iron tools similar to that of the Nok people indicate that Nok craftspeople had come to this site. It was discovered by archeologist in 1977.

247 B.C. - Li Ssu left Ch'u and traveled to Ch'in, a kingdom where Legalist doctrines were practiced. He found employment with Lu Pu-wei, the king's grand councilor, who was compiling an encyclopedia. Lu Ssu soon became tutor to Prince Zheng, heir to the throne of Ch'in.

247 B.C. - Start of Parthian Dynasty (ab. 247 B.C.-A.D. 226) which was one of longest in history

246 B.C. - Jan 9, Ptolemy II Philadelphus, 2nd king of Egypt's Ptolemaic Dynasty, died.

246 B.C. - In China the Ch'in completed the Chengkuo canal connecting the Ching and Lo rivers. This created a key agricultural and economic area in western Szechuan. About the same time the last Chou ruler was deposed.

246 B.C. - Qin Shihuangdi (13), became the head of Qin, one of 7 major Chinese states.

246 B.C. - 222 B.C. - Ptolemy III Eeuergeter served as Egypt's 3rd ruler of the Ptolemaic Dynasty.

246 B.C. - In Antiochus 11th year Parthians shook off Macedonians, and Ephtalite king's son is new ruler. All nations of Eastern and Northern Asia accepted his rule. King Arsac had four sons. One received Ephtalites, second Hindus, third Parthians, fourth Armenians.

241 B.C. - The Battle of Aegusa in which the Roman fleet sank 50 Carthaginian ships occurred.

241 B.C. - The Romans incorporated Sicily as a province.

240 B.C. - Jun 19, Eratosthenes estimated the circumference of Earth using two sticks.

239 B.C. - 169 B.C. - Ennius, Roman poet: "A friend in need is a friend indeed."

238 B.C. - The Romans occupied Sardinia.

238 B.C. - 227CE The Parthians (238 B.C.-A.D. 227) ruled the Persian Empire despite attempts by the Roman Republic (133-27 B.C.), the Roman Empire (27 B.C.-A.D. 476) to conquer it. During the centuries-long struggle, border towns and provinces in the Near East passed back and forth like Alsace-Lorraine or the Polish Corridor would in nineteenth-and twentieth-century Europe. Rarely in the history of human conflict has a feud such as the one between the empires of Rome and Persia lasted so long and accomplished so little.

234-149 B.C. - Cato, Roman statesman and historian: "If you are ruled by mind, you are a king; if by body, a slave."

233 B.C. - General Quintus Fabius Maximus led a Roman victory against the Ligurian tribes northwest of Italy.

232 B.C. - King Agron died, the Illyrian throne was occupied by Queen Teuta.

231 B.C. - King Qin Shihuangdi (28), head of one of 7 major states, embarked on a series of campaigns that in 10 years created China. The king of Ch'in invaded Han.

231 B.C. - Parthian Arsac, lost to Persian king Selecud and retreats amongst Aspasiac Scythians, near Aral Sea. With their aid he reconquers his empire

230 B.C. - Touman (Tumen, 240 - 210 B.C.), of clan Suylyanti with a bull totem establishes Hunnic Empire

230 B.C. - Celtic warriors were repelled at Pergamon. The king of Bithynia had invited some 20,000 Celts as mercenaries and after 50 years of pillaging they were repelled and settled in Galatia.

230 B.C. - The capital of Han fell. Its king and entire extended family were massacred. Han was absorbed by Ch'in and under Li Ssu's direction was transformed into a Legalist state.

228 B.C. - The Kingdom of Chao fell to the Ch'in.

225 B.C. - The Kingdom of Wei fell to the Ch'in.

225 B.C. - Polybius, a Greek historian, described the naked gaesatae, Celtic spearmen, at the Battle of Telamon, northwest of Rome where the Romans defeated the Celts.

224 B.C. - An earthquake purportedly broke the Colossus of Rhodes at his knees.

223 B.C. - The Kingdom of Ch'u fell to the Ch'in. Li Ssu had the royal family spared.

222 B.C. - The Kingdom of Yen fell to the Ch'in. The royal family was slaughtered.

222 B.C. - 205 B.C. - Ptolemy IV Philopater served as Egypt's 4th ruler of the Ptolemaic Dynasty.

222-196 B.C. - The Romans showed up at the site of Milan and subdued the Gauls after 26 years of butchery. Mittaland was Latinized to Medioland, i.e. middle of the plain, and later transformed to Milano.

221 B.C. - unification of China and beginning of Qin Dynasty of Kings (China)

221 B.C. - great wall of China built

221 B.C. - The Kingdom of Ch'i fell to the Ch'in and Li Ssu advised King Zheng that there were no other countries worth conquering. King Zheng proclaimed himself Shi Huangdi, "First Emperor of the World Under Heaven."

221 B.C. - The Qin (Ch'in) unified China at the end of the "Warring States." King Zheng engaged in a process of unifying 7 kingdoms in China under a central bureaucracy. He killed most of the people in the 6 rival kingdoms and buried alive 400 scholars whose loyalty he questioned. The 1998 Chinese film "The Emperor's Shadow" was directed by Zhou Xiaowen. It was a historical drama of the first emperor (Ying Zheng or Jiang Wen) of a united China. The 1999 film "The Emperor and the Assassin," directed by Chen Kaige, was about Zheng.

221 B.C. - 206 B.C. - Qin Shi Huang ruled as the first emperor of China. His tomb is in X'ian, one of the ancient capitals of China, and is guarded by thousands of life-sized terra-cotta soldiers. He fixed Chinese script of 2,500 characters. The Great Wall of China was completed under Shi Huangdi and his minister Li Ssu. In 2001 it was found that the Great Wall extended into Gansu province to Xinjiang and measured 4,470 miles. The wall was extended during the Ming Dynasty. In 1990 Arthur Waldron authored "The Great Wall of China."

218 B.C. - The Romans renewed their efforts against Carthage as Carthage expanded into Spain. This 2nd Punic War lasted 16 years (202 B.C. -) at the end of which Carthage was forced to surrender all of its territory to Rome except for its capital city in North Africa.

218 B.C. - Hannibal crossed Portugal on his way to storm Rome.

218-201 B.C. - Numidia, ancient Roman name for part of northern Africa roughly equivalent to modern Algeria. In the Second Punic War (218-201 B.C. -) between Carthage and Rome, western Numidia supported Carthage. King Masinissa of eastern Numidia joined the Romans. With the victory of Rome, Masinissa controlled all Numidia.

217 B.C. - Jun 21, Carthaginian forces led by Hannibal destroyed a Roman army under consul Gaius Flaminicy in a battle at Lake Trasimenus in central Italy. Hannibal of Carthage attacked Roman Consul Flaminio at Tuoro on Lake Trasimeno in Umbria. Hannibal's army of Numidians, Berbers, Libyans, Gascons, and Iberians was down to one elephant after crossing the Alps with 39. His army of 40,000 drove the Romans into the lake where 15,000 died as opposed to 1,500 of Hannibal's men. Two nearby towns were named Ossaia (boneyard) and Sanguineto (bloodied).

217 B.C. - During the Second Punic War Rome appointed Quintus Fabius Maximus as dictator to stave off Hannibal's Carthaginian army.

216 B.C. - Aug 2, Hannibal Barca of Carthage won his greatest victory over the Romans at Cannae. Hannibal seized a grain depot in the small village of Cannae in order to lure the Romans to battle. Having crossed over the Alps, Hannibal's forces defeated the Romans at the Trebia River and also at Lake Trasimene. Thereafter, the Romans were unwilling to commit a large force to attacking Hannibal. However, Hannibal's spies had learned two Roman consuls shared command of the legions and attempted to goad the more impetuous of the two into battle at Cannae.

214 B.C. - In China the building of the Great Wall was begun. It was designed to keep out the destitute and starving nomadic Hsiung Nu people.

214 B.C. - Guangdong province became a part of China.

214 B.C. - Chinese ruler Si Huang Ti (259-210 B.C.) builds Great Chinese Wall against attacks of Huns

213 B.C. - Minister Li Ssu convinced Ch'in King Zheng to outlaw all philosophies except Legalism. Some 500 Confucian scholars resisted and were buried alive. A number of Confucian and Taoist libraries were burned.

212 B.C. - Archimedes (b.287 B.C. -), Greek mathematician, died. Legend holds that he was killed by a Roman soldier during an invasion of Syracuse, because he was too busy doing calculations to obey the soldier's orders.

211 B.C. - Roman legions overran the Greek settlement of Morgantina on Sicily.

210 B.C. - Qin Shihuangdi, the first emperor of China, died. He was buried near the city of Xi'ab in Central China with some 7-8,000 larger-than-life terracotta soldiers. The soldiers had real weapons and each had distinct facial features. The army was discovered in 1974. [see Jul 11, 1975]

210 B.C. - Crown Prince Fu Su, an anti-Legalist, committed suicide on orders from a forged message. Prince Hu-hai was installed as the Second Emperor. Chief eunuch Chao Kao and Li Ssu shared power at first but Chao Kao gained the backing of Hu-hai.

209 B.C. - Touman died (Tumen, 240 - 210 B.C.), accession to throne of Maotun (Batur, 210 - 174 B.C.), founder of Hun Empire. Expansion of Hun Empire.

208 B.C. - Ch'in Chief eunuch Chao Kao had Li Ssu arrested and condemned to death. Most of Li Ssu's reforms, including standardized writing, measurement and money, survived for over 2,000 years.

207 B.C. - In China the Ch'in Dynasty ended.

207-195 B.C. - In China Han Kao-tzu (Liu Ping), a man of humble origins, became the first ruler of the Former Han Dynasty. The dynasty lasted to 9CE.

206 B.C. - Rome destroyed Carthaginian forces at the Battle of Metaurus in northern Italy.

206 B.C. - 25CE In 2003 China's Xinhua News Agency reported that archaeologists in western China had discovered five earthenware jars of 2,000 B.C. - year-old rice wine in an ancient Han dynasty tomb (206 B.C. - 25CE), and its bouquet was still strong enough to perk up the nose.

206 B.C. - Han Dynasty of Kings founded (China)

206 B.C. - 220CE - The Han Dynasty ruled in China. The Western Han period. In the early Han period Prince Liu Sheng had a jade suit made of 2,498 pieces sewn together with gold thread for his death. Jade was also used to make plugs for his bodies orifices.

205 B.C. - 180 B.C. - Ptolemy V Epiphanes served as Egypt's 5th ruler of the Ptolemaic Dynasty. He became ruler at age 5 following the death of his father. He married Cleopatra I and died at age 29 while putting down insurgents in the Delta. His wife became regent for their young son.

204 B.C. - The sacred stone of Cybele, the Great Mother, was brought to Rome, and her worship was established.

204 B.C. - 202 B.C. - Greece and most of Asia Minor came under the control of the Romans after the Roman victory over Carthage in the 2nd Punic War.

204 B.C. - HUN EMPIRE

204 B.C - 216 A.D. - Founder - Mete (Bagatir, Maotun, Batur) Area - At north, Siberia; south, Tibet - Kashmir; east, Pacific Ocean; west, Caspian Sea, (Total Area - 18,000,000 Km 2)

203 B.C. - Hannibal and his army returned home to defend Carthage against Roman forces.

203 B.C. - Quintus Fabius Maximus, Roman general and dictator, died shortly before Hannibal's final defeat. The name Fabian has come to mean "using a cautious strategy of delay and avoidance of battle."

202 B.C. - The Han Dynasty began in China.

202 B.C. - Roman forces under Scipio Africanus defeated Hannibal of Carthage on the Plains of Zama in northern Tunisia.

200 B.C. - Hopewell Culture (North America)

200 B.C. - silk road opened

c200 B.C. - Trade between the Arabs and East Africans on the Indian Ocean was established. It took this long to learn the seasonal winds known as the monsoons to sail across the Indian Ocean. Between Nov. and March the monsoon blows from the northeast. Between April and Oct. the monsoon blows from the southwest.

200 B.C. - The Chinese natural history classic "Erya" said that the Yangtze River was teeming with baiji, a freshwater white dolphin. By 1998 the baiji were on the verge of extinction.

c200 B.C. - At this time the Chinese were using the sternpost rudder to steer their ships.

c200 B.C. - The Egyptian priest Hor cared for the ibis galleries. His writings explained that hundreds of people were involved in the animal mummification business at Saqqara.

c200 B.C. - The Greek Venus de Milo statue of marble was sculpted about this time. It was found in 1820 on Melos and is now in the Louvre. [2nd source says 2,500 years old]

200 B.C. - In Greece Skepticism arose under the influence of the Carneades. It had close ties to Sophism and taught that because all knowledge is achieved through sense perception, nothing can be known for sure. [see Heisenberg 1901-1976]

c200 B.C. - Drawings in stone of this time showed women milking elk in what later became northern Iran.

c200 B.C. - In Mexico migrations began toward the area north of Lake Texcoco where the urban center of Teotihuacan developed.

c200 B.C. - A Sanskrit marriage manual dates back to this time

200 B.C. - 100 B.C. - The excavation of Pergamon (now Bergama), Turkey, in 1876 by German archeologist uncovered a monument called the Great Altar with a frieze of the mythological hero Telephos. The Telephos Frieze recounts the story of Telephos, a son of Herakles and legendary founder of Pergamon. It is viewed as political propaganda legitimizing the rule of Pergamon's Attalid lineage (after Attalos, its first king's father).

200 B.C. - 100 B.C. - The Silk Road made the city of Ashgabat, Turkmenistan rich. Spice and silk merchants stopped here on their way from China to Europe.

200 B.C. - 500CE The Tunisian city of Leptiminus was a major port for the shipment of olive oil throughout the Roman Empire. The ancient city is today largely covered with olive groves. The entire surface of the city (some 150 hectares) has been surveyed by teams from the Univ. of Michigan. Two kinds of pottery were made there: African Red Slip Ware and amphorae.

c200 B.C. - 650CE Caves at Ajanta, India, were painted and sculpted during this period with court scenes and tales from the Jataka and Bodhisattvas.

200 B.C. - Emergence of Huns (Hsiung-nu) on western borders of China.

200 B.C. - A strong stone and mortar wall surrounds capital Neapolis Scythia of Royal Scyths in 200 B.C. - Of note is a mausoleum that contains seventy-two richly furnished tombs, which are probably representative of royal Scythian house

199 B.C. - 150 B.C. - Greco-Bactrian kingdom. Now Afghanistan, it was then a major stop on the silk route between Rome and China.

199 B.C. - 150 B.C. - Early in the 2nd century B.C. - the Romans made Macedonia into a province and obliterated the city of Corinth.

c196 B.C. - In Egypt the Rosetta Stone, found in 1799, was inscribed about this time. It affirmed the rule of Ptolemy V (age 13) in 3 languages.

195 B.C. - China's 1st Han Emperor Liu Pang died and his empress Lu Zhi took the empire for her own family.

190 B.C. - In the US state of New Mexico a volcanic lava flow occurred at the 114,000 acre El Malpais National Monument and covered wood that was later dated to this time.

190 B.C. - Hipparchus was born in what is now Turkey. He calculated the length of a year to within 6 1/2 minutes and was the first to explain the Earth's rotation on its axis. He also compiled the first comprehensive catalog of the stars. [see 160-125 B.C. -]

c190 B.C. - 120 B.C. - Hypsicles of Alexanderia, mathematician. He wrote "On the Ascension of Stars," in which he was the first to divide the Zodiac into 360 degrees.

184 B.C. - In Rome Cato the Censor (234-149) was elected as one of two censors, i.e. assessors of property and moral conduct. He aimed to preserve Roman ways and tried to extirpate Greek influences.

184 B.C. - In India the Maurya dynasty ended when the last ruler was assassinated by an ambitious army commander.

183 B.C. - 182 B.C. - Hannibal, Carthaginian general, committed suicide. Some reports said that a comet in the night sky was an omen of his death.

180 B.C. - The Liu clan regained control of China and enthroned Emperor Wen, a surviving son of Liu Bang.

180 B.C. - The state of Meroe in Nubia was a great cultural center whose scribes developed an alphabet to better express the Nubian language around this time.

180 B.C. - 164 B.C. - Ptolemy VI Philometor served as Egypt's 6th ruler of the Ptolemaic Dynasty. His regent mother died around 176 B.C. - and Ptolemy ruled under the control of his guardians, Eulaeus and Lenaeus.

177 B.C. - Mete Khan (Maotun) letter to Chinese government describes that 26 nations are in Türkish sate and all of them became "nations stretching bow-string", or Huns

175 B.C. - 164 B.C. - King Antiochus IV, Seleucid tyrant, ruled Syria.

174 B.C. - Kokkhan (174-161 B.C.), Huns (Hsiung-nu) attack Tocharians (Yüeh-chih), driving them from Gansu

170 B.C. - The rebel Maccabees were able to gain victory in Jerusalem occupied by Antiochus IV During the re-dedication of the temple they stretched a days worth of oil out to 8 days for which the holiday of Hanukkah is celebrated.

170 B.C. - Lucius Accius, Roman poet, wrote "Has oderint dum metuant" (Let them hate us, so long as they fear us). This became a favorite phrase of Emperor Caligula.

170 B.C. - 160 B.C. - The Bactrian--Parthian era of Afghanistan.

168 B.C. - Rome conquers Macedonia

168 B.C. - Illyria and Epirus were conquered by Rome.

168 B.C. - Syria's Seleucid king Antiochus IV Epiphanes ruled over Israel and tried to outlaw Judaism. He tried to Hellenize the Jews by erecting idols. The Jews resisted and began the Maccabean revolt. The Maccabees were successful until internal dissension tore them apart.

167 B.C. - Antiochus IV, the Hellenistic tyrant of the what later became called the Middle East, began to increase religious persecution against the Jews in Palestine and outlawed observance of the Torah. This included the circumcision of males, dietary restrictions and observance of the Sabbath. He installed a cult of Zeus in the Temple in Jerusalem. The Jewish priest Mattathias of Modin defied Antiochus, escaped outside Lydda with his 5 sons and began a revolt.

167 B.C. - Rome presented to Athens the island of Delos, whose prosperous slave and commodities market brought large profits.

165 B.C. - Romans captured King Gent of Illyria and sent him to Rome. Illyria went under Roman control.

165 B.C. - Jerusalem and sacred temple of Judah were recaptured by the Maccabees. They used guerrilla tactics and elephants as tanks to throw off the tyranny of the Greco-Syrian oppressors. During the cleanup they found one container of the sacred oil used to light the temple's candelabra known as a menorah. They gathered to light the oil which was expected to last only a day, but lasted eight nights. The event was memorialized in the celebration of Hanukkah (rededication), the Feast of Lights. [see 164 B.C. -]

164 B.C. - Ptolemy VI Philometor went to Rome and left Egypt under the rule of his brother Ptolemy VII Euergetes II Physcon.

164 B.C. - The Temple of Jerusalem was recaptured by forces under Judah Maccabee, religious traditionalists from the countryside. [see 165 B.C. -] The restoration of Jewish law was also a victory over Jewish factions who wanted to turn Jerusalem to a city modeled after the Greek pagan city-states.

163 B.C. - 145 B.C. - Ptolemy VI Philometor was called back to Egypt and agreed to split their rule. Physcon assumed rule of the western province of Cyrenaica and Philometor ruled Egypt.

161 B.C. - 137 B.C. - The legendary King Duthagamani ruled Sri Lanka. He began construction of the Ruvanvali stupa. His brother Saddhatissa completed the project.

161 B.C. - Kunkhan (161 - 126 B.C.)

160 B.C. - 125 B.C. - Hipparchus, Greek mathematician and astronomer, often

called the father of modern astronomy. He attempted to calculate the distance to the moon and the sun. His estimate for the distance to the moon was 67r vs. the modern value of 60.267r. He estimated the sun to be 37 times farther than the moon and at least 12 times greater in diameter than the Earth. His figures were accepted for 17 centuries until the invention of the telescope and precise astronomical instruments. Together with Ptolemy he graded the visible stars into six magnitudes. The first magnitude was comprised of about 20 of the brightest stars. He compiled a stellar catalogue in Alexandria which shows the position of 1080 stars. [see 190 B.C. -]

160 B.C. - –220CE The Weerdinge Couple, 2 men dating to this period, were found in a Holland bog in 1904.

156 B.C. - 141 B.C. - In China Han Ching-ti ruled the Han Dynasty.

155 B.C. - 213 Some evidence has it that the Ark of the Covenant was brought to Ethiopia during this period. The 1992 book "The Sign and the Seal" by Graham Hancock presents the evidence.

154 B.C. - In China Han Ching-ti wrote the laws of inheritance that made all sons coheirs of their father's estate.

c150 B.C. - Agora's Stoa of Attalos, a massive colonnaded monument at the foot of the Acropolis, was dedicated by King Attalos of Pergamon.

c150 B.C. - The craft of paper making was developed in China around this time. Paper was made by soaking flattened plant fibers and then allowing them to dry on a screen.

c150 B.C. - Cival was a large and sophisticated Mayan city of some 10,000 people.

150 B.C. - In 2005 archaeologists at the San Bartolo site in Guatemala led by Guatemalan Monica Pellecer Alecio found the oldest known Maya royal burial, from around 150 B.C. - . Excavating beneath a small pyramid, that team found a burial complex that included ceramic vessels and the bones of a man, with a jade plaque, the symbol of Maya royalty, on his chest.

150 B.C. - 200CE In Oman triliths, small, 3-stone monuments, were set in rows in the Mahra tribal territory. Many were inscribed with an undeciphered south Arabic script. The Mahra and Shahra are Semitic, non-Arabic speaking tribes in the Dhofar Mountains that even today control much of the frankincense region.

150 B.C. - Rise of Hun Empire's puts pressure on territory of Iran dislodging many Scythian nations who were pushed west, including Saka-Uraka whose kings' title was Makar.

150 B.C. - Migration of a part of Sarmats (Bulgarians) from Northern Caucasus to Cis-Caucasus.

149-146 B.C. - Rome and Carthage fought the 3rd Punic War that resulted in the total defeat of Carthage. All inhabitants of Carthage were sold into slavery and the city was burned to the ground. As a result of the Punic wars Rome expanded its empire to cover Spain, North Africa, Greece, Asia Minor and Egypt.

146 B.C. - Roman forces breached the walls of Carthage. All inhabitants were sold into slavery. The city was burned to the ground and the land was sown with salt.

146 B.C. - 30 B.C. - All Hellenistic territory became subject to Rome over this period.

146 B.C. - Roman conquest of Carthage in North Africa

146 B.C. - 30 B.C. - Roman civilization as a result of the Punic Wars witnessed a series of cultural conflicts and assassinations.

145 B.C. - In China Su-ma Ch'ien, the historian and author of the "Records of the Historian," was born. He included social and economic consideration in his history but mentioned nothing of Han Wu-ti and his administration. He was eventually castrated by Wu-ti after writing an apology on behalf of the Hsiung Nu. He died around 90 B.C. - .

141 B.C. - Wu Di (15) became China's 5th Han emperor.

141 B.C. - The Romans incorporated Macedonia as a province.

141 B.C. - 141-128 B.C. - Tochars (Yüeh-chih), fleeing from Huns (Hsiung-nu), overrun Greco-Bactrian kingdom, which is renamed Tocharistan.

133 B.C. - China's Emperor Wu Di declared war on the Xiongnu, a nomadic people in northwest China.

133 B.C. - In Rome Tiberius Gracchus was elected as tribune. He and his brother, elected in 123 B.C. - , strove for reforms in the Roman Republic, but failed due to the conservative customs of the upper class and their resistance to change. Marius and Sul-

la, 2 military leaders, followed the attempts of the Gracchi.

133 B.C. - Attalus III of Pergamon bequeathed his kingdom to Rome. It became the province of Asia.

130 B.C. - The Huns pushed the Kushan and Scythian nomads west across the Central Asian steppes.

130 B.C. - The Great Silk Road opened from China to the West.

126 B.C. - El Chishi (126 - 114 B.C.)

124 B.C. - Asi (Yazig), Pasiani (Budini/Beçen/Peçenek), Tocharian, Sabir (Sabaroi) tribes break into Sogdiana and Baktria. In next five years two Parthian emperors loose their lives in wars. They also later conquer Sakauraka tribe.

123 B.C. - In Rome Gaius Gracchus was elected as tribune. [see 133 B.C. -]

123 B.C. - The Romans won a victory over the Gauls near a 3,000 foot peak that was named Mt. Sainte-Victoire in commemoration. It established a marker between civilization and barbarism.

121 B.C. - Chinese, under General Ho Chuping, defeat Huns (Hsiung-nu).

c119 B.C. - The Huns invaded China.

117 B.C. - In China the original salt monopoly was set up during the Han dynasty.

116 B.C. - 27 B.C. - Marcus Terentius Varro, a Roman scholar and author.

114 B.C. - Ovi (114 - 105 B.C.)

113 B.C. - The army of John Hyrcanus, leader of the Hasmonean rulers in Judea, burns down a Samaritan Temple and the surrounding city. The temple is thought to be copy of the Second Temple of Jerusalem. Archeologists in 1995 find stone fragments inscribed with the Ten Commandments written in the Samaritan script, similar to an ancient form of Hebrew known as Paleo-Hebrew.

108 B.C. - 62 B.C. - Catiline, tyrant of Rome. He was defeated by Cicero. This was a period when civil conflict had become epidemic.

106 B.C. - Jan 3, Marcus Cicero (d.43 B.C. -), Roman orator, statesman and author, was born. He was elected Consul in 63. He chose to support Pompey over Caesar and was murdered by Mark Antony: "What is more unwise than to mistake uncertainty for certainty, falsehood for truth?"

106 B.C. - 48 B.C. - Pompey. He was a rival to Caesar for Roman power.

105 B.C. - The Jihong Bridge across the Lancang River in Yunnan, China, was built. It linked 2 portions of the Southern Silk Road.

105 B.C. - The heart of ancient Numidia lay in the eastern region of what is now Algeria in Northern Africa. The Numidians were originally nomadic horsemen. They were defeated by Roman troops in the Jugurthine War in 105 B.C. - and conquered by Rome in 46 B.C. - . The Vandals and Byzantines ruled successively before Arabs conquered the area in the seventh century AD. Jugurtha was the king of Numidia.

104 B.C. - Rome faced a slave retaliation in Sicily.

103 B.C. - Tribe Pu-ku/Bu-gu is repeatedly mentioned in different Chinese sources from 103 B.C. - up to 8-th century A.D.. They inhabit W and E parts of Central Asia, N and NW of Tien-Shan, Semirech'e and W of rivers Syr Darya and Amu Darya.

103 B.C. - One of tribal lords of Pu-ku - Sofu sulifa Kenan Bain, bears title sulifa, attested later among Dagestan Bulgarians.

100 B.C. - most of the Dead Sea scrolls written over the next hundred years (Near East)

100 B.C. - rise of the Roman Empire

100 B.C. - Diodorus Siculus, 1st c. B.C. - Scythians "lived in very small numbers at Araks River....they gained country in mountains up to Caucasus, in lowland on coast of Ocean (Caspian Sea) and Meot Lake (Azov Sea) and other territories up to Tanais River.

100 B.C. - "They won for themselves a country "behind Tanais River up to Egyptian Nile River" (Diodorus II, 43).

c100 B.C. - Jul 12, Gaius Julius Caesar (d.44 B.C. -), Roman general and statesman, was born.

c100 B.C. - Camulodunum (later Colchester in southeastern England) was established about this time as a fortress dedicated to the Celtic god of war.

c100 B.C. - The Bantu-speaking people began expanding and moving southeast. It is thought that they originated in the Congo basin (now Zaire) or the mountains of Cameroon. They used iron, grew millet and kept goats.

100 B.C. - In 2005 archaeologist William Saturno said he was awe-struck when he

uncovered a Maya mural not seen for nearly two millennia. Discovered at the San Bartolo site in Guatemala, the mural covers the west wall of a room attached to a pyramid.

c100 B.C. - The Shilla Dynasty began in southeastern Korea and grew to become a top-heavy feudal system that covered most of South Korea for almost 900 years.

c100 B.C. - The community situated on an island in the Seine River was known by the Romans in the first century B.C. - as Lutetia. At the time, it was occupied by the Gallic tribe called Parisii. As the city grew into a Roman trading center, it came to be known as Paris.

c100 B.C. - The area around Palenque (Mexico) was 1st occupied.

100 B.C. - 1 B.C. - A Roman fortified citadel was built about this time in Moldova. It may have protected a town occupied by a late-era Sarmatian king.

100 B.C. - 1 B.C. - The painted cave of Naj Tunich in the Peten of Guatemala began attracting pilgrims.

c100 B.C. - 1 B.C. - Diodorus Siculus, Greek historian of the late 1st century.

100 B.C. - 100CE The Mayan site of Palenque was settled by farmers over this period.

100 B.C. - 500CE The Hopewell Mounds of Ohio were erected by a mound building culture of this period that dominated the eastern US.

100 B.C. - 668CE The Three Kingdoms era of Korea.

96 B.C. - 81 B.C. - The Circus of Domitian was built in Rome. It later became the Piazza Navona.

95 B.C. - 55 B.C. - The Artaxiad King Tigranes I extends the Armenian state from Georgia in the north to Mesopotamia and Syria in the south.

95 B.C. - 51 B.C. - T. Lucretius Carus author of the epic poem "On the Nature of Things", about the science of physics, yet dedicated to pleasure. He was a devoted follower of Epicurus.

94 B.C. - 56 B.C. - Tigranes (Dikran) the Great, a scion of the Eastern Dynasty, ruled. He welded the two Armenian satrapies into one kingdom, and so created the first strong native sovereignty that the country had known since the fall of Urartu five centuries before.

90 B.C. - After centuries of decline, Etruscans become Roman citizens.

89 B.C. - Roman general Cornelius Sulla sacked Clusium, the Etruscan capital.

89 B.C. - 80 B.C. - Mithridates, ruler of Pontus in the north of Asia Minor, made war on Rome and overran much of Asia Minor and parts of Greece. The Athenians joined Mithridates and was consequently besieged by the Roman Gen'l. Sulla.

87 B.C. - Chinese Emperor Wu Di died. Sima Qian, historian of the era, had been castrated by Wu Di for daring to stand in support of a disgraced general.

87 B.C. - Haley's comet was observed.

c81 B.C. - 30 B.C. - Mark Antony had Cicero murdered. He cut off his hands and had them nailed to the senate rostrum as a warning to other men who might wish to speak the truth.

80 B.C. - Cicero journeyed to Greece and Asia suffering from pthisis [tuberculosis], and returned cured after 2 years.

75 B.C. - Scythian nomads from Central Asia conquered Kabul River Valley, with Taxila and Pushkalavati as their twin capital cities in Gandhara, from Greek kings of Bactria

74 B.C. - According to Pliny the Roman General Lucullus introduced cherries to Europe. Greeks had cultivated cherries hundreds of years before this.

73 B.C. - Rome faced a 2nd slave uprising in Sicily.

70 B.C. - Virgil (d.19 B.C. -) [Vergil] (Publius Vergilius Maro), Roman poet, was born in Mantua. He wrote about the mythical founding of Rome in the Aeneid, which told the legend of Rome's founder and was considered a national epic.

70 B.C. - 15 B.C. - Vitruvius, author of De Architecture, translated to Italian in 1531.

69 B.C. - Cleopatra (d.30 B.C. -), daughter of Ptolemy XII, was born. She was queen of Egypt from 51 B.C. - 49 B.C. - , 48 B.C. - 30 B.C. - . During her reign she declared earthworms to be sacred and her subjects were forbidden to kill them.

69 B.C. - The Roman Gen'l. Lucullus experienced an attack by the Samosatans with a flammable mud called maltha (semisolid petroleum and gases). The event was lat-

er recorded by Pliny the Elder (23-79CE), a Roman naturalist.

66 B.C. - Tigranes I, King of Armenia was forced to become a tributary of Rome.

65 B.C. - Dec 8, Quintus "Horace" Horatius Flaccus (d.8 B.C. -), Roman poet and satirist best known for his three books "Odes," was born. "Drop the question what tomorrow may bring, and count as profit every day that Fate allows you."

63 B.C. - Sep 23, Caesar Augustus (63 B.C. - 14CE) was born in Rome. Augustus, first emperor of Rome, ended the era of the Roman Republic and introduced the Pax Romana, the era of peace. Augustus held power but shared administrative tasks with the Senate, consuls, and tribunes who continued to be elected: "Make haste slowly."

63 B.C. - Cicero was elected Consul of Rome. During this time he suppressed a conspiracy to murder the entire Senate.

63 B.C. - The Romans conquer the Jews The Jews appealed to Pompey to settle internal dissention. The Romans intervened and began their occupation of Palestine.

63 B.C. - Caesar's troops plundered Terena in Portugal's Alentejo province.

61 B.C. - Jul 7, Commagene, a small kingdom of the upper Euphrates, under the reign of King Antiochus, had a citadel area in front of which a lion was sculpted in relief with recognizable constellations on or near the lion's body. Prof. Otto Neugebauer of Brown Univ. studied the marks and identified the date of the sculpture.

59 B.C. - 52 B.C. - Caesar's legions battled the Gallo-Celtic tribesmen of King Vercingetorix in northern Burgundy.

59 B.C. - Chinese conquest of Central Asia

56 B.C. - First split of Hun Empire into Western and Eastern branches Qoghoshar (Khukheniy I) (56 - 36 B.C.)

55 B.C. - Aug 26, Roman forces under Julius Caesar invaded Britain.

55 B.C. - Pompey dedicated his theater, the first to be constructed of stone in Rome.

54 B.C. - The Eburons, A Belgian tribe under the command of their King Ambiorix, won a victory against the Roman Legion.

54 B.C. - The Romans under Julius Caesar fought the first skirmishes with the Celts in England.

54 B.C. - Chinese chronicles mention Ogurs as separate people in vicinity of Edisu

53 B.C. - Parthian nomads from east of Caspian Sea conquered Kabul River Valley, with Taxila and Pushkalavati as their twin capital cities in Gandhara, from Scythians. After defeating Greeks in 53 B.C., Parthians ruled northern Pakistan area. Parthians promoted art and religion, developed Gandhara school of art with Greek, Syrian, Persian and Indian art influences

53 B.C. - Sep 23, Augustus, the first Roman emperor, or Caesar, was born. His ascension to the title of emperor marked the end of true Roman democracy, even though the Senate survived for generations. [see 63 B.C. -]

53 B.C. - The Persians defeated the Romans in the Battle of Carrhae. Some 20,000 Romans under Crassus were killed by the Parthian army and 10,000 were captured. The Parthians then used the Romans as guards on their eastern frontier in what later became Turkmenistan.

52 B.C. - Pompey dedicated his Temple of Venus Victrix.

c52 B.C. - Cicero defended Titus Milo for the murder of Publius Clodius. The setting is the background for the historical detective novel: "A Murder on the Appian Way" by Steven Saylor.

52 B.C. - Caesar climaxed his conquest of Gaul at Alesia in northern Burgundy where he vanquished Celtic forces under Vercingetorix.

51 B.C. - 49 B.C. - Cleopatra was queen of Egypt from 51 B.C. - 49 B.C. - and 48 B.C. - 30 B.C. - .

51 B.C. - Huns (Hsiung-nu) split into two hordes, with Eastern Horde subject to China.

50 B.C. - Dionisios Periegetos says, already in 1st century B.C., Huns dominate over all Caspian lands

50 B.C. - Jun-Aug, In Egypt the "Zodiac of Dendera," a map of the stars of this period, was carved in stone. It is now in the French Louvre.

50 B.C. - Virgil first described the Damask Rose.

50 B.C. - Maastricht, Netherlands, began as a Roman settlement.

49 B.C. - Jan 11, Julius Caesar led his army across the Rubicon, plunging Rome into civil war. [see Jan 12, Mar 10]

49 B.C. - Jan 12, Julius Caesar crossed the Rubicon River signaling a war between Rome and Gaul. [see Jan 11, Mar 10]

49 B.C. - Mar 10, Julius Caesar crossed the Rubicon and invaded Italy. The event was noted by Suetonius in the phrase: "The die is cast." [see Jan 11]

49 B.C. - Mauretania (now northern Morocco and Algeria) became a client kingdom of Rome.

48 B.C. - Aug 9, Julius Caesar defeated Gnaius Pompey at Pharsalus.

48 B.C. - Sep 28, On landing in Egypt, Pompey was murdered on the orders of King Ptolemy of Egypt.

47 B.C. - Aug 2, Caesar defeated Pharnaces at Zela in Syria and declares "veni, vidi, vici," (I came, I saw, I conquered).

47 B.C. - Julius Caesar adopted a modified form of the Egyptian Calendar. Together with Sosigenes, an astronomer from Alexandria, the new calendar spreads the last 5-6 days of the Egyptian calendar amongst alternate months. March 1 began the year as a carry over from the old Roman calendar.

47 B.C. - The library at Alexandria was ravaged by fire.

46 B.C. - Caesar's calendar went into effect at the time of the first new moon after the winter solstice.

46 B.C. - The heart of ancient Numidia lay in the eastern region of what is now Algeria in Northern Africa. They were conquered by Rome in 46 B.C. - . The Vandals and Byzantines ruled successively before Arabs conquered the area in the seventh century CE.

45 B.C. - Jan 1, The Julian calendar took effect.

45 B.C. - Feb 29, The first Leap Day was recognized by proclamation of Julius Caesar. Under the old Roman calendar the last day of February was the last day of the year.

c45 B.C. - Colonia Julia Equestris, a Roman veterans' colony, was founded in what is now Nyon, Switzerland. Nyon is derived from the Celtic name Noviodunum.

44 B.C. - Mar 15, assassination of Julius Caesar in Rome Roman Emperor Julius Caesar (b.100 B.C. -) was murdered by Brutus, Cassius and other conspirators on the Ides of March. He had defeated Pompey in battle and had Pompey murdered in 48 B.C. - . He was perceived as a big threat to the Roman Aristocracy and so his murder was supported by Cicero and most Romans.

44 B.C. - Quintilis, the fifth month was changed to Julius in honor of Julius Caesar. A bright comet was declared by the Romans to be the soul of Julius Caesar ascending to join the gods.

43 B.C. - Mar 20, Ovid (d.17?18CE), Publius Ovidius Naso, Roman poet, was born. His writings included: "The Art of Love."

43 B.C. - Apr 21, Marcus Antonius was defeated by Octavian near Modena, Italy.

43 B.C. - Nov 27, Octavian, Antony and Lepidus formed the triumvirate of Rome.

43 B.C. - Dec 7, Cicero (b.106 B.C. -), considered one of the greatest sons of Rome was assassinated on the orders of Marcus Antonius. Cicero, elected Consul in 63, had chosen to support Pompey over Caesar. He translated Greek works that they might be understood by his fellow Romans, and tried to apply Greek ethical thought to Roman business and politics. His last work was "On Duties," where he propounds a common solution to all social problems i.e. "Always do the right thing... that which is legal... that which is honest, open and fair... keeping your word... telling the truth... and treating everyone alike. In 2002 Anthony Everitt authored "Cicero," a biography based on his letters.

42 B.C. - Oct 23, Marcus Junius Brutus, a leading conspirator in the assassination of Julius Caesar, committed suicide after his defeat at the Battle of Philippi. Octavian and Mark Antony defeated Brutus and Cassius at Philippi in Macedonia.

42 B.C. - Nov 16, Tiberius Claudius Nero (d.37CE, Roman Emperor, was born. Tiberius was chosen by Augustus in 4CE as emperor of Rome.

37 B.C. - King Herod (d.4 B.C. -) reigned over Judea. During his reign underground support structures were built for an expansion of the Temple Mount in Jerusalem. The Wall of King Herod's Second Temple is the famed "Wailing Wall."

37 B.C. - 448CE The Koguryo kingdom straddled what is now North Korea and part of South Korea and the northeastern Chinese

region of Manchuria. It spread Buddhism throughout the region.

33 B.C. - Agrippa called for the construction an aqueduct, 500 fountains and 700 basins for central Rome.

32 B.C. - Pompey's theater was damaged in a storm and repaired by Augustus who especially noted that in repairing it he nowhere recorded his own name.

32-23 B.C. - Octavian ruled as Consul over Rome by self election.

31 B.C. - Sep 2, The Naval Battle of Actium in the Ionian Sea, between Roman leader Octavian and the alliance of Roman Mark Antony and Cleopatra, queen of Egypt. Octavian soundly defeated Antony's fleet which was burned and 5000 of his men were killed. Cleopatra committed suicide. The rivals battled for control of the Roman Empire in the naval battle of Actium, where Cleopatra, seeing Antony's navy being outmaneuvered by Octavian's, ordered her 60 ships to turn about and flee to safety.

c31 B.C. - Augustus founded the city of Nikopolis in Epirus (northwestern Greece) to commemorate his victory over Antony and Cleopatra at Actium.

31 B.C. - Rome under Emperor Augustus annexed the Carthage territory.

31 B.C. - An earthquake occurred at the Qumran caves by the Dead Sea when Herod ruled in Jerusalem. This was the site where fragments of scrolls from the books of Psalms and Numbers were later found, as well as a human skeleton beneath boulders from the earthquake.

30 B.C. - Jul 30, Mark Antony, lover of the Egyptian queen Cleopatra VII and claimant to the Roman throne, stabbed himself when faced with certain defeat at the hands of his rival Octavian. Antony expected to be named the heir to Rome after the assassination of his friend and confidant Julius Caesar, but had not counted on Caesar naming his adopted son Octavian as his successor. Shaken by his loss at Actium and abandoned by his allies, Antony committed suicide. Cleopatra followed him in death shortly afterward when she allowed herself to be bitten by a venomous asp.

30 B.C. - Aug 30, Cleopatra, the 7th and most famous queen of ancient Egypt, committed suicide about this time.

30 B.C. - Rome gained control over Egypt. The wheat fields of Egypt became one of Rome's main sources of food. Antony and Cleopatra committed suicide.

30 B.C. - Construction began on the Temple of Isis in Sabratha, Libya. It was completed in 14CE.

29 B.C. - Cicero complained that "Two of my shops have fallen down... The tenants have fled... Even the mice have migrated." [see 43 B.C. -]

28 B.C. - Oct 9, The Temple of Apollo was dedicate on the Palatine Hill in Rome.

27 B.C. - The Roman senatorial province of Achaea was established. It comprised all of Greece south of Thessaly.

27 B.C. - 14CE Octavian, adopted son of Julius Caesar ruled as Rome's first emperor. He was given the name Augustus (revered or exalted one) and put an end to the chaos and power struggles that had occurred after Caesar's assassination. He also expanded the empire by conquering the territory that ran along the Rhine and Danube rivers.

25 B.C. - Augustus received two trade groups from India.

25 B.C. - Strabo, a geographer and scholar from Alexandria, made the most comprehensive map of the known world.

19 B.C. - Sep 20, The Roman poet Virgil (Publius Vergilius Maro, b.70 B.C. -) died. His epic "The Aeneid" became one of the great classics of Western literature. The story it tells runs from the end of the Trojan War to the start of the Roman Empire.

19 B.C. - Agrippa had the Aqua Virgo built in Rome.

19 B.C. - A wine jug bearing reference to King Herod was found in an ancient garbage dump near the synagogue at Masada, Israel. The cone-shaped, two-handled jug held about 20 gallons of wine and had been shipped from Italy.

19 B.C. - Romans turned Ghadames, Libya, into a garrison town.

16 B.C. - Flying Swallow (16) became empress to China's Emperor Cheng.

15 B.C. - King Herod of Judea built the coastal settlement of Caesarea. It was razed to the ground in 1265.

12 B.C. - Aug 31, Caligula (Gaius Caesar), 3rd Roman emperor (37-41 CE), was born.

10 B.C. - Aug 1, Claudius (d.54CE)., Roman Emperor, was born. Tiberius Claudius Nero Caesar Drusus, the nephew of Tiberius and

grandson of the wife of Augustus, was made emperor after Caligula.

08 B.C. - Augustus, emperor of the Roman Empire. The Roman Senate changed the name of the month Sextilis to Augustus, and an extra day was added while subtracting a day from February.

08 B.C. - Augustus Caesar ordered a census under the consulship of Gaius Censorinus and Gaius Asinius. 4,233,000 Roman citizens were counted.

08 B.C. - Horace (b.65 B.C. -), Roman poet, died. In 2002 J.D. McClatchy edited "Horace: The Odes, New Translations by Contemporary Poets.

c07 B.C. - Dionysius of Helicarnassus, Greek rhetorician and historian in Rome, died. He said that history is philosophy learned from examples.

06 B.C. - Apr 17, Jupiter was in a rare alignment with the constellation Aries and marked an important date for ancient astrologers. Jesus was believed to have been born in this year.

06 B.C. - In China Confucius suggested that effigies be used to be buried with a dead emperor instead of real people.

06 B.C. - 4 B.C. - Publius Quinctilius Varus served as Roman governor of Syria.

c05 B.C. - 65CE Seneca, Roman statesman: "Malice drinks one-half of its own poison."

c04 B.C. - The Second Temple in Jerusalem was rebuilt a few years before the birth of Jesus under King Herod. Jerusalem at this time had a population of about 100,000 people.

04 B.C. - Birth of Christ: one of several dates for the

04 B.C. - Publius Sulpicius Quirinus served as Roman governor of Cilicia, which was annexed to Syria.

04 B.C. - King Herod the Great died. He governed Judea from 37 B.C. - .

04 B.C. - 40CE Herod Antipas, son of Herod the Great, tetrarch of Galilee for this period. He examined Jesus at the request of Pilate. He executed John the Baptist. Pontius Pilate served as governor of the island of Ponza before he was made procurator of Judea.

04 B.C. - 65CE Lucius Annaeus Seneca, Roman intellectual born in Spain. He was a Stoic philosopher and playwright and wrote a version of "Medea." Seneca was Nero's teacher. Nero had Seneca compose his speeches. Seneca and his colleague were ordered by Nero to contrive the murder of Agripinna. He was forced to commit suicide after the conspiracy of Caius Piso to murder Nero. His wife Paulina cut her wrists together with Seneca but Nero ordered that she be saved. Seneca's blood did not flow well and he asked for poison which was refused. He then requested a hot bath to increase the blood flow and apparently was suffocated by the steam.

03 B.C. - Sep 14, Jupiter appeared to pass very close to the star Regulus, "the King's Star."

03 B.C. - 2 B.C. - Astronomical events occurred at this time and coincided with the probable birth of Jesus Christ. During the conjunctions of 3 B.C. - , Jupiter, the King Planet, came into contact with the King Star, Leo the Lion, which was also the sign for the Jewish tribe of Judah. REGULUS

02 B.C. - Feb 17, Jupiter again appeared to pass very close to the star Regulus, "the King's Star."

02 B.C. - May 8, Jupiter appeared to pass very close to the star Regulus, "the King's Star" for a 3rd time in recent months.

02 B.C. - Jun 17, Jupiter and Venus drew close together and appeared to fuse as a single star. This was later thought to be the Biblical star of Bethlehem.

02 B.C. - Heratosthene of Greece drew a map that showed 3 continents about equal in size labeled: Europe, Asia and Libya.

02 B.C. - The Maccabeans built an aqueduct in Jerusalem.

01 B.C. - Mar 1, Start of the revised Julian calendar in Rome.

01 A.D. - construction of Moche pyramids begins (South America)

01 A.D. - invention of paper in China

01/100

01/100 A.D. - import of pepper to Rome from India

01/100 A.D. - improved farming methods (China)

06 A.D. - Illirian rebelion (6-9 A.D.). Introduction of Roman provincial rule in Pannonia

20 A.D. - Strabo (c. 64 B.C. - - A.D. 20): Massagetae, [meaning hero-tribe] who also live in Balk are Kush. According to Armenians Baktria is land of Kush and Balkh is its capital city, where great Arsac set up his throne.

20 A.D. - Strabo: Parthian Scythians became Persian and Armenian kings from which even Byzantines received capable rulers. In Armenia Arsac dynasty ruled for about 600 years.

21 A.D. - Rebellion in Thrace and Gaul

3536 A.D. - Alanian participation in Ibero-Parphian war on side of Iberia.

48 - WESTERN HUN EMPIRE

48 - 216 A.D. - Founder - Panu Area - area over present Central Asia

50 A.D. - Kujula Kadphises unites (Yüeh-chih) to establish Kushan Empire, stretching from Persia to Transoxiana to Upper Indus.

50 A.D. - 1st century A.D. (first half) Alans (Alani =Tr. 'field') mentioned by written sources of Ancient Rome (?) for first time.

50 A.D. - Apostle Paul (Saul) begins spreading Christianity to the gentile world. Start of Christianity as a world event

64 A.D. - Kushana king Kujula, ruler of Central Asian nomads, overthrew the Parthians and took over Gandhara. Kushans extended their rule into northwest India and Bay of Bengal, south into Bahawalpur and short of Gujrat, and north till Kashghar and Yarkand. They made their winter capital at Purushapura, City of Flowers, now called Peshawar, and their summer capital north of Kabul

72 A.D. - Alans invade Transcaucasus

78-144 Reign of King Kanishka over Kushan Empire (territory extended to include Tarim Basin), with Buddhism as dominant religion.

79 A.D. - eruption of Vesuvius buries Pompeii and Herculaneum

93 A.D. - Western (Northern) Huns suffer a major defeat from Mongols (Hsien-pi) and start westward migration (93-c.380).

97 A.D. - Chinese armies reach Caspian Sea.

100 A.D.

100 A.D. - kingdom of Funan in Vietnam

117 A.D. - library built at Ephesus (Turkey, Library of Celsus)

106 A.D. - Jornand recalls that Nocopol on Danube was founded by Trayan after victory over Sarmats

122 A.D. - building of Hadrian's Wall in Britain

124 A.D. - Dionysius Periegetes (the guide) Orbis terrae descriptio map showing Huns (Unni), Caspii, Massagets, Sacii, Alani, Scyths, Hyrcanii, Sarmats, Taurii

124 A.D. - Dionisus Periegetes (end of 1st - beginning of 2nd c.) maps and talks that on Northwestern side of Caspian sea live Scythians, Uns, Caspians, Albanians, and Kaduses, of Huns living next to Caspian Sea Sak (Gr. Sacae)=Türkco-Persian saka=water carrier

128 A.D. - Kanishka, the greatest of Kushans, ruled from 128 to 151 A.D.

135 A.D. - Alanian campaign in Transcaucasus and Media

139 A.D. - Dionisus Periegetes: Huns living next to Dniepr in Eastern Europe. Calls them Khuni (Chuni) and Suni. (Khuni is clan/national designation while Suni is probably from Senü, their ruler)

139 A.D. - Ptolemy (83?-161? A.D.) writes that in European Sarmatia 'below Agathyrsi (Akatsirs, Tr. Agach-ers 'forest people') live Savari (Türkic Suvars), between Basternae (Tr. Bash-t-er 'head people') and Rhoxolani (Tr. Uraksy Alans, i.e. 'Alans-farmers') live Huns

150 A.D. - Mid. 2nd century Alans defeated by Roman army at Olvia (Olbia)

150 A.D. - Pyramid of the Sun in Teotihuacan (Central Mexico), Reading on the Pyramid of the Sun

155 A.D. - End of Huns as a major power in inner Asia.

200 A.D. - ca. A.D. 200-370: Invasions by Goths., who colonize and mix with local populations. Tervingi branch consolidated their realm between Dniestr and Danube, and became known as 'Visigoths'. Greutungi dominated west of Dniestr and became known as Ostrogoths

200 A.D. - Yamato State founded (Japan)

200 A.D. - Bantu-speaking people in South Africa

220 A.D. - Han Empire breaks into many pieces (China)

213 A.D. - Roman war with German and Danubian tribes. Caracalla defeats Alemans

214 A.D. - Edessa becomes a Roman colony

216 A.D. - End of HUN EMPIRE

216 A.D. (from 204 A.D.) - Founder - Mete (Bagatir) Area - At north, Siberia; south, Tibet - Kashmir; east, Pacific Ocean; west, Caspian Sea (Total Area - 18,000,000 Km 2)

216 A.D. - End of WESTERN HUN EMPIRE

216 A.D. (from 48 A.D.) - Founder - Panu Area - area over present Central Asia

226 A.D. - End of Parthian Dynasty (ab. 247 B.C.-A.D. 226), it was one of longest in history

234 A.D. - Roman war against Alemans. Maximin, a Thracian, is proclaimed Emperor by Pannonian army (ñ 235 to 238)

235 A.D. - period of military anarchy in Roman Empire

236 A.D. - Roman war against Sarmatians and Dacians

236 A.D. - Gothic invasion across Danube and invasion of Dacian Carps

260 A.D. - In 60's of 3rd c, Caucasian Huns served in Persian army

266 A.D. - Unification of China. Hun rebellion is suppressed

275 A.D. - EUROPEAN HUN EMPIRE

275 - 454 A.D. - Founder - brothers Muncuk, Oktar, Rua & Aybars

Area - S Russia, Romania, N Yugoslavia, Hungary, Austria, Czechoslovakia, S& C Germany. From E France to Urals; from N.Hungary to Byzantine Empire

(Area - 4,000,000 Km2)

290 A.D. - In 90's of 3rd c, Armenian sources write about Hun's wars in Trans-Caucasus (N.Caucasus)

293 A.D. - Sasanid (Persian) inscriptions dated by 293 mention name of one of Türkic khakans from Caucasus

300 A.D. - start of the Maya Classic Period (Yucatan, Mexico)

300 A.D. - Tele left early Huns Horde, keeping patriarchal relations and nomadic life. They were not Sinadized. They move in steppes on carts with high wheels.

300 A.D. - Tele have 12 clans, each governed by aldermen, all living in peace

300 A.D. - Sirs and Türks live at Ordos

300 A.D. - Bulgars and Khazars are blood relatives, with a common or similar language.

301 A.D. - In 4-7c. Seyanto (Sir + Yanto) occupied steppes between Mongol Altai and E. Tianshan

304 A.D. - Huns and Syanbinians conquered from China Khan Empire northern part and established a sequence of kingdoms. Toba tribe led predominantly Chinese population.

309 A.D. - Hun's raid eased by rebellion of (Chinese) people against officials

309 A.D. - Intrigues of Emperor Huai-di against Sym Yuy. Aliance with Tabgach Khan Ilu against Huns

311 A.D. - Defeat of Sym Yuy. Fall of Loyan, Huns take Chanan

311 A.D. - Christianity made official religion of the Roman Empire

312 A.D. - Small Syanbinian tribe with Khans from Muyun family moved from southern Manjuria to west and settled in proximity of lake Kukunor. They fought Tibetans successfully and Tobases unsuccessfully.

312 A.D. - Syanbinian tribe with Muyun Khans were organized into kingdom Togon and became vassals of Empire Wey.

312 A.D. - Chinese displace Huns from Chanan

320 A.D. - Muyun Khoy becomes Great Shanuy

321 A.D. - Tsu Ti dies, and Chinese advance against Huns stopped

325 A.D. - China loses lands north of river Huai

330 A.D. - Constantinople was founded (Turkey)

334 A.D. - First mention of Bulgars, they live in basin of Tanais and Cuban

336 A.D. - Beg. 4th c. Invasion of Armenia by Hun-Maskuts (Gr. Massagets), together with Sakas, led by king of Massagetae Sanesan (Tr. Sen-esen=you+storming (man))

337 A.D. - Hun' s vanguard reached Tanais, displaced Ostgoths, who displaced Visigoths and Sarmats into Roman territory. Death of Constantine the Great leads to formal division of Roman Empire into Western and Eastern Empires

338 A.D. - Tele tribes subjugated by Tobases Khan. They live west of Ordos

350 A.D. - invention of stirrup (China)

350 A.D. - Ügülüy from Syanbinian cavalry organizes a band and joints neighboring nomads.

350 A.D. - Tele are living of animal husbandry, in a weak confederation of tribes, fighting for their independence.

354 A.D. - Earliest known European record about Bulgarians is "Anonymous chronograph", a list of tribes and peoples in Latin. He mentiones a certain 'Ziezi ex quo Vulgares'.

360 A.D. - Huns cross Volga and attack Alans. Part of Alans retreat to N. Caucasus, part is absorbed in Hun's Horde, part retreat to N. Donets. Most likely, after conquest a part of Bulgars joins Huns, and a part remains

360 A.D. - Uhuans and Syanbins become subjects of Fu Tsyan II, who moves them beyond Chinese Wall

363 A.D. - In 363, Armenian, Roman and Persian authors write about necessity of fortifying Caucasian passages, especially Derbent passage, against Huns, who make repeated raids and campaigns against Persians, Armenians and peoples of Middle East

364 A.D. - Goth's invasion of Thrace

367 A.D. - Valens twice crossed Danube with his troops and devastated much of Goths' territory

370 A.D. - Huns defeat Goths (Germans)

370 A.D. - Romans hired Hunnic warriors as auxiliary troops and paid them a yearly tribute, partly for services rendered and partly as a bribe to keep them from raiding provinces

370 A.D. - Huns were a genetic hybrid between Mongoloid, Altaic (Siberian), and Central Asian Türkic stocks. Typical Hunno-Bulgars probably had a squarish face, high cheekbones, and slanting eyes. Term 'Bulgar' comes from Türkic 'bulgha' = 'to mix'. These nomadic horsemen groups were mainly composed of As - Ossetians, Eastern Antes - Iranian-Slavic blend, Khazars - a mixed Türkic group, and a people known as Sarmatians, an Iranian group.

370 A.D. - Huns defeat Ostrogoths. Death of Germanarix. Vinitari (Vitimir?) becomes new Ostrogothic king. Ostrogoths retire to Lower Dniepr. Geruls and Burgundians part of Ostrogoths.

370 A.D. - 370-376 War between Alans and Goths.

370 A.D. - Huns control N. Pontic, Tanais, and N. Caspian steppes. Alans who live there join Huns.

370 A.D. - Guylüchoy, successor to Ügülüy, organized a horde, move along all Khalka to Khingan, subordinated to Tobas Khans, paid tribute in horses, sable and martens.

370 A.D. - Guylüchoy life and organization are primitive and organized by regiments of 1000 men. No changes for 200 years. All efforts went to rob neighbors.

370 A.D. - 2 migrations of Bulgarians from Caucasus to Armenia. 1st during Armenian ruler Vaharshak, immigrants of Vh' ndur Bulgar Vund, lands named Vanand.

370 A.D. - 2nd migration during Armenian ruler Arshak, disturbances ... in land of Bulgars, many of whom migrated and settled south of Kokh, because of expansion of Huns in E European steppes

372 A.D. - After crushing, or compelling alliance of, various nations Alpilzuri, Alcidzuri, Himari, Tuncarsi, Boisci, Huns reached Alani, Don Alans crushed by Huns. Part of Alans joins Huns in advance to Europe

374 A.D. - Retreating to Dnieper Ostrogoths fight with Ants living there. After a number of battles and defeats, Ostrogoths captured Antian King Boz (Bus, Bog?) and executed him

375 A.D. - Jordanes, XLVIII, 249. Battle between Alans under Balamber and Ostrogoths at river Erac (present Tiligul). After death of Vitimir, young Vidirix bacame a King. Alatey and Safrac ruled under his name. Ostrogoths retreated to Dniestr.

375 A.D. - Ammianus Marcellinus: After his (Hermanaric) departure, Vitimir was made a King, and resisted Halans for some time... But after many defeats he suffered, he was subdued by arms and died in battle

376 A.D. - Huns captured Atilkuzu (Bessarabia). Alans remained in Dacia. Vestgoths and Ostrogoths, defeated by Huns and Alans, retreated to Danube.

376 A.D. - Vestgoths and Ostrogoths Goths fled from Huns, asked help from Emperor Valens, who allowed them cross Danube to guard borders, and entered Roman Empire. Poor control of crossing, extractions by of-

ficials caused rebellion. Rome faced Gothic invasion.

376 A.D. - Goths who crossed Danube became Visigoths, and Goths who remained behind and became subjects of Huns were designated Ostrogoths. Ostrogoths who cross Danube joined Vestgoths. Entire Alaric's Visigothic population is estimated to be around 100,000 people

377 A.D. - Hunnish-Bulgarian association during period of Hunnish hegemony in Central Europe. Attilla's combat power consists mostly from mounted Bulgarian troops. Attila' dynasty is continued for Bulgars.

377 A.D. - A detachment of Huns crossed Kerch straight from Caucasus, displaced Goths in Crimea to center of peninsula, and went to join main army in Dniestr estuary

378 A.D. - At a victory celebration Bulümar (360??---378) dies, his son Alyp-bi becomes Khan of Huns (378-390)

378 A.D. - Oldest son of Hun's Bulümar (Balamber) Alyp-bi defeats Sadumes (Scandinavians), crossed Danube, and with Visigoths, Ostrogoths and Alans defeats 80K Byzantium army at Andrianopol

378 A.D. - Valens acted alone and engaged a massive Gothic force of estimated 200,000 warriors near Adrianople. Result was a catastrophe, Valens army was completely annihilated, he perished (9 August A.D. 378). His body was never found

380 A.D. - Western (Northern) Huns in westward migration (93-c.380) take possession of lower Tanais river valley and north of Meotida

380 A.D. - New Roman Emperor Theodosius settles Gothic problem diplomatically. Goths become federates, and Alans move north.

380 A.D. - 380-395 Alans clear Dacia and Atilkuzu from Vestgoths, Taifals, Gepids, Burgunds and other peoples. Huns went to Pontic steppes

386 A.D. - Creation of Tabgach-Northern Wey Empire

390 A.D. - Tele move north, to Djungaria, and spread in West Mongolia to Selenga.

390 A.D. - Alyp-bi (378-390) dies, is buried on Kuyantau mountain (current Kiev) under Baltavar stone with Ψ sign. His son Aybat (Eur. Mundzuk) becomes Khan of Huns (390-434)

395 A.D. - Hun campaign in Cis-Caucasus and even raid Syria. Alans, Ostrogoths and Geruls, retreated earlier to Cis-Caucasus, subordinate to Huns

395 A.D. - Rebellion of Alarics and Visigoths

400 A.D. - Syanbian language, ancient Mongolian, becomes inter-tribe language for Türk's allied tribes. "Türk" = "strong", "powerful".

400 A.D. - Alans and Bulgars live between Itil and Don

400 A.D. - In Danube area, evidently, arrived Huns. They killed Byzantian federate Gain, expelled by rebels from Constantinople.

400 A.D. - Arab and Persian authors mention town Varachan (Belenjer), capital of Hun state, in Sulak valley near Upper Chir-Ürt in Dagestan. Later authors refer to Balanjar as native land of Khazars.

400 A.D. - Ancestors of Khazars among Huns called selves Basils (Bas, head; il/el, people--ruling people)

402 A.D. - Ruler of Western Empire Stilihon allied with Huns and Alans, who help Stilihon to fight off attack of German tribes.

405 A.D. - New help by Huns and Alans to Stilihon to fight off attack of German tribes (Suewes).

406 A.D. - Alans join Vandals in invasion to Gallia (modern France).

406 A.D. - Radagais leads Vandals, Suebis, Kuads, Burgonds, Saxsons, Almants, is captured at Fiesol by Huns under Ulduz (?-410?), supposedly, ruler of right, eastern wing of Hunnish army, allied with Romans, and is executed (Aug 406). Vandals cross Rein, retreat to Gaul

409 A.D. - Alans and Vandals moving from Gaul to Spain.

409 A.D. - Uldiz, ruler of right, eastern wing spread from Balkhash to Volga, tells to ambassador of Byzantium, governor of Thrace, "I can capture all lands to sunset"

410 A.D. - Syanbinian Jujan Khan Shelun Deuday died (?-410), his brother Khulüy (410-414) becomes Khan.

410 A.D. - Syanbinian Jujan Khan Shelun Deuday unlimitedly controlled steppes from Khingan to Altai. Tele were subjugated. Central Asian Huns, after winning battle at river Ili, recognized suzerainty of Syanbinian Jujans and bought peace by submissiveness.

410 A.D. - Huns attack Roman Empire and sack Rome. Huns introduce pants to Roman Empire, which replace traditional togas

410 A.D. - Goths attack and sack Rome

410 A.D. - After death of Uldiz (?-410?) Karaton (410-422?) becomes Khagan of Huns. In 412 Karaton receives Byzantian ambassador Olimpiodors. Karaton rules mostly eastern part of empire. No information till 422 A.D. - 412 A.D. - Byzantian embassy to Huns in Pontic area

414 A.D. - Syanbinian Jujan Khan Khulüy (410-414) died, his cousin Datan (414-?) becomes Khan

418 A.D. - Syanbinian Jujanes penetrated Tarbagatay area

420 A.D. - Toba tribe unites Northern China into a kingdom known under Chinese name of Empire Wey

420 A.D. - Huns settle in middle Danube. Rulers were Roila (Rugila), Mundzuk and Oktar

420 A.D. - WHITE HUN (EPHTALITE) EMPIRE

420 - 552 A.D. - Founder - Aksuvar (Aksungur)

Area - Half of Northern India, Afghanistan, parts of Turkistan, Eastern Turkestan but also significant parts of Central Asia (Tokharistan, Chaganian, Samarkand, Bukhara, Kesh, Ferghana, Chach (Total Area - 3,500,000 Km2)

420 A.D. - Ephtalites were divided into White Chions and Red Chions

424 A.D. - Jujan Khan Datan (?-424) with 60K cavalry invades Empire Wey. In 425 Tobases of Empire Wey expel them to behind Gobi

430 A.D. - Major campaign by Tabgach Empire Wey army, under Emperor Tay-u-di (Toba Dao) disperses Syanbinian Jujanes. Datan disappears, leadership taken by his son Udi (430-445). Udi agrees to pay tribute to Empire Wey

430 A.D. - Huns reach Rein. Yabgu Roila (Ruga) keeps friendly relations with Rome, lending troops to suppress Bagauds in Gaul

432 A.D. - After Oktar, Ruga (432-437) becomes Hun Khagan

434 A.D. - Akatzirs are subjects to Huns under Hunnish Khan Ruga (432-437)

434 A.D. - Aybat (Eur. Mundzuk) (390-434) dies. His son Attila becomes Yabgu of W. Huns (Kara Bulgar) (434-445). His son Bleda becomes ruler of E. Huns (Ak Bulgar) (434-445).

434 A.D. - Roman bishop of Margus crossed Danube and robbed royal Hun graves, stealing their burial treasures. War broke out

434 A.D. - Attila forces Eastern Roman Empire to recognize the superiority of Huns. Constantinople gives many concessions in treaty of Margus: Hun merchants' rights, military alliance conducts, the return of Hun fugitives, and increases tribute to 700 pounds of gold to be paid each year

434 A.D. - Possibly during Byzantine campain Ruga (Rua, Roila, Rugila) dies (?-434), Atilla and his brother Bleda are elected, his nephew Attila becomes ruler of left (western) wing of empire

437 A.D. - Syanbinian Jujanes under Udi resume attacks on Empire Wey. In 439 Empire Wey counterattacks, without decisive battle. In 440 Udi attacks border and flees. Then again in 445.

439 A.D. - In 439 Tobases had victory over Huns and joined Khesi to Wey Empire, Khan Ashina with 500 families fled to Syanbinian Jujanes and settled south of Altai mountains and produced iron for Syanbinian Jujanes.

439 A.D. - An horde of warlike Syanbinians retreated to Tibet from Khesi. Coming to a rich, but disunited country, Syanbinian leader attracted Kyans, i.e. occupied a dominating position between ever-hostile tribes.

439 A.D. - In Tibet, descendants of Syanbinian leader had title Tsenpo, meaning in between King and Head of Government, supported by Syanbinians who are the only real force in country.

439 A.D. - Huns stand in Dunkhuan and battle against Shanshan

440 A.D. - Atilla has a full control in N. Caucasus. Treaty with Persian Shakh Yazdagar

440 A.D. - Hephthalites (White Huns, later known in West as Avars) move south from Altai region to occupy Transoxiana, Bactria, Khurasan, and eastern Persia

441 A.D. - Huns are again on Danube border, took Singidun (Belgrad)

442 A.D. - Ultimatum by Atilla to Theodosius II, who rejects it.

442 A.D. - 442-447 Huns invade Byzantium. Destruction of cities in Illiria and Thrace, capture and inclusion of vast territory in Hunnish state.

443 A.D. - Peace between Theodosius II and Atilla. By peace of Anatolius (the mediator of the treaty negotiation) Romans were to pay 6,000 pounds of gold immediately, and yearly tribute set at 2,100 pounds of gold, and immediate release of Hun fugitives

444 A.D. - Atilla, Kara Bulgar Yabgu, becomes Hun Kagan (445-453) upon death of Kagan Bled (434-445), the highest ruler from Caucasus to Danube. Per Priscus, Bleda had honor burial and three-day giant feast attended by all nobles in Kaganate

445 A.D. - Syanbinian Jujan Khan Udi (430-445) died, his son Tukhechjen becomes Khan. Empire Wey undertakes punishment raids into steppes against Syanbinian Jujanes.

447 A.D. - 2-nd peace of Anatolius between Byzantiun and Huns. Big tribute to Huns. Hun commander Edeco assented to assassinate Atilla for 50 pounds of gold

448 A.D. - Byzantian embassy to Atilla, described by Priscus. Byzantian attempt to organize Atilla's murder.

448 A.D. - Akatzirs are reported by Priscus living near Black Sea and subjects to Huns. Attila (7) (437-453) installs Karidach (Kuridach) as Akatzirs Khan.

450 A.D. - In written sources, Huns are identified with Scythians and Cimmerians, and specifically with "Royal Scythians". Scythian ethnonym "As-kishi", or its stem "as" is retained in written sources, especially old Georgian documents, in Huns' name as "ovs", "os"

450 A.D. - Hunnish society attained progress thanks to contact with Roman civilization. In dwelling place of Onegesios, in Attila's court, for example, prisoner from Sirmium constructed baths

450 A.D. - Priscus: "because Scythians are mixed and besides their own language, they try to speak language of Huns, or Goths or Ausoni, when some of them have to do with Romans"

450 A.D. - Per Priscus, Sabirs conquered lands of Onogurs, Saragurs and Ugors in steppes around north-western Caspian coast.

450 A.D. - Death of Theodosius II Flavy on a hunt (10.4.401). Markian, a son of a plain soldier, becomes Emperor, formally as a husband of Pulheria. 450 Markian refuses to pay tribute to Huns.

450 A.D. - Huns were called Os in 5th century, during their raids in Georgia in time of king Vakhtang. Word "ovs" of Georgian sources is actually a slightly deformed name of a Türk tribe "As"

451 A.D. - Attila heads great army, size of Hunnic army has been variously estimated at between 300,000 and 700,000, crossed Rhine and swept across Europe looting, pillaging, and burning. Aetius battles Attila on Rein in June at Battle of Chalons on Catalaunian Plains

451 A.D. - 451.06.15 "Battle of Peoples" at Catalaun ravine near present Trua. On Atilla's side are Huns, Geruls, Ostrogoths and part of Franks, on Aecius side Roman legions recruited from Gaul and Germany, Vestgoths, Burgunds, Franks, Armorician Alans headed by San. No definite result.

451 A.D. - Jordanes: In a direct fight battled strongest troops on both sides, without surprise attacks. Mighty tribes were killed, 165K on each side, plus 15K Gepids and Franks who fought at night, killing each other, Franks on Roman side, Gepids on Hun's side

451 A.D. - Atilla prepares a campain in Italy

452 A.D. - Italian campain of Atilla, ending with peace. In spite of large conquests, Atilla agreed to peace because of epidemy in his army.

453 A.D. - Atilla (434-453) weds young German Ildico. Next morning he is found dead. End of Hunnish hegemony in Central Europe. Atilla is given state funerals. Ellak becomes Hun Kagan (453-454).

453 A.D. - Vestgoths, headed by Torismud, son of killed in Catalaunian Plains Theodorix, defeat Huns and expell them from their territory.

453 A.D. - Coalition of Germanic clans defeats and kills Ellak in battle at Nedao.

453 A.D. - Gepids under Ardaric battle Huns under Ellak. Tingiz ((Dengizik/Diggiz) and Bel-Kermek (Hernach) retreat to a military camp and defend for 2 years. Negotiations allow Tingiz and Bel-Kermek leave with Bulgars, remaining defenders are surrendered to Ardaric

453 A.D. - To Ellak, eldest of brothers, given Sabir ulus, to 2-nd son Tengiz given Kutrigur

ulus, to Bel-Kermek, 3-rd son, given Utigur ulus

453 A.D. - 454-565 Gepids control Pannonia. Gepidian reign is established in Dacia (current day Transylvania)

454 A.D. - Several Hunno-Bulgar uluses outside of three main Hunnic hordes joined with Byzantines with obligation of military services, and were given land to settle as protectors against their northern cousins

454 A.D. - Coalition of Germanic clans defeats and kills Ellak in battle. Sabirs without Ellak retreat to East, through Pontic Steppes, to Daghestan. Kutriguri and Utiguri under Bel-Kermek (Hernach), fell back to 'Ugol' place that corresponds to Bessarabia

454 A.D. - 454 - 455 Rebelion in Hun's state. German tribes of Gepids, Rugs, Geruls rebelled. Battle at Nedao (Nedava, tributary of Sava). Coalition was composed of Gepids, Scires, Suaves, Ruges, Herules and Ostrogoths

454 A.D. - Jordanes: You could see Goth with lances, Gepids mad with sword, Rug breaking spears in his wounds, and Svev bravely acting with bat, and Hun with arrow, Alan with heavy, Gerule with light weapons.

454 A.D. - Atilla's son Ellak tried suppress rebelion, was defeated and died in battle. Remains of Ellak's army retreated east of Carpathians. Two other sons Dengizik and Ernak remained in Dacia and Bessarabia. Alans led by ruler Kandak were forced to go to Dobrudja

454 A.D. - Ostrogoths take part on losing side in battle at Nedao where Gepids under Ardaric crush last Hun coalition. Ostrogoths become sovereign and settle in Pannonia

454 A.D. - End of EUROPEAN HUN EMPIRE

275 - 454 A.D. - Founder - brothers Muncuk, Oktar, Rua & Aybars

Area - S Russia, Romania, N Yugoslavia, Hungary, Austria, Chekoslovakia, S& C Germany. From E France to Urals; from N Hungary to Byzantine Empire (Area -4,000,000 Km2)

455 A.D. - Tingiz and Bel-Kermek (Hernach) (455-465) lead Bulgars, on way from Pannonia to estuary of Buri-chai (Dnieper) are attacked by Gallidjians (Scandinavians). Tingiz is killed. Bel-Kermek raises red flag of Asses and breaks through to lower Dnieper.

455 A.D. - Bel-Kermek, 3rd son of Atilla, leads Bulgars to settle between Crimea and estuary of Buri-chai (Dniepr), and proclaims a beylik of Altynoba, with Bel-Kermek as Baltavar (Lord of Beys) (455-465).

455 A.D. - Bel-Kermek with Hun's Sadagariem and other tribes remain in Dobrudja (Little Scythia) and Lower Moesia. Later known as Sacromontizies and Fossatizies.

455 A.D. - Two other Attilla's sons, Emnetzur and Ultzindur lead from Crimea tribes of Ultzindzur and Ultzindgur to Byzantium on right bank of Danube

455 A.D. - Jews from Armenia and Persia begin immigration to North Caucasus

459 A.D. - Hephthalites conquer Kushans and invade India

460 A.D. - Bulgarian tribes Ultinzur, Bittugur and Bardor of Pannonia join Altynoba, with Bel-Kermek as Baltavar (Lord of Beys). Huns adopt name Bulgars, Bulgars use Hun's language.

463 A.D. - Ogur Türkic tribes, including Onogurs (Onoghur = 10 Ogur Confederation), Saragurs (White Türks) and Uturgurs (Utigurs) (Uturgur = 30 Ogur Confederation) cross Itil and enter Europe.

463 A.D. - Priscus Rhetor: In 463 Byzantium was visited by an embassy of Saragurs, Urogs and Onogurs, who, dislodged by Avars drive to west, conquered conquered lands of Akacirs and asked for a union with Byzantium

463 A.D. - Destunis G.C.: Saragurs, Urogs and Onogurs sent embassy to Byzantine. They said that they were expelled by Savirs, who fled Avars, who fled from people living on shores of ocean. Saragurs subjugated Akacirs and want to become Roman federates

463 A.D. - Gumilev suggests that after fall of Hun's Empire Bulgars take a lead and decimated Akacirs, finishing fall of Hun's Empire

465 A.D. - Bulgars led by Bel-Kermek control lands of Akacirs and asked for a union with Byzantium

465 A.D. - Altynoba's Bel-Kermek (455-465) dies, his older son Djurash Masgut becomes Baltavar (465-505).

465 A.D. - Agaçeris crossed Caucasus and invaded Media. Agaçeris are included in Five Ogur confederation which also includ-

ed Karluk, Kangly, Kalaç and Kipchak nations

468 A.D. - Tengiz (Dengizik) and Bel-Kermek (Hernach) sent ultimatum to Byzantium, when it is rejected, Dengizik invades Thrace, but is defeated under command of Byzantians Anagast and Aspar. Dengizik dies in battle.

468 A.D. - Bulgar Kutigurs fight Byzantine (468-469). Bysantine's Anagast procured Khan Dengizik's head after he was killed and sent it to Constantinople where it was displayed atop of a spear. Kutrigurs never forgot Utigur Hernach's refusal of help.

468 A.D. - 468 - 469 Danube war between Huns and Byzantium. Bel-Kermek (Hernach) after Dengizik death leads army. Byzantium beats off invasion with difficulty. Byzantium mercenary army consists of Slavs and Alans commanded by Aspar, whose father was Alan.

468 A.D. - Vernadsky G.V.:"in some respect Danube war of 468 - 469 was a war of Alans and Ants against their former masters, Huns." After Byzantian victory Huns left Dacia and Bessarabia. These provinces opened for Slavic colonization.

469 A.D. - Western Hunnish clans retreated. Utigurs to Azov-Taman SE of Sea of Azov. Kutrigurs to between Dniepr and Don Rivers, NW from Sea of Azov Utigurs. Sabirs in Daghestan SE of other two Hunnic hordes, between Daryal Gorge and Kuma River on Caspian Sea.

469 A.D. - 469 - 488 movement of Bel-Kermek army back to Meotian-Taman region. They call themselves descendents of Hernach and are known as Utigurs (Kulakovsky "Alans")

469 A.D. - Remnants of Tengiz (Dengizik) horde follow Utigurs to Dniepr and settle between Dniepr and Meotian Sea. They were called Kutigurs.

470 A.D. - Peace between Syanbinian Jujan and Tabgach-Northern Wey Empire

480 A.D. - Promulgation of first Sinicization decree in Tabgach-Northern Wey Empire

481 A.D. - Ioanes Antiochenus: First written agreement of Byzantium emperor Zeno (474-475,476-491) with Bulgars' Djurash Masgut (465-505), allying them in war against Ostrogoths Goths of Theodoric (493-526), son of Triarius [Must be 475]

485 A.D. - Syanbinian Jujan Khan Üychen (?-485)died, his ...??... Doulun (485-492) becomes Khan.

486 A.D. - Bulgars fight again against Goths as allies of Byzantium

488 A.D. - Bulgars settle in Moesia, Thrace and Macedonia after expelling Theodoric Ostrogoths (488).

488 A.D. - Khazarian khalifa begins rule over Georgia and Abania in S. Caucasus

488 A.D. - Bulgars fought again against Goths as allies of Gepids.

488 A.D. - Bulgarians had been regarded as a brave and invincible in war people

488 A.D. - Chersonesus ruler decided to restore walls and towers damaged by earthquake, scared of Kutugur's raids

492 A.D. - Syanbinian Jujan Khan Doulun (485-492) killed, end of Syanbinian Jujan overlordship over steppes and Tele. Nagay (492-493) becomes Khan

492 A.D. - Kutigur Bulgars invade Thrace, defeat Byzantine army and kill their leader Julian.

493 A.D. - Syanbinian Jujan Khan Nagay (492-493) died, his son Futu (493)becomes Khan.

493 A.D. - 493-499 Altynoba's Djurash Masgut Kutigur Huns start raiding Thrace, possibly with Slavs. They took advantage of a civil war in Byzantium.

495 A.D. - Publication of Sinicization decree in Tabgach-Northern Wey Empire prohibiting use of Tabgach language.

498 A.D. - Altynoba's Djurash Masgut in winter 498-499 annihilate Byzantium Illyrium army and extends to left bank of Danube. Altynoba subordinates to Avar overlordship.

499 A.D. - Toba conquerors assimilated and switched to Chinese language

500 A.D. - Camels well established as a means of desert transport in North Africa

500 A.D. - kingdom of Chenia in Cambodia

500 A.D. - Gaochan in Turfan oasis, under ethnically Chinese lord, under overlordship of Syanbinian Jujanes, breaks with their allies Syanbinian Jujanes.

500 A.D. - Earliest settlement on site of city of Bolgary dates to about A.D. 500 A.D. - 502 A.D. - Altynoba's Djurash Masgut Kutigur Huns Bulgars plundered all of Thrace

504 A.D. - Buddhism proclamed a state religion in China.

504 A.D. - Altynoba's Djurash Masgut Kutigur Huns raid Thrace, possibly with Slavs

505 A.D. - Altynoba's Djurash Masgut (465-505) dies, Tatra (505-) becomes Bulgarian Baltazar subordinated to Avar overlordship.

505 A.D. - Sabirs from Pannonia immigrate to North Caucasus and Itil valley

505 A.D. - Sabirs created a powerful federation of akin tribes, "Kingdom of Huns". They were populous and had an army of 20,000 well equipped cavalrymen. They were masters of art of war and build siege machines unknown even to Persians and Byzantines.

508 A.D. - Teles (Teleutes) Khan Mivotu in vassalage to Ephtalites. Helps Empire Wey 's 3K army defeated Syanbinian Jujanes at lake Puley, after being paid 60 pieces of silk by Empire Wey. Futu dies in struggles. Mivotu is rewarded with musical instruments.

508 A.D. - Cheunu (508-520) becomes Syanbinian Jujan Khan.

513 A.D. - Altynoba's Tatra Bolgarian raids against Byzantium become annual. Huno-Bulgars aid in Vitalians Revolt (514).

513 A.D. - Buddhism penetrates to Syanbinian Jujanes. Khan Cheunu converts to Buddhism. Religious divisions in ruling clan

516 A.D. - Syanbinian Jujan Khan Cheunu attacks Tele's kingdom Gaogüy, captures Tele (Teleut) lord Mivota, Tele escape to Ephtalites.

516 A.D. - Slavs raid Macedonia and Illiria

518 A.D. - Cheunu sends an embassy to Empire Wey, received by emperor Syao-mindi, re-establishes vassalage to Wey.

518 A.D. - Justin I repulsed Slav hordes beyond Danube

519 A.D. - Syanbinian Jujan Khan Cheunu makes a treaty with Ephtalites, gives Eftalite lords his princesses as wives. Allies with Korea (Gao-Guyli) against Empire Wey, and together smash Manju tribe Dideugan.

519 A.D. - Empire Wey recognized suzerainty of Turfan's Gaochan, and Syanbinian Jujanes continue to trade with them, receiving bread and cloth. Iron goods are provided to Syanbinian Jujans by their Türk (Türkstuku) vassals in Altai.

520 A.D. - Syanbinian Jujan Khan Cheunu (508-520) killed by his mother, installed her another son, Anahuan, replaced by Polomyn.

521 A.D. - Teles rebel and defeat remaining Syanbinian Jujanes under Polomyn, and Polomyn moves to Empire Wey with remains of his Horde. Anakhuan escaped to Empire Wey in 520, so both branches of Syanbinian Jujan horde ended up in Empire Wey.

521 A.D. - Polomyn's horde is resettled within Empire Wey by lake Kukunor, and Sinifa, brother of Anakhuan, is resettled beyond border, north of Dunkhuan.

525 A.D. - Anahuan leads Empire Wey expedition against rebel fortress Bo-ye and defeats rebels. Receives rewards and absolution from Empire Wey.

525 A.D. - Togon's Syanbinian prince Kualüy pronounces himself Khan.

527 A.D. - Procopius Caesariensis: Hephthalites are people from Unn tribe, but they do not mix with them... they are not nomads like other Unn tribes, but live since ancient times in a fruitful country... Among all other Unns they are the only ones with white bodies and not repulsive faces

527 A.D. - Procopius: Chosroes sent army of Huns into Roman Armenia, to create a diversion there, had fallen into hands of Valerian and his Romans, and these barbarians had been badly beaten in battle, and most of them killed

530 A.D. - Procopius gives first historical accounts about invasions of Slavic tribes across Danube. These invasions started during first half of 6th century during Roman emperors Justinian (527-565) to Heraklios (610-641)

530 A.D. - Migrations of Slavs were frequently led by Türks, shown by archaeological finds (oldest pieces of Slavic pottery and metal art objects are borrowed from Türkic peoples), and by numerous Türkic loanwords concerning state organization and cultural life

530 A.D. - Second army of Romans in Caucasus consists of Saracens (sary chechle - yellow haired, or Kipchaks) under Arethas, ruler of Saracens,

531 A.D. - Gao-Khuan revolted, defeated Tobases and split Empire Wey into East Wey and West Wey, both controlled by Chinese military leaders under a nominal Syanbian Emperors.

531 A.D. - With split of Empire Wey Syanbinian Togon became free.

531 A.D. - Khazarian khalifa loses rule over Georgia and Abania in S. Caucasus to Persian Sasanid Chosroes I (531-578)

531 A.D. - Procopius Caesariensis: "Huns and Ants, Sklavens already crossed Danube many times and caused unrecoverable damage to Romans". Attack of Altynoba's Tatra Huns and Slavs on Byzantium. After next raid Justinian appoints Ant (Slav) Khvalibud a Roman commander on Danube

534 A.D. - Anahuan with his horde attacks Tele's kingdom Gaogüy, defeats it. Tele's lord Ifu killed by his brother Üegüy, who continues resistance, is defeated, killed by Ifu's son Bidi.

537 A.D. - Goths siege of Rome. To help Belisarius came army of Altynoba's Tatra Bulgars, Sklavens and Antes. Byzantines drive Goths from Rome with help of Bulgar troops (537-538).

538 A.D. - Slavic soldiers are mentioned in Roman army

539 A.D. - Altynoba's Tatra Bulgar Huns raid to Thrace. Byzantium runs 3 wars

540 A.D. - Tele's kingdom Gaogüy under Bidi is defeated and Gaogüy stops existing.

540 A.D. - Split of Empire Wey makes Syanbinian Jujan Khan Anakhuan a gegemon for both halves of Empire Wey.

540 A.D. - Altynoba's Tatra Kutigur Bulgars take and plunder not only rural areas, but take forts (539-540). In Illyrium alone, in 540, Kutigur Bulgars seized 32 forts.

540 A.D. - Syanbinian Khan Kualüy sends embassy to Gao-Khuan in Syanbinian Eastern Wey, becoming an enemy of Syanbinian Western Wey.

540 A.D. - Togon occupied considerable territory, had cities (protected settlements), had organized government, maybe copied from Tobases, had extensive cattle growing economy, low in culture, and under strong dominance of Khans.

540 A.D. - Türkic autonomy is recognized by Western Wey

540 A.D. - Byzantine use of treacherous politics cause Utiguri and Kutriguri to unite against them

543 A.D. - outbreak of plague ravages southern Europe, Turkey to Ethiopia

545 A.D. - Altynoba's Tatra (505-545) dies, Boyan Chelbir (545-590) becomes Baltavar subordinated to Avar overlordship

545 A.D. - Syanbinian Jujan lord Anakhuan, allied with Syanbinian Eastern Wey, together with Eastern Wey's emperor Gao Khuan, and Togon's king Kualüy, attack Syanbinian Western Wey, but do not defeat Syanbinian Western Wey decisively.

545 A.D. - Emperor of Syanbinian Western Wey Ven-di sends ambassador An Nopanto to Türk lord Bumyn. Bumyn displays disloyalty to their suzerain Syanbinian Jujanes and sends a reciprocating embassy to Syanbinian Western Wey capital Chanan.

545 A.D. - Türks under lord Bumyn become allies of Syanbinian Western Wey and its successor Bey Chjou.

546 A.D. - Bey Chjou dynasty was not of Chinese, but of Syanbinian roots and relied on assimilated Syanbinian elite.

546 A.D. - Ephtalite embassy came to W. Wey

550 A.D. - West Tele tribes revolt against Syanbinian Jujan dominance, and attack from western Djungaria toward Khalka in Syanbinian Jujan heartland.

550 A.D. - West Tele tribes are intercepted on the march by Türkic army coming from valleys of Gobi Altai in lined formations, covered by armored plates, on well fed war horses. West Tele army, surprised by unintended enemy, pledged submission to Türkic Lord Bumyn.

550 A.D. - Bumyn, by accepting West Tele tribes vassalage displays another unloyalty to Syanbinian Jujanian suzerainty.

550 A.D. - Descendant of Gao-Khuan, Gao Yan, establishes his own dynasty in Syanbinian Eastern Wey named Bey-Tsi.

550 A.D. - Mid. VI century Period of king Sarosius' government in Alania. Establishment of tight contacts between Alania and Byzanthia.

551 A.D. - Türkic Khan Bumyn (1) provokes Syanbinian Jujanes to a war by asking for a Syanbinian Jujan princess as a wife. Anakhuan refuses, calling him slave-smelter daring for such an offer.

551 A.D. - Boyan Chelbir Bulgars and Slavs led by Khagan Zabergan (558-582) cross Danube, loot Thrace and Macedonia, and attack Constantinople. Military losses, Byzantine bribes, and attack of Bulgar homeland by Avars causes Khagan Zabergan to withdraw his forces.

551 A.D. - Boyan Chelbir Kutriguri Bulgars break through Antian border guard into Byzantine

551 A.D. - Zachariah Ritor: Bulgars and Alans are mentioned once as settled populations with towns, and once as nomads. Bulgarians towns were in territory immediately next to Caspian gates, while nomads - in steppes north of Caucasus.

551 A.D. - Zachariah Ritor: Thirteen peoples Avnagur (Onogur), Avgar, Sabir, Burgar, Alan, Kurtargar, Avar, Hasar, Dirmar, Sirurgur, Bagrasir, Kulas, Abdel and Hephtalit live in tents, earn their living on meat of livestock and fish, of wild animals and by their wea

551 A.D. - Onogurs had towns - in earlier times they had built town of Bakat.

551 A.D. - Boyan Chelbir Kutrigurs raid Thrace. Byzantium, with a skillful diplomacy, incite Uturgurs against Kutrigurs, and Uturgurs attack Kutugurs

552 A.D. - Buddhism introduced to Japan

552 A.D. - Türkic Khan Bumyn executes Syanbinian Jujan's ambassador, and in winter of 552 attacks Syanbinian Jujanes and defeats them.

552 A.D. - Bumyn Il Khan (1) dies in 552, his son Kolo Isigi (3) becomes Khan (552-552) under name of Kara Issyk Khan (3) , his uncle Istemi (2) remains Istemi-Yabguu.

552 A.D. - Syanbinian Jujanes, defeated by Türks, elect Anakhuan's uncle Dynshuttsy Khan and continue fight. In a battle near mountain Lyanshan they are defeated by Kara Issyk Khan.

552 A.D. - Anakhuan commits suicide, his son Yanlochen flees to Syanbinian Eastern Wey under dynasty of Bey-Tsi. Bumyn takes title of Il Khan, but dies in same 552 A.D. - 552 A.D. - Kipchaks were members of Türkic Kaganate, Boma were not members of Türkic Kaganate

552 A.D. - Kipchaks lived in Altai, valley of Chjelyan = Djilan = Snake, so Snake mountain and city Zmeinogorsk. Probably same as Boma of Dinlin Belonged to Türkic Kaganate, lived in Alashan, mixed with Kangals, became Koman/Kuman/Cuman Russ. Polovets)

552 A.D. - Kara Issyk Khan (3) dies in 552, his younger brother Kushu (4) becomes Khan as Mugan Khan (553-572).

552 A.D. - Huns and Syanbinians conquered from China western part of Shansy province. Local people were submitted to Hunnish Khan Mugan, who controlled Chesi area west of Ordos, between bends of Chuanche and Nanshan.

552 A.D. - GOKTÜRK EMPIRE

552 - 743 A.D. - Founder - Bumin Khan (Tumen) Area - From Black Sea across Asia along northern borders of Mongolia and China almost to Pacific Ocean, and valleys of Altay Mountains (Ergenikon) (Total Area - 18,000,000 Km 2)

552 A.D. - End of WHITE HUN (EPHTALITE) EMPIRE

420 - 552 A.D. - Founder - Aksuvar (Aksungur) Area - Half of Northern India, Afghanistan, parts of Turkistan, Eastern Turkestan but also significant parts of Central Asia (Tokharistan, Chaganian, Samarkand, Bukhara, Kesh, Ferghana, Chach (Total Area - 3,500,000 Km2)

552 A.D. - Sabirs switch from Iran to Byzantium and conquer Agvania. Byzantium conquer Italy

552 A.D. - 2 Nestorian monks smuggle silkwarm eggs from China to Byzantium, and by early 7-th c silk industry is well established in Asia Minor

553 A.D. - Syanbinian Jujanes are defeated by new Goktürkic Khan Mugan Khan. They flee to Syanbinian Eastern Wey under dynasty of Bey-Tsi, who accepted them and repulsed Goktürkish pursuit.

553 A.D. - 553-568 Goktürks and Sassanids ally to destroy Hephthalite Empire (Avars?).

553 A.D. - Ephtalite embassy to W.Wey

553 A.D. - Kidanes defeated and subordinated by Emperor Ven-di of Eastern Wey under dynasty of Bey-Tsi. Rest of Kidanes fled to Kogurio (Korea) or subordinated to Goktürks, who reached Yellow Sea.

554 A.D. - Syanbinian Jujanes do not have their herds, and are unable to work. They terrorize and rob population, and Syanbinian Eastern Wey Bey-Tsi sends an army against Syanbinian Jujanes.

554 A.D. - Thirty Tatar tribes (Chinese Shi Wey), Tatabs (Khi by Chinese), and Kidanes are east of emerging Goktürk Khaganate. All three people were close in culture and life, spoke dialects of Mongolian language, but had hostile relations.

554 A.D. - Tatabs lived on west slopes of Khingan and were allied with Eastern Wey under dynasty of Bey-Tsi.

554 A.D. - Destruction of Syanbinian Jujanes weakened Syanbinian Eastern Wey Bey-Tsi. At same time, Syanbinian Western Wey Bey-Chjou was growing and more powerful.

554 A.D. - Persians defeat Sabirs in Agvania.

554 A.D. - Jujans started looting in Tsi, but are repelled by Chinese. 555 Jujans flee from Bey-Tsi to W Wey, given to Goktürks and decimated. Lyan attacks Bey-Tsi

555 A.D. - Syanbinian Jujanes are expelled from Syanbinian Eastern Wey by Bey-Tsi army to steppes. Syanbinian Jujanes are beaten by Goktürks and Kidanes.

555 A.D. - Goktürks defeat Avars (Abars). First encounter of Goktürks with Ephtalites.

556 A.D. - Syanbinian Jujanes flee to Syanbinian Western Wey, which surrenders 3K army to Goktürk's ambassador, who orders decapitation of all except children and servants. End of Syanbinian Jujan dominance of steppes.

557 A.D. - Avar's ambassador Kandikh to Byzantium Justinian demands lands and tribute.

557 A.D. - Emperor Justinian (527-565) began a huge fortification program in Balkans, in an attempt to slow, if not stop, invasions across Danube

557 A.D. - Assimilated Syanbinian, Üyvyn Tay, establishes his own dynasty in Chanan of Syanbinian Western Wey.

557 A.D. - 557-561 Türks and Sasanians ally to destroy Hepthalite state in Central Asia, which had ruled, among other places, Sogdiana.

558 A.D. - Bulgars living along lower Dniepr and Don are Kuturgur Huns. Bulgars living along Kuban are Uturgur Huns. Kuturgurs raid Byzantium's Thracia, Byzantium incites Uturgurs to fight with Kuturgurs.

558 A.D. - Avars then confederated Kuturgurs and proceeded to attack Byzantium. Perso-Avar union lasted to 628 and almost destroyed Byzantium.

558 A.D. - Avars devastate Thessalia, Hellas, Epirus, Vetus, and Attica, invad Peloponnese and kill "noble and Hellenic race". Avars ruled over Peloponnese for 218 years

558 A.D. - Kutugurs under Zabergan raid Byzantine on Balkans and come to walls of Constantinople.

558 A.D. - Avars smash Bulgars/Uturgurs, loyal allies of Byzantine, and Zals (?) living along lower Don. Kutugurs supported Avars.

558 A.D. - Istemi Yabgu stops at Itil (Itil), allowing Vars and Huni, both from North of Aral Sea, to escape to west and become known as Avars. Istemi: When I finish with Ephtalites, I will go after Avars, they can't escape

558 A.D. - Vars (Ugrian tribe, related to Hungarian ancestors Ogors/Ugrs which lived between Itil and Yaik (Ural) rivers, and to Hungarians living in Bashkiria up to 13 c.) and Huni (Khionites = Sarmato-Alanians), both from North of Aral Sea, become known as Avars.

558 A.D. - Avars first crushed Türkic Sabirs, allies of Byzantine, who lived on Kuma river and in Dagestan. Avars then crushed Uturgurs, a Bulgarian tribe and also allies of Byzantine, living between Itil and Don, then crushed Zals and Ants on both sides of Don.

558 A.D. - Avars negotiate with Persia and Byzantium to find an ally. Avars conclude agreements with both Persia and Byzantium. Avars proceed to play in their own interests.

558 A.D. - Invading Avars attack Hunno-Bulgars. Utiguri, Kutriguri, and Sabiri are conquered (559-560).

558 A.D. - Goktürks conquered Itil and Yaik areas. Remains of Huni, Var, and Obr tribes went west to Danube, creating united Avar people. Their first task was to escape from Goktürk enemy. They managed it only because Ephtalites in C Asia distracted Istemi Yabgu

558 A.D. - Türkic coins with Türkic inscriptions 'Khagan' and 'Yabgu' are minted in Soghd, Chach and Ferghana. Terminated by Arab conquest of Mawaranahr and consequent introduction of new kinds of coins, in Semirech'e issue of Türkic coins continues into 9th to 10th

558 A.D. - Hephthalites (Avars) move west to Black Sea steppe to form Avar Khanate

558 A.D. - Slavic warriors may have taken part in a Bulgar invasion to Greece

558 A.D. - AVAR EMPIRE in Europe

558-805 A.D.

Founder - Khan Bayan

Area - Pannonia, Balkans, Bessarabia, N. Pontic steppes to Tanais and Itil (Total Area - 2,500,000 Km2)

Seat of Avar kaghan and his warlords east of Danube in Pannonia, known as Rhing

558 A.D. - Discovered in Mongolia late in 20c inscription Var-guni (Bar-guni) mention Europian Avars. Majority of Avar's time skeletons from Hungary are Mongoloids, Bayan was probably Mongolian word, evidence that Avars were Mongol Jujuns

558 A.D. - Avarian embassy to Byzantium. Avars defeat Sabirs and Ants.

558 A.D. - Avars led by Khan Bayan invaded N Caucasus and faced Byzantium's allies. In Byzantian sources first time they are mentioned

558 A.D. - Avars show up on Danube.In Jan-Feb embassy of Kagan Bayan negociates in Constantinopole. Justinian hires them to guard agains "barbarians", the same Türkic nomadic hordes as Avars, who continued to erupt from N China.

559 A.D. - Utugurs under Sandilch attack returning Kutugurs, and start a war. War weakens both peoples.

559 A.D. - Kutugur Bulgars under Zabergan, with Avars, made a treaty with Sklavins(?), cross Danube on ice, raid Byzantine, in three directions. Via Macedonia to Ellada to Thermopile, to Thracian Chersones, under Zabergan through a break in Long Wall to Constantinop

559 A.D. - Velizarius led defense and repulsed Kutugurs. Kutugurs remained in Thracia until paid off and received "gifts" on same conditions as Utugurs. Kutugurs leave Thracia.

559 A.D. - After unsuccessful storm of Constantinopol Bulgars and Slavs were trapped. Byzantians cut their retreat. Justinian magnificiently spared them. Velizarius pushed them behind Long Wall. Zabergan retreated because Avars were coming fron east.

560 A.D. - Avar Khaganate extended from Itil to mouth of Danube. Bulgars are split, with Kuturgur Huns (also listed are Onogundurs (10 Ogur Confederation), Hunnogurs, Sabirs belonging to Avar Khaganate, and Utugur Huns (30 Ogur) and Khazars loyal to W. Khaganate

560 A.D. - Avars invaded land of Utigurs on east shore of Meotida. Utigurs recognized Avarian rule. Avars invaded Kutigurs. Kutigurs defeated and became Avarian vassals too. Bayan proclames himself Kagan.

560 A.D. - Goktürkic ambassadors to Iran killed by Ephtalites on the road

561 A.D. - Embassy from Kucha to Bay-Chjou

561 A.D. - Avars captured Bessarabia, execute local ruler Mesamer

561 A.D. - Sosroi Nushirvan crushes Sibirs

562 A.D. - Last incursion by Kutigur Bulgars into Byzantium, stopped by Byzantium's instigating internecine wars between two most powerful branches, Kutigur (Kutrigur) and Utigur.

562 A.D. - Second Avarian embassy to Byzantium

562 A.D. - Avars came to Dobrudja and settle there

562 A.D. - Persians defeat Ephtalites

563 A.D. - Western Wey dynasty Bey-Chjou was of Syanbinian descent, and relying on support of Syanbinian elite transformed into large landlords. They assimilated and used Chinese language.

563 A.D. - Goktürkic emissary in Constantinopole

563 A.D. - Goktürkic armies, supported by Khosrov, attack Balkh, invade Ephtalite lands south of Amudarya. Per 'Shah-Name', decisive battle near Bukhara. Ephtalite army of King Gatifar is crushed

564 A.D. - Army service was made compulsory for simple people of Empire Wey, and two armies were organized. Army of nobles - fubin - was balanced by army of people. Fubin came from military organization of Syanbinian tribe Toba, who conquered Northern China in 4 c.

564 A.D. - Service in army was mandatory for Syanbinian clansmen. In reward they received land parcels, and were released from any other obligations. Service was inherited, and with time soldiers become a privileged caste.

564 A.D. - Initially army consisted exclusively of Syanbinians, but later it was supplemented by rich Chinese from Shansi and Shensi who accepted foreign dynasty after it adopted Chinese culture and language.

565 A.D. - Avars under Khan Bayan (c. 565-602) subjugate Hunnugur and Sabir, and other Hunnic hordes, assimilating them under Avar Khaganate.

565 A.D. - After defeat of their forces by Avars, Khazars took lead in Sabir-Khazar federation. Part of Sabirs move north, to Middle Itil region, among settled there Bulgarian tribes. Their main city Suvar is a great center of Itil Bulgaria.

565 A.D. - Pannonia came under pressure from Avars, Lombardian new king, Alboin, found support from Constantinople less then he had hoped for.

565 A.D. - Langobards destroys Gepidian Reign

565 A.D. - Goktürkic Khagan Mugan Khagan and Istemi Yabgu defeat Ephtilites at Neseph. Considered fall year of Ephtilite state. Ephtilites traces lost in history

565 A.D. - Hephthalite territory divided between Iran and Goktürk Khaganate. Border between them ran west of Balkh and east of Murgab

566 A.D. - Between 566 and 571 Istemi Yabgu subjugated peoples Bandjar, Balandjar (Belendjer) and Khazar. Barandjar (Balandjar) = Onogur = Utigur Bulgars. Khazar influence increased as Khazars became Goktürks' closest allies and assistants.

567 A.D. - Goktürks capture Bosphorus

567 A.D. - Gepidic kingdom defeated by Avars

567 A.D. - Avars ally with Longobards

567 A.D. - Goktürk embassy to Sasanids, with a request for Silk Route transit trade through their territories is rejected

568 A.D. - Sirs live in towns and have ports in Djurdjan, across Amu-Darya

568 A.D. - Avars occupy Panonia

568 A.D. - Lombardian King Alboin led a host of Lombards, Gepids, Sarmatians and other peoples (including Hunnic Bulgars, per Paul the Deacon) from Pannonia to Italy. Others, amongst them Bavarians, Saxons and Taifali, joined invasion en route

568 A.D. - As Lombardian King Alboin advanced, vacuum left behind them was filled by Avars, Bulgars and Slavs

568 A.D. - Goktürk embassy to Constantinople led by a Soghdian Maniakh, proposing to ally against Sasanians

569 A.D. - Goktürks invade and conquer Sirs.

569 A.D. - Zemarkh embassy to Goktürks, with five further embassies exchanged by 576 A.D. - 569 A.D. - Goktürk war agains Sasanians; penetration of Kabul and Gandhara regions

570 A.D. - Kutugurs, as all people on Itil ruled by Goktürks, are encouraged by rise of Avars as alternative to Goktürk suzerainty.

570 A.D. - Syanbinian Jujan horde keeps robbing neighbors. Language = Syanbinian Consider themselves to be ethnically Tobases.

570 A.D. - Khazars are ruled by Western Goktürk Khaganate (570-659)

570 A.D. - Goktürk rulers receive 100,000 pieces of silk tribute a year from China. Goktürks are the first Eurasian steppe empire to extend from Roman/Byzantine world in west, Iranian/Sasanian in south and Chinese in East

572 A.D. - 572-591 Goktürks and Byzantines ally against Sassanians

572 A.D. - Goktürks subjugate Utiguri until about 581.

572 A.D. - Western Goktürk Khaganate's "Ulus" on lower Itil and Yaik

572 A.D. - Mugan Khan (4) dies in 572, his younger brother Tobo (5) becomes Khan (572-581)

572 A.D. - Peace between Bey-Tsi and Goktürks

574 A.D. - Embassy from Khotan to Bey-Chjou

575 A.D. - Istemi Yabgu (2) dies, his son Dyangu (Tardu) Kara ChurinTürk (7) becomes Tardu Yabgu (575-603).

575 A.D. - Uturgurs are allied with W. Goktürk Khaganate.

575 A.D. - Alliance between Goktürks and Uturgurs

576 A.D. - Tardu Yabgu sends Bokhan to attack Byzantine in Crimea and Panticapeum (Kerch) as a leader of Utigur Huns under chief Anagai (576-590).

576 A.D. - Utugurs under Khan Anagai, as auxiliaries of Goktürks, take Bospor. Utugurs remain on N. Caucasus from Dagestan to Derbent, under W. Goktürk Khaganate suzerainty

576 A.D. - Goktürks establish Khazar Khanate.

576 A.D. - Bulgars of lower Itil and Kuban are loyal to Goktürkish dynasty Ashina

576 A.D. - Goktürks are on both sides of Kerch straight. Goktürkic army leader (Tma Tarkhan) on Taman peninsula, giving name to city Tmutarkhan

577 A.D. - Goktürks invade Crimea

578 A.D. - Slavs invade Ellada

578 A.D. - Bysantium allies with Avars. Avars defeat Slavs, killing their Prince Davrit

578 A.D. - Regions along lower Danube were in 6th and 7th centuries inhabited by Sclavinae, Antes, and Huns (probably Bulgarians). Moldavia and northeastern Muntenia were populated by Slavic tribe of Antes.

579 A.D. - Avarian ultimatum by Kagan Bayan to sessede city Sirmiy. Tiberius refuses. Avars capture Sirmiy after a two tear siege

580 A.D. - Presence in Istria of hostile to Bysantium Slavs and Avars. Avars were partly responsible for southward migration of Serbs and Croats

580 A.D. - Slavic chieftain sacked Corinth

580 A.D. - Avars conquered and plundered cities and strongholds in Hellas

580 A.D. - Goktürks invade Lasica

580 A.D. - Peace of Bay-djou with Kaganate

581 A.D. - Tobo (5) dies, Shetu (9) becomes Khagan (581-587).

581 A.D. - Tardu Yabgu sends Bokhan to attack Cheronesus as a leader of Utigur Huns under chief Anagai.

581 A.D. - Goktürks at Chersonessus walls

581 A.D. - 581-584 Devastating raid of Slavs through Thrace, Macedonia and Ellada. Settlement of Slavs in Thrace

581 A.D. - Khans Ashina are Türks and are" wolves". Syanbian quean describes her husband Shabolio as Wolf by his personality.

581 A.D. - Chinese revolt against Syanbinian dynasty. New dynasty received name Suy. Sinadized Syanbinian elite survived.

582 A.D. - Avar Khagan Bayan attacks Byzantium in Thrace.

582 A.D. - Kuturgur Hun Bulgars settle in Bessarabia and Wallachia, from which they will move to Moesia under pressure from Magyars, and make it Bulgaria.

582 A.D. - Hunnic Khan Zabergan (558?-582) dies, Gostun becomes Hunnic Khan ruling over Kutigurs.

582 A.D. - Shetu Kagan appoints Gostun Kutigurian Khan

582 A.D. - Goktürkic Khaganate officially breaks up into Western and Eastern Khaganates. Khwarezm (lower part of Amu Darya R., S. of Aral Sea) and Sugd/Sogdiana (Zerafshan and Kashka Darya R., including area around Samarkand) likely autonomous kingdoms to become independent in next century with Tang defeat of Goktürks

582 A.D. - 582 - 602 Rule of Byzantine Emperor Maurice. First mention of Khazars in Byzantine annals, along with Bulgars and Barsils. Noted their coming from Bersilia, supposedly in Caspian steppe

583 A.D. - Avarian attack on Byzantium

584 A.D. - Hunnic Khan Gostun (582-584) dies, Orchona becomes regent of his nephew Kubrat (584-594).

584 A.D. - New Emperor recognizes queen Khan's wife as daughter, thus Shetu as son, thus recognizing previous traditions of trading with Goktürks as a form of paying tribute, and confirming privileges of Syanbinian elite. Shetu acknowledges vassalage to empire.

584 A.D. - New Slav attack on Constantinople. Defeat and retreat

586 A.D. - Avars and Slavs besieged Thessalonica

587 A.D. - Shetu (9) dies, Moho (14) becomes Khagan, followed by Tulan (Ün-Ulug) (16) (587-599). Tulan has anti-khan Tuli (Jangar) (18) (600-609) supported by empire.

587 A.D. - Byzantium peace with Avars

588 A.D. - Shetu Khan (19) dies, Ün Ulug (Tulan) (Dulan) (16) (587-599) becomes Khan

588 A.D. - China open markets for trade with Türks

588 A.D. - 582? Separation of Goktürkic Empire into East (Mongolia) and West (Turkestan) parts

589 A.D. - W. Goktürk Khaganate campaign against Persia in Caucasus, with Khazars but without Bulgars. Both Khazars and Bulgars

are confederated (jointed voluntarily, not as conquered) into W. Goktürk Khaganate.

589 A.D. - W. Goktürk Khaganate's Khazars supply military contingents and participate in division of captured wealth. Bulgars man western border with Avars and don't benefit from captured wealth.

589 A.D. - Invasion of Khazars, Greeks and Georgians to Agvania is repelled by Persians

590 A.D. - Under dynasty Suy position of fubin worsened. Soldiers were moved from "military" lists to "Civil household lists", thus exemption from taxes ended. This was aimed against Syanbinian privileges left from Syanbinian overlordship.

594 A.D. - Hunnic Regent Orchona (584-594) dies, Kubrat accends to Khanship (594-642).

594 A.D. - Judging from some eparchial lists from end of 7-th or beginning of 8-th century, in 7-th century there was an Onogurian episcopate in Gothic eparchy. This attests early spread of Christianity among Onogurs

594 A.D. - Theophanes Confessor and Constantinus Porphyrogeneus explicitly state that Bulgarians, settled on Balkans, had been called earlier Unogundurs

594 A.D. - Byzantine patriarch Nicephorus calls ruler of Great Bulgaria khan Kubrat "ruler of Unogundurs"

594 A.D. - Heir of throne, Tulan Khagan's cousin, Tuli (Jangar), with a title of Toleses' Khan = Tuli Khan, was Khan of north-east territory. Tuli Khan had vassals ShiWey (Tatars), Kidanes, Khi (Tatabs).

598 A.D. - Kara Churin embassy to Constantinipole

599 A.D. - Tulan (Ün-Üylüy) (16) is killed, Kara Churin Türk (7) becomes Khan with title Boke Khan (599-604)

599 A.D. - Chinese fight successfully in Ordos

600 A.D. - Tulan (Ün-Üylüy) (16) dies, Jangar (Tuli) (18) (600-609) assumes control of all Eastern Goktürk Khaganate, in vassalage of Chinese empire.

601 A.D. - Byzantians defeat Avars

601 A.D. - Priskos, Byzantine general, defeated Avars in Banat and collected 9.000 prisoners, 3000 Avars, 800 Slavs, 3200 Gepidae, and 2.000 Abarbarians

602 A.D. - Byzantium general Priscus defeats Avars. Bayan (c. 565-602) dies. Next Khan rules (602-630).

602 A.D. - HAZAR EMPIRE

602-1016 A.D. - Founder - no historical data for founder, its greatest ruler was Hakan Yusuf.

Area - Hazars separated from Goktürks and formed a state from Caucasian Mntns to Danube and N. Pontic area

603 A.D. - Tardu Khan (7) dies in 603, his grandson Buri-Shad (13/14/15) becomes Khan of partitioned Western Goktürk Khaganate, controlling westernmost part. Chulo (10) controls eastern part.

603 A.D. - Kushans rebel against Iran with help from Goktürks. Tocharistan separates from Iran

604 A.D. - Rebellious Tele in basin of Selenga area pacified, but Djungaria and basin of Tarim did not return to Eastern Goktürk Khaganate.

604 A.D. - New dynasty treat carefully descendants of Tobases (Syanbinians). Assimilated Syanbinians live along Great Wall from Khebey to Chanan. There were many large landowners and professional military pushed from power by Chinese landowners who took power.

604 A.D. - Kara Churin Türk Boke Khan (7) dies, Goktürk Kaganate split into West and East. Tuli (Jangar) (18) becomes Khan of Eastern Goktürk Kaganate, Taman (28) becomes Khan of Western Goktürk Khaganate (604-610).

604 A.D. - Nominally Djungaria and basin of Tarim entered Western Goktürk Khaganate. However Kibi on northern slopes of East Tian-Shan and Seyanto on S. Slopes of Altain-Nuru crest fought western Goktürks for 2 years (605-606) and gained freedom.

605 A.D. - Kidanes revolt against Goktürk suppression

606 A.D. - New state was created in Djungaria, under Kibi leadership, with a vast territory and including settled population necessary for nomadic state, in oasises Karashar, Turfan and Khami. Kibi's Prince Gelen took title Mokhe-Khan.

606 A.D. - Leader of Seyantos Ishibo subordinated to Gelen but retained control over his tribe. State was likely a tribal union.

607 A.D. - Order about outlawing a free trade of Chinese with Goktürks

608 A.D. - Wars between Tele and Goktürks of Western Khaganate end.

608 A.D. - Troops of Empire Suy attack Togon and destroy it.

608 A.D. - Jangar Khan (Tuli) (18) (-608) died, his son, Shad Dugi, becomes Khan of East Goktürk Khaganate in vassalage of Empire Tan, under name Shibir (Shipi) Khan (25) (609-620).

609 A.D. - Troops of Empire Suy attack Tele and Western Goktürk Khaganate

610 A.D. - 610-620 Avar Slavs raided Thessalia, Hellas, Aegean Islands, Achaia, and Epirus

610 A.D. - Marquart: Leader of Unugurs (Unogundurs) Organa, founder of Bulgarian Dynasty Dulo, uncle of Kubrat Dulo, related to Ashina by female line, of most-western ulus, is baptized in Constantinople. Kubrat is not baptized.

610 A.D. - Future Sibir-Khan (14), Mokhodu, of most western ulus is baptized in Constantinople. This starts his fight with Buri Shad (34) (610-618) and Tardu Yabgu (Tun-djabgu) (23) (618-630). Kubrat is not baptized.

610 A.D. - Taman Yabgu (28) dies, Buri Shad Yabgu (34) becomes Khan of Western Goktürk Khaganate (610-618). Chulo (26) = anti-Khan (610-611).

615 A.D. - Tobases living along northern border of Western Wey stopped being Tobases long ago, but did not become Chinese yet. They are equally distanced from steppes and China, and equally close to both. Goktürks called them Tabgach.

615 A.D. - In time of revolt Tabgaches participated because of warlike ancestry, but acted aimlessly, because lost organization and unity.

617 A.D. - 617(?) A defeat from Byzantines resulted in deterioration of situation for Avar's Khakan. Alburi killed at court of Avar's Khakan.

617 A.D. - Shi Wey, along with Kidan, Togon and Gaochan submitted to Shibir Khan Khagan (25).

618 A.D. - Buri Shad Yabgu (34) dies, Tung Yabgu (23) becomes Khan of Western Goktürk Khaganate (618-630).

618 A.D. - Bu-Yurgan refused to be elected Baltavar, saying, that he will be a bolyar, i.e. a cleric. On his advice, Kara Bulgars elected Alburi's senior son Kurbat a Baltavar

619 A.D. - Kubrat allies with Byzantium against Avars.

619 A.D. - Both Tele leaders, Kibi's Mokhe-Khan and Seyanto's Inan, subordinate to Tung Yabguu Khan = Yabgu of Shenuy. Djungaria returned to Western Goktürk Khaganate.

619 A.D. - Sirs are controlled by Tung Yabgu Khan directly.

619 A.D. - Baptism of "Hunnish Khan" in Constantinopole. Avars reach Constantinopole.

619 A.D. - China breakes union with Goktürks. Capture of Khesi. Lyan Shi-du and Lyu U-Chjou invade N China with Goktürkic support

620 A.D. - Shambat, younger brother of Baltavar Kubrat, on Kubrat order, builds in aul Askal on mountains Kuyantau city-fortress named Bashtu, present Kiev. Other names Askal, Kuk-Kuyan, Shambat, Kyi.

620 A.D. - Shibir Khagan (25) (609-620) dies, Kat Il Khan (27) becomes Khan of Eastern Goktürk Khaganate, free from vassalage of empire (620-630).

620 A.D. - In 200 years descendants of Syanbinians assimilated in Tibet. Tsenpo was an inherited position, he received income from lands, taxes, tributes, confiscations and executions. But he could be dismissed at any time because he did not have support or real pow

620 A.D. - Tibet army was under a special advisor. Tsenpo Nimry (570-620). In following history there is no Syanbinian role,

620 A.D. - Avarian retreat from Constantinople

622 A.D. - The Hijra. Start of Islam as a world event

622 A.D. - Union of Lu Shey-da with Goktürks

623 A.D. - Several successfull uprisings of Slavic tribes against Avars are recorded, for example revolt of Vends in 623.

623 A.D. - Avars reigned over a vast territory between Alps, Adriatic Sea and Black Sea

623 A.D. - Shambat starts war against Avars, with Ulchis (Slavs) and Ugrs. Shambat captures Pannonia and calls his ulus Duloba (623-658). Baltavar Kubrat calls him Kyi (Separated).

623 A.D. - Slavs attacked Crete

623 A.D. - Byzantine authors recorded ethnic composition of Avar Empire as Avars, Gepids, and Slavs

623 A.D. - Birth of Samo state, first political formation of Slavs, first mentioned in writing in 623 A.D. - 625 A.D. - Exchange of embassies between Byzantium and Western Goktürkic Khaganate

626 A.D. - (Onogur?) Bulgars live in Trans-Caucasus on right bank of Kuban' to Don Different fr and rival to Khazars

626 A.D. - Avars controlled all Kuturgur Hun lands Uturgur (Onogur?) Bulgars did not participate in Khazars' war raids into Caucasus Uturgur (Onogur?) Bulgars guarded western border of Western Kaganate Uturgur (Onogur?) Bulgars are allied with Tele (Dulu).

626 A.D. - W. Goktürk Khaganate campaign against Sasanian Persia in Caucasus, with Khazars but without Bulgars

626 A.D. - Khazars and (Onogur?) Bulgars confederated (voluntarily, not conquered) into W. Goktürk Khaganate. Khazars supply military contingents and participate in division of captured wealth. Bulgars man western border with Avars and don't benefit from captured we

626 A.D. - Kubrat proclaims independence from W. Goktürk Khaganate and assumes title of Khagan.

626 A.D. - While Heraclius with W, Goktürk Khaganates fights Persians in Caucasus, Persians with Avars attack Constantinople. Avars retreat with heavy losses and in disgrace. Kubrat suggests sucking Avar Khagan and replacing him. End of Avar-Persian union.

626 A.D. - Khazars ally with Byzantine under Emperor Heraclius (626-630)

626 A.D. - Li Shi-min coup. Peace with Goktürks at river Vey

626 A.D. - Greeks and Goktürks seige Tbilisi

626 A.D. - Avars suffered a crushing defeat at Constantinople in 626 A.D. - 627 A.D. - Seyanto tribe and Djungaria left Western Goktürk Khaganate and joined Eastern Goktürk Khaganate Kat Il Khan

627 A.D. - Cinese embassy to Tun-Yabgu Khan stopped by Kat Il Khan

627 A.D. - Seyanto and Uygurs, both Tele tribes, help each other in Goktürk Khaganate. Seyanto's Inan and Uygur's Pusa support each other.

627 A.D. - Series of revolts against Avars start among subjugated tribes. Uprising of western Slavs, led by Samo, a Frankish merchant, resulted in founding of a Slavic state on territory of present-day Czech Republic and Slovakia.

627 A.D. - Avars and Perians beseige Contantinopole

628 A.D. - Khazars capture Tbilisi

628 A.D. - Seyanto tribe with 70K yurts gains independence.

629 A.D. - Chinese take fortress May in Ordos. Counterattack by Goktürks on all fronts. Srontsangambo enthroned in Tibet

630 A.D. - Bulgars/Barsils are incorporated into elite of W. Goktürk Khaganate horde.

630 A.D. - Great Bulgaria north of Black Sea under Kubrat (630-660)

630 A.D. - End of rule of Khazars by Goktürk W Khaganate

630 A.D. - Seyanto pursue Goktürk Chebi Khan who finds refuge in Altai valley with 30K army.

630 A.D. - Avars treat Bulgars/Barsils badly as conquered people. Western Bulgars/Kuturgurs move to Bavaria, and are annihilated by Frankish king Dagober. Eastern Bulgars/Kuturgurs joint with Bulgars/Uturgur

630 A.D. - Avar Khagan (602-630) dies. Next Khan rules (630-?).

630 A.D. - Sibir-Khan (14) recognized independence of Bulgaria under Kubrat of Dulo dynasty, his nephew of feminine line.

630 A.D. - Qarluqs rebel, Tung Yabgu (23) dies, W. Goktürk Khaganate split, SW and NE. SW run by Nushibis, under Irbis Bolun Yabgu (31) (631-631), installed by Nishu Khan Shad (32), son of Baga Shad (24). NE run by Tele (Dulu), under Sibir Khan Yabgu (14) (630-631).

630 A.D. - Chinese Tang defeat Eastern Goktürkic and occupy Eastern Goktürkic Khanate (Mongolia). Kat Il Khan (27) taken prisoner by Tang army, Eastern Goktürk Khaganate is ruled by Tang Empire for 50 years (630-682)

630 A.D. - 630-640 Chinese subdue Tarim Basin

630 A.D. - Türks of Ordos become known as Gok Türks (Blue Türks), different from their northern neighbors - Tele

630 A.D. - 80 K Chinese living with Goktürks are captured

630 A.D. - Tardu Tong Yabgu of Western Goktürk Khaganate (619-630), per Chinese chronicle Tanshu, subjugated Toleses between rivers Orkhon and Tola, and Lake Aral, Iranians, advanced to Khandagar in south. His army has hundreds of thousands of good bow-shooters.

630 A.D. - W. Goktürks invade Armenia and defeat Persians. W. Goktürks clear S Caucasus

630 A.D. - Xuanzang visits court of W. Türk kaghan Tung Yabghu near Lake Issyk-Kul

631 A.D. - Seyanto tribe keeps independence.

631 A.D. - Seyanto under China = 70K wagons

631 A.D. - Uygur leader Tumidu, heir of Pusa, defeated Seyantos and seized their ranges. Emperor Taitszun sent an embassy to Seyanto leader Inan and recognized him as Khan, as a counterweight to Uygurs. Uygurs subordinated and recognized new Khan.

631 A.D. - Seyanto state organized like Türk's. Khan's sons are Shads, leading Tolos (North) and Tardush (South). Army numbered 200K lances, smaller than was 1,000K of Gokürks' Shibir Khan.

631 A.D. - Seyanto state successfully controlled all Türkic leaders except for Ordos Türks under Chinese protection. Some Ordos Türks move north into Seyanto state.

631 A.D. - Irbis Bolun Yabgu (31) replaced by Nishu Khan Shad (32) as Dulu Khan (631-634). Sibir Khan Yabgu (14) killed. W. Goktürk Khaganate reunited.

631 A.D. - New Seyanto state spread from Altai to Khingan and from Gobi desert to Baikal.

631 A.D. - Kutugur's rebelion against Avars and defeat of Kutugurs by Avars

631 A.D. - Samo Slavs in 631 beat Frank Army of King Dagobert near Vogatisburg and gain their independence from Franks and Avars

632 A.D. - Seyanto gave a blow from behind. Ashina Chuni, loyal to traditions of Eastern Kaganate, raised his army against Seyanto. He had 50K army without success.

632 A.D. - Yishbara Tolis Shad (33) is not trying to re-subjugate Bulgars

632 A.D. - Kipchaks are not in 10 arrows of Western Kaganate

633 A.D. - Kubrat unites Bulgar Kuturgur and Uturgur tribes and liberated from W. Goktürk Khaganate.

633 A.D. - Kubrat organizes state, 2nd=kavkhan, 3rd=Ichirguboyl ??

634 A.D. - Seyanto tribe with 70K wagons keeps independence.

634 A.D. - Dulu Khan (32) (631-634) dies, his younger brother Tong Shad becomes Yabgu as Yshbara Tolis-Shad Yabgu (634-639).

635 A.D. - Kubrat escaped dominance of Goktürks and Khazars, by supporting Sibir-Khan in 630. He became independent, defeated Avars. Controlled near- Black Sea steppes

635 A.D. - Kubrat sent embassy to Constantinople and received title of Patrician. Kubrat's Bulgaria joins Byzantium as Federatae. Byzantium becomes a bordering state with Khazaria of W. Goktürk Khaganate, controlling former Khazar territories.

635 A.D. - In W Goktürk Kaganate nations that did not receive autonomy were Karluks, Yagma (YanNyan), Kipchaks, Basmals, and Hun (Dulu) tribes Chue, Chumi and Shato

635 A.D. - Yshbara Tolis-Shad Yabgu reorganizes W. Goktürk Khaganate into 10-arrow Goktürks, of 5 Nushibi and 5 Tele (Dulu) tribal leaders, recognizing them as Shads (blood prince).

636 A.D. - Bulgaria hostile with Khazars of W. Goktürk Khaganate on East, with Avars on West, with Byzantium on South.

636 A.D. - NE of Western Goktürk Khaganate controlled by Tele Khan Tong Shad Yabgu, who attempts to unite W. and E. Goktürk Khaganates.

639 A.D. - Seyanto ally with Gaochan in defense of Gaochan from aggression of Empire Tan. Gaochan is attacked and occupied.

639 A.D. - Yishbara Tolis Shad (33) died, then (42), then cousin Bagadur, title = Irbis Yshbara Yabguu Khan (37)

639 A.D. - Capital of 'South Horde' at Chu & Ili

641 A.D. - Türks in service of Tan Empire are moved to north bank of Khuankhe and serve as a barrier against Seyanto.

641 A.D. - Seyanto Khan Inan organized expedition against restored Goktürk vassal Khaganate on north bank of Khuankhe. Seyanto army demolished 80%.

641 A.D. - Kipchaks have 100K people, 40K army, 90 K horses

641 A.D. - Irbis Yshbara Yabgu Khan executed (37), his brother Yugu-Ukuk (38) selected Khan of Western Goktürk Khaganate (641-651)

641 A.D. - Kipchak on Altai subordinated to Khan Ükuk Yabgu,

641 A.D. - Boma on Enisey subordinated to Khan Ükuk Yabgu.

642 A.D. - First Khazar - Arab war (642-652) against Abd Al Rahman

642 A.D. - Imperial Chinese garrison in Khami deafeats W Goktürks of Irbis Dulu Khan

645 A.D. - Seyanto Khan Inan died.

646 A.D. - Remains of Seyanto Horde loose to Empire Tan army and are dispersed. Uygurs fought Seyanto with Empire Tan and become loyal subjects and fight in all wars for Empire.

646 A.D. - Seyanto Khanate was destroyed by Empire and their allies Uygurs, people were mercilessly wiped out. Remains of Seyanto dispersed by slopes of Beyshan, and joined Goktürks.

646 A.D. - Empire Tan breakes relations with W Goktürkic Khaganate

649 A.D. - Türk Chebi Khan horde is resettled in East Khanganate vacated by Seyanto.

650 A.D. - Irbis becomes first Kagan of Khazar's Kaganate (650?-....).

650 A.D. - Kipchaks move to Upper Irtysh and E. Kazakhstan steppes under pressure from China and Uygurs

650 A.D. - Langobards conclude conquest of whole Italia, excluding Ravenna, South Italia and Sicilia.

650 A.D. - In village Nagi Szent Miklos in Hungary is found famous treasure, 23 golden cups with Türkic inscriptions, dated by Avar period (c 650)

650 A.D. - Migration of Bulgars to middle Itil, attested to by burial sites in Shilovka and Brusyany. Burials are of Türkic nobility with complex rites and rich implements.

651 A.D. - With loss of W.Goktürk Khaganate rule, former confedrate Khazaria with attached Bulgar Kutugurs, Alans, Slavs and Itil Bulgars gain independence. Khazars keep Kagan from Ashina dynasty.

651 A.D. - Defeat of Khazar-Alan army by Abd Al Rahman Arabs in Euthrates battle.

651 A.D. - W. Goktürks take Tinchjou (Bishbalyk = Head City)

652 A.D. - End of first Khazar - Arab war (642-652) against Abd Al Rahman

653 A.D. - Ükuk (38) died, son Chjenchu (39) (653-659)

655 A.D. - Khazars allied with Alans.

656 A.D. - Murder of Calif Osman. Civil war in Califate.

656 A.D. - Founded Khazarian state

656 A.D. - Advance of Chinese inperians against W Goktürkic Khaganate. Rebelion of Baiyrku, Sige, Bugu and Tonra against Empire Tan. Sogdiana occupied by Chinese (657-700)

658 A.D. - Great Bulgaria, Baltavar Kubrat's state, is divided into 2 uluses, Western Kara Bulgar and Eastern Ak Bulgar Yorty, separated by river Shir (Don).

658 A.D. - Kara Bulgar extended from estuary of (Danube) to Shir (Don). Ak Bulgar Yorty extended from Shir (Don) to estuary of Itil (Volga). Border went by river Aksu, including aul Kharka (current Kharkov). Bulyar was included as semi-autonomous beylik.

658 A.D. - Great Bulgaria's capital Bandja, renamed fron Onoguria (Gr. Phanagoria). Summer stan is Khorysdan or Batavyl (Lord's stan), present Putivl. In between are two more stans, Tiganak and Baltavar, present Poltava.

659 A.D. - Tang defeat last rulers of first Goktürkic empire. Chjenchu (39) executed, end of dynasty. Western Goktürkic Kaganate ceased to exist forever. Yshbara Khan died

660 A.D. - Khan Kubrat Dulo (24) (618-660) died, is buried 13 km from Baltavar, present Poltava, burial excavated in 1912, no anthropological, forensic examination.

660 A.D. - Kubrat's 1st son Bayan (Batbayan) is elected Baltavr and remains in Great Bulgaria, confederated with Khazars

660 A.D. - Kubrat's 2nd son Kotrag resettled his Kuturgurs (Kotrags) West of Don, and in 730-740 they spread to E. Azov area to join Kuban Bulgars. Kotrag domain consisted of groups Barsula, Eskel and Bulkar (Bulgar).

660 A.D. - Kubrat's 3rd son, Atilkese, nicknamed Asparukh (Khan Asparukh) heads Onogurs (Utigurs)

660 A.D. - Agvanian Djevanshir defeats Khazars

662 A.D. - Tibetians penetrate Western region to support rebelling Türks

662 A.D. - Arabs fight Khazars for Derbent

663 A.D. - Dismemberment of Great Bulgaria - Divided up among Kubrat's five sons, third of which was Asparukh, Khan of Utiguri.

665 A.D. - With death of Prince Samo first Slavic state is re-intrgrated into Avar Khaganate in 665 A.D. - 665 A.D. - Kutlug (56) restores E. Goktürk Khaganate, becomes Elteres Khagan (665-691).

667 A.D. - 150K Kumans, Turkmens, Gok-Oguses and Kyrgises, confederated with Khazars, cross Itil from the east. Shambat and Asparukh battle Khazars, loose and flee to Bashtu, present Kiev.

667 A.D. - Arabs defeat Peroz, last Sassanian shah, and cross Oxus River (Amu Darya) for the first time

668 A.D. - Peace treaty between Khazars' Kagan Kaban and Kara Bulgar's Baltavar Bat-Boyan. Kara Bulgar is subordnated to Khazar.

669 A.D. - Split of Kara Bulgar into W. and E. of Dniepr. West is controlled by Shambat and Asparukh, and East, including Bulyar, by Baltavar Bat-Boyan

670 A.D. - Bat-Boyan Bulgars are defeated by Khazars. Khazars recover territory with east Bulgar (Utugur) and Alan populations.

670 A.D. - Khazars under Alp-Ilitver defeat Bulgars

671 A.D. - Large Horde of Kubrat's 3rd son, Atilkese, nicknamed Asparukh, after death of Shambat in 670, moved west with Onogurs (Utigurs) and some Turkmen (Byzantian historians call them Bolgars from now on), to Danube and Pannonia district Kashan, between rivers B

673 A.D. - Arab raids to Bukhara, across Oxus River

675 A.D. - Bulgars arrive on Danube under Asparukh

678 A.D. - Kubrat's 4th son Kuber (Ultzindur?) (Balkor?) moved from S of Crimea his Ultzindurs and Ultzingurs of Hunnish stock to Pannonia under Avars (678-679)

678 A.D. - Kubrat's 5th son Emnetzur (Altsek) moved his Alciagirs, Alcildzurs and Alpidzurs from Crimea to Italy under Byzantines, to duchy of Benevetto/Abruzi region, Pentapolis at Ravenna.

679 A.D. - Byzantine's Constantine IV attacks Asparukh Bulgars. Bulgars retaliate, take Scythia and lower Moesia, Pliska becomes Khans' new headquarters.

679 A.D. - Chuvash may be descendants of Utugur Bulgars and Volgo-Kama Bulgars. Tatars may be descendants of Utugur Bulgars and Volgo-Kama Bulgars.

679 A.D. - Territorially, Bulgar's split is along Kutugur/Utugur uluses, with Kutugurs independent of Avar and W. Goktürk Khaganates, and Utugurs remaining in W. Goktürk Khaganate sphere.

679 A.D. - Kubrat's Bulgaria is split into independent (Byzantium Federatae) west Khanate under Asparukh, controlling from Donets on East to Danube on West, and Eastern Ak Bulgar Yorty, subject to Khazar Kagan from Itil to Donets, with capital Onogoria (Gr. Phanago

679 A.D. - Kipchaks restored Goktürk Kaganate, second component = Sirs, descendants of Seyanto, became 'Kok Goktürk' = Blue Türks, known as Kipchaks from that time

679 A.D. - Revolt Against Tan Empire

679 A.D. - Asparukh Bulgars invade Thrace

680 A.D. - Asparukh Khaganate includes Slavs. Asparukh Khaganate spreads into Dobrudja south of Danube.

680 A.D. - Asparukh 680 treaty with Slavs recognizes their self-government and territory. Slav princes participate in people assembly along with Bulgarian nobles. state administration consists of a Khan and 12 Great Boyls.

680 A.D. - Slav's obligation to Bulgars is to pay tribute and supply military contingents. state capital established in Pliska in Moesia.

680 A.D. - Empire of Avars peaked at end of 7th century (680 A.D.), after devision of Kubrat Bulgaria between Avars and Khazars, when it reached from Volga to Danube

680 A.D. - In Avaria, men were laid down in tombs with their horses, arms, and horse-trappings. Tomb objects are characterized by geometrical ornaments pressed upon a

print, with a certain degree of Byzantine influence

680 A.D. - Arab raids to Khwarizm, Samarkand

682 A.D. - Albanian missionary bishop Israel describes "Kingdom of Huns" (Belendjer) capital Varachan located north of Derbent, and Tangri cult of Northern Dagestan Barandjar (Balandjar) = Onogur = Utigur Bulgars, subordinated to Khazars.

682 A.D. - Kutlug is proclamed Khagan, title Ilterish (Country Creator) and oranized a second Khanate, appointing his brother Kapagan as Shad, and another brother Tosifu as Yabgy

683 A.D. - Successful Türkic rebellion led by Kutlug Ilterish (56) and Tonyukuk, restoration of Türkic Goktürk Khaganate

683 A.D. - Khazar raid to Armenia

684 A.D. - Khazar raid to Cis-Causasus

688 A.D. - Greek occupation of Cis-Causasus

689 A.D. - Otuz-Tatars are hostile to Kutlug Khan state

690 A.D. - Bulgar Khan Bat-Boyan (660-690) dies, succeeded by his son Bu-Timer (690-700) in vassalage of Khazars

691 A.D. - Kutlug Khan (56) (682-691) died, succeeded by his brother Mochur (Bakchor) (Mochjo) (Mochur) (57) (691-716) as Kapagan Khan.

692 A.D. - Boma live N. of Kyrgyz Khanate

692 A.D. - Kutlug Khan subordinated Khalka

692 A.D. - Kipchaks mixed with Kangar (Besenyos, Russ. 'Pecheneg') between Black Irtysh and Syr-Darya in Desht-i-Kipchak

694 A.D. - Embassy from Kurykans arrived to China. Rebellion of Ashina Suytsy and his alliance with Tibetians. Chinese imperial troops crush Tibetians, Turgeshes and W Goktürks

700 A.D. - Khazars are frequently allied with Huns of North Caucasus. Alp Elteber of Huns of North Caucasus is a vassal of Khazars. Huns capital city is Varachan (late 10 c).

700 A.D. - Tatars lived north of Tatabs and Kara-Kibi, on Kerulen tributary of Amur river, in those times mostly engaged in fishing.

700 A.D. - Oguz tribe federation relocates in great numbers from Orkhon area to vicinity of Talas, then to Syr Darya. Oguz dialect separates from Eastern Türkic, and by 11th century Oguz language of Syr Darya differs from Eastern Türkic in lexicon and pronounciation

701 A.D. - Khan Asparukh (679-701) of Danube Bulgaria dies, his son or grandson Terval (702-718) succeeds him

703 A.D. - Busir (Ibousir-Glavan) becomes Kagan of Khazar's Kaganate (703?-....).

703 A.D. - Khazar royal princess ..... marries Bysantine emperror Justinian II to become Empress Theodora.

704 A.D. - Ashina Khayn subjugated Semirechye for Empire Tan. Shato subdued without fight. Western Goktürks are subjugated, and Karluks, Huvu and Shunishes accede

705 A.D. - Khan of Danube Bulgaria Tervel aids Justinian II in regaining his control of Constantinople after a rebellion. Afterwards, Terval is crowned "Caesar"

705 A.D. - Beginning of systematic Arab conquest of Transoxania. Qutaiba ben Muslim becomes Governor of Khurasan

706 A.D. - Chinese break negociations with Goktürks

708 A.D. - Chinese built three fortresses north of Huanhe against Goktürks

709 A.D. - 709 Arabs capture Bukhara and Samarkand. 711 Arabs capture Khiva. 712 Arabs subdue Khwarezm and recapture Samarkand. 713 Arabs sack Kashgar.

711 A.D. - Khazars help to install Phillipicus as a Byzantine Emperor

711 A.D. - Goktürks suppress rebelion of Turgeshes. Divisions in Khorezm

712 A.D. - Khan-Caesar Tervel, after leaving Justinian II to his doom, sees fit to avenge his death by raiding and looting southern Thrace.

712 A.D. - Kuteyba subjugates Khorezm and takes Samakand. Emperor appoints Mohedo Tutuk a ruler of Samakand

713 A.D. - Arab embassy to China

714 A.D. - Chinese, under emperor T'aitsong, defeat Goktürks at Lake Issyk-Kul.

714 A.D. - Khazars loose Derbent to Arabs

714 A.D. - Trurks are defeated at Byshbalyk. Shato subordinate to Empire Tan

715 A.D. - Chinese beat back Goktürkic attacks on Beytin, and Arabs and Tibetians on Fergana 716 Luchen is taken from Kidanes.

Turgeshes rebel against Empire and defeat Chinese and Karluks

715 A.D. - Ases, and then Yasygs, are cruelly suppressed by Kapagan Khagan

716 A.D. - Mochur (Bak-chor) (57) (691-716) Qapagan Khan died, after defeating Bayirku of upper Kerulen but killed on return trip. He was succeeded by Mogilyan (Mokilien) (63) (716-734), elder brother of Kul-tegin, installed by Kul-tegin. Peak of second Goktürk empire (716-734)

718 A.D. - Danube Bulgars under Khan Tervel as federats of Byzantium defeat Arab invasion and save Byzantium. Khan-Caesar Terval (26) (702-718) dies, ?.. becomes Khan (718-725).

718 A.D. - Orkhon Inscriptions on Tonyukuk slella are created, describing events and providing Türkic perspective. Inscriptions are bilingual, in Kipchak language in Türkic alphabet, and in Chinese language in Chinese characters. Sources

718 A.D. - Khazars invade Azerbaijan.

720 A.D. - Goktürks' victory over Chinese imperians. Kashmirian Radj is given title Van

722 A.D. - Second Khazar - Arab war (722-737) First campaign of Arabian troops led by Zh. Jirrah in Northern Caucasus against Alans and Khazars

722 A.D. - Son of Türk Bilge Khagan, Tengru Khan, has 300K army

723 A.D. - Khazars lose Balanjar to Arabs, move capital to Samandar

723 A.D. - Start of massive Jewish emmigration to Khazaria (723-944)

724 A.D. - In Avaria, after about 40 years, i.e., after 720 A.D., figures of plants and animals were used more frequently, were cast and decorated. New art shows Türkic Asian features, probably a new population coming from east took place of earlier one

724 A.D. - Second Jirrah's campaign in Northern Caucasus.

725 A.D. - Danube Bulgar Khan ..?. (718-725) dies, end of Dulo dynasty. Sevar becomes Khan (725-740). Danube Bulgar Khanate expands.

727 A.D. - Khazars invade Azerbaijan. Muslam's raid against Khazars

730 A.D. - Khazar's Barjik leads 300K army to raid Azerbaijan (Albania?). At Arbadil, Khazars defeat entire Arab army.

732 A.D. - Orkhon Inscriptions on Kul Tegin slella with a large and small inscriptions, and on Tonyukuk slella. Inscriptions are bilingual, in Kipchak language in Türkic alphabet, and in Chinese language in Chinese characters. Sources

732 A.D. - Otuz-Tatars moved from Goktürks to Amur-area taiga.

732 A.D. - Khazar princess Chichek marries Bysantine emperror Constantine V to become Empress Irene.

734 A.D. - Mogilyan Khan (63) poisoned, his son Yollyg-Tegin (Yijan) (65) died, his brother Bilge Kutlug Khan (66) succeeded as Tengri Khagan (66) (734-741).

735 A.D. - Fubin annulled statuary. Chinese and foreign (Syanbinian) stratification was fixed and joining Chinese people was impossible. This started a new ethnical substrate. All non-Chinese could only join border army, hated by Chinese element.

735 A.D. - Campaign of Arabian military leader Mervan Kru in Alania. Alan king Itaz.

737 A.D. - Arabs force conversion to Islam. …... becomes first Kagan of Khazar's Kaganate to convert to Islam for political reasons (703?-….).

737 A.D. - Khazars loose Samandar to Arabs, move capital to Itil.

737 A.D. - Goktürks attack Kucha

740 A.D. - Danube Bulgaria Khan Sevar (725-740) dies, Kormisos becomes Khan (740-756)

740 A.D. - Ashina Sin is appointed a ruler of ten tribes, sent west and killed. After his death Dumochji, Yabgu of three tribes is appointed Dumochji, Yabgu of three tribes

740 A.D. - UYGUR EMPIRE

740 - 1335 A.D. - Founder - Kutlug Bilgekul Khan (Bilge Kutlug Tengri Khan)

Area - Central Asia and Northern Mongolia

743 A.D. - END OF GOKTÜRK EMPIRE

552 - 743 A.D. - Founder - Bumin Khan (Tumen)

Area - From Black Sea across Asia along northern borders of Mongolia and China almost to Pacific Ocean, and valleys of Altay Mountains (Ergenikon) (Total Area - 18,000,000 Km 2)

744 A.D. - Ozmysh Khagan (68) (742-743) killed by Basmils. Basmils failed to take control of E. Goktürk Khaganate, and Uygurs,

with Karluk help, set Kuli Peilo Khan as Kutlug Bilga Khagan (11) (Tengrida Bolmish El, Qutluq Bilge Qaghan) (742 - 747). Creation of Uygur

744 A.D. - Uygurs substituted one Türkic people for another, closely related, for hegemony of Mongolia, in the next century (744-840)

747 A.D. - Khan Marduan of Daghestani Bulgars, Burjans, build a small wooden city, named city Marduan. Khazars called it Mardukan. Present Bulgar (Great Bulgar)

747 A.D. - Tatars lose a battle to Uygurs N-W of Selenga. Tatars were caught at Keyre spring and river Tri- birkyu, and lost half of army.

747 A.D. - Ay Tengrida Qut Bolmish, Tutmish Bilge Qaghan (11) dies. Bayanchur (12) (747 -759).

747 A.D. - Created Shine-usu, Terkhin and Tes inscriptions. Inscriptions are in Old Uygur?? language in Türkic alphabet. Kagan Bayanchur (747-759) relates 6-th c events with "QSR=QASAR". Sources

750 A.D. - Bulgars live along north-western shore of Caspian Sea

750 A.D. - After living as neighbors of Chuvash people for over 1,000 years, a part of Hungarians moved south to "Levedia" in approximately 750 A.D., while others remained between Itil River and Ural Mountains

750 A.D. - Kengeres/Pecheneg/Kangar/Besenyos living west of Uygurs and are hostile with them

751 A.D. - Defeat of Chinese armies at Talas river by a combined forces of Goktürks, Arabs and Tibetans. End of Chinese control over Turkestan. Paper starts spreading to Arabs and on to Europe

752 A.D. - Tatars lived on eastern border of Uygyria.

753 A.D. - Ilmish Kutlug Khan is Kara Khan of Goktürks

755 A.D. - Constantine V (son of Leo III) builds a chain of forts along Bulgarian border. War begins between Danube Bulgars and Byzantines. After initial success, Bulgars are defeated.

755 A.D. - Created Orkhon Inscription on Mogilyan Bilge Khan slella. Inscriptions are bilingual, in Kipchak language in Türkic alphabet, and in Chinese language in Chinese characters. Sources

756 A.D. - Danube Bulgaria Khan Kormisos (740-756) dies, Vinekh becomes Khan (756-761)

759 A.D. - El Tutmish Alp Qutluq Bilge Qaghan. El Tekin (13) (759 - 779).

760 A.D. - Khazar Khagan Boghatur (760?-...)

760 A.D. - Bulgar Khan Tat-Ugek renames city Marduan to Bulgar, which becomes a center of small Burjan kingdom.

761 A.D. - Khan Vinekh of Danube Bulgaria (756-761) and all his kin assassinated. Teletz of Ugain clan and a leader of conspiracy is elected new Khan (761-763).

762 A.D. - Khazars, led by As Tarkhan, invade and re-conquer Cis-Caucasia. 764 Khazars take Tbilisi

763 A.D. - Danube Bulgaria Khan Telets seizes southern Thrace. Bulgars loose battle of Anchiel. Khan Telets (761-763) is murdered by hostile Boils for his failure. Umar, then Bayan (763-765) is elected new Khan

765 A.D. - Danube Bulgaria Khan Bayan (763-765) is replaced by Toktu, then Magan, then Telerig (c.765-777) assumes Bulgarian Khan-hood.

772 A.D. - War between Greeks and Danube Bulgars. Khazaria unites with Alania

775 A.D. - Leo IV "Khazar" emperor of Byzantine Empire (775-780)

777 A.D. - Danube Bulgaria Khan Telerig (c.765-777) is replaced by Kardam (c.777-c.803)

779 A.D. - Alp Qutluq Bilge Qaghan. Tonga Bagha (14) (779 - 789).

780 A.D. - Leo II, greatson of Khazar Kagan, ruler of Abkhazia. (780-....)

786 A.D. - Khazars help Abkhazia to free from Byzantine, and Abkhazia becomes Khazarian dependency

789 A.D. - Tengride Bolmish Qutluq Bilge Qaghan. Taras (15) (789 - 790).

790 A.D. - Qutluq Bilge Qaghan. Aychur (16) (790 - 795).

790 A.D. - Shato subordinate to Tibet. Tibetians take Beytin and Kucha (Ansi) 791 Tibetians take Khotan

791 A.D. - Franks met resistance on their campaign in area of Austria and Slovenia

792 A.D. - Franks met with little resistance on their 2 campaigns in area of Austria

and Slovenia because of Avar/Bulgar/Slav draught and famine

792 A.D. - Avar leaders fought each other between 792 and 795, but Kaghan and Yugrush, his fellow ruler, were killed by their own men, who blamed them for draught and famine

794 A.D. - Tibetians defeat Uygurs 795 Tatabs and Tatars are defeated by Chinese

794 A.D. - According to archaeological evidence, Avars populated Banat, Crishana, and parts of Transylvania. Their number in Transylvania is not very high, but this is difficult to estimate. As in other territories, they probably lived together with Slavic tribes

795 A.D. - Avars power broken, Franks destroyed residence of Kaganat. Nestor chronicle stipulates that all Avars died, but some retired to east of Tisza. Last reliable mention of Avars is from 822, and in 873 there is a record of uncertain character.

795 A.D. - Ay Tengride Ulugh Bolmish Alp Qutluq Bilge Qaghan. Qutluq (17) (795 - 805)

796 A.D. - Avar Kaghan and his warlords abandoned their capital Rhing before Frankish host reached it in 796, but 90 per cent of Charlemagne's horses that advanced as far as Gyõr in 791 also perished of famine

796 A.D. - Avar state, weakened by internal dissent, was destroyed by a combined Frankish and Bulgarian Khan Kardam attack in 796.

803 A.D. - Danube Bulgaria Khan Kardam (c.777-c.803) is replaced by Krum (38) elected to Bulgarian Khan-hood (803-814). Bulgars under Khagan Krum unite with Franks to crush Avar Khaganate.

804 A.D. - Khan Krum's army has 30,000 chain armored heavily armed cavalry, vs. Byzantium's less than 400.

804 A.D. - Khan Krum venture to become independent suzerain, lays off federatae status, become Tzar, and absorbs Slavic and Avar territories and populations. Policy program for next half century.

804 A.D. - Charlemagne and then Pepin defeat and subjugate Avar Khan in Pannonia, rob 2 centuries of treasuries. In 805 Avar Khagan Zodan baptized with name Theodore. Theodore continued ruling as a subject of Charlemagne

804 A.D. - Joint forces of Bulgars and Franks crush and annihilate Avar Khaganate.

805 A.D. - End of AVAR EMPIRE in Europe

558-805 A.D. Founder - Khan Bayan Area - Pannonia, Balkans, Bessarabia, N. Pontic steppes to Tanais and Itil (Total Area - 2,500,000 Km2)

Seat of Avar kaghan and his warlords east of Danube in Pannonia, known as Rhing

805 A.D. - Ay Tengride Qut Bolmish, Qutluq Bilge Qaghan. Unknown (18) (805 - 808).

806 A.D. - Manicheans arrive to Chanan from Uygurs

807 A.D. - Danube Bulgars and Greeks fight.

808 A.D. - Ay Tengride Qut Bolmish, Alp Bilge Qaghan. Unknown (19) (808 - 821).

813 A.D. - Bulgars take Adrianopole.

813 A.D. - In 813, Krum led a large army of Slavs and Avars against Byzantium and besieged Constantinople without success. He died in following year.

814 A.D. - April 13, 814 While preparing another attack against Byzantines, Khagan Krum (38) bursts a blood vessel and dies. Khagan Omurtag (41) assumes Bulgarian Khan-hood (814-814). Boils rule Bulgaria - Chok (?) (?_?).

814 A.D. - Khan Ditsen (40) (814-816)

816 A.D. - Chok and Boils Danube Bulgars conclude a peace treaty with Byzantines to last thirty years, to be renewed every ten years.

816 A.D. - Khan Omurtag (41) (816-831)

817 A.D. - Inhabitants of Samandar revolt against attempts by Khazar Khagan Karak introduce Judaism

817 A.D. - Manichean missionaries are exiled to Uyguria

818 A.D. - Danube Bulgars thrust to north as far as Kiev (818-820).

819 A.D. - Kara Bulgarian Khan Aydar (819-855)

820 A.D. - Khazars found Sambata (sam = high, bat = stronghold) and Kiev (kui = low, ev = settlement), settled by Khazars and Magyars.

821 A.D. - Preslav is completed - new Bulgarian capital.

821 A.D. - Kun Tengride Ulugh Bolmish, Kuch Kuchluk Bilge Qaghan. Unknown (20) (821 - 824).

824 A.D. - Tengride Qut Bolmish, Kuch Bilge Qaghan. Hazar Tekin (21) (824 - 832).

827 A.D. - Danube Bulgars and Franks fight.

830 A.D. - Khazar Khagan Khan-Tuvan (Dyggvi) (830?-…)

830 A.D. - Construction of Sarkel fortress by Khazars with Byzantium's help

830 A.D. - Khzarian Kabars rebel against Bek (830-862).

830 A.D. - First Rus Khaganate is established as ulus by Itil Bulgarian Khan Aydar (819-855)

831 A.D. - Danube Bulgaria Khan Malamir (42) (831-837)

832 A.D. - Danube Bulgars and Franks sign peace treaty.

832 A.D. - Tengride Qut Bolmish, Kuchluk Bilge Qaghan. Kho Tekin (22) (832 - 839).

833 A.D. - Khan-Tuvan (Dyggvi) sends an embassy to Byzantine asking to send engineers-fortificators to build fortresses against Rus' attacks.

836 A.D. - Danube Bulgar Khan Presijan (43)(836-852)

837 A.D. - Magyars crossed Dnieper from east around 837, occupying steppe as far as Danube by year 860 A.D. - 837 A.D. - Atelkuzu, largely consisting of Ukraine, Moldavia and Eastern Wallachia, favoured survival at time of warming. As drought spread, it was possible to move flocks up-river to cooler, wooded regions, where fishing provided an extra food for semi-nomads.

837 A.D. - Magyar tribes, and chiefly ruling caste, moved up river as far as Kharka, Bashtu, and Galich

839 A.D. - Kho Tekin (22) (832 - 839) dies. Kichik Tekin (23) (839 - 840)

840 A.D. - Destruction of Uygur Orkhon Empire by Kirgizes. End of Uygur leadership of E. Goktürkic Khaganate

840 A.D. - E. Goktürk Khaganate Kichik Tekin (23) dies

840 A.D. - In about 840-850 A.D., Hungarians were forced to move westwards to Atelkuzu (Etelkoz) and they then occupied Carpathian Basin in 896 A.D. living there to this day

841 A.D. - Kyrgyz ambassador arrived in China

842 A.D. - Muhamad ibn Musa Al Khwarizmi works in Khazarian Kagan's palace, sent there by Caliph Al-Wathiq.

850 A.D. - Bashkorts used prior to 9c antroponym 'Ishtek/Istek' (Asses, Ossian/Yassian people), and from 9 c became known antroponym 'Bashkort' from (according to Arab author Salam Tardjman) Khan Bashgird, whose horde lived in present area.

852 A.D. - Khan Presijan (43) (836-852) controls Danube Bulgaria extending from Panonnia, Transilvania, Wallachia, Moldavia, Moesia, Thrace and Macedonia, to Donets ??, with numerous inhabitants (Slavs, Bulgars, Thracians (Vlach, Wallach, Dacian, Get)

855 A.D. - Kara Bulgarian Baltavar Khan Aydar (819-855) died, Gabdulla Djilki (Shilki) becomes Khan (855-882)

859 A.D. - Khan Shilki lost battle to Khazar Kagan Iskhak at Baltavar (Poltava)

859 A.D. - Kara Bulgar Khan Gabdulla Djilki (Shilki) lost Bashtu (Kiev) and Urus (Novgorod) uluses to Khazars. Khazars oganize them as ulus Rus. Khagan Iskhak appoints Norman leader Dir (Bulg. Djir) of Slavic militia in Bashtu a ruler of Rus and Norman Ascold (Bulg. As-Khalib) a Viceregent of Rus

859 A.D. - Shilki settles in c. Karadjar (Chernigov) with territory

859 A.D. - Shilki's brother Lachyn becomes Khan of remaining Kara Bulgar with a capital in Khorysdan (Putivl)

859 A.D. - Kara Bulgar Bashtu becomes Khazarian Kiev

861 A.D. - Religious debate in Khazarian court (khazarian Polemic) between Cyril and Methodius, Rabbi Yitzhak Ha Sangari, and Muslem cleric Farabi Ibn Kora.

861 A.D. - Khazar Bulan Bek, nobility and some common people convert to Judaism.

862 A.D. - Chronist Nestor gives 862 as year of creation of Rus. Ruses are rulers of Slavs. Ruses live in military settlements and "feed" by spoils, a part of which was rendered to Jewish Khazars. Slavs are engaged in agriculture and animal husbandry. Russes are eth

862 A.D. - Viking warrior Hrorekr (Riurik) leads expedition to Staraya Lagoda and occupied city in 862 A.D. - 862 A.D. - Hrorekr (Riurik) (862-879) takes Novgorod, the other brothers take two other cities. Eventually Riurik gained all three cities. Gradual conquest of surrounding Slavic states, raided as far as Constantinople. At his death, his son Ingvar is too young to ru

863 A.D. - Khan Shilki re-unites Bashtu and Karadjar with Kara Bulgar. Knyaz Dir (Bulg Djir) submits to Shilki, Ascold (Bulg As-Khalib) escapes to Galidj (Novgorod? Galich?) Shilki restores himself as Baltavar of Kara Bulgar with capital at Baltavar (Poltava)

865 A.D. - Khan Barys of Itil Bulgaria beylyk founded by Tat-Ugek, died, and Shilki, Khan of Kara Bulgar with a capital in Baltavar (Poltava) is proclamed Khan of Itil Bulgaria (865-882).

865 A.D. - City Bulgar becomes a capital of Itil Bulgaria.

865 A.D. - Shilki proclames Itil Bulgaria an Islamic state, without a Califate recognition

866 A.D. - Established Kara Bulgar station Kolyn (Khlynov, Vyatka)

868 A.D. - First revolt of Türkish soldiers against Abbasid Calif al-Mutaawakkil (847-861)

868 A.D. - Ahmad ibn Tulun, a Türkish praetorian of Abbasid Califate, becomes an independent ruler of Egypt and extends his rule to Syria

875 A.D. - Khazars built a glass factory in Hrodna (present Belarus)

879 A.D. - 879-882 Post Riurik (862-879), pre-Olaf period in Rus ulus

882 A.D. - Khan Shilki (855-882) died, Bat-Ugyr becomes Khan of Itil Bulgaria (882-895).

882 A.D. - Khan Alabuga of a Baryn line of Sabans starts a city, named later Bilyar.

882 A.D. - Olaf (Russ. Oleg) (882-913) First serious Rus expansion. Dominated several E. Slav tribes as tribute states.

889 A.D. - After 889, Besenyos break through Khazarian border guards and replace Magyars from Levedia

893 A.D. - Catastrophically cold winter of 892-893 froze Itil and Don, made it possible for Besenyos, whom Oguzes attacked, to flee across frozen rivers into Atelkuzu, although some of them were stuck east of Yaik river

893 A.D. - Besenyos stop their pusuit of Majars at Dniepr, spend winter near mouth of river Buh

894 A.D. - Majar Prince Levente leads Khazar Kabars against Bulgaria

894 A.D. - Besenyos in alliance with Bulgars start a second attack of Majars, forcing them to leave Atilkiji (Itil-Kiji, Atelkuzu) for Transylvania and Upper Tisza region

895 A.D. - Bat-Ugyr (882-895) abdicates. Baltavar (Elteber) Almush (Almas), eldest son of Shilki, becomes Khan of Itil Bulgaria, accclamed in city Bulgar (895-925).

895 A.D. - Khan Almush Kara Bulgar census lists 550K, 200K are Saban-speaking Bulgars, 180K-Ars (Udmurts, Finno-Ugors), 170K-Modjars

895 A.D. - Alans and Bulgars freed from Khazar power

895 A.D. - Some Khazar Kabars settle in Transilvania/Hungary with Majars.

895 A.D. - Avaria (Pannonia) is divided between Slavic state of Great Moravia under Svyatopolk, and Türkic Khanate of Bulgaria. Bulgar Onogundur (or Onogur) settle there, possibly giving name to Hungary.

900 A.D. - Ibn Ruste lists three branches of Itil Bulgars: "first branch was called Bersula, second - Esegel, and third - Bolgar".

902 A.D. - Varangian Rus mercenaries are mentioned serving in Byzantine naval expedition to Crete. Rus mercenaries also serve Khazars

904 A.D. - Olaf (Russ. Oleg), Prince of Kiev (882-916), remains a vassal of Avar Khaganate, divided between Bulgarian principalities.(In 859 to Khazars??)

909 A.D. - Rus raiders (druzhina) with Varangian (Varyag) allies captures Khazarian fort Abezgun on Caspian Sea

910 A.D. - First missions of Christian preachers from Byzantium to Alania. Establishing Alan arch-episcopate. Peter as first archbishop of Alania.

913 A.D. - Kengeres, once a part of confederation of W. Goktürk Khaganate, were driven toward lower Syr-Darya and Aral Sea by Karluk Türks. They were grazing their herds between Yaik and Itil rivers.

913 A.D. - North of Sea of Azov Kengeres occupied Levedia, taking it from Majars, and then drove them from Atilkiji area between Dniepr and Lower Danube

913 A.D. - Ingvar (Russ. Igor) (913-945) re-established control over Eastern Slavs

913 A.D. - Khazars demolish Rus marauding expedition fleet

915 A.D. - Besenyos appear before Kiev for first time in force. Prince Ingvar (Russ. Igor)

signs peace treaty with them establishing a frontier between Don and Dniester

920 A.D. - Khazars fight with Burtas (Steppe Alans or Asses), Oguz, Byzantines, Kengeres and Kara Bulgars.

920 A.D. - Itil Bulgar Baltavar Almush (Almas) allies with Caliphate as counterbalance to Khazars. Beginnng of minting of Bulgarian dirkhems

922 A.D. - Itil Bulgars congress of Bulgarian tribes adopted Islam as state religion, built mosques and schools. Itil Bulgars start transition to Arabic script from Türkic script

922 A.D. - Baltavar Almush takes a title 'Emir' as obligation to rule in accordance with Quran

922 A.D. - City Bilyar becomes a province Baityuba capital and a 3rd sized city after Bulgar and Bandja

922 A.D. - City Nur-Suvar (922-1246). Present Tatarskiy (Sham-Suar).

922 A.D. - Established city Tukhchi, renamed in 1219 Djuketun (Chistopol)

925 A.D. - Governor of province Mardan-Ballak Balus starts a city, named later Banja (Banja-Burtas). Present Syzran.

925 A.D. - Almush (895-925) died, Khasan becomes Khan of Itil Bulgaria (925-930). Almush is buried in Fortress Gulistan.

930 A.D. - Seljuks are from tribe Kynyk - one of 24 Oguz tribes. Oguzes live between Syr Darya, Caspian and Aral seas. Kynyks live near delta of Syr Darya.

930 A.D. - Yabgu rules Oguzes. Leader of Seljuk clan, Temir-Yalyg, nicknamed Dukak (Dokak), has a high position. He objects to a raid by Yabgu against other Türkic tribes, and sours relations with Yabgu. He and his tribe may be Moslems.

930 A.D. - Itil Bulgaria has 30 cities. Khasan built: Matak Nukrat Bandja (Samara) (Center of Mardan-Bellak ulus) Bulyar (citadel in Bilyar) Kamysh Simbir Gazan-Deber Kashan Tukhcha Tau-Kerman (Sviyajsk) Tash-Bulgar Subash-Simbir Karadjar Djilan

930 A.D. - Khasan (925-930) died, Yalkau Michail becomes Khan of Itil Bulgaria (930-943).

930 A.D. - Khazars ally with Alans who adopt Judaism, and arrange a dynastic marriage

932 A.D. - KARAHANID (Karahanli, Ilek (ilig)-khanid, al-Hakaniye, el-Haniye, al-Afrasiyab)

932 - 1212 A.D. - Founder - Saltuk Bugra Han

Area - All Trans-Oxus area including area between Issyk and Balkash Lakes Initial center in Kashgar

932 A.D. - Khazars ally with Oguzes.

934 A.D. - Kengeres join in Hungarian invasion of Byzantian Thrace.

939 A.D. - Khazar Baliqchi Pesakh defeats Rus

943 A.D. - Yalkau Michail died (930-943), Mohammed becomes Khan of Itil Bulgaria (943-976).

944 A.D. - Kengeres join in Prince Ingvar of Kiev raid on Byzantium.

945 A.D. - Helga (Russ. Olga) (945-962) is energetic in subjugating Slavs, exacting terrible revenge upon Drevlians, burying alive and burning their most distinguished men alive in a bath in Kiev, massacring 5,000 at her husbands funeral feast, burning Izkorosten with many killed or enslaved

944 A.D. - All Gothic cities-colonies are robbed to foundation in raid of Prince Ingvar of Kiev

945 A.D. - Start of Itil Bulgar-Turkmen 15 year war

949 A.D. - Talib, junior son of Khan Gazan, and grandson of Almush, organizes a regular army in Itil Bulgaria.

950 A.D. - There is information about Bashkir Confederation in 9-12c under Masim Khan, starting with Khan Bashkort. Bashkir 'Shejere' listed Khans Muyten Bey and Maiky Bey at approx. 1220, witha list of 10 predesessors covering 9-12c.

950 A.D. - Al Mas'udi (died in 956) describes 4 Türkic peoples: Ydjni, Badjkurt (Maskurts, Masguts, called by Herodotus (5-th c. B.C.), Strabo (c.64 B.C. - - A.D. 20), and C. Plinius Secundus (62-113 A.D.) Massagetae Scythians), Badjanak (Besenyos), Nukardi

950 A.D. - Conversion of Karakhanids and Uighurs from Buddhism to Islam under Satuq Bughra Khan (d.955)

950 A.D. - Magyars living in Lebedia are vassals of Khazars.

960 A.D. - End of Itil Bulgar-Turkmen 15 year war. Chief Turkmen Khan Arslan is beheaded by Bulgar sardar Kukcha Amir.

960 A.D. - Besenyos live in Moldova (10th cent.-1171)

960 A.D. - ...... becomes second Kagan of Khazar's Kaganate to convert to Islam (960?-....).

960 A.D. - Karahanid Satuk's son, Musa (Baytas) defeated eastern Khan Arslan Han and carried off this branch of dynasty. Entire Karahanli State becomes Muslim (960). Afterwards, forced diffusion of Islam among C. Asian Türks turned into holy war. First case among Türks to abandon tradition of freedom of convitions and to force conversion of subject populations

961 A.D. - After Dukak death, Oguz Yabgu appoints Dukak's son Seljuk Syu-Bashi as head of army. Seljuk evacuates his tribe to Sugura, near Jend (Hojdent), bordering with Moslem countries. Relocation may be caused by Kipchak wictory over Oguz State or shotage of pastures

961 A.D. - Seljuks (Salchukiyans, Sakachikas) together with Kynyk clan and other Oguz clans leave winter capital of Oguz State Yenikent (Ruins of present Jankent) between Caspian and Aral, with their cattle of horses, camels, sheep and cows, to Maverannakhr .

961 A.D. - M Kashgari: To live with Moslem Türks, multitudes of Seljuk tribes adopted Islam. Seljuk adopted Islam for political possibilities, and asked neighboring Bukhara and Khorezm to send Moslem scholars. Prior, they were called Turkmens, Karluks and Oguzes

961 A.D. - Oguz Yabgu's Oguses arriving in Jend to collect annual taxes are driven out by Seljuks under pretext "We are not paying taxes to infidels", and started juhad war against Oguz State with Seljuk's title Gazi. Start of independent Seljuk Beylyk in Jend.

962 A.D. - Svyatoslav (962-972) first Rus Prince with Slavic name. Numerous campaigns to assert his authority over eastern Slavs. Invaded Khazaria and destroyed its capitl Itil, and its major fortresses Samander and Sarkel. Allied with Constantinople against Danube Bulgars

962 A.D. - Türkic Ghaznavid dynasty is established in Afghanistan

962 A.D. - GAZNELI EMPIRE

962 - 1183 A.D. - Founder – Alptekin

Area - from Trans-Oxus to Ganges River, from Caspian to steppes of Pamir (Total Area - 4,700,000 Km 2)

964 A.D. - Kengeres seriously threaten Khazaria

965 A.D. - Byzantine governor (strategos) of Chersonesus asks Svyatoslav for aid against Khazars. Svyatoslav campaign to Don. En route he attacks Volga Bulgars. He raids Sarkel, Itil, and Tmutarkhan, also captures Chersonesus

965 A.D. - Svyatoslav possibly signed agreement with Besenyos before crossing their territory. He allies with Oguzes. Purpose to gain tribute from Viatchi on Oka by removing their Khazar overlords. He also conquers Yasians and Kasogians in Taman-Kuban area.

965 A.D. - Kkazar Kagan temporarily converts to Islam for political reasons

965 A.D. - Itil Bulgars gain independence after defeating Khazars.

966 A.D. - Bandja (Fanagoria), capital of Great Bulgaria in VII c, destroyed by Kiev Knyaz Svyatoslav. Escaped inhabitants established New Bandja in Jiguli on Itil (Murom setlement).

966 A.D. - Khan Mohammed established fort Simbir (Simbirsk)

967 A.D. - Knyaz Svyatoslav of Kiev seizes Khazar capital Itil

969 A.D. - Khazaria, broken by Svyatoslav (called Barys by Bulgars), is divided between Itil Bulgaria and N. Caucasus Saklans.

969 A.D. - Inflow of silver dirhams from Bulgaria and Khazaria stops

969 A.D. - Saklans receive territory S. of rivers Sal and Kum, Shir (Don), Kuper-Kubar (Khoper), Boryn-Inesh (Voronej). Khin (Sarkel, Belaya Veja) is a province ruled by Bulgar's vali.

970 A.D. - Khan Mohammed established fort Balyn (Suzdal) in Mary land

972 A.D. - 8 Besenyo (Bedjenek) tribes, under Khan Kura, of Kipchak stock with Oguz element, freed of Khazar dominance, defeat Rus prince Svyatoslav and make a drinking cup of his scull. Bedjenek's continuous figts with Khazars, Byzantines and Russ.

976 A.D. - Mohammed died (943-976), Talib becomes Khan of of Itil Bulgaria (976-981).

981 A.D. - Itil Bulgaria Khan Talib (976-981) died, Timar becomes Khan (981-1004).

985 A.D. - Türkic Karakhanid and Gaznevit, and Iranian Samanid states surround Seljuk Beylyk. Seljuks fight with Karakhanids and Samanids. Samanids give Karakhanid Yabgu Arslan Israel with Oguzes control of Nur, near Bukhara.

985 A.D. - Seljuq Türks, a ruling tribe of Oguz, move to vicinity of Bukhara.

986 A.D. - Khazars present Judaism to Knyaz Voldemir (Russ.Vladimir) of Kiev, Itil Bulgars present Islam.

988 A.D. - Voldemir consolidates his possession of conquered city-states through adoption of single state religion. He orders conversion of subject people and launches built-up of Christian churches. Negotiations for military aid with Emperor Basil II end in agreeme

994 A.D. - Formation of Türkic-Ghaznavid dynasty in present day Afganistan

999 A.D. - Destruction of Persian Samanid dynasty by Türkic tribes.

1000 A.D. - Some Khazars in Kievan Rus are Slavicized and adopt East Slavic language (1000-1300).

1004 A.D. - Itil Bulgaria Khan Timar (981-1004) died, Masgut becomes Khan (1004-1006).

1006 A.D. - Itil Bulgaria Khan Masgut (1004-1006) died, Ibragim becomes Khan (1006-1025).

1010 A.D. - Kipchaks are pressed by Kumosi- Kimaks and then by Kidanes and move west

1016 A.D. - Last Khazar Khagan Georgius Tzul is cuptured by combined army of Byzantine Basil II and Sfengus, brother of Kiev's Grand Prince Voldemir. Khazaria loses last independence and territories of Crimea and Taman.

1016 A.D. - End of HAZAR EMPIRE

602-1016 A.D. - Founder - no historical data for founder, its greatest ruler was Hakan Yusuf. Area - Hazars separated from Goktürks and formed a state from Caucasian Mntns to Danube and N. Pontic area

1020 A.D. - Kipchaks occupy Middle and Lower Donets basin, lower Don and N.Azov. Earliest Kipchak gravestone monuments are located west of Itil

1024 A.D. - Lavrentiev Chronicle dates establishment of Suzdal in Merya land

1025 A.D. - Itil Bulgaria Khan Ibragim (1006-1025) died, Azgar becomes Khan (1025-1028).

1025 A.D. - One of Seljuk chiefs, Arslan Israil Yabgu, serves as auxiliary to Karakhanid's Ali-Tegin, against Ghazavids.

1026 A.D. - Kengeres invasion of Byzantium is repulsed by Constantine Diogenes..

1028 A.D. - Itil Bulgaria Khan Azgar (1025-1028) abdicated, Ashraf becomes Khan (1028-1061).

1029 A.D. - Kipchaks control steppes from Itil to Irtysh

1032 A.D. - Torgul-beg , with Daud and Arslan Israil Yabgu, acquires control of E. Iran.

1035 A.D. - Itil Bulgaria Khan Azgar established fort Khazar (Voronej)

1036 A.D. - Itil Bulgaria Khan Azgar established city Tyumen, center of Tubdjak ulus (Tyumen)

1040 A.D. - SELCUK EMPIRE

1040 - 1157 A.D. - Founder – Seljuk

Area - East, Balkash and Issyk Lakes and Tarim Derya; West, Aegean and Mediterranean; North, Aral, Caspian Sea, Caucasian and Black Sea; South, area including Arabia (Area - 10,000,000 Km 2)

1051 A.D. - Kengeres invade Byzantium.

1054 A.D. - Seljuks, under Tügral Beg, capture Baghdad, Abbasid capital, from Buwayhids, establish Seljuq Sultanate, and become official protectors of Caliphate.

1054 A.D. - Rus chronicles record appearance of Guz people, pushed by Kipchaks - a branch of Kimaks of middle Irtysh and of Ob.

1055 A.D. - Rus claims that majority of Kipchak tribes have crossed Itil and occupy E. Europian steepes.

1055 A.D. - Ipatian Chronicle reports first arrival of Kipchaks at border of Pereyaslav principality

1059 A.D. - Yabgu Arslan Israel with Oguzes fights Karakhanids, and withdraw with booty, leaving Samanid heir Ismail El Muntasyr, who loses war with Karakhanids,and dies. Samanid state desintegrates, Karakhanids take over Maverannakhr, and Gazavids take Horasan.

1060 A.D. - Kipchaks replace Besenyos (Bedjenek) from N Caucasus steppes. Stan of Kipchak Khans is located on river Sunj.

N Caucasus steppes is an important component of Deshti-Kipchak.

1063 A.D. - Beginning of reign of Seljuc Alp Arslan

1064 A.D. - Kengeres invade Byzantium, across Thrace to gates of Constantinople..

1065 A.D. - 600K Oguzes crossed Danube, devastated Balkans to Thessalonica. Emperor Constantine X Ducas, and then Kengeres and Bulgars, who were ruled at that time from Byzantium, annihilated them. Remains of Oguzes were subjugated, eliminated or assimilated by Kipch

1065 A.D. - Visit of Alanian king Durguleit Great to Georgian king Bagrat IV in Kutais.

1065 A.D. - Three Türkic peoples inhabit steppes N. of Lake Balkhash: Oguz (Ghuz, Torks, Ouzoi, Uzes, Türkmen), Kimaks/Kipchak of middle Enisey of Ob, and Kirghiz. Ogur group is distinguished from Oguz Türkic people that they had Y mutated to J (DJ).

1169 A.D. - Prince of Suzdal, Andrei Bogoliubskii, sacked Kiev, then moved seat of Great Prince to Vladimir, capital of Suzdal

1070 A.D. - Turks in Karahanli State engage in cultural and scientific activities. Turkish written with Uighur and Arabic alphabets becomes literary language and literature spread for the first time. Karahanli people exchange with Gazneli and other state sultans in Turkish written in Uighur letters

1070 A.D. - Most ancient monument of Islam era in Türkic is "Kutadgu Blig" written by Yusuf Has Hacib in 1069-1070 in Ughur and Arabic letters about ideal administration system of a state

1071 A.D. - Kengeres, in service of Byzantium, desert Emperor Romanus Diogenes V (1067-1071) in favor of Oguz Sultan Alp Arslan.

1072 A.D. - Beginning of reign of Seljuc Malik Shakh.

1072 A.D. - Marriage of Maria of Alania to Byzantine emperor Michael VII Duca Parapinaces (1071-1078 d. 1078). Marriage of Georgian king George III with Alanian princess Burduhan

1073 A.D. - Probably grandson of Mohammed b. Yusuf Kadir Han, Great Khan of Eastern Karahanli State, Mahmut Kashgari work, titled "Divan-i Legat it-Turk" written in Baghdad in 1073-1077, gave examples of dialects of various Türkic peoples ranging from Byzantine borders to borders of China. He wrote about geography of Türkish cities, political and economical life of Türks and their beliefs, gave examples of literary works and ancient epics and folk literature that did not survive

1076 A.D. - Itil Bulgaria Khan Akhad (1061-1076) deposed, Adam becomes Khan (1076-1118).

1076 A.D. - Capital of Itil Bulgaria is transferred from city Bulgar to city Bilyar

1077 A.D. - HARZEMSHAH

1077 - 1231 A.D. - Founder - Kudrettin Mehmet (Harzemshah) Area - Persia, Southern Caucasia, Dagestan, Afghanistan and most of Central Asia. (Total Area - 5,000,000 Km 2)

1078 A.D. - Daughter of Burduhan and George III is crowned as Queen Tamar on Georgian throne

1087 A.D. - Kengeres invade Byzantium across Thrace, are driven back, and defeat Alexius Comneus.

1088 A.D. - Former Khan, Emir Akhad Moskha built in Batyshes' (Russ. Vyatiches) land fort Moskha (Caw), now Moscow (Moskva).

1089 A.D. - King of Ovs (As, Alans) David Soslan's son marries Queen Tamar

1091 A.D. - Kipchaks under Togortak and Maniak are allied with Byzantium under Alexius Comnenus, and together crush Kengeres army.

1096 A.D. - Rabbi Nissim: Seventeen Khazarian communities join nomads (Kengeres, Bulgars, Oguses)

1099 A.D. - Formation of Karachai-Balkarian (Alan) people completed.

1099 A.D. - Tatars are beaten by Kerayit Türks' Khan Torgul, son of Khan Cyriacus(Qurjaquz), son of Marcus(Marguz) Buyiruq

1099 A.D. - Tatars lived since at least 8th cent. on south bank of Kerulen river near Bor Nor to Khingan range. On north bank of Kerulen to Onon river roved neghbouring Mongols. On west bank of Selenga river to Black Irtysh river roved neighboring Naiman Türks.

1099 A.D. - 200,000 Kerayit Türks, Nestorian Christians since 1009, roved neighboring south of Selenga river, on upper Orkhon, to Karakorum. Tatars are confederated as Tokuz Tatars (Nine Tatars) and Otuz Tatars (Thirty Tatars).

1099 A.D. - Tatars are redoubtable warriors and ranked among fiercest of all people.

1099 A.D. - Tatars constitute a serious danger to Sino-Tungustic kingdom of Kin. Kin used early Chingiz Khan to attack Tatars from Northwest.

1100 A.D. - Kipchaks are subdivided into hordes: Dniepr, Don, Lower Itil (Kipchak-Saksin), Eastern (Kipchak).

1103 A.D. - Established settlement Uchel (Kazan)

1103 A.D. - W. Kipchaks are raided and defeated on river Suten (Molochnaya) by Voldemir Monomakh and Svyatopolk Izyaslavich of Kiev. 20 Kipchak princes died. Kipchaks retreat from Bug.

1109 A.D. - Don Kipchaks are invaded and defeated by Rus Princes.

1110 A.D. - Kipchaks stone monuments spread in Dniepr basin, Crimea, N.Azov, Don, itil, N Caucasus

1111 A.D. - Don Kipchaks are again invaded and defeated by Rus Princes.

1116 A.D. - Don Kipchaks are again invaded and defeated by Rus Princes. Cities Sharukhan, Sugrov and Balin with Alano-Bulgar populations are taken.

1116 A.D. - (1116-1236) End of Russo-Kipchak wars. Kipchaks ally with Rus Principalities and join in in Rus intestine wars. In 120 years Kipchaks participate in 16 Russo-Russo wars, with only 6 Russo-Kipchak invasions and 6 Kipchak-Russo invasions.

1117 A.D. - Kipchaks under Khan Otrok retreat to N Caucasus steppes. Kipchak Khan Syrchan remains in Don Steppes. Kipchaks under Khan Otrok on way to N Caucasus destroy Sarkel, last known as Itil Bulgarian domain. Its inhabitants with Besenyos (Bedjenek) and Oguz Tür

1118 A.D. - Itil Bulgaria Khan Adam (1076-1118) died, Shamgun (Sain) becomes Khan (1118-1135)

1118 A.D. - Old capital city Bulgar becomes capital of Itil Bulgaria instead of city Bilyar.

1118 A.D. - Kipchaks make peace with Alans. Khan Otrak has 40K army and is allied with Georgian King David IV the Builder and participates in war with Seljuks. A number of Kipchaks settle in Georgia.

1120 A.D. - Capital of Itil Bulgaria is again transferred from city Bulgar to city Bilyar

1122 A.D. - As-Tarkhan established settlement As-Tarkhan (Astrakhan)

1122 A.D. - Russes defeat Cumans

1123 A.D. - Scyths/Besenyos (Bedjenek) reported as really wiped out by Byzantine Emperor John II in 1123.

1124 A.D. - Formation of Kara Kitai Empire in Transoxania.

1130 A.D. - 1130-1150 Kipchaks participate in intercine wars of Rus principalities.

1135 A.D. - Itil Bulgaria Khan Shamgun (Sain) (1118-1135) died, Khisam Anbal becomes Khan (1135-1164).

1136 A.D. - Established station Omek (Omsk)

1137 A.D. - Established station Kazgyn (Novosibirsk)

1150 A.D. - Bulgars had their own scientists and poets. Jakub ibn-Nogman who wrote "History of Bulgaria" lived in first half of XII century. Scholar Burchan ibn-Bulgari wrote book on rhetoric and medicine.

1152 A.D. - Kipchak lands are defined in Ipatievsk Chronicle and Chronicle of Igor. Itil, N Black Sea, Sula, Crimea (Suroj and Korsun (Kerch), Tmutarkhan (NW Fore-Caucusus)

1155 A.D. - Tatars capture Mongol Qutula Khagan's brother Okin-barqaq and cousin Ambaqai and deliver them to Kin, who executed them by nailing to a wooden donkey.

1161 A.D. - Tatars, allied with Kin, defeat Mongols at Bor Nor, in retaliation for Mongol Qutula Khagan raids, plunder of Kin. First Mongolian royalty is destroyed, Qutula Khagan's sons Jochi and Altan don't have titles, and people reverted to old tribal order.

1161 A.D. - Once victory made Tatars masters of Eastern Gobi, they incessantly harassed frontiers of Kin.

1164 A.D. - Itil Bulgaria Khan Khisam Anbal (1135-1164) is captured, Otyak becomes Khan (1164-1178).

1167 A.D. - Tatars poisoned baghatur Yesugei, father of Chingiz Khan and a chief of Mongolian Kiyat clan, at a friendly meal in steppe. Chingiz Khan is born about 1167 on right bank of Onon, in region of Dulun-Boldaq (Russia).

1171 A.D. - Besenyos lose control of Moldova to Cumans (1171-1241)

1175 A.D. - Kipchaks consolidate into 2 confederated hordes, Dniepr and Don. Al Mansuri and An Nuvayri mention Burjogly and Toksoba confederations.

1178 A.D. - Itil Bulgaria Khan Otyak (1164-1178) died, Gabdulla Chelbir becomes Khan (1178-1225).

1183 A.D. - GAZNELI EMPIRE

1183 A.D. (from 962 A.D.) - Founder - Alp Tekin

Area - from Trans-Oxus to Ganges River, from Caspian to steppes of Pamir (Total Area - 4,700,000 Km 2)

1184 A.D. - Dniepr Kipchaks are again attacked and their Khan Kobyak is captured. Kobyak is from line Toglyy/Izay/Osoluk/Kobyak

1185 A.D. - Don Kipchaks are again attacked, unsuccessfully, by Igor Svyatoslavich of Novgorod-Severskiy.

1185 A.D. - A number of Kipchaks, in 10's K, settle in Georgia in times of George III (1152-1184) and Quinn Tamara (1184-1214).

1195 A.D. - 1195- Kipchaks participate in intercine wars of Rus principalities.

1198 A.D. - Kin re-oriented and allied with Kerayit Khan Torgul. Torgul, accompanied by Chingiz Khan, attacked from northwest, and Kin from southeast, and defeated Tatars at Bor Nor. Torgul, with Chingiz Khan, chase Tatar chief Megujin SeUltu along Ulja river.

1201 A.D. - Tatars join anti-Wamg-Khan an Chingiz Khan coalition that included 8 Mongol clans, and Türkic Markit, Oirat, Naiman.

1202 A.D. - After subjugating Mongolian clan Tayichi'ut, Chingiz Khan turns to Chaghan Tatars and Alchi Tatars. Tatars vanquished and were massacred and were distributed among Mongol tribes. Chingiz Khan choosed two beautiful Tatar women, Yesui and Yesugan.

1202 A.D. - Further east, Solons, of river Nonni, acknowledge Chingiz Khan as tributaries.

1203 A.D. - Chingiz Khan is in control of eastern Mongolia. Naimans under Khan Tayang remain in control of western Mongolia.

1203 A.D. - Türkic tribes Markit, Oirat, Tatars, with rebel Mongolian clans, unite against Chingiz Khan, but he is warned about war by Ongut-Türks' Alaqush-tegin, invited into alliance to outflank Chingiz Khan.

1203 A.D. - Chingiz Khan calls quriltai and starts a war against Naimans and allies.

1206 A.D. - Chingiz Khan calls quriltai and is proclaimed Khagan of all Turco-Mongol peoples.

1206 A.D. - Khazar Jews are reported to use a form of Cyrillic script.

1209 A.D. - Uighurs, under Barchuq, submit to Mongol rule

1212 A.D. - End of KARAHANID Empire

932 – 1212A.D. - Founder - Saltuk Bugra Han

Area - All Trans-Oxus area including area between Issyk and Balkash Lakes

1218 A.D. - Chingiz Khan starts western campaign.

1219 A.D. - Chingiz Khan grants Muyten Bey yarlik for Bashkir? Kipchak? Ulus from Yaik and Agizel (Belaya), tributary of Kama, to Irtish.

1220 A.D. - Chingiz Khan conquest of Bukhara, Samarkand, Tirmidh and Gurganj

1220 A.D. - Uchel (Kazan) renamed Gazan

1220 A.D. - Rus Knyaz George II of Vladimir raids Itil Bulgars, captures Oshel and other cities along Kama. Bilyar city was saved by paying rich ransome

1221 A.D. - Chingiz Khan conquest of Balkh, Merv, Heart and Nishapur.

1222 A.D. - Defeat of Alans and Kipchaks in first fight against Mongol-Tatars. Mongol-Tatars seizing capital of Alania Magas (Meget).

1223 A.D. - Itil Bulgaria Khan Gabdulla Chelbir makes a deal with Juchi to help him in taking Khwarezm, Persia and Caucasus in exchange of not attacking Itil Bulgaria

1223 A.D. - An important Russo-Kipchak force was defeated on , at battle of Kalka.

1223 A.D. - War Council in Kiev: Kipchak Khan Kotyak Galicia Knyaz Mstislav Mstislavich Udaloy (Brave) Kiev Knyaz Mstislav Romanovich Chernigov Knyaz Mstislav Svyatoslavich Volyn Knyaz Daniil Kursk Knyaz Oleg Smolensk Knyaz Vladimir Former Novgorod Knyaz Vsevolod

1223 A.D. - 80K Russo-Kipchak force was defeated by 20K, 3 tumen force of Subetai on June 16, (May 31?) 1223, at battle of Kalka.

1223 A.D. - Gabdulla Chelbir collects 24K army, of 5K Kursybays, 3K militia of Dair Tetush, 6K Kazanchies, 10K Bashkorts. Staged at Kermek, NW of Mardan-Sember (Simbirsk), Left bank of Itil. Subetai had 20K Tataro-Mongols, and 50K Turkmen and Kumans.

1223 A.D. - Second son of Subetai Uran Kytai led a battle at Kermek and ordered a surrender to Gabdulla Chelbir of 38K surviving troops. Subetai lost 4K dead, and ransomed captured in exchange for sheep.

1223 A.D. - Chingiz Khan army penetration as far as Novgorod.

1225 A.D. - Itil Bulgaria Khan Gabdulla Chelbir (1178-1225) dies, ?? becomes Khan ()

1227 A.D. - Juchi dies, Batu becomes Ulus Juchi (Kipchak) Khan (1227-1255)

1227 A.D. - Cuman prince Barc and 15,000 of his people baptized in Transylvania.

1228 A.D. - First bishopric of Cumania established in Transylvania and King Béla IV of Hungary assumed title "king of Cumania"

1229 A.D. - Itil Bulgaria Khan ?? died, Gazi Baradj becomes Khan (1229-1246)

1229 A.D. - Chingiz Khan dies in 1229, Ogodei becomes Khan (1229-1241).

1235 A.D. - Eastern Desht-I Kipchak from Altai to Idel are included in Tataro-Mongol Empire Kipchak Kaganaate

1236 A.D. - 5 November 1236 Capital of Itil Bulgaria Bilyar is taken by Batu

1237 A.D. - Capture of Bulgar city and Voronej by Batu Tataro-Mongols, and subjugation of Bulgar population

1237 A.D. - Batu founded his capital, Sarai Batu, in city Saksin-Bolgar on lower stretch of Itil. Capital was later moved upstream to Sarai Berke, which at its peak held perhaps 600,000 inhabitants.

1237 A.D. - Batu Khan becomes ruler of Kipchak Kaganate (Altyn Urdu)

1237 A.D. - Batu army invades Asses and Kipchaks in N.W. Caspian and N. Caucasus. Leading Kipchak warrior Bachman killed, Khan Kotyan retreat beyond Tanais. Batu starts encircling maneuver going through Burtases, Erzya, Moksha, and Rus.

1237 A.D. - KIPCHAK KHANATE (ALTYN URDU) (GOLDEN HORDE)

1224 - 1502 A.D. - Founder - Batur Han

Area - Eastern Europe, Western Ural Area, Crimea and area to north of Itil

1238 A.D. - Capture of Moscow, Vladimir and Suzdal.

1239 A.D. - King Béla IV of Hungary granted asylum to Cumans and their prince Kuthen, who had earlier unsuccessfully tried organize Rus resistance to Mongols

1239 A.D. - Assimilation of Alania into Ulus Juchi

1240 A.D. - Batu Khan controls Kipchak, Bulgar, Rus Principalities

1240 A.D. - Batu Khan sack and burn city of Kiev in 1241, and subjugate S.Slavic population

1240 A.D. - Türkic tribes concentrated on animal husbandry in steppes, while their subject peoples, Russ, Mordvinians, Greeks, Georgians, and Armenians, contributed tribute

1240 A.D. - Cumans' leader Kuthen, considered a dangerous alien, is murdered. Cumans left Hungary but resettled there by Béla IV in 1245.

1241 A.D. - Death of Ogodei (1229-1241), Shiramon becomes Khan (1241-1242), then Toragana (Regent) (1242-1246)

1241 A.D. - Mongols defeat Hungarians and European knights.

1241 A.D. - Cumans lose control of Moldova to Mongols (1241-1286)

1242 A.D. - End of Daghestani Khazar kingdom.

1243 A.D. - Great Prince Yaroslav II of Vladimir calls a meeting of Rus princes, suggests recognizing Khan Batu as Tsar, and concluding a treaty with Bordjugins clan of Batu, to find a protection from conquering by Teutons and Lithuania.

1243 A.D. - City Saksin-Bolgar is renamed Sarai Batu

1243 A.D. - MONGOL EMPIRE

1229 – 1405 A.D. - Founder - Chingiz Khan

Area – From Mideterranian to Pacific, from Baltic to Indian Ocean

1246 A.D. - Guük becomes Mongol Khan (1246-1248), then Oghul Ghaimish (Regent) (1248-1251)

1246 A.D. - Itil Bulgaria Khan Gazi Baradj (1229-1246) died.

1246 A.D. - City Nur-Suvar destroyed (922-1246). Present name Tatarskiy (Sham-Suar).

1248 A.D. - Appointment of metropolitan for Khanbalik (Peking)

1249 A.D. - Establishment of Kipchak Türkic Mamluk dynasty in Egypt.

1249 A.D. - 1249-1345 Date of inscriptions on Nestorian gravestones near Bishkek

1250 A.D. - City Bolgary became most important trade and craft center of Kipchak Khanate

1250 A.D. - Kipchaks spoke a Türkic language whose most important surviving record is Codex Cumanicus, a late 13th-century dictionary of words in Kipchak, Latin, and Persian, compiled by Christian missionaries

1250 A.D. - Presence in Egypt of Kipchak-speaking Mamluks also stimulated compilation of Kipchak-Arabic dictionaries and grammars written in Egypt and Syria

1250 A.D. - Béla IV's son, future Stephen V, married Cuman princess, and, under rule of their son (Ladislas IV [László]; 1272–90), Cuman influence in Hungarian affairs was great

1250 A.D. - Cumans did not completely assimilate into Hungarian society for centuries

1250 A.D. - Bulgars had their own scientists and poets. Poem by Kul-Gali "Tale about Yusuf" (13-th century) was well known far from Bulgaria and greatly influenced development of Bulgarian and Tatar literature

1251 A.D. - Alexander Nevsky comes to Sarai Batu, befriended and bebrothered Sartaq, become his anda, and an adopted son of Khan Batu. Aleksnder returns with Tatar army that defeats Teutons. Aleksander receives yarlyk for Rus' Great Prince, in vassalage of Kipchak Khanate

1251 A.D. - Rus is allied with Kipchak Khanate as an autonomous vassal without loss of culture or religion. Rus' principalities refusing protection of Tatars are eventually captured by Lithuania

1251 A.D. - Vassalage tax paid by Rus is 5,000 R a year to XV c and 7,000 R after XV c, or 1.6 kg of grain per person in a country of 5 mln.

1251 A.D. - Mongke becomes Mongol Khan (1251-1258)

1255 A.D. - Hulegu recaptures Samarkand

1255 A.D. - First Buddhist-Taoist debate in Karakorum

1255 A.D. - Kipchak Khan Batu dies (1227-1255), Sartaq the Christian becomes Khan (1255-1257), then Ulagchi the Child (1257-1257)

1257 A.D. - Kipchak Khan Ulagchi the Child dies (1257-1257), Berke the Moslem becomes Khan (1257-1266)

1258 A.D. - After Mongke (1251-1258) Ariq-Buqa (1258-1260) becomes Mongol Khan

1258 A.D. - Second Buddhist-Taoist debate in Karakorum.

1259 A.D. - Crusader offensive by Ariq-Buqa Khan on Jerusalem. In Ain-Djalud battle noyon Kit-Buga is defeated by Mamluk army

1260 A.D. - After Ariq-Buqa (1258-1260) Kublai becomes Mongol Khan (1260-1294)

1261 A.D. - Kipchak Khan Berke exchanges ambassadors with Mamluk Egypt

1262 A.D. - First war between Kipchak Kaganate and Il Khans

1263 A.D. - Kipchak Khan Berke alliance with Mamluk Egypt

1263 A.D. - Kipchak Khanate carried on an extensive trade with Mediterranean peoples, particularly their allies in Mamluk Egypt and Genoese

1265 A.D. - 20,000 horsemen against Byzantium

1266 A.D. - Kipchak Khan Berke the Moslem dies (1257-1266), Mangu Timur becomes Khan (1266-1280)

1269 A.D. - 50,000 horsemen to help Qaidu

1278 A.D. - Mongol-Tatars and Rus allies seize Alanian town Dediakov.

1279 A.D. - Kipchak Khanate Khan Mangu Timur installed Kipchak (Cuman) George Terter I Khan of Danube Bulgaria (1280-1292)

1280 A.D. - Kipchak Khanate Khan Mangu Timur (1266-1280) dies, Tode Mangu the Moslem becomes Khan (1280-1287)

1281 A.D. - War between Mamluks and Mongols. Destruction of Mongol fleet off Japanese coast

1286 A.D. - Mongols lose control of Moldova to Lithuania (1241-1286)

1287 A.D. - Kipchak Khanate Khan Tode Mangu the Moslem (1280-1287) dies, Tole Buqa becomes Khan (1287-1290)

1290 A.D. - Kipchak Khanate Khan Tole Buqa (1287-1290) dies, Tokhtaga becomes Kipchak Khan (1290-1312)

1295 A.D. - Accession of Ghazan to Il Khanid throne. June 19: Public conversion of Ghazan to Islam.

1297 A.D. - Adoption by Il Khanid Ghazan of Islamic state symbols.

1299 A.D. - OTTOMAN EMPIRE

1299 - 1922 A.D. - Founder - Osman Bey Area - Algeria, Tunisia, Libya, Egypt, Arabia, Jordan, Israel, Syria, Iraq, Anatolia, Caucasia, Crimea, Bessarabia, Romania, Yugoslavia, Bulgaria, Greece, Cyprus, Hungary, Sudan...Black Sea, Mediterranean Sea and Red Sea were for a time Türkish Lakes (Total Area - 20,000,000 Km 2)

1300 A.D. - Descendants of Jewish Khazars in Eastern Europe adopt Yiddish language (1300-1500).

1300 A.D. - Kipchaks live east of Itil and in southern Urals

1300 A.D. - Kipchaks who settled from Itil to Lower Ilek rivers left modest earthen kurgans with rectangular burials facing east, with a hide or a mummy of harnessed and saddled horse.

1300 A.D. - Kipchak men grave goods have bark quivers with cut arrows, knifes, flints, and women have bronze or silver earrings, rings, pendants, scissors, bronze mirrors and headdress ornaments (bark tubes "bokks")

1303 A.D. - Mamluks stop last Mongolian invasion of Syria

1304 A.D. - Khan Tokhtaga summons Rus princes for meeting in Pereyaslavl to stop feudal infighting and swear allegiance to Kipchak Khan

1309 A.D. - Hungarian Christian clergy edicts that Catholics cannot marry "Khazars".

1312 A.D. - After Kipchak Khan Tokhtaga (1290-1312), his nephew Giazetdin-Sultan Mukhammed-Uzbek (Özbeg) (1312-1341) becomes Khan. He gives yarlyks to Rus princes to collect taxes instead of former Tatar baskaks

1315 A.D. - Kipchak Khan Uzbek summons Prince Yuri III (1303-1325) of Moscow to Sarai Berke. Yuri marries Usbek's sister Konchaka (Russ. Agrafia), becoming brother-in law of Khan Uzbek, and lives 2 years in Sarai Berke

1320 A.D. - Kipchak Khan Uzbek gives princess (Tughay? D. 1348) to Mamluk Sultan al-Nasir Muhammad of Bahri Mamluk dynasty (1293-1341) as wife

1321 A.D. - Lithuanian Duke Gedemin defeats coalition of Kipchak Rus vassal princes and captures Kiev, leaving his vassal prince as governor

1324 A.D. - Lithuanian Duke Gedemin annexes all Black Rus (Ukraine) and Podlyakhia into his Lithuanian domains

1327 A.D. - Kipchak Khan Uzbek sent 50,000 horsemen against Prince Ivan I Kalita (Moneybag) (1328-1340) of Moscow

1327 A.D. - Ivan I Kalita with Tatar help subdued anti-Mongol uprising in Tver. Thousands of Tverians were sent to China to join Rus volunteer recruits, conscripts, and captured prisoners serving as special guards for Mongol Emperor

1334 A.D. - Partition of Chagatai Khaganate

1335 A.D. - End of UIGUR EMPIRE

1335 A.D. (from 740 A.D.) - Founder - Kutlug Bilgekul Khan

Area - Central Asia and Northern Mongolia

1336 A.D. - Birth of Timurlan

1339 A.D. - Join campaign of Ivan I Kalita and Khan Uzbek to take Smolensk.

1339 A.D. - Kipchak Khanate is gradually Islamized

1340 A.D. - Grand Prince Ivan I Kalita with all Rus princes called to gather in Sarai Berke. Khan Uzbeg approves Ivan's son as next Rus Grand Prince

1341 A.D. - After Kipchak Khan Uzbek (1312-1341), Tini Beg is murdered (1341-1341), Jani Beg I becomes Kipchak Khan (1341-1356)

1341 A.D. - Dmitry (future Donskoi), Great Prince of Vladimir and Moscow, son of Ivan I Kalita, mints "denga" coins with "Es-Soltan-El-Egzem" on one side and Seal Of Great Prince Dm on another side

1346 A.D. - Black Death struck in 1346-47 A.D. - 1349 A.D. - Black Death struck in 1349. Beetwen 1364 and 1425. Rus looses 1/3 of population

1349 A.D. - Hungarian Jews, partly of Khazar origin, resettle in Poland and Austria.

1352 A.D. - Black Death struck in 1352-1353 A.D. - 1356 A.D. - Kipchak Khan Jani Beg I (1341-1356), last member of House of Juchi to rule over Kipchak Kaganate, dies, Berdi Beg becomes Khan (1356-1359)

1359 A.D. - Kipchak Khan Berdi Beg (1356-1359) dies, Qulpa becomes Khan (1359-1360)

1360 A.D. - Kipchak Khan Qulpa (1359-1360) dies, Nauruz Beg becomes Khan (1360)

1360 A.D. - Kipchak Khan Nauruz Beg (1359-1360) dies, Hizr becomes Khan (1360-1361). General Khan Mamai controls western half of Kipchak Khanate

1360 A.D. - Black Death struck in 1360 A.D. - 1361 A.D. - City Bolgary was destroyed by Ak Urdu Khan Bulak-Timur.

1361 A.D. - Kipchak Khan Hizr (Ak Urdu - White Horde) dies, Temur Hoja becomes Khan (1361-1362)

1361 A.D. - Gazan (Kazan) renamed Bolgar-al-Djadid (New Bolgar)

1362 A.D. - Kipchak Khan Temur Hoja (1361-1362) dies, Murad becomes Khan. He gives yarlyk to Dmitri of Moscow (future Donskoi), who is also a favorite of rebellious Khan Mamai

1364 A.D. - After Kipchak Khan Murad (1362-1364), Abdullah (1364 d1370) becomes Khan, civil war and multiple khans following him

1364 A.D. - Black Death struck in 1364-1366 A.D. - 1369 A.D. - After Kipchak Khan Abdullah (1362 d1370), Jani Beg II becomes Khan (1369-1370)

1369 A.D. - EMPIRE OF TIMUR KHAN

1369 - 1501 A.D. - Founder - Timur Gurgani

Area - West, Balkans; North, Volga, South, Indian Ocean; East, Central Asia

1370 A.D. - After Kipchak Khan Jani Beg II (1369-1370) dies, Mohammed Buluq-Khan becomes Khan (1370 d)

1370 A.D. - Mohammed Buluq-Khan (1370 d) dies, Tulun Beg-Khanum (fem) becomes Khan (1370-1373)

1371 A.D. - Grand Prince Mikhail again goes and obtains yarlyk from pretender Khan Mamai, while Dmitri obtains competing Grand Prince yarlyk from Khanum Tulun Beg at Sarai Berke

1372 A.D. - 1372-75 Renewal of war between Tver, joined with Lithuania allied with Khan Mamai, and Moscow, allied with Sarai Berke Tatars. Dmitry of Moscow concludes separatist peace with Lithuania. Pretender Khan Mamai sacks Riazan in revenge (1373)

1373 A.D. - Tulun Beg-Khanum (fem) (1370-1373) dies, Ai Beg becomes Kipchak Khan (1373 d 1376)

1373 A.D. - Dmitry of Moscow repulsed Khan Mamai punitive incursion

1374 A.D. - Black Death struck in 1374 A.D. - 1375 A.D. - Kipchak Khan Ai Beg (1373 d 1376) dies, Hajji Cherkes (in Sarai Berke) becomes Khan (1375-1376)

1376 A.D. - Dmitrii Donskoi of Moscow open campaign against Kazan

1376 A.D. - Hajji Cherkes (in Sarai Berke) (1375-1376) dies, Urus-Khan becomes Kipchak Khan (1376-1378)

1377 A.D. - Khan of Ak Urdu Tokhtamysh assumes control of Kipchak Kaganate.

1378 A.D. - Urus-Khan (1376-1378) dies, Arab Shaykh (restored)(in Sarai Berke) becomes Kipchak Khan (1378-1379)

1379 A.D. - Arab Shaykh (restored)(in Sarai Berke) dies, Mamai becomes Kipchak Khan (1379-1380)

1380 A.D. - Dmitrii Donskoi of Moscow and Rus princes in 1380 won a signal victory over Kipchak Army under rebelious general Mamai at Battle of Kulikovo

1380 A.D. - Tokhtamish, son of a minor Tatar prince, won fight with Mamai and ascended throne of Kipchak Khaganate. Mamai dies, Tokhtamish becomes Kipchak Khan (1380-1397)

1382 A.D. - Tokhtamish sack Moscow, restored Rus vassalage

1388 A.D. - Tamerlane (1336 - 1405) assumes title of Sultan

1393 A.D. - Tamerlane captures Baghdad and Shiraz.

1395 A.D. - Tamerlane defeated Tokhtamish, demolished Tana, Hajji-tarkhan (Astrakhan) and burnt Sarai Berke. He systematically annihilated Sarai Berke, Azov, and Kaffa.

1395 A.D. - Tamerlane, who invaded Horde's territory in 1395, destroyed Sarai Berke, and deported most of region's skilled craftsmen to Central Asia, thus depriving Horde of its technological edge over resurgent Moscovy. Ak Horde never recovered.

1395 A.D. - Tamerlane defeats Tokhtamysh. Türkish Emir Edigu takes over control of Kipchak Kaganate.

1395 A.D. - Tamerlane army invasion in Northern Caucasus, mass murder of Alanian population

1396 A.D. - Black Death struck in 1396 A.D. - 1398 A.D. - Emergence of Great Nogay Horde of Ak Urdu's Temnik Nogay, inbetween Itil and Yaik rivers

1398 A.D. - After Kipchak Khan Tokhtamish (1380-1397) dies, Temur Qutlugh becomes Khan (1398-1400)

1399 A.D. - Lithuania fought and lost a major battle against Golden Horde in Crimea in 1399 A.D. - 1400 A.D. - After Kipchak Khan Temur Qutlugh (1398-1400) dies, Shadi Beg becomes Kipchak Khan (1400-1407)

1400 A.D. - Tamerlane defeats Mamlukes in Syria

1402 A.D. - War between Tamerlane and Ottoman Empire.

1405 A.D. - Death of Tamerlane (1336 - 1405), Shah Rukh becomes Turkestan Khan(1405-1447)

1407 A.D. - Shadi Beg (1400-1407) dies, Pulad becomes Kipchak Khan (1407-1412)

1412 A.D. - After Kipchak Khan Pulad (1407-1412) dies, Jalal Al-Din becomes Khan (1412-1413)

1413 A.D. - After Kipchak Khan Jalal Al-Din (1412-1413) dies, Karim Berdi becomes Kipchak Khan (1413-1414)

1414 A.D. - After Kipchak Khan Karim Berdi (1413-1414) dies, Kebek becomes Kipchak Khan (1414-1417)

1417 A.D. - After Kipchak Khan Kebek (1414-1417) dies, Jabbar Berdi becomes Kipchak Khan (1417-1419)

1419 A.D. - After Kipchak Khan Jabbar Berdi dies, Ulugh Mehmed becomes Kipchak Khan (1419-1420 d 1434)

1419 A.D. - Death of Edigu. Beginning of civil war in Kipchak Kaganate

1420 A.D. - After Kipchak Khan Ulugh Mehmed dies, Devlat Berdi becomes Kipchak Khan (1420-1421)

1421 A.D. - After Kipchak Khan Devlat Berdi dies, Baraq becomes Kipchak Khan (1421-1428)

1423 A.D. - Crimean Khaganate separates from Kipchak Khaganate under Khan Mengli Girei

1423 A.D. - After Kipchak Khan Baraq dies, Kuchuk Mehmed becomes Kipchak Khan (1423(36?)-1459)

1428 A.D. - After Kipchak Khan Kuchuk Mehmed dies, Ulugh Mehmed (restored) becomes Kipchak Khan (1428-1434)

1430 A.D. - Kazan Khaganate separates from Kipchak Khaganate.

1430 A.D. - Hajji Girei formed Crimean Khaganate

1431 A.D. - Bolgar-al-Djadid (Kazan) renamed Kazan

1434 A.D. - After Kipchak Khan Ulugh Mehmed (restored) dies, Sayyid Ahmad I becomes Kipchak Khan (1434-1436)

1432 A.D. - Kipchak Khan Ulugh Mehmed's envoy enthroned Vasili II on throne of Moscow instead of Vladimir. This is last time that Tatar envoy participated in coronation of Grand Prince of Russia

1436 A.D. - Formation of Khanate of Kazan

1438 A.D. - ?... died, Ulugh Mohammed becomes Kazan Khanate Khan (1438-1446)

1440 A.D. - Ulugh Beg (1393-1449), a preeminent astronomer and mathematician of fifteenth century, published a new star catalog, correcting many errors in Ptolemy's work

1443 A.D. - Formation of Crimean Khanate

1446 A.D. - After Kipchak Khan Ulugh Mohammed died, Mahmudek becomes Kazan Khanate Khan (1446-1466)

1447 A.D. - Shah Rukh dies (1405-1447), Tamerlane grandson Ulugh Beg becomes Turkestan Khan (1447-1449)

1459 A.D. - After Kipchak Khan Sayyid Ahmad I dies, Mahmud becomes Kipchak Khan (1459-1466)

1466 A.D. - Mahmudek died, Khalil becomes Kazan Khanate Khan (1466-1467)

1466 A.D. - After Kipchak Khan Mahmud dies, Ahmad becomes Kipchak Khan (1466-1481)

1466 A.D. - Formation of Astrakhan Khanate

1467 A.D. - Khalil died, Ibrahim becomes Kazan Khanate Khan (1467-1479)

1469 A.D. - Kazan Khanate becomes a Rus vassal

1470 A.D. - Struck last bilingual Tatar-Russian coins

1479 A.D. - Ibrahim died, Ilham becomes Kazan Khanate Khan (1479-1485 d. 1487)

1480 A.D. - Ivan III of Moscow "liberates" Russia by refusing to pay tribute to Kipchak Khan, but continues collecting trubute taxes

1481 A.D. - Ahmad dies, Sayyid Ahmad II becomes Kipchak Khan (1481-1502)

1485 A.D. - Ilham replaced, Mohammed Amin becomes Kazan Khanate Khan (1485-1486 d. 1518)

1486 A.D. - Mohammed Amin replaced, Ilham (restored) becomes Kazan Khanate Khan (1486-1487)

1487 A.D. - Ilham (restored) died, Mohammed Amin (restored) becomes Kazan Khanate Khan (1487-1496 d. 1518)

1490 A.D. - Kazakh Empire is established in Central Asian steppes

1496 A.D. - Mohammed Amin (restored) died, Mamuk becomes Kazan Khanate Khan (1496-1497)

1497 A.D. - Mamuk died, Abdul-Latif becomes Kazan Khanate Khan (1497-1502)

1501 A.D. - End of EMPIRE OF TIMUR KHAN

1369 - 1501 A.D. - Founder - Timur Gurgani

Area - West, Balkans; North, Volga, South, Indian Ocean; East, Central Asia

1502 A.D. - Abdul-Latif died, Mohammed Amin (re-restored) becomes Kazan Khanate Khan (1502-1518)

1502 A.D. - Mengli Girei of Crimea destroyed Kipchak Kaganate capital Sarai Berke. Crimean Khanate seizes leadership of Kipchak Kaganate as a successor of Sarai Berke, starting a disintegration spiral

1502 A.D. - End of KIPCHAK KHANATE (ALTYN URDU) (GOLDEN HORDE)

1224 - 1502 A.D. - Founder - Batur Han

Area - Eastern Europe, Western Ural Area, Crimea and area to north of Itil

1504 A.D. - Kazan Khanate threw off Rus subjugation

1518 A.D. - Mohammed Amin (re-restored) died, Shah 'Ali (see Kasimov) becomes Kazan Khanate Khan (1518-1521 d. 1567)

1521 A.D. - Shah 'Ali (see Kasimov) died, Sahib Girai becomes Kazan Khanate Khan (1521-1525)

1525 A.D. - Sahib Girai died, Safa Girai becomes Kazan Khanate Khan (1525-1532 d. 1549)

1526 A.D. - EMPIRE OF BABUR

1526 - 1858 A.D. - Founder - Babur Shah

Area - Afghanistan and India (Total Area - 2,700,000 Km 2)

1532 A.D. - Safa Girai replaced by Jan 'Ali (see Kasimov) becomes Kazan Khanate Khan (1532-1535)

1535 A.D. - Jan 'Ali (see Kasimov) died, Safa Girai (restored) becomes Kazan Khanate Khan (1535-1546 d. 1549)

1546 A.D. - Shah 'Ali (restored) died, Safa Girai (re-restored) becomes Kazan Khanate Khan (1546-1549)

1546 A.D. - Safa Girai (restored) died, Shah 'Ali (restored) becomes Kazan Khanate Khan (1546 d. 1567)

1549 A.D. - Safa Girai (re-restored) died, Utemish Girai becomes Kazan Khanate Khan (1549-1551)

1551 A.D. - Utemish Girai died, Shah 'Ali (re-restored)(see Kasimov) becomes Kazan Khanate Khan (1551-1552 d. 1567)

1552 A.D. - Shah 'Ali (re-restored) (1551-1552 d. 1567) captured, Yadiger Mohammed becomes Kazan Khanate Khan (1552)

1552 A.D. - Rus Ivan IV of Moscow conquers Kazan Khanate and subjugates Türkic population.

1554 A.D. - Capture of Astrakhan Khanate by Russ and subjugation of Türkic population. Start of methodical destruction of Sarai-Batu city

1555 A.D. - Beginning of "Friendship" treaties between Moscow and Great Nogay horde turning horde into a mercenary (Kazak) state.

1558 A.D. - Beçens (Beçen/Becen "Peçenek") are still living in same area in 16th c, river Kama [branch of Volga] is called Vachen, live in wilderness without house or habitation

1558 A.D. - Beginning of Russian penetration of Central Asia.

1563 A.D. - 1563-98 reign of last Shaybanid ruler of Siberian Khanate, Kuchum Khan

1571 A.D. - Crimean Tatars sack Moscow

1574 A.D. - Ivan IV (1576-1584) mints bilingual Tatar-Russian coins, struck at a time of no Tatar vassalage

1590 A.D. - Kazakh Empire divides into three hordes: Great Horde (east), Middle Horde (center), and Lesser Horde(west).

1650 A.D. - 1st half 17 century Balkarians and Karachais first mentioned in Russian documents.

1662 A.D. - Bashkir revolt of Sary Mergen against Russian domination (1662-1664).

1662 A.D. - Bashkir revolt of Seit against Russian domination(1681-1684).

1680 A.D. - 1680-1718 Rule of Khan Teuke over reunited Kazakh hordes

1690 A.D. - End of use in Hungary of Türkic 32 character alphabet with 4 suplemental letters a,f,h,l from Greek.

1690 A.D. - 2nd half 17 - beg. 18 century Kabardins populate plains of Alania

1704 A.D. - Bashkir revolt of Aldar and Kusüm against Russian domination (1704-1711).

1735 A.D. - Bashkir revolt of Kilmyak, Akai andYusup against Russian domination(1735-1736).

1737 A.D. - Bashkir revolt of Tülkuchur, Bepen, Kusyap and Seit-bey against Russian domination(1737-1738).

1739 A.D. - Bashkir revolt of Karasakal, Allanziangul and Mandar against Russian domination(1739-1740).

1773 A.D. - Refer to Bashkir Encyclopedia for multiple Bashkir revolts, including Pugachev.

1775 A.D. - Rissian army destroys Sich of Zaporozhian Cossaks on an Island on Dniepr

1778 A.D. - Catherine I of Rissia deports Tatar speaking Crimean Goths to Azov area. They establish Mariupol (akin to Mariampol near Bakhchisarai)

1804 A.D. - 9 May 1804 Kabardins, Balkarians, Karachais and Ossetians battle with troops of general G. I. Glazenap on river Chegem.

1810 A.D. - Kabardins and Balkarians encounter with troops of general Bulgakov.

1822 A.D. - General A. P. Ermolov's raid in canyons of Balkaria.

1822 A.D. - 20 October 1822 Karachais battle with troops of general G. A. Emanuel at Hasauk. Karachai included in Russia.

1858 A.D. - End of EMPIRE OF BABUR

1526 - 1858 A.D. - Founder - Babur Shah Area - Afghanistan and India (Total Area - 2,700,000 Km 2)

1893 A.D. - B. Tomsen, dean of comparative linguistics at Cponhagen University deciphers Orkhon Inscriptions

1922 A.D. - End of OTTOMAN EMPIRE

1299 - 1922 A.D. - Founder - Osman Bey Area - Black Sea, Mediterranean Sea and Red Sea were for a time Türkish Lakes. (Total Area - 20,000,000 Km 2)

Notes 1

SAPPHOS

We don't know the date of her birth or death, but we do know that Sappho lived some six hundred years on the island of Lesbos, before Mary Magdalene, between 610~570 B.C.

Like the Magdalene, born of wealthy merchants her surroundings and home would have been luxurious, and she would have had access to beautiful clothes and jewelry.

Sappho spent much of her adult life in Mytiline.. According to Herodotus, who lived about150 years after her death. He records her fathers name as Scamandronymous. Her three brothers, Charaxus, Larichus, and Eurygius were of noble standing. This much is evident from inferences made in historical fragments. Although the details of her third brother Eurygius remain a mystery, enough information survives to paint a picture of her familial surrounds. The renowned wine of Lesbos was exported to Naucratis in Egypt by her brother Charaxus, a merchant who was married to a wealthy Egyptian woman named Doricha. Larichus was cup-bearer at Mytilene, an honorary office open only to aristocracy. "

A wellspring of lyric poetry sprang from Lesbos where women were well respected and their cosmopolitan society allowed them to move freely weaving in and out of various religious circles and schools of thought. Other famous poets of Lesbian fame included Terpander and Alcaeus, as well as several other female poets.

Being rather outspoken, Sappho, like the Magdalene, lived in exile for a period; an event evidenced in writing. A block of marble found at Paros is engraved with a chronology of events during this period. Sappho fled to Sicily when the intimidators rose to power and Aristocles ruled the Athenians.

Her biography and poetry bear mention and further study.

RELICS OF THE AMERICAN MOUNT-BUILDERS

First Published in 1898

SECTION II., 1898. [3] TRANS. R.S.C.

Recently Discovered Relics of the American Mound-Builders

By JOHN CAMPBELL, LL.D.,
Professor in the Presbyterian College, Montreal.

(Read 25th May, 1898.)

During the past winter there have been sent for my inspection, and if possible, for my decipherment, photographs of caskets, inscribed tablets, and other objects, that were found some six years ago in some mounds in Michigan. The first to send me these photographs was Mr. O.H. Roberts, of Paris, Ont., a gentleman until then entirely unknown to me, who was led to consult me by his study of my volumes on The Hittites. Mr. Roberts was under the impression that the objects were of great antiquity; that the characters of the inscriptions were cuneiform; and that one pictured tablet represented the Deluge. Any one who has seen the photographs will admit that, however improbable these conclusions may seem, there is much in the aspect of the articles portrayed to justify them. As a photograph, however well taken, is poor material for the epigrapher, I induced Mr. Roberts to furnish me with accurate drawings of such mound inscriptions as were in his possession, either as originals or as casts of the originals. He kindly provided me with four complete inscriptions and several fragments. Of the four inscriptions, two short ones belong to separate sides of a terra cotta casket; the other two are on tablets, one of which contains the supposed Deluge scene.

On a careful examination of the workable material before me, I saw that I had to deal with something that was only new in the matter of grouping, in other words, with the old Turanian syllabary. This syllabary I was led into acquaintance with through Hittite studies, and, having mastered its various forms and their phonetic equivalents, I have published many decipherments of inscriptions made in its protean characters. Among these may be mentioned contributions to the Canadian Institute of Toronto on the Etruscan, Siberian, Lat Indian, American Mound-Builder, and Sinaitic inscriptions. The Celtic Society of Montreal published an article on the Turanian Inscriptions of the Isle of Man. For the Rev. Wentworth Webster, the author of Basque

Legends, M. Henri O'Shea, author of La Maison Basque, La Tombe Basque, &c., and M. Victor Stempf, the Vasconist of Bordeaux, I have translated several so-called Celt-Iberian inscriptions found in various parts of Spain. During the past winter, I deciphered for SeÃ±or Don Juan Bethencourt Alfonso of Tenerife a number of similar inscriptions found in Hierro, one of the Canary Islands. And, at the meeting of the Australasian Association for the Advancement of Science, held last January in Sydney, N.S.W., Dr. John Fraser submitted my translation of a few characters inscribed upon a figure painted on the wall of a cave on the Glenelg river, which was the work of ancient ship-wrecked Japanese, as far back as the twelfth century A.D. The Association accepted my explanation, and Japanese and Basque scholars favour my translations, in the east of the Lat Indian and Siberian inscriptions, and the west of the Etruscan, Celt-Iberian, and similar documents. Unfortunately, among philological ethnologists there are few Basque and Japanese scholars. I mention the above facts, not as a matter of ostentation, but as a justification, rendered necessary by much incredulity, of my ability read the old Turanian character.

The oldest civilizations of the world were Turanian, that is, they were neither Semitic nor Aryan. Semitic writing is old, and Semitic speech was adopted by non-Semitic peoples, such as the Phoenicians. But the rulers of men were Turanians. Such were the primitive Egyptians whom we would now call Malays; and the Accadians of Chaldea, who might be termed Uralians. The latter, representing the Northern Turanians of postponing grammar, and vocabulary that mediates between the Basque and the Japanese, are popularly supposed to have had no other form of writing than the cuneiform of Babylonia, and the Hittite hieroglyphics. This is a radical misconception. They possessed a phonetic syllabary, not an alphabet, from before the time of the patriarch Abraham. Over 3,000 inscriptions in it are found from the Sinaitic Peninsula, and East of Jordan up into Syria. They have been called Sinaitic, Nabatean, and many other names, and, because men have failed to decipher them, they have been set aside as worthless. Most of the native syllabaries of Asia Minor, such as the Phrygian and Lydian, are of the same character. The inscription of Lemnos belongs to their category, with the Etruscan and other non-Pelasgic documents of Italy; and to these must be added the Celt-Iberian of Spain and the Canary Islands. When the Turanian was driven into the north, as the Esthonian, the Finn, the Lapp, and the Pict, he carried his runes with him, even as far as Greenland in the west. The Teutonic and perhaps the Celtic peoples seem to have borrowed these from him, changing the phonetic staff, and turning the syllabic into the alphabetic to suit themselves; but most of the runic inscriptions are not Norse, Gothic, and Anglo-Saxon, as their translators who make them yield unhistorical rubbish falsely imagine. Their authors and their languages were and are Turanian, and the best key to them is the Basque.

Besides this westerly movement of Turanian peoples and letters, there was a more extensive eastern one. When it first began we are not yet in a position to tell, but we know that it received a great impetus towards the end of the eighth century B.C., when Sargon of Assyria broke up the Hittite empire in Syria, Mesopotamia and the adjoining countries. The Turanians held their own in Parthia, and exercised sovereignty there from 255 B.C. till 226 A.D., when Persian rule was restored. They filled the rest of the Persian empire, in which scattered remains of their script may be found; but it was in northern India that their empire, arts, civilization, and letters revived under the religious forms of Buddhism. There were no royal Aryans then in India; they were simply for a time Brahman priests and councillors of Kshattriya or Turanian kings. When Buddhism was revived by the Sakya prince who was called Gotama, the occupation of the Brahman was gone, and he became a merchant, a seaman and an agitator. The name of Prince Sidhartta has nothing to do with the keeping of cows, as the Sanscritists translate Gautama; it is pure Japanese, Go tama, the excellent master. The Buddhist inscriptions of India are in a form of the old Turanian character; they are the work of royalty, not of mendicant monks, as Prinsep, Cunningham and others have made them out to be; and their language, as I have shown, is pure Japanese. It is not in vain that Japanese historians derive their race from India. An interesting fact to us in Canada is that, in the Andhra* [*Andbra?] dynasty of Magadha, there reigned four Satakarnis and two Skandaswatis, names we are familiar with as those of two founders of the league of the Iroquois, Shadekaronyes and Skandaswati.

From before the Christian era on to the fifth century A.D., the Brahmans worked to overthrow Turanian and Buddhist rule; not driving all the Turanians out, but subordinating them as the three inferior castes, and imposing on all a modified Brahmanism that contained many elements of Turanian heathenism. As late as the seventh century, Brahman kings were few and weak in authority. But, as early as the fifth century, the literary Turanian betook himself from northern India to Siberia, carrying his Buddhism and his Buddhist scribes with him.

About the head waters of the Yenisei, and west and east of them, he built his wooden cities, heaped his mounds, and engaged in the chase and in war. Still his inscriptions are in the same character, if a little ruder in form, and their Japanese is less archaic than that of India. The chief monarchs who reigned in Siberia appear in the Japanese annals, which do not tell, as do the rocks of the Yenisei, that they ruled over the Raba and the Yoba Kita. It is hard to decide, from the diverse data furnished by the Corean, Japanese and Chinese historians, when the Turanians of Siberia descended upon Corea and northern China, over which they ruled for about two centuries. The rule of the Khitan in China is said to have ended in 1123, and is supposed to have begun before the middle of the tenth century; but they were in Corea before the end of the seventh. The Corean alphabet is a much modified form of the Lat Indian and Siberian syllabary, and, with the Cypriote syllabary and the Aztec hieroglyphic system, constituted my material for fixing the phonetic values of the Hittite characters.

Tho Turanian writers must have been in Japan long before their brethren conquered China, probably as early as the sixth century. This we know, not from the Japanese annals, full of Siberian, Indian and still more western and ancient monarchs, going back to 660 B.C., but from the mound-builder inscriptions of America, and from the history of Mexico. The most ancient date of Mexican history is 717 A.D., and the oldest monuments on American soil which are dated are the two stones from Davenport, Iowa, engraved in 793 and 795. Their dates are Buddhist, reckoning from the death of the sage in 477 B.C. Copies of inscriptions in the Turanian character from Japan havo been sent to me, but they were too much weathered to yield any satisfactory result. The Japanese are said to have replaced their ancient form of writing by modifications of the Chinese in 285 A.D., under the advice of the wise Wonin. This is quite fabulous, as the Japanese were at that time in India. But it is probable that the change of script took place during the period of Khitan rule in the celestial empire, which lies somewhere between the sixth and the twelfth century. The mound builder inscriptions of America are all in the old character, although their dates extend from 723 to 1261, and I am not aware of the existence of any American inscription in the Japanese modifications of the Chinese form of writing. Ban Nobutomo's work on old Japanese alphabets shows that the Japanese are now ignorant of their ancient form of written speech: yet I have a shrewd suspicion that it may be preserved among the arcana of Buddhist priests in the land of the chrysanthemum. At any rate, it is perfectly evident that there is not knowledge enough of this old Turanian writing in the world to enable any one to forge it, as it has been charged over and again to have been done by American antiquarians, who have thus sought to shield their own ignorance.

I must not be unjust in this matter, nor leave it to be understood that America alone produces sceptics. Mr. Roberts sent his photographs and some memoranda with which I had furnished him to the head of one of the departments of the British Museum, who returned for answer this remarkable piece of dogmatism: "In my opinion, the objects shown in the photographs have not the least scientific interest or importance, and nothing founded on them can be of the slightest value." The same gentleman favoured me with a note, cautioning me against the discovered objects. Mr. Roberts's reception by the authorities of the Smithsonian Institution was equally chilling. At the same time, so convinced is he of the genuineness and unique character of the remains taken from the mounds, that he wished to keep the secret of their discovery, and gave me nothing more than the general statement that they came from a part of Michigan which had not been explored by Professor Cyrus Thomas and his mound-visiting coadjutors of Washington. With this meagre information I should have been compelled to rest content, had not a second set of photographs arrived about the middle of March, this time not from Paris, but from Leamington, Ont. They were sent by a respected minister of that town, who was formerly one of my best students. It will hardly be violating the confidence of private correspondence to transcribe that part of his letter which relates to the photographs. In regard to these the writer says:

"The story of them is briefly this. A young man visiting in this section recently brought these pictures to me, thinking that possibly I might be able to decipher them. Of course I was unable to do so, and expressed the desire that he would leave them with me, and I would get your opinion about them. As far as I could learn from him, they were found, about six years ago, at a place called Wyman, near Mount Pleasant, Michigan. The circumstances connected with the discovery were as follows: A man was digging holes in the ground for the purpose of erecting a fence, and about three feet below the surface his spade struck a stone, which appeared to give forth a hollow sound. He dug around it, and unearthed a casket, which when opened he found to contain some tablets, with curious inscriptions engraved on them. The tablets when taken out of the ground were soft like clay, but when exposed to the sun became quite hard. Of course, when this discovery was made, the whole community was aroused, and they began to dig in several other places, and on one spot, which was mound-shaped, they found the largest casket, containing other tablets. This one was very much below the surface of a mound on which there grew a pine tree over four hundred years old. The tablets were preserved, and a photographer from Mount Pleasant took views of them, copies of which I am sending you; This, in brief, is about all the information I could get about them. He--that is, the man who brought them to me--said the people living around there believed they were placed there by the Chaldeans, but I told them that in all probability they were similar to the tablets found in Mexico and Peru."

From the two sets of photographs, which are not identical, showing that the collection taken must have been larger than that in the possession of either of my correspondents, and from Mr. Roberts's communications, I gather that the terra-cotta caskets, surmounted by sphinx-like and couchant winged animal figures, were at least five in number; that either in or near them were found complete specimens of pottery, stone dies for stamping the figures on the clay, pieces of copper larger than a cent, having the appearance of coin, and some six tablets, of which one is an effigy thoroughly mound builder in character. As I have already stated, I have made no attempt to decipher any of the tablets but the two of which Mr. Roberts sent me faithful copies, nor of the legends of the caskets beyond two which he also sketched for my benefit. In the uninitiated they are calculated to inspire incredulity. Sphinxes and cuneiform characters, together with a deluge scene, seem out of place in Michigan. Yet, sphinxes with men's faces such as these belong to the art remains of Buddhist India, and doubtless are known in Japan. The supposed cuneiform characters are not really such, those that have a wedge appearance being few, and scattered among the ordinary types of the Turanian syllabary. There are also some hieroglyphic or ideographic symbols with which I am not familiar. The deluge scene is misnamed, as investigators might have learned had they only taken the trouble to look at the object near the human figure on the top of the left side of the tablet. It is the stump of a tree, and indicates that the three lower compartments are stages in the Buddhist under-world.

The chief peculiarity in the writing on tablets and caskets, which, in this old Turanian syllabary throughput the world, I have met but rarely, is the grouping of characters, either by simple superposition or by adhering to a staff representing an open vowel or an aspirate syllable, such as o, ha, ye . As the documents are ecclesiastical rather than historical, consisting of what might almost be called charms, this mode of writing may have been an invention of the monks to add mystery to the formulas of their creed. A few ideographs occur in the tablets under consideration, such as the figure of a man, hito , and that of a deer, skika . These are simple enough; but more difficult are two conventional characters of much importance that play a considerable part in the funeral ritual. One of them is a crenelle, not unlike the Egyptian hieroglyphic for water, ma . But in Turanian script, such a crenelle has the consonantal value of n rather than of m , and has no relation to water directly. It may, however, represent the first syllable of the Japanese nami , a wave, which rises and falls. With reduplication, this would give anon , tranquillity, the Stoic frame of mind which Buddhism exalts, although it is hard to see how the restless wave is its type. The other ideograph resembles a crown, but whether crowns were in use among Turanian monarchs or not, I have not found its representation symbolic in their writing. It rather sets forth a mountain range, the Basque meta, mendi the Japanese yama, yamato , the Iroquois onontes , applied to supreme power, and the mata or mito , by which I have rendered a somewhat similar hieroglyphic in the inscription of the Cilician king Tarkutimme. It probably represents the title amida applied to Buddha by the Japanese. The historians of Japan indicate that Amida was an ancient god of the Sintoists; possibly the eponym of Japan or yamato, whose name, as indicating supreme divinity, was transferred by the Buddhists to their object of worship. In the Siberian inscriptions Buddha is occasionally called Anata , doubtless the Japanese ando , tranquillity, but this is a quite different word.

I have already referred to my translations of Mound Builder inscriptions in the Transactions of the Canadian Institute. On the 15th of December, 1897, the paper containing these was read, and it set forth seven inscribed stones; that of Yarmouth, Nova Scotia; the so-called Northman's Written Rock near West Newbury, Mass.; the Grave Creek stone of West Virginia; the Plain Township and Brush Creek Stones of Ohio; and two tablets from Davenport, Iowa. All these have been cried down as forgeries by men who have or had the public ear, and who united to a dogmatic assertion, that the aboriginal American never rose above the stage of pictorial illustration, the epigraphic ignorance that enabled them to brave it out. Since my paper on Aboriginal American Inscriptions in Phonetic Characters was written, I have received copies of others. Mr. A. Cameron, President of the Summer School of Science for the Atlantic Provinces of Canada, wrote me on the 16th of September, last year, to the following effect: "I write in regard to the inscription on page 50 of the '96 Volume of Trans. R.S.C. That stone has been known since 1812. About three weeks ago, another graven stone was found near the shore, about a mile southwest of where the first one was found. The inscription is in two lines. The upper line is the same as the old one. The lower line contains only three charcters: Y.V.H. Will you be good enough to tell me what this second line means?" I immediately replied to Mr. Cameron's letter, informing him that these three characters have the value of ku-be-ka , and that they denote the fact that Katorats, whom the stones commemorate, was a chief of the Kubekas, or, in modern parlance, of the Cayugas, whose ancient name solves the long vexed problem of the origin of Quebec.

In the spring of last year, if I remember aright, Miss Cornelia Horsford, of Cambridge, Mass., was kind enough to send me a volume of the Transactions of the Societe Royale des Antiquaires du Nord, from the library of the poet Longfellow; This volume is of May 14, 1859, and on page 23 contains an engraving of the Monhegan stone, found by Augustus Hamlin, of Bangor, in 1856, on Monhegan island, near the coast of Maine. It is cut on a slab of rock. The lower line is to be read first, and the whole legend is:

No. I No. II THE MONHEGAN STONE]

aka toi ha ka obe mi to ra bei de to to a re to ku 3 fu 1 to 3. That is to say:

(1) Akatoihaka ofi mito Raweideto to ari toki 73 : Quatoghie, aged king Raweideto, who has years 73. Placing this legend in English order it reads: "Raweideto, aged chief of the Quatoghies, whose years were seventy-three." The Quatoghies were a Wyandott or Huron tribe that were known historically as dwelling on the south side of Lake Michigan, and who sold their lands to the English in 1707. They may have been in Maine under Raweideto, when the Cayugas under Katorats were in Nova Scotia, but unhappily no date accompanies these monuments to tell us when that was. The characters of the Monhegan stone are precisely of the same nature as that of those of Yarmouth, N.S.

I now proceed to an examination of the Wyman inscriptions of Michigan, of which I possess copies that justify an attempt at interpretation. By reference to the illustrations, it will be seen that I have first presented the inscriptions as they stand, and secondly, have analysed the compound groups into their individual parts, furnishing also a list of characters with their phonetic values, which, so far as the vowels go, follow not the English, but the European continental pronunciation. The first inscription, which is very irregular, is the key to the whole. It is from a side of one of the caskets. That part of it which occupies the principal space reads as follows:

No. I.

hi ka ye o te o be ha ka ka de

Hikaye Ote obe haka ka de Hikaye Ote chief tomb house from

That is: "From the house of the tomb of the chief of the Ote (Utes or Otos), Hikaye."

Hikaye in Japanese means, "The Forbearing." The three compound characters in the margin read:

ko i go ta fu ki fa ri koi gotafu ki furi prayer whole-body spirit to expel

"A prayer to expel the spirit from the whole body." Of greater interest is the second side of the casket, which has two lines of some length each.

No. II.--hi ka ye go ha ra ni se ha ra se ha ra yo he da te ru shi ta be i yo bu da mi shi ta be i yo anon ya fu ya me no amida bu da yo miHikaye gohara nisehara jahara yo hedateru Hikaye anger spirit false-spirit depraved-spirit from separates.

hita bei yo Buda me shita bei yo anonya fuyame no dead warrior from Buddha eye dead warrior from Anonya hasten will

Amida Buda yomi Amida Buddha writing

"Hikaye. The Buddhist writing Anonya separates between the spirit of anger, the spirit of falsehood, the spirit of depravity, and the dead warrior; and between the eye of Buddha and the dead warrior; and the character Amida will hasten it."

The second line is:

hi ka ye shi ri r to shi 1 fu hi do ha ra go ha ra ha da mi ha ra shi ta ta yo fu ya me no be da ta ru anon amida bu da yo mi

Hikaye, shi ri 2 toshi 1 fu. Hidohara, gohara, hadamihara Hikaye 4 300 2 year 1 20. Cruel spirit, anger spirit, naked body spi rit.

shitata yo fuyame no hedateru Anon Amida Buda yomi love from hasten will to separate Anon Amida Buddha writing.

"Hikaye, 12 hundred, 1 score, and 2 years. The Buddhist characters Anon and Amida (tranquillity and contemplation) will hasten to separate from the love of the spirit of cruelty, the spirit of anger, and the spirit of the naked body."

Here we have a dated inscription, perfectly clear and definite. The date consists of 4 ri-toshis , which, as I have indicated in my essays on the Siberian and Buddhist-Indian inscriptions, are periods of 300 years, 1 fu , futachi or 20, and 2 units, making in all 1,222 years. The only Buddhist era is that of the death of the founder of their religion, or his attainment of Nirvana, which was 477 B.C. As he died in his eightieth year, his birth must have been in 557. The 1222nd year of Buddha was A.D. 745, when western Europe was in a state of barbarism. It was only 28 years later than 717, the most ancient date that American history presents, and 48 years earlier than the period of the Davenport inscriptions. As pure Japanese is found in many much later inscriptions than this, but so far there has come to light no other trace of Buddhist ritual, nor any such elaborate work of art as the Michigan mounds have furnished. A war- rantable conclusion seems to be that Hikaye and his tribe, though so far in the east, had not been long out of Japan, and that, with a boldness almost unparalleled, though resembling the movements of the Huns in Europe and Asia, they had, with meagre appliances, traversed the vast extent of country from Oregon to Michigan in a single generation. They may have been an offshoot of the Utes, after whom the state of Utah was named.

The third inscription is that accompanying the supposed Deluge scene. The Leamington photographs also include such a scene, but the characters upon it are quite different from those on that furnished by my Paris correspondent, although both bear the name of Hikaye. All the complete lines begin, like those already deciphered, on the left, but the first is continued boustrophedon. The characters as separated read:

No. III.

he da te o be yo go ha ra yo hi ka ye he da te ru anon ya bu da i da hito ri do shika ri do

he da te ru to he da te hi ye bu da

ro ku yo ku ya do ri he da te o be fu ri ta te ra yo hi ka ye ri yo tera yo

(3) Hedate obe yo gohara, yo Hikaye hedateru Anonya separated chief from anger spirit from Hikaye separates Anonya

Buda ida hito ri do shika ri do Buddha embracing man profit way as profit way

"Anonya (tranquillity) separates between Hikaye, the departed chief, and the spirit of anger; the path of profit of the man embracing Buddha as the path of profit."

Hedateru to hedate hi ye Buda to separate door departed evil defilement Buddha.

"The door to separate the defilement of sin from the departed (is) Buddha."

Roku yoku yadori hedate obe furita tera yo Hikaye six lusts indwelling departed chief has driven away temple from Hikaye riyo tera yo kingdom shining from

"The departed chief has driven away the six indwelling lusts from the temple, from the resplendent kingdom of Hikaye."

The last inscription is irregular. The first line reads from left to right, and so does the second, but the third reverses the order. The fourth is like the first and second, but the fifth follows the third, while the sixth and seventh agree with the fourth, second and first. I have not included in these lines that which simply contains the name Hikuye.

No. IV.

he da te ru ri go i bu da yo mi fu ya me no shi ma i ma ye fu ho ma ni ni yo

go fu amida fu annai ri

ko to ta ri shi ta te ri yo he da te ba i fu mi no to i ta yo shi ri yo shi ta te ri yo

i de he da te ba i mu ma ye shi ta shi ta be i yo he da te yu re i na o shi ta shi ta

ta ri o dzu fu mi no na o shi ta shi ta yu re i yo

shi ta ni ni ta dzu wa shi ta ri yo te ra te ra

na o shi fu mi no ri yo shi ta he da te yu re i ta tsu i de shi mu ho ba i yo i to me ba i

The translation of this more extensive document is as follows:

1. Hedateru rigai Buda yomi fuyame no shimai maye separate gain and loss Buddha writing hasten will put away former fuho ma nin yo wicked devil man from

2. gofu Amida fuannai ri charm Amida unacquainted law

3. koiotari shitate riyo hedate bai fumi no toi taye satisfy lower world separating wall writing of request sustains shiriyo shitate riyo spirit lower world

4. ide hedate bai mumei shita shita bet yo hedate go out separating

wall dishonourable dead dead warrior from separated yurei naoshi tashita spirit heal perfectly

5. tariodzu fumi no naoshi tashita yurei yo unworthy writing of heal perfectly spectre from

6. shita nin tadzuwa shita riyo tera tera dead man participates dead kingdom resplendent

7. naoshi fumi no riyo shita hedate yurei tatsu ide healed writing of world lower separated spirit rises goes out shi muho bei yo itoma bei dead wicked warriors from free warrior.

The following is a free, but, at the same time, an exact English rendering of the above:

HIKAYE.

Distinguishing gain and loss, the writing of Buddha will hasten to put away from the man former wicked devils, (namely) the charm of the law of the unacquainted with Amida. To satisfy the separating wall of the lower world, the request of the writing sustains the spirit to go out of the lower world. The separating wall (delivers) the dead warrior from the dishonourable dead (and) the separated spirit it heals perfectly, Through the writing, the deficient are perfectly delivered from spectres. The dead man participates in the resplendent kingdom of the dead. Healed by the writing, the separated spirit of the lower world rises and goes out from dead wicked warriors, a free (discharged) warrior."

These documents enlighten us in regard to the character of Buddhist worship in the eighth century. It seems to have been largely a matter of magic or charms, the priestly writings in the name of Buddha being efficacious to deliver the soul of the dead from any relation to the dead body, from the six lusts of the Buddhist six senses, from spectres, from the wicked and unaided dead, and from the various stages of the lower world. Our Indians of northern Asiatic origin have long ago lost all the Buddhism their ancestors may have possessed, yet many of them still retain veneration for written documents which have in their eyes the value of a fetish. It is of course possible that the priests practised and taught the people to practise the virtues which are the opposites of the vices their writings Condemn. The vices condemned are anger, falsehood, cruelty, depravity, whatever that may stand for, and the naked body-spirit, which probably was simply the savage instinct that rejects clothing. The eighth century Buddhist priests had at any rate a mental acquaintance with sin in various forms, with its punishment in a future state, and with the possibility of redemption from that punishment. But, in regard to the last of these, the only means specified is the Buddhist charm, a document written by priestly hands. Apparently, the larger the number of these charms the friends of the deceased could afford to bury with his body, the more assured was his salvation. Hikaye, being a man of note, had a large number of such passports to the under-worlds, and the copper pieces found in one of his caskets were no doubt the fee of the Buddhist Charon who was to ferry him over the Styx in the vessel mistaken for Noah's ark.

There is every reason to believe that American history began, not in Mexico in the south, but in the north, and at first in the distant west. Brasseur de Bourbourg says that the Othomis occupied the mountains and valleys of Anahuac long before the Nahuas and the tribes afterwards known as the Toltecs. Their chief city was Otompan. The Davenport, Iowa, inscriptions, dated 793 and 795, are chiefly concerned with a chief named Maka-Wala, whose town or country I have transliterated as Atempa. This reading of the name of Maka-Wala's kingdom arose out of the poverty of the old Turanian syllabary in America, which, like ancient Semitic and modern Arabic, paid little attention to vowel sounds. Atempa may be, with equal justice, read Otompa, which in Japanese would be O tomo fu, or "the city of the great companion." The Otomos were a great feudal family in Japan. Titsingh in his annals mentions Otomo-no-Osi, son of the thirty-ninth emperor Tentsi, in the seventh century, and Otomo-no Sin, the younger, brother of Saga-no-teno, the fifty-second emperor, in the ninth. Saganoteno is the Sakata of the Siberian inscriptions, and the Shekingtang of Chinese history, who heads the Khitan dynasty of China, and his brother, on the Siberian monuments, is called Mi tomo, the honorific prefix mi taking the place of the equally honorific prefix o . The Old Testament student is familiar with the Othomi name in its Hebrew form Eshtemoa, the head of the Maachathites or Massagetae (I. Chronicles iv. 19.) He was the son of Naham of Caleb of Jephunneh of Ephron the Hittite, who sold the cave of Machpelah to Abraham. Machpelah, after whom the cave was called, was Ephron's father; Zochar, who in Genesis xxiii. 8 takes his place, being a remote ancestor; and the name Machpelah is that of the king of Atempa or Otompan, namely, Maka-Wala, who was killed by the Mekushi and the Tolaku, under the chief Mashima, in 792.

Ottumwa in Iowa is some distance from Davenport, near which the Iowa tablets were found; but it marks the site of Maba-Wala's ancient principality; and, on American ground is the original Otompan of the Mexican historians. The Mekushi who fought against Maka-Wala were the ancestors of the Mexicans proper, and when, by way of the Mississippi, they made their way southward, they carried with them the record of this tribal conflict in the north. From these considerations I was disposed to regard Iowa as the first theatre of American history as distinguished from barbaric wanderings. But Michigan now puts in a claim of forty-eight years' priority, in the person of Hikaye of the Otos or Utes, who appear to have been the same race as the Aztecs of Mexico. The Mexicans were a branch of the Aztecs, and they again of the Chichimecs, now represented by the Shoshonese of the Rocky Mountains. It is not impossible that the Otos, who, like the Iowas, belong to the great Dakota family, represent the descendants of Hikaye's tribe in retrogression, for no trace of them is to be found in the east; but the probability is that the Dakotas belong to a much later, tide of immigration, subsequent to that of the Huron-Iroqnois-Cherbkee stock, which was by no.meansone of the

The poverty of the following syllabary will explain apparent inconsistency in the rendering of vowel sounds and aspirates, and in the consonantal forms k, t and s, replaced by g, d and j.

[Illustration: PLATE VI.] earliest to seek the shores of the New World. Whether Hikaye's tribe was exterminated, or lost its identity in some larger invading force, or moved southward as the germ of Aztec monarchy to overthrow the Toltec power in Mexico, we cannot for the present tell; but the ancient records so far brought to light encourage us to hope that, before long, from many valuable fragments, there may be built up a consistent mosaic of American aboriginal history.

ANALYSIS OF THE INSCRIPTIONS.

(1.) Akatoihaka , the Huron tribe called by the English Quatoghies. ofi , archaic form of the Japanese oi , aged. mito , J. mi and to , the honourable door or Sublime Porte, of the same signification as mi-kado . Raweidato , the name of the Huron chief, which may be equivalent to the Iroquois Rawendio, "The Master." to ari , original form of verbal suffix tari , "who is." toki means a season or time, and here stands for toshi , a year. fu is an abbreviation of futachi , now hatachi , twenty. The numeration of the Turanians was by scores. to , ten.

(2.) Hikaye , the Forbearing, name of a dead chief. Ote or Oto , name of his tribe. obe , old form of kobe , head or chief. Omo has the same signification. haka , the tomb. ka , the house. de , postposition, with, by, from. koi , desire, prayer. gotafu , archaic form of gotai ,the whole body. Many original endings in fu have been reduced to i . See Aston's Japanese Grammars. gohara , anger, but composed of go , anger, and hara , mind or spirit. nisehara , composed of nise , to falsify, and hara . jahara , composed of ja , depraved, and hara . yo , old postposition, from, now yori . hedateru , to separate. shita , dead. bei , old form of hei , a soldier. Many Japanese labials have been reduced to aspirates. yo , see above. Buda or Futa , Buddha. me , the eye. shita , see above. bei see above. anon-ya , the place or manner of tranquillity. fuyame , now hayame to hasten. no , sign of futurity. Amida , a Japanese title of Buddha which the lexicons fail to explain. yomi , writing, reading; written character. shi , four. ri or more fully ri-toshi , a cycle of 300 years. See my Siberian Inscriptions, Transactions of the Canadian Institute, April, 1892, p. 279. toshi , a year. fu , see end of Note 1. hidohara , composed of hido , cruel, and hara , spirit. gohara , see Note 1. hadamihara , composed of hadami , naked body, and hara . shitata , now shitai , shitaota , love, long for. yo , fuyame , no , hedateru , see above. Anon , a Buddhist charm, meaning literally "rest," ease, tranquillity. Amida , see above. Buda yomi , see above.

(3.) hedate , from hedateru , to separate, distinguish. obe , see Note 2. ida , abbreviation of idaki , to embrace. hito , a man, a Hittite. ri , profit, victory, law, right, principle. do , a way, path. shika , as, thus, so. to , a door. hi , evil. ye , defilement, pollution. roku , six. yoku , lusts, sensuality. yadori , to sojourn, lodge, dwell in. furita or furitta , preterite of furi , to drive away. tera , a Buddhist temple or monastery. riyo , kingdom, dominion, estate, rule. tera , perhaps teri , to shine, or abbreviation of tera-tera , shining.

(4.) rigai , profit or loss. shimai , to end, put away. maye , former. fuho , wicked, unlawful. ma , a devil. nin , a man. gofu , "a charm, or small piece of paper on which a sentence from the Buddhist sacred books is written by a priest."--Hepburn. fuannai , unacquainted with. ri , law. kototari , to content, satisfy. shitate , subordinate, lower. bai , old form of hei , a fence, partition or wall, as seen in the compounds ita-bei , a board fence, ishi-bei , a stone fence. no , genitive post-position. toi , question, inquiry. taye , part of the verb tayeru , to support, sustain. shiriyo , the spirit of a dead person. riyo , dominion, territory. ide , part of the verb ideru , to go out. mumei , nameless, dishonourable. shita , dead. yurei , a ghost, spectre. naoshi , to heal, cure, mend, rectify, deliver from. tashita or tasshita , perfect. tariodzu , old and more perfect form of taradzu , incompetent, lacking, insufficient, unworthy. tadzuwa , now tadzusawa-ri , to join, participate in. tera-tera , shining. tatsu , part of the verb tachi, tatsu , to stand up. ide , see above. muho , lawless, wicked. See fuho , above; fu and mu are negatives. itoma , freedom, liberty from service, honourable discharge.

Notes

Notes

Notes

HOW WE THINK
DIFFERENTLY

LaVergne, TN USA
09 August 2010
192646LV00004B/88/P